Story

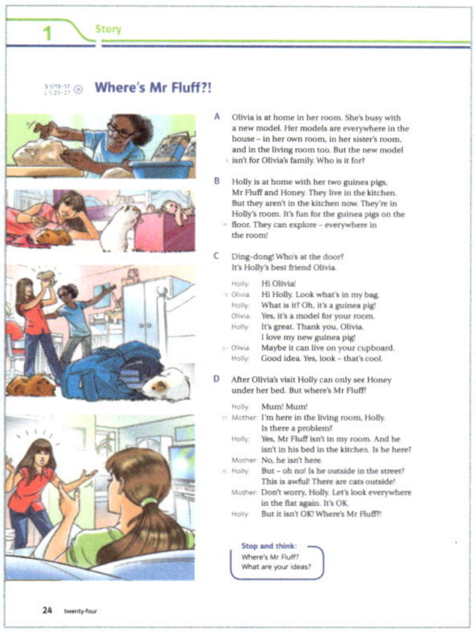

Lustige und spannende Texte über die fünf Lehrwerkskinder aus Greenwich erwarten dich auf den **Story**-Seiten.

Check-out

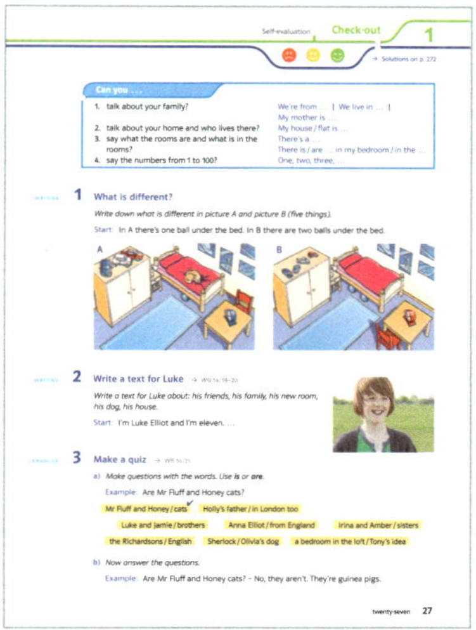

Mit diesen Übungen am Ende der *Unit* kannst du deinen Lernfortschritt selbst überprüfen. Die Lösungen stehen dir im Anhang zur Verfügung.

…wischen den Units

Across cultures, Revision und Focus

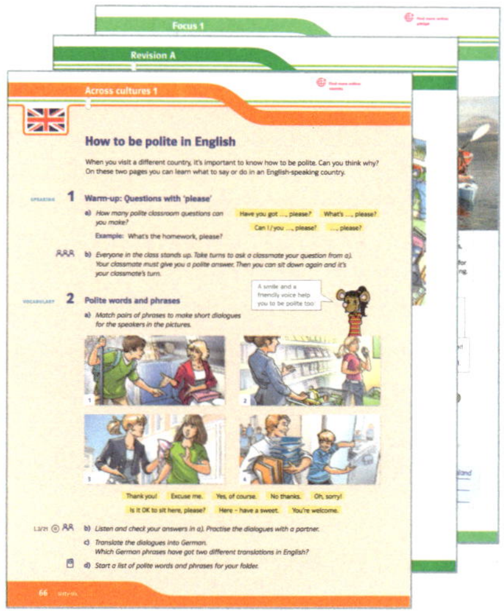

Zwischen den *Units* findest du **Across cultures** zum Kennenlernen der britischen Alltagskultur, **Revision** für die Wiederholung des Lernstoffs und **Focus** mit spannenden Sachthemen.

Üben und Nachschlagen am Ende des Buches

Practice pool

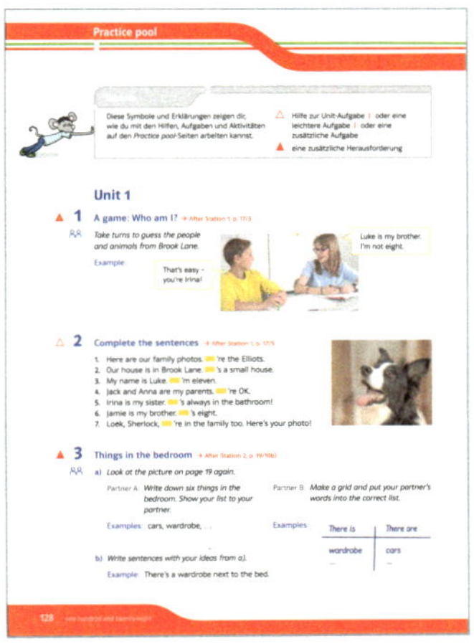

Die roten Dreiecke zeigen dir, dass du hinten im **Practice pool** weitere Übungsmöglichkeiten findest.

Grammar

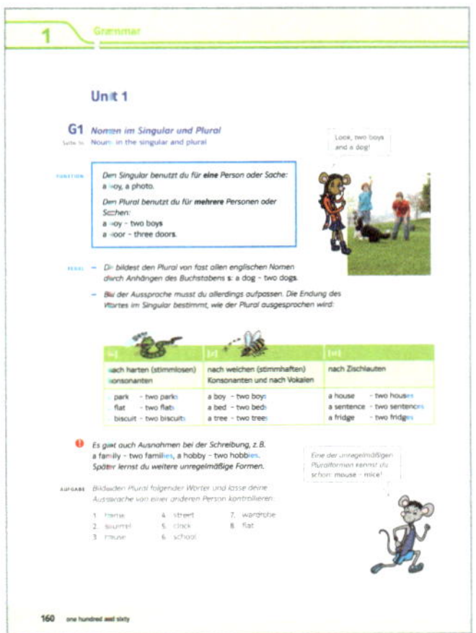

Im Anhang **Grammar** findest du viele Beispiele, Regeln, Tipps und Übungen zum grammatischen Lernstoff aus den *Stations*.

Und im Anhang findest du auch das Vokabular, eine alphabetische Wortliste (E→D/D→E) und vieles mehr …

Jule K. Weiss

Symbole

- → △ 130/1 zusätzliche / leichtere Aufgabe im Practice pool
- → ▲ 130/2 anspruchsvollere Aufgabe im Practice pool
- → WB 7/4 Übung im Workbook
- → G2 Grammatik im Anhang
- Partnerarbeit
- Gruppenarbeit
- Produkt für dein Portfolio
- S1/23 Schüler-CDs (Audio)
- L1/35 Lehrer-CDs (Audio)
- Lehrer-DVD (Film)

Green Line 1
Lehrerfassung
für Klasse 5 an Gymnasien in Bayern

Autorinnen und Autoren: Louise Carleton-Gertsch M.A., München; Marion Horner M.A., Ipswich; Carolyn Jones M.A., Beckenham; sowie Elizabeth Daymond M.A., Kiel; Paul Dennis M.A., Lahnstein; Rosemary Hellyer-Jones M.A., Ehingen (Donau); Harald Weisshaar, Bisingen; unter Mitwirkung von Michael Mattison, Stuttgart

Beratung: Dr. Thomas Becker, Nürnberg; Christel Beck-Zangenberg, Erlangen; Elmar Beyersdörfer, Gräfelfing; Wolfgang Funk, Bamberg; Michael Kleis, Geltendorf; Berit Möckel, Nürnberg; Uli Nürnberger, München; Wolfram Scharrer, Laaber; Harald Weisshaar, Bisingen

Für besondere Unterstützung danken wir herzlich Ms Susan Bolton von der **Thomas Tallis School**, London, und den Schülerinnen und Schülern der **Wigbertschule Hünfeld**.

Zusatzmaterial für Schülerinnen und Schüler zu diesem Band:

Workbook + Audio-CDs + Übungssoftware
978-3-12-803016-6

Workbook + Audio-CDs
978-3-12-803015-9

Trainingsbuch Schulaufgaben mit Lösungsheft und Audio-CD
978-3-12-803011-1

Vokabellernheft
978-3-12-803076-0

sowie eine Reihe von abgestimmten
English Readers

Zusätzliche Informationen in der Lehrerfassung

Produktiver Lernwortschatz
Rezeptiver Wortschatz
Neue Grammatik

△→ ▲→ **Help with/Instead of/After …:** Verweis auf unterstützende/alternative/weiterführende Aufgaben im *Practice pool* des Schülerbuchs für leistungsschwächere bzw. -stärkere Schüler/innen.

HA: Vorschlag zur Hausaufgabe.

Folie 1: Hier können Sie Folie 1 des Folienordners einsetzen.

KV 1: Hier können Sie Kopiervorlage 1 des Lehrerbands einsetzen.

Voc.: Hier sind Verweise auf Wortschatzhilfen im Schülerbuch und Workbook (WB) angegeben.

Lösung: Hier finden Sie Lösungen bzw. Erwartungshorizonte (EH) zu den geschlossenen und halboffenen Aufgaben.

1. Auflage 1 5 4 3 2 1 | 2021 20 19 18 17

Redaktion: Monique Kunhar, Rebecca Keller;
Lektorat editoria: Cornelia Schaller, Fellbach; Gaby Bauer-Negenborn, Weßling
Herstellung: Marietta Heymann

Gestaltung: Petra Michel, Essen
Umschlaggestaltung: know idea, Freiburg; Koma Amok, Stuttgart
Illustrationen: Peer Kramer, Düsseldorf; jani lunablau, Barcelona *(Maskottchen und Story)* sowie Christian Dekelver, Weinstadt *(Karten)*
Satz: Satzkiste GmbH, Stuttgart
Reproduktion: Schwaben-Repro, Stuttgart
Druck: DBM Druckhaus Berlin-Mitte GmbH, Berlin

Printed in Germany
ISBN 978-3-12-803012-8

9 783128 030128

Green Line 1

Lehrerfassung

von
Louise Carleton-Gertsch
Marion Horner
Carolyn Jones
Elizabeth Daymond
Paul Dennis
Rosemary Hellyer-Jones
Harald Weisshaar

Ernst Klett Verlag
Stuttgart · Leipzig

Inhalt

Legende

VOC Vocabulary — 🧩 Kompetenzaufgabe — 🇬🇧 Across cultures — ‹› Fakultativ

Inhalt

Legende

VOC Vocabulary — Kompetenzaufgabe — Across cultures — 〈 〉 Fakultativ

Inhalt

Inhalt

Legende

VOC Vocabulary — Kompetenzaufgabe — Across cultures — < > Fakultativ

Inhalt

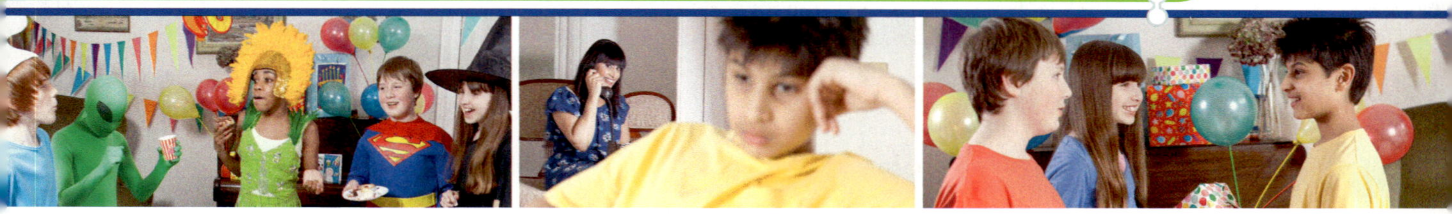

S1/1 L1/1

Pick-up A

I'm from Greenwich ['grenɪdʒ]

In Pick-up A findet keine Kognitivierung der Grammatik statt.
(G1 Nomen im Singular und Plural)
(G2 Die Personalpronomen und die Formen von *be*)

Look, two boys and a dog in Greenwich Park. Dogs are my friends, but not cats! I'm a mouse.

Tony

LISTENING **1** **Hello** → Folie 1

L1/2 *Listen. Who is it?* Dave Pia Luke Tony Sherlock

Lösung *Tony, Dave, Pia, Luke, Sherlock*

SPEAKING **2** **Characters**

Partner A: You're a character in the photo story.
Partner B: Close your book. Guess the character.

Example: A: I'm here with my parents. B: Oh, you're Pia!

SPEAKING **3** **Your turn: Talk about yourself**

My name is … | I'm German / … |
I'm from Regensburg / … | I'm …

SPEAKING

4 Dialogues → KV 1

L 1/3 a) *Listen and repeat the dialogues. Partner A is Tony. Partner B is Lou.*

b) *Your turn: Talk to different partners.*

Voc.: Numbers, p. 199

Hello.
My name is Tony.
I'm English.
I'm from Greenwich.
I'm one.
I'm a mouse.

WRITING

5 Your turn: Your profile → WB 4/1 → HA, KV 2

Look at Tony's card. Make a card with your photo and information.

SPEAKING **6** **Hi!** → Folie 1

Look at photo 10. Introduce a classmate.

SPEAKING **7** **A puzzle: Tony's rhyme**

a) *Find the right order and make a rhyme.*

Start: I don't like …

I'm not scared of dogs, But I'm scared of cats!	I don't like squirrels And I don't like rats.
Yes, they're my friends – They don't eat mice!	Worms are OK And rabbits are nice.

L 1/4 **b)** *Listen and check the right order.*

Lösung *I don't like … I'm not scared of dogs … Worms are OK … Yes, they're my friends – …*

SPEAKING **8** **Your turn: Talk about animals**

a) *Write words for animals on cards.*

b) *Put all your cards face down. Take turns to choose a card and talk.*

Voc.: Animals, p. 200 / Animals, Word bank (WB), p. 2

Worms / … are OK. | I don't like worms. | I love …

I don't like … | I'm scared of … | I like …

VOCABULARY **9** **Sports** → WB 4/2

S 1/2 L 1/5 **a)** *Listen and repeat the words.*

football skateboarding
cycling volleyball
skating badminton

b) *Name more sports. Then make a class poster.*

Sports

SPEAKING **10** **Find words in the story with the same sound** → Folie 1

[ɒ]	[əʊ]	[aɪ]	[eɪ]
dog holiday …	Oh …	I …	name …

VOCABULARY **11**

A colours puzzle

What are the colours? Write the words in the correct colour.

Lösung *green, brown, red, white, yellow, purple, orange, black, blue, pink, grey*

Voc.: Colours, p. 201

yellow white red orange purple green

brown grey blue pink black

enger wrnob edr thewi lewyol

lurpep garoen clakb elbu npik ryeg

LISTENING **12**

The boating lake

→ WB 5/3–5 → HA, Folie 2

L 1/6

Look at the picture and listen. Find the people and point.

0	1	2	3	4	5	6	7	8	9	10	11	12
zero ('oh')	one	two	three	four	five	six	seven	eight	nine	ten	eleven	twelve

Voc.: Numbers, p. 199

SPEAKING **13**

What can you see? → WB 6/6

What can you see in the picture? Talk about people, things, colours and numbers.

Boat number eight is pink.

I can see Sherlock.

Pia is with …

I can see …

VOCABULARY **14**

A numbers quiz → WB 6/7

Roll two dice. What's the number? Read the question.

Example:

A: Four and six is ten. Number ten, please.

B: Can you name four sports?

A: Football, …

2 How old are you? | **3** Where is Greenwich? | **4** Say your phone number. | **5** What's your name? | **6** How old is Tony? | **7** Where is Pia from? | **8** What's your favourite colour? | **9** What's Luke's favourite sport? | **10** Can you name four sports? | **11** What colour is Sherlock? | **12** Where is the boating lake?

SPEAKING **15**

S 1/5 L 1/9

Voc.: The alphabet, p. 201

Alphabet rap

a) *Listen and say the alphabet rap.*

b) *Who is your favourite star? Spell his or her name.*

M-I-C-K-E-Y
M-O-U-S-E

A B C - RAP

A B C D E F G
Rap the alphabet like me.
H I J K L M N
Zero, two, four, six, eight, ten.
O P Q R S T U
Mice are nice – Lou, I love you.
V and **W X Y Z**
My favourite colours
are blue and red.

VOCABULARY **16**

Word puzzles → Diktat-/Transfertext

a) *What numbers and colours are the letters?*

Examples: D is a pink 'one'. – P is a green 'three'.

b) *Find the letters and write the words.*

1. 1 3 2 = F U N
2. 2 1 2 2 3
3. 3 1 1 1 2 3
4. 1 4 1 2 2 2 1

c) *Make three more word puzzles for your partner.*

Lösung *1. fun 2. hello 3. rabbit 4. cycling*

	1	2	3	4
(blue)	A	H	O	V
(green)	B	I	P	W
(black)	C	J	Q	X
(pink)	D	K	R	Y
(red)	E	L	S	Z
(white)	F	M	T	
(yellow)	G	N	U	

Find more online: e84yd7

Unit 1

S1/6 L1/10 It's fun at home

This is Brook Lane in Greenwich. Here's Luke with Sherlock – and that's Holly, a girl from school. Holly and her family live in a flat in the street, and Luke and his family live in the house with the green door.

LISTENING **1** **Luke and Sherlock** → Folie 3

L 1/11 **a)** *Listen and point to the photos.*

b) *Where are Luke and Sherlock?*

Start: 1. In photo A they're …

in the living room | in the bedroom | in the kitchen | in the bathroom | in the street

That's my house too. It's a good house for a mouse – the biscuits under the table are nice!

TV chair sofa table
shower bath toilet bed
clock wardrobe cupboard cooker

In Unit 1 lernst du

… über deine Familie und dein Zuhause zu sprechen. Dazu lernst du:

- Wortschatz zum Thema sowie Zahlen über zwölf
- zu fragen und zu sagen, was es an einem Ort gibt und wo sich etwas befindet *(there is / there are)*.

VOCABULARY

2 What is it? → WB 7/1–2

Voc.: Rooms at home, p. 202 / In my room, Word bank (WB), p. 3

a) *Pick-up: Look at the four rooms. How many things can you name? Match the words and the things.*

b) *Copy the mind map for 'bathroom'. Make mind maps for more rooms.*

Vocabulary skills

Mind maps help you to collect new words.

bathroom – bath, shower, toilet

SPEAKING

3 A quiz → WB 7/3 → Folie 3, HA

Ask your partner quiz questions.

big / small / white / …

in the kitchen / bedroom / …

Example: A: It's in the bedroom. It's big. What is it?
B: It's the wardrobe.

G1 Nomen im Singular und Plural
G2 Die Personalpronomen und die Formen von *be*
G6 Die Possessivbegleiter

S1/7 L1/12

This is my family

Greenwich – ['grenɪdʒ]

Zajac – ['saɪjæk]
Cracow – ['krækau]
Jan – [jɑːn]

Hi! I'm Luke Elliot. I'm from Greenwich. I live with my parents, my sister and my little brother. My father is English, but my mother is from Poland. The Zajacs (her family) live in Cracow. My cousin Jan is an only child, like my dad. Jan is twelve – and cool! I'm eleven.

My parents are great, and my sister is OK too. Her name is Irina and she's thirteen. It isn't always easy with my brother Jamie. He's eight. But it's fun at home with our crazy dog Sherlock!

READING

1 Find the speaker in Luke's family tree

→ WB 8/4 → G1, 6 → Folie 4

Example: "Luke and Jamie are my brothers." – That's Irina.

brother – brothers

Lou

1. "My parents live in Poland. I live in Greenwich."
2. "Luke is my big brother."
3. "I'm eleven and my cousin is cool!"
4. "Anna is my sister."
5. "My parents are Henry and Carol."
6. "Luke is my cousin."
7. "I'm eight. I'm crazy!"

Lösung 1. That's Anna. 2. That's Jamie. 3. That's Luke. 4. That's Damian. 5. That's Jack. 6. That's Jan. 7. That's Jamie.

VOCABULARY

2 Word power

→ HA, KV 3

a) *Find family words in Luke's text.* Start: parents, …

b) *Pick-up: Collect more family words. Write down pairs: brother – sister* | …

SPEAKING **3**

→ 128/1
→ After

Voc.: Adjectives, p. 204

Your turn: Names in your family → Folie 4

Write down names in your family – animals too! Take turns to ask about the names.

Example:

Tell me about Sven, please.

He's my brother.
He's thirteen.
He's cool.

Michael
Inge
Susi
Sven
Benni

LISTENING **4**

L1/14

Holly and her family → WB 8/5

a) *Listen and point to the people in the photos.*

b) *Listen again. Find two sentences for the people and the names.*

Start: 1. Holly: She's the quiet sister. She's …

They're the parents. He's in London too.
She's fifteen. They're guinea pigs.
She's crazy. She's the quiet sister.
They're friends. She's eleven.
They're in the kitchen. He's cool.

Lösung Holly: *She's the quiet sister. She's eleven.* Sally and Steve: *They're the parents. They're friends.* Mr Fluff and Honey: *They're guinea pigs. They're in the kitchen.* Amber: *She's fifteen. She's crazy.* Steve: *He's in London too. He's cool.*

Holly Richardson and her family

LANGUAGE **5**

→ 128/2
→ After …

Tony in Brook Lane → G2

Copy the text and make short forms.

I'm a good mouse. My house is in Brook Lane. **It** 1 a good house for a mouse. I love the biscuits under the table – **they** 2 nice! The girl in the house is thirteen. **She** 3 OK. I like the boys too – **they** 4 great! The dog is great too. **He** 5 big and **I** 6 only small. But **we** 7 friends. And Lou is a new friend. **She** 8 my favourite mouse! **It** 9 fun with her.

Lösung *1. It's 2. they're 3. she's 4. they're 5. he's 6. I'm 7. we're 8. She's 9. It's*

I am = I'm
we are = we're
he / she / it is = he's / she's / it's
you are = you're
they are = they're

Tony

G3 Die Verneinung von *be*

LANGUAGE

6 The Richardson family

→ WB 9/6 → G3

Lösung *1. are 2. is 3. isn't 4. are 5. is 6. are 7. isn't 8. aren't 9. is 10. aren't*

a) *Put in: **is** – **isn't** – **are** – **aren't***

Sally and Steve [1] the parents in the Richardson family. Steve [2] in London too, but he [3] with his family. Amber and Holly [4] with Sally in a small flat in Greenwich. Holly [5] a quiet girl. Mr Fluff and Honey [6] her guinea pigs. The flat in Brook Lane [7] big, and small flats [8] good for big animals. The flat [9] OK for Mr Fluff and Honey. They [10] big animals.

Lösung *1. Holly isn't five. She's eleven. 2. Mr Fluff and Honey aren't rabbits. They're guinea pigs. 3. Luke and Jamie aren't sisters. They're brothers. 4. Brook Lane isn't in Hamburg. It's in Greenwich. 5. The Elliots aren't from Germany. They're from England. 6. Sherlock isn't pink. He's black and white.*

b) *Correct the sentences.* → HA

Example: A mouse is big. → A mouse **isn't** big. It's small.

1. Holly is five. 2. Mr Fluff and Honey are rabbits. 3. Luke and Jamie are sisters. 4. Brook Lane is in Hamburg. 5. The Elliots are from Germany. 6. Sherlock is pink.

What's the rule for negative forms?
is – isn't
are – aren't

c) *Partner A: Make 'wrong' sentences. Partner B: Correct them.*

WRITING

7 Your turn: Your family

→ WB 9/7–8

Write a text about your family like this. Put it in your English folder.

I'm Steffi Kurz. I'm ten. I live with my parents and my brother. My brother is eight. His name is Alex. He's OK. Our dog is Susy and she isn't crazy. She's great!

Useful phrases

I'm … | I live with …
My parents are … | They …
My sister / brother is / isn't …
Her / His name is … | She / He …
My dog … / Our rabbit …

MEDIATION

8 An e-mail for Pia from Olivia

→ WB 10/9

Was erzählt Pia ihren Eltern über den Inhalt der E-Mail von Olivia? Wähle aus den Sätzen unten die richtigen aus.

Hi Pia. Thanks for the photos. Your family's flat is very nice. I love the crazy wardrobe in your bedroom – it's COOL! :-))) Here are some photos of my family. Please say hello to your parents too. XOXO, Olivia

Lösung Olivia bedankt sich für die Fotos. Meine Fotos gefallen ihr sehr. Sie findet unsere Wohnung schön. Sie lässt grüßen.

Olivia bedankt sich für die Fotos. | Ihr geht es gut. | Meine Fotos gefallen ihr sehr. | Sie findet unsere Wohnung schön. | Sie hat mir Fotos von ihrer Familie gemailt. | Deutsche Wohnungen sehen anders aus. | Ich soll bald wieder schreiben. | Sie lässt grüßen.

S1/11 L1/17

What's the problem?

There's a nice garden behind the Elliot family's house. But their house is small. There are only three bedrooms: one for Mr and Mrs Elliot, one for Luke's sister Irina, and one for Luke and his brother Jamie. Oh no! Now there's a problem with the two boys.

Dad: Boys! Quiet, please! What's the problem? Are Jamie's cars everywhere again?
Jamie: No, they aren't!
Luke: Yes, they are! Look, they're on the floor, next to my bed, under the chair, behind the door, in front of the cupboard, on the –
Jamie: *Your* things are on the floor too!
Dad: OK, OK. It's a small room for two big boys. But listen: Here's your mother's idea. A new bedroom!
Luke: A new bedroom? Where?
Dad: In the loft. Is that a good idea?
Jamie: Yes, it is. It's a cool idea.
Luke: Great! My own room in the loft!
Jamie: No, *my* room!
Dad: Please, boys! Not a *new* problem!

READING **9**

Talk about the problem → Folie 5

1. What's the problem with the boys?
2. What's Mrs Elliot's idea?
3. What's the new problem?

LANGUAGE **10**

What's in the bedroom? → WB 10/10–11 → G7 → Folie 5

Voc.: Prepositions, p. 205

a) *Talk about the picture.*

Examples: **There's a** clock. **There are** two beds.

→ ▲ 128/3
→ △ 129/4
▲ → After
△ → After

b) *Where are Jamie's cars? Write sentences.*

Example: There are two cars **on** the table.

in | under | in front of | behind | next to | In the middle of … there's | on | On the right / On the left there's …

SPEAKING **11**

Your turn: What's in your bedroom? → WB 11/12 → KV 4, HA

→ ▲ 129/5
▲ → After

Start like this: There's a clock on the …

VOCABULARY

12 Numbers

a) *With a partner, say the numbers from 13 to 100.*

Voc.: Numbers 13–100, p. 206

13 thirteen	**19** nineteen	**25** twenty-five	**60** sixty
14 fourteen	**20** twenty	…	**70** seventy
15 fifteen	**21** twenty-one	**29** twenty-nine	**80** eighty
16 sixteen	**22** twenty-two	**30** thirty	**90** ninety
17 seventeen	**23** twenty-three	**40** forty	**100** a / one hundred
18 eighteen	**24** twenty-four	**50** fifty	

→ △ 129/6
△→ Help with …

b) *Read three numbers to your partner. He / She writes the number words down. Take turns to read and to write.*

c) *What number is your house or flat?*

Example: I live at Birkenweg 17.

Across cultures

Über seine Adresse würde Luke sagen: "I live at 254 Brook Lane." Schau dir nun die Adresse links an. Was ist bei einer deutschen Adresse anders?

LISTENING

13 The house in the loft

L 1/19

a) *Look at the pictures. Listen to Tony and Lou. Is A or B Tony's house? Explain your answer.*

Start: 1. … is Tony's house. His sofa is … 2. There's … / There isn't …

Lösung 1. A is Tony's house. There's a yellow living room with a green sofa. 2. A (shower). 3. B (big fridge with two doors). 4. B (40 new mouse houses).

b) *Write sentences about Tony's house. Here are some words to help you.* → HA

Voc.: Things in my room, p. 206 / In my room, Word bank (WB), p. 3

Start: Tony's house is… | Tony's living room is … | …

Tony's house | living room | bedroom | kitchen is	yellow | blue | red | green | nice | crazy | great | …	
There's a | There isn't a | There are | There aren't	yellow | blue | red | green | nice | crazy | cool | …	wall(s) | bath | shower | loft | room(s) | chair(s) | table(s) | fridge | …

SPEAKING **14**

Your turn: Talk about your house → HA, KV 5

Voc.: My house, p. 207

Say where you live. Describe your house and your room. These phrases can help you.

Useful phrases

I / We live at Birkenweg 17 / at …
My address is Färbergasse 7.
Our flat / house is small / OK / …
There's a kitchen / There isn't a …

There are two / … bedrooms.
The living room is big / nice / …
There's / There isn't a garden.
My brother's room is crazy / cool …

LANGUAGE **15**

People in Greenwich → WB 11/13 → G6

Voc.: Pronouns, p. 206

Put in the right words: ***my – your – her – his – its – our – their***

1. They're the Elliots. **Their** house is in Brook Lane.
2. Holly and Amber are sisters. ▬ flat is in Brook Lane too.
3. She's Holly. ▬ guinea pigs are Mr Fluff and Honey.
4. He's the dog in the Elliot family. ▬ name is Sherlock.
5. We're brothers. ▬ room is a problem!
6. I'm Olivia Fraser. ▬ friend Pia is from Germany.
7. It's a nice park. ▬ name is Greenwich Park.
8. Are you new in Greenwich? What's ▬ name?

Lösung *2. Their 3. Her 4. His 5. Our 6. My 7. Its 8. your*

Lou

LANGUAGE **16**

Questions and answers → WB 12/14 → G4

Yes, it is. / No, it isn't.
Yes, they are. / No, they aren't.

Match the questions and answers and make dialogues.

1. Is your bedroom nice?
2. Are the walls in your room white?
3. Is your wardrobe new?
4. Is it your sister's room too?
5. Are your things in the cupboard?
6. Are your sister's things a problem?

a) No, they aren't. They're on the floor.
b) Yes, it is. It's a small room, but it's nice.
c) Yes, it is. There are two beds in the room.
d) Yes, they are! They're always everywhere.
e) No, it isn't. It's my mother's old wardrobe.
f) No, they aren't. They're green.

Lösung *2. f) 3. e) 4. b) 5. a) 6. d)*

LISTENING **17**

Luke's new room → WB 12/15 → G7

L 1/20

Remember:
There is (There's) … = one!
There are … = two or more!

a) *What's in Luke's new room in the loft?*

Start: There's one / a … | There are two …

→ △ 130/7
△ → After …

b) *Take turns with a partner to ask and answer questions about Luke's room. Use short answers.*

Start: Is there a …? – Yes, there is. / No, there isn't.
Are there …? – Yes, there are. / No, there aren't.

Tony

G5 Fragen mit Fragewörtern

SPEAKING **18**

Your turn: Your partner's room

→ KV 6, Diktat- und Transfertext
→ WB 12/16 → G5, 7
→ △ 130/8
△→ Instead of …

a) *Ask your partner about his / her room.*

Is Are	+	your room big | …? the walls pink | …? your name on the door? it your own room? your things on the floor | …?
Is there Are there	+	a table | a sofa | … in …? two | three tables | chairs in …?
Where is Where are	+	your bed | your chairs | …?

Is your room big?

Yes, it is.

Across cultures

A: Are you from Greenwich?
B: No.

Das war leider keine sehr höfliche Antwort! Eine Antwort wie ***Yes, I am*** oder ***No, I'm not*** klingt höflicher als ein bloßes ***Yes / No***:

~~"Yes." / "No."~~ ☹
"Yes, I am." / "No, I'm not." ☺

b) *Write four sentences about your partner's room.*

Maria's room is small. Her name is on the door. The walls are white. Her things are in the wardrobe.

LISTENING **19**

< A song: Holly's family song >

L 1/21–22

This is my mum, Sally is her name,
This is my dad, football is his game,
This is my sister, she's a crazy kid.
Together we are a family.

Honey's in the kitchen, Mr Fluff is with her too,
They like our flat – what about you?
I love my pets, and they love me,
Together we are a family.

Chorus:
Mum and Dad, my sister and me,
Together we are a family.
Mum and Dad, my sister and me,
This is my family.

Hi, I'm Holly. What's your name?
Hello, nice to meet you.
Where are you from?
Oh, that's great!
Hey, can you sing? Yes?
Let's sing together!

(Chorus)

Musik und Text: T. Dorsch / P. Hoke

My fantasy house

Draw and write about a fantasy house for you and your family.

Think of all the house and family words from **Pick-up A** and **Unit 1**. Remember?

Step 1

Collect ideas

Make a mind map with your ideas. Look at Lou's ideas too.

friends
colours
things in the house / garden / …
family
animals
rooms

MY FANTASY HOUSE
- *my brother*
- *my parents*
- *my friends*
- *a boating lake*
- *a room for skateboarding*
- *different colours for different rooms*

Step 2

Draw your fantasy house

Draw a picture or a plan of your house.

For your text, use 'there is', 'there are' and useful phrases.

Step 3

Write a short text

Write five or six sentences about your fantasy house.

Step 4

Present your fantasy house

a) *Take turns to show your pictures and read your texts to your classmates. Talk about the houses. Ask and answer questions.*

Your house is crazy / nice / … The kitchen / Your sister's room is cool / …

I like your house / picture. Is the bathroom / …?

Where's …? What's in the …?

You know how to ask and answer questions. Remember? Look back at **Station 2**.

b) *Make a class display with your fantasy houses. Then put your work in your folder.*

S 1/13–17 L 1/23–27

Where's Mr Fluff?!

→ Folie 6

A Olivia is at home in her room. She's busy with a new model. Her models are everywhere in the house – in her own room, in her sister's room, and in the living room too. But the new model isn't for Olivia's family. Who is it for?

B Holly is at home with her two guinea pigs, Mr Fluff and Honey. They live in the kitchen. But they aren't in the kitchen now. They're in Holly's room. It's fun for the guinea pigs on the floor. They can explore – everywhere in the room!

C Ding-dong! Who's at the door? It's Holly's best friend Olivia.

Holly: Hi Olivia!
Olivia: Hi Holly. Look what's in my bag.
Holly: What is it? Oh, it's a guinea pig!
Olivia: Yes, it's a model for your room.
Holly: It's great. Thank you, Olivia. I love my new guinea pig!
Olivia: Maybe it can live on your cupboard.
Holly: Good idea. Yes, look – that's cool.

D After Olivia's visit Holly can only see Honey under her bed. But where's Mr Fluff?

Holly: Mum! Mum!
Mother: I'm here in the living room, Holly. Is there a problem?
Holly: Yes, Mr Fluff isn't in my room. And he isn't in his bed in the kitchen. Is he here?
Mother: No, he isn't here.
Holly: But – oh no! Is he outside in the street? This is awful! There are cats outside!
Mother: Don't worry, Holly. Let's look everywhere in the flat again. It's OK.
Holly: But it isn't OK! Where's Mr Fluff?!

Stop and think:
Where's Mr Fluff?
What are your ideas?

E 35 Ding-dong! Here's Olivia again, and there's a guinea pig in her bag again too. But it isn't a model. It's Mr Fluff! Guinea pigs explore everywhere – in bags too!

READING

1 The story → WB 13/17 → Folie 6

a) *Match the sentence parts. Write down the sentences.*

1. Olivia is busy with
2. Holly is at home with
3. The girl at the door is
4. The new model is a guinea pig for
5. After Olivia's visit there's
6. Mr Fluff isn't in Holly's room
7. Here's Olivia again –

a) and he isn't in the kitchen.
b) Holly's room.
c) her two guinea pigs.
d) with Mr Fluff in her bag!
e) a new model.
f) a problem.
g) Holly's best friend Olivia.

Lösung 1. e) 2. c) 3. g) 4. b) 5. f) 6. a) 7. d)

b) *Can you match the sentences in a) with the pictures in the story?*

Start: Sentence 1 – "That's …"   That's picture A / …   There isn't a picture.

Lösung 1. A; 2. B; 3. –; 4. C; 5. D; 6. D; 7. –

READING

2 Find the right headings for parts A – E

It's Mr Fluff!   What is it?   Where's Mr Fluff?!   Models everywhere   Fun for the guinea pigs

Lösung A: Models everywhere; B: Fun for the guinea pigs; C: A new model; D: Where's Mr Fluff?!; E: It's Mr Fluff!

WRITING

3 Make a dialogue for part E → WB 13/18 → HA, Folie 6

Find the right order for a dialogue. Start like this: Olivia: Hi Holly.
Holly: …

- Right! It's your crazy guinea pig!
- Yes, I'm here with my bag again.
- Look. What can you see?
- Oh, hello Olivia. It's you again!
- What's in your bag now?
- Hi Holly. ✔
- Oh, it's Mr Fluff!

Lösung O: Hi, Holly. H: Oh, hello, Olivia. It's you again! O: Yes, I'm here with my bag again. H: What's in your bag now? O: Look. What can you see? H: Oh, it's Mr Fluff! O: Right! It's your crazy guinea pig!

SPEAKING

4 Your turn: Talk about the story → Diktat- und Transfertext

Say what you like and don't like.

Examples: I like Olivia. She's a good friend. | The ending is …

Useful phrases

I like … / I don't like …
Olivia / Holly / Mr Fluff is …
The guinea pigs are …
Holly's room is …

Around the house[1]

VIEWING

1 Who's who?

1 *Watch the film. Who are they? Talk about the photos.*

father | brother | sister | friend

Start: Photo 1 – That's Laura. She's Nathan's …

Lösung *1. That's Laura. She's Nathan's sister. 2. That's Parule. She's Laura's friend. 3. That's Nathan. He's Laura's brother. 4. That's Mr Beckett. He's Laura's and Nathan's father.*

1. Laura ['lɔːrə]

2. Parule [pə'ruːl]

3. Nathan ['naɪθən]

4. Mr Beckett

SPEAKING

2 Who's your favourite?

Say who you like / don't like.

Examples: Partner A: I like Nathan. He's … What about you?
Partner B: I like Nathan too. I don't like …

I like … | I don't like … | What about you? | I like … too. | He's / He isn't … | She's / She isn't … | cool | crazy | great | nice

WRITING

3 What's the problem? → HA, KV 7

A

B

C

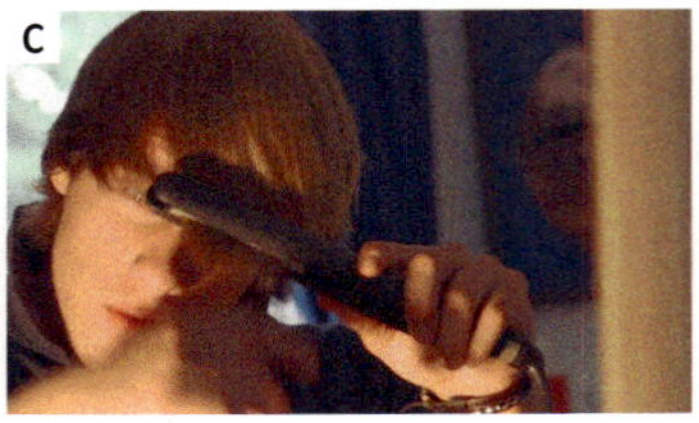

Write sentences for the photos. **Example:** There it is! My hair straightener[2]!

WRITING

4 Our house → KV 7

Watch the film again. Write about Laura and Nathan's house. What is / isn't there in the house?

SPEAKING

5 Brothers and sisters → KV 8

Partner A is Laura, Partner B is Nathan. Make and act a dialogue.

Start like this: A: Where's my pink T-shirt? Is it in your wardrobe? | B: No, it isn't. Maybe it's …

1 **around the house** [əˌraʊnd ðə 'haʊs] zu Hause | 2 **hair straightener** ['heə ˌstreɪtnə] Glätteisen

→ Solutions on p. 272

Can you …

1. talk about your family?	We're from … | We live in … | My mother is …
2. talk about your home and who lives there?	My house / flat is …
3. say what the rooms are and what is in the rooms?	There's a … There is / are … in my bedroom / in the …
4. say the numbers from 1 to 100?	One, two, three, …

WRITING

1 What is different? → HA

Write down what is different in picture A and picture B (five things).

Start: In A there's one ball under the bed. In B there are two balls under the bed.

A

B

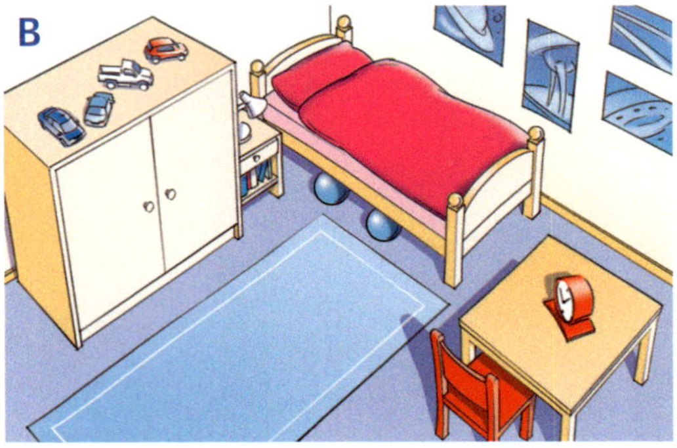

WRITING

2 Write a text for Luke → WB 14/19–20 → HA, KV 9

Write a text for Luke about: his friends, his family, his new room, his dog, his house.

Start: I'm Luke Elliot and I'm eleven. …

LANGUAGE

3 Make a quiz → WB 14/21 → HA, KV 10

a) *Make questions with the words. Use* ***is*** *or* ***are****.*

Example: Are Mr Fluff and Honey cats?

Mr Fluff and Honey / cats ✓ — Holly's father / in London too — Luke and Jamie / brothers — Anna Elliot / from England — Irina and Amber / sisters — the Richardsons / English — Sherlock / Olivia's dog — a bedroom in the loft / Tony's idea

b) *Now answer the questions.*

Example: Are Mr Fluff and Honey cats? – No, they aren't. They're guinea pigs.

In **Pick-up B** findet keine Kognitivierung der Grammatik statt. Rückgriff auf/Erweiterung von Grundschulwissen.

S 1/18
L 1/28

Pick-up B
This is fun!

→ Folie 7

→ WB 15/1 → Folie 8

READING

1 In Greenwich with the friends → WB 15/2 → Folie 7, Folie 8

Lösung
1. That's photo 7.
2. That's photo 2.
3. That's photo 1.
4. That's photo 2.
5. That's photo 9.
6. That's photo 5.

a) *Who are the people in the photos on pages 28–29? What can you see?*

b) *Say which sentences match the photos.*

1. Holly and the new boy are sorry.
   – "That's photo …"
2. Luke isn't happy.
3. Olivia and Holly are happy.
4. It's a text message from Dave.
   He can't meet Luke.
5. It's Holly's lucky charm.
6. Holly is fast.

VOCABULARY

2 What can you say? → WB 16/3

Lösung
1. c) 2. a) 3. c) 4. b)

*Match the phrases to the pictures. (Two of the phrases match **one** picture!)*

1. Don't worry.
2. She's cute.
3. I'm sorry.
4. No thanks.

VOCABULARY

3 Holly, Olivia, Luke and Dave

Lösung *Olivia: cycling, inline skating; Holly: skating; Luke: to play with friends, football; Dave: computer games*

Lösung *I love …; My favourite sport is …, I like …, … is so cool.*

Voc.: Hobbies, p. 209 / Free time activities, Word bank (WB), p. 4

a) *Look at the photo story again.*
What hobbies can you find in the text?
Write a list for the four friends.

Example: Olivia: cycling

b) *Here's a phrase from the story to talk about hobbies: **I'm into** (football / sports / skating / …).*
Find four more phrases in the story to talk about hobbies. → HA

LISTENING

4 Interviews

L 1/29

Lösung *Girl 1: Sport, Music; Boy 1: Music, Computers; Boy 2: Reading, Computers; Girl 2: Reading, Sport*

Listen. What are their hobbies?
Make a grid like this:

	Reading	Sport	Music	Computers
Girl 1		✔		
Boy 1				
Boy 2				
Girl 2				

VOCABULARY

5 More hobbies → WB 16/4

Lösung 1. draw/paint picture 2. read books 3. take photos 4. listen to music 5. go swimming 6. play with my cat

a) *Look at the pictures and match the hobbies.*

1

2

3

4
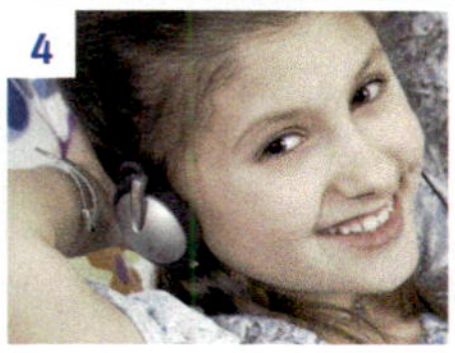
5

6

play with my cat | draw / paint pictures | go swimming | read books | take photos | listen to music

Lösung b) play in the garden/cards/ computer games/ with my friends/badminton/basketball; watch TV, DVDs; read magazines, things on the internet; go skateboarding/ cycling

b) *Make pairs with the verbs on the left and the other words on the right. Write the pairs down.*

c) *Act your hobby. Can your classmates guess it?*

play watch read go	+	in the garden | cards | skateboarding | magazines | TV | things on the internet | DVDs | computer games | with my friends | badminton | cycling | basketball

SPEAKING

6 Your turn: Talk about a hobby → WB 16/5–6 → HA

Tell a partner about a hobby.

Example:
I love drawing pictures.
It's fun to draw with my favourite colours. I can draw …

Useful phrases

My hobby is / My hobbies are…
Swimming / reading / … is one of my hobbies.
I'm into sports / reading / …
I like / love …ing. – Me too.
I can read … / play …
It's fun to read / to …
Animals / … are fun.

SPEAKING

7 Role play: What's fun? What's boring?

Make dialogues.

Example:
A: Bikes are cool! Let's go cycling.
B: No, that's a silly idea. But we can play with my rabbits in our garden.
A: Yes, OK! Animals are fun.

WRITING

8 Your turn: Write about your hobby → HA, Diktat- und Transfertext

Write a short text about one of your hobbies. Put it in your English folder.

Example: My favourite hobby is listening to music. I'm into …

Find more online: n6627i

Unit 2

S 1/20 L 1/31 I'm new at TTS

1

2

LISTENING

1 Luke, Dave and the new boy → Folie 9

L 1/32

Before you listen, read the speech bubbles in photos 1–6. Then listen to the tutor (Mr Swindon) and the boys, and look at the photos again. Say where the boys are.

Lösung EH *cafeteria (picture 3), recording studio (picture 6), school shop (picture 4), Art room (picture 5)*

VIEWING

2 Schools in the UK → KV 11, KV 12

2

Watch the film. Say what you can see. Then write sentences for the different scenes.

In Unit 2 lernst du

… vieles über die Schule und über Schüler in Großbritannien. Du lernst:

- Wortschatz zum Thema
- zu sagen, was jemand hat *(have got, 's, s')*
- zu sagen, was man tun darf und was nicht *(can / can't, don't)*
- auf Rechtschreibung zu achten.

VOCABULARY

3 Make a classroom quiz

→ KV 13, HA
→ WB 17/1–3

→ ▲ 131/1
▲ → After …

a) *Pick-up: With your partner, write down school words from the photos. Add more words from primary school.*

b) *Classroom quiz: Point to things in the classroom. Ask a classmate what they are.*

What's that?

It's a chair.
It's a …

Across cultures

Alle Schülerinnen und Schüler an britischen Schulen tragen eine Schuluniform. So ist die Zugehörigkeit zur Schule auf einen Blick erkennbar. Was würdest du von einer Uniform für deine Schule halten?

G8 Der unbestimmte Artikel
G9 Der bestimmte Artikel
G10 Besitz und Zugehörigkeit mit *have got* ausdrücken
G11 Die Verneinung von *have got*

S 1/21
L 1/33

Have you got questions for Jay? → Folie 10, KV 14

Holly isn't happy. She's got a problem. There's an English test today, and she hasn't got her lucky charm with her in the classroom. Where is it? Maybe it's in her schoolbag. Oh, but here's the tutor, Mr Swindon, with Luke, Dave – and a new boy in the tutor group.

Olivia: Holly, look – it's the cute boy again!
Mr S: Good morning, everyone. We've got a new student. This is Jahangir Azad.
Jay: Oh, you can call me Jay. [dʒəˈhʌŋgɪə əˈzɑːd]
Mr S: Maybe you've got questions for him. – Is an interview OK, Jay?
Jay: Cool. No problem.
Luke: (Oh, he's *so* cool.)
Mr S: Have you got a question, Luke?
Luke: Oh, er – where's your old school?
Jay: In Enfield. But I live in Greenwich now.
Dave: What are your hobbies? I'm into computers.
Jay: I like singing and dancing.
Olivia: Wow!
Luke: (Oh, wow!)
Mr S: Singing? That's great for our new project in the recording studio!
Olivia: Has your old school got a recording studio too, Jay?
Jay: No, it hasn't. But I'm at Thomas Tallis now – and that's great!
Luke: (That isn't great for *everyone*.)
Olivia: You now, Holly.
Holly: No, Olivia – please!
Mr S: Have you got a question, Holly?
Holly: No, I haven't. Well – yes, I have. What's your favourite colour?
Jay: Hi Holly. I haven't got a favourite colour. But I've got something for the girl in pink. Wait and see …

READING

1 Work with the text → WB 18/4

a) *Complete the information.*

1. The new student's name is …
2. His hobbies are …
3. His old school hasn't got …
4. Holly has got …
5. Jay hasn't got …

Lösung 1. … Jay Azad.
2. … singing and dancing.
3. … a recording studio.
4. … a problem.
5. … a favourite colour.

b) *What are your ideas?*

1. Who's 'the girl in pink' (line 35)?
2. Where's Holly's lucky charm? – It's …
   - in her schoolbag.
   - in the computer room.
   - …

LISTENING 2 — *A* or *an*? → WB 18/5 → G8

L1/35

Lösung 1. an 2. a 3. an 4. a 5. an 6. an 7. a 8. An 9. an

Here's [1] exercise book. And here's [2] pencil-case. This is [3] English book. And this is [4] pen. It's [5] orange pen. It isn't [6] old pen. Holly has got [7] lucky charm – but where is it? [8] interview is OK for Jay. Mr Swindon has got [9] idea.

a ruler
an English book
Find the rule.

LISTENING 3 — The: [ðə] or [ði]? → WB 18/6 → G9

L1/36

Listen and write the words in two lists. [ðə] pencil, …
[ði] old ruler, …

the [ðə] **new boy**
the [ði] **old school**
Find the rule.

VOCABULARY 4 — Things in schoolbags → Folie 10

→ △ 131/2
△ → After …

a) *Play a game:*
Partner A: *Look at Holly's things. Then close your book and say what she has got.*
Partner B: *Check and then take turns.*

She's got three books. She's got a …

b) *Pick-up: What have you got in your schoolbag?* → HA

Start: I've got a / an …

LANGUAGE 5 — Find the right forms → WB 19/7 → G10–11 → KV 15

Lösung 1. has got 2. have got 3. hasn't got 4. has got 5. haven't got 6. has got, hasn't got 7. have got

haven't got | have got | has got | hasn't got

1. My new school **has got** a big cafeteria.
2. The students here ___ a cool recording studio.
3. My old school ___ a recording studio.
4. Everyone at TTS ___ a blue uniform. Boring!
5. It's OK for teachers – they ___ a uniform.
6. The school shop ___ pens and things, but it ___ sweets.
7. Schools everywhere ___ silly rules!

LANGUAGE 6 — Put in the short forms → G10 → HA

Lösung 1. we've got 2. He's got 3. It's got 4. I' ve got 5. It's got 6. She's got 7. you've got

1. Dave: We're in a good tutor group – we ___ a nice tutor.
2. Luke: Mr Swindon is OK. He ___ great ideas for projects.
3. Jay: TTS is a cool school. It ___ a big computer room.
4. Dave: I love computers. I ___ a computer at home too.
5. Luke: This is our classroom. It ___ a new whiteboard.
6. Jay: Look at Holly's pencil-case. She ___ a pink pen too!
7. Dave: Wow, Jay, you ___ a cool phone!

I have got	→ I've got
you have got	→ you've got
he has got	→ he's got
she has got	→ she's got
it has got	→ it's got
we have got	→ we've got
they have got	→ they've got

G12 Entscheidungsfragen und Kurzantworten mit *have got*
G13 Die Fragewörter *who, what* und *whose*

SPEAKING

7 TTS and your school
→ WB 19/8a) → Folie 11

→ △ 131/3
△ → Help with …

Voc.: School subjects, p. 211 / Subjects, Word bank (WB), p. 5

a) *Make two groups. Group A: You're students at TTS. Group B: You're at your school.*

Useful phrases

Our school has / hasn't got …
We've got … too, but we haven't got …
There's / There isn't a … at our school.
I like / don't like …
The … is / are cool / not so good / …

b) *Your turn: Write about TTS and your school.* → HA

LANGUAGE

8 Short answers: Ask and answer questions about Jay
→ WB 19/8b) → G12 → KV 16

Example: Has Jay got a favourite colour? – No, he hasn't.

Lösung Has Jay got a favourite colour? – No, he hasn't. Have Jay's mum and dad got jobs? – Yes, they have. Has his uncle got a restaurant? – Yes, he has. Have Jay's grandparents got a house in Pakistan? – Yes, they have. Etc.

[dʒəˈhʌŋgɪə əˈzɑːd]

Jahangir "Jay" Azad (11)

- **parents:** from Enfield / London; office jobs
- grandparents from Pakistan; house there
- **hobbies:** singing, dancing, talent shows
- friends at his old school send Jay text messages
- **favourite foods:** 'gajar ka halwa' (carrot pudding) from his uncle's Tandoori restaurant! (Jay and his brother Shahid help at restaurant with small jobs for pocket money)
- **favourite colour:** no
- **lucky charm:** no

[ʃɑːˈhiːd]

Has	Jay got a favourite colour? Jay's mum and dad got jobs? his uncle got a restaurant? Jay's grandparents got a house in Pakistan?
Have	his parents got a restaurant? Jay got friends at his old school? his old friends got Jay's phone number? Jay and Shahid got jobs? Jay got a lucky charm?

Yes, he has. Yes, they have.
No, he hasn't. No, they haven't.

SPEAKING

9 Talking in the classroom
→ WB 20/9–10

With a partner, match the dialogue parts.

Lösung 1. d) 2. e) 3. b) 4. f) 5. c) 6. a)

Partner A:
1. Let's draw something.
2. Have you got a red pen?
3. Can I use your rubber, please?
4. I've got a problem.
5. Is that your pen on the floor?
6. My ruler isn't in my bag.

Partner B:
a) Don't worry, here's one for you.
b) Yes, here you are.
c) Oh – thank you!
d) Yes, that's a good idea.
e) Sorry, only green.
f) Maybe I can help.

LANGUAGE 10 Questions with *who* and *what* → G13

a) *Look at the picture and answer the questions.*

1. Who is in the photo?
2. Who can you see in the photo?
   → *What is* ***who*** *in German?*
3. What is on Olivia's table?
4. What has Olivia got on her table?
   → *What is* ***what*** *in German?*

b) *Now look at the picture again. Ask and answer more questions with a partner.*

Example:
A: Who can you see next to Luke?
B: I can see Dave and Olivia.

A: What is on the table? – B: …
A: What has Dave got? – B: …
A: What colour is Olivia's pen? – B: …

SPEAKING 11 Let's play a game

All of the students put something into a bag. Now take something out of the bag and ask, "Whose … is this?" The other students guess whose it is. Take turns.

> Remember:
> *Whose* and *who's (who is)* are not the same!

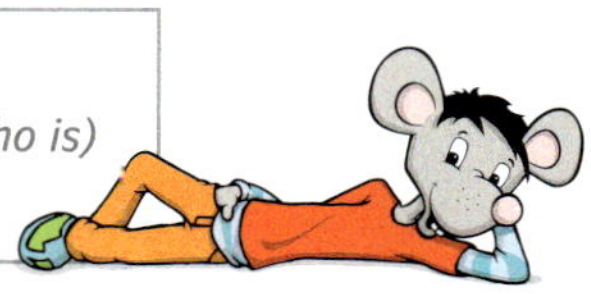

SPEAKING 12 Who's in the picture?

→ WB 21/11

→ △ 132/4
△→ After …

Ask and answer questions about the picture. Take turns with a partner.

Use ***who, what*** *and* ***whose.***

Example:
Who's under the table?
Whose bag is blue?
What's next to …?

MEDIATION **13**

A student from Britain
→ WB 21/12

Mediation skills

Don't translate word for word in mediation.
Look at the examples. What's different in English and German?

Englisch ***macht*** *Spaß.* – English **is** fun.
Es gibt *eine nette Schülerin an unserer Schule.* – **There's** a nice girl at our school.
Wie ***heißt*** *du?* – **What's** your **name**?
Welche Farbe ***hat*** *dein Füller?* – What colour **is** your pen?

Lösung EH
Alex: *Yes, no problem. My name is Alex. What's your name?*
Alex: *Are you new at our school?*
Alex: *Yes, we have got a new building.*
Alex: *Are there computer rooms at your school too?*
Alex: *There are old schools in Germany too.*
Alex: *What colour is your school uniform?*
Alex: *Thank you. English lessons are fun!*

Ein Mädchen aus Großbritannien ist zu Besuch an Alex' Schule. Was sagt Alex auf Englisch? Das Beispiel in Blau und die Ausdrücke in Gelb helfen dir.

Girl: Hi. Sorry, my German is awful. Is English OK?
Alex: *(Ja, kein Problem. Ich bin Alex. Wie heißt du?)*
Yes, no problem. My name is Alex. What's your name?
Girl: My name is Julie. I'm from London.
Alex: *(Bist du neu an unserer Schule?)*
Julie: No, this is only a visit. But your school is nice.
Alex: *(Ja, wir haben ein neues Schulgebäude.)*
Julie: I can see that. The computer rooms are so cool!
Alex: *(Hat deine Schule auch Computerräume?)*
Julie: Yes, but the school is old. I like German schools.
Alex: *(Es gibt auch alte Schulen in Deutschland.)*
Julie: Well, maybe. But German students are lucky – they haven't got a school uniform!
Alex: *(Welche Farbe hat deine Uniform?)*
Julie: It's brown. – Hey, your English is good, Alex.
Alex: *(Danke. Englischunterricht macht Spaß!)*

- What colour is …?
- … computer rooms too?
- we've got …
- … name?
- English lessons are …
- There are …
- … at our school?
- … new building

READING **14**

< School poems >

L 1/38

Read the poems. Maybe you can write a riddle too …

A school riddle[1]
What am I?
My first[2] is in rhyme, but not in rule.
My second's[3] in house and home and school.
My third[4] is in ruler but not in bike.
My fourth[5] is in building, picture and like.
My fifth[6] is in friend, in student and dice.
My sixth[7] is in teacher, but not in nice.
My seventh[8] is in happy and easy and crazy.
In school or not – don't be lazy![9]

First day at school
Tell us
About yourself
Your hobbies and your friends
The students here are cool and fun
Or quiet

1 **riddle** ['rɪdl] Rätsel | 2 **first** [fɜ:st] erster *(hier: Buchstabe)* | 3 **second** ['seknd] zweiter | 4 **third** [θɜ:d] dritter | 5 **fourth** [fɔ:θ] vierter | 6 **fifth** [fɪfθ] fünfter | 7 **sixth** [sɪksθ] sechster | 8 **seventh** ['sevnθ] siebter | 9 **lazy** ['leɪzi] faul

S1/24 L1/39

Don't stare! It's rude.

→ Folie 12

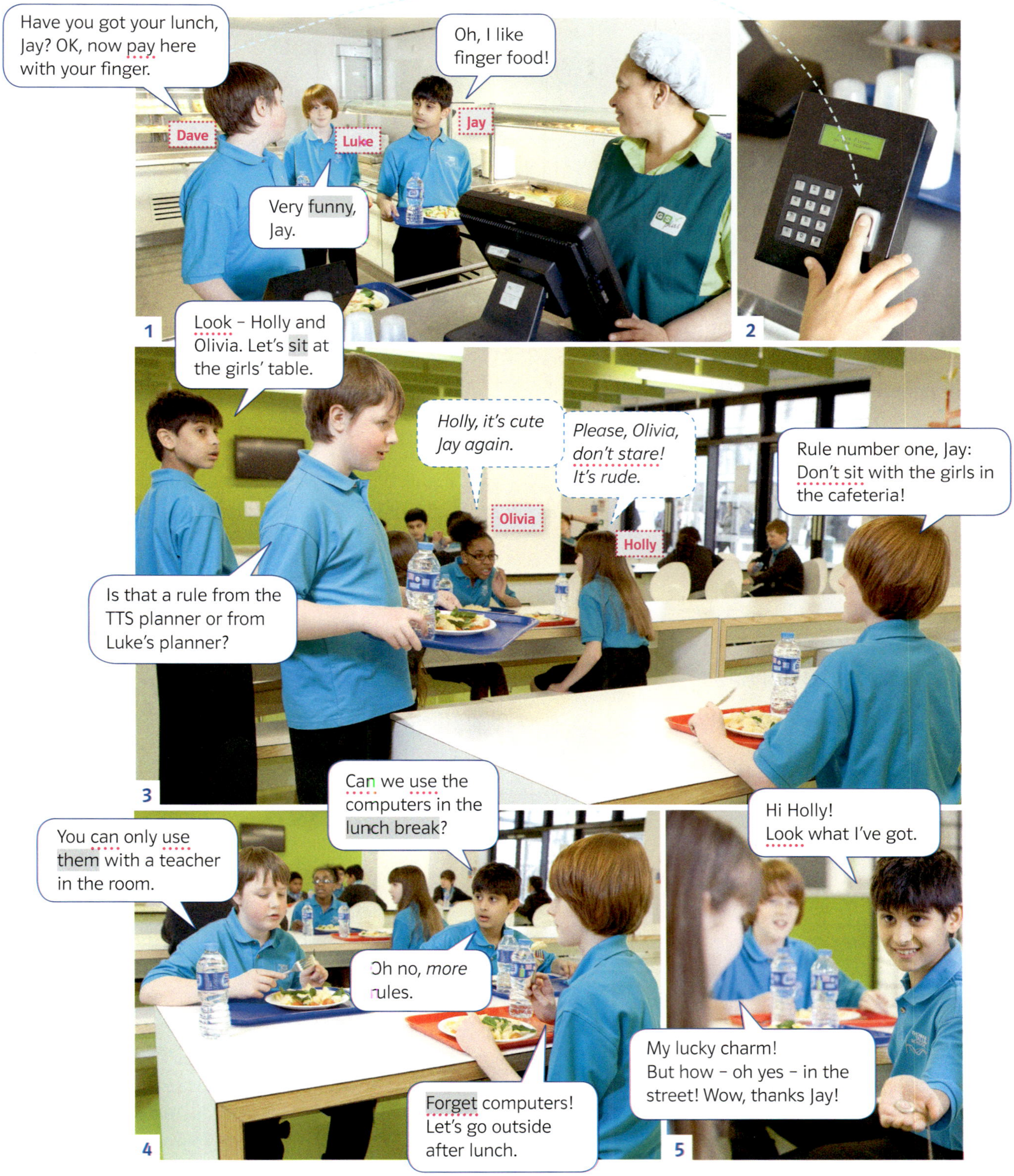

SPEAKING **15**

Jay and his new friends → Folie 12

Talk about the story photos on page 39. These phrases can help.

Luke is … | Dave, Luke and Jay … | Holly is … | The girls have got … | Jay has got … | …

LANGUAGE **16**

Information about TTS → G14

a) *What can Dave tell Jay? Make sentences with the right information.*

Lösung … go into a computer room alone. We can draw nice pictures in Art lessons. We can sing in the recording studio. We can't play with balls in the classroom. We can't use phones at school. We can go outside in the lunch break. We can't bring skates to school.

- do fun things with computers ✔
- go into a computer room alone ×
- draw nice pictures in Art lessons ✔
- sing in the recording studio ✔
- play with balls in the classroom ×
- use phones at school ×
- go outside in the lunch break ✔
- bring skates to school ×

Start: We can do fun things with computers. ✔
We can't … ×

b) Partner A: *Ask and answer questions about what students can do at TTS.*
Partner B: *Close your book.*

Example: Partner A: Can they use phones …?
Partner B: No, they can't. / Yes, they can.

LANGUAGE **17**

School rules → WB 22/13, 23/14–15 → G14–15

a) *Look at these phrases from pages 39–40. There are two different ways to talk about rules. What is the difference?*

We **can go** outside in the lunch break.
We **can't go** into a computer room alone.

Pay here with your finger.
Don't stare, it's rude!

Lösung Be polite. Don't be late for school. Wear the TTS uniform. Don't forget your planner. Bring your books. Don't run in the school building. Do your homework.

b) *Look at the different rules on page 39, in exercise 16 and on the right. Now make rules for the TTS planner. (Think! Which rules start with '**Don't …**'?)*

be polite | be late for school | wear the TTS uniform | forget your planner | bring your books | run in the school building | do your homework

Start: Be polite.
Don't be …

→ ▲132/5
▲→ After …

c) *Rules can be a problem for Jay. Write a list of funny rules for him.* → HA

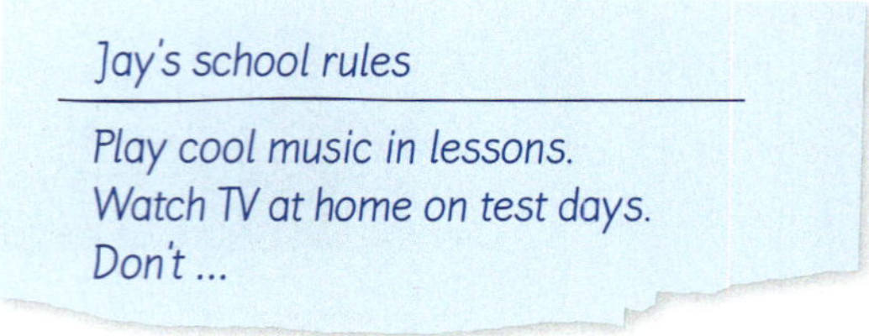

SPEAKING **18**

Your turn: Say what you can and can't do at your school → HA

Lösung EH We can play football outside. We can look at a book in lessons. We can't use our phones in the classroom. We can't play computer in the lunch break. Etc.

We can We can't	play look at use bring buy eat …	 …	at our school. to school. in / after lessons. in the lunch break. in the classrooms / … in the school building. outside. alone / with a teacher. …

SPEAKING **19**

Make a quiz → WB 23/16

a) *Write 6–8 quiz questions about Thomas Tallis School. Use information from the texts and pictures in Unit 2.*

b) *Find new partners, then ask and answer each other's questions. Which pair has got more correct answers?*

Useful phrases

How can the students…?
Where can the students …?
What's the name of …?
Where can you see / play / …?
What colour is …?
What's the rule for computers / …?
Where's Tony's …?

LANGUAGE **20**

Possessive forms: 's or s'? → WB 24/17 → G16

a) *Read part 1 of Tony's e-mail to his brother Terry.*

Hi Terry. I'm not in the Elliot**s'** loft now. My new house is at Thomas Tallis School. It's my friend**'s** idea. Her name is Lou, and Lou**'s** house is at TTS too, behind the door …

b) *Here are two phrases from page 39:* *Luke's planner* | *the girls' table*
Now look at the rules below. Match the parts.

1. When the word / name has already got an **s** …
2. When the word / name **hasn't** got an **s** …

a) you add **'**.
b) you add **'s**.

c) *Now put in **'s** or **s'** in part 2 of Tony's e-mail.*
(But first look and see which gaps need a plural form!)

Lösung 1. the students' classroom 2. Lou's pictures 3. Mr Swindon's cupboard 4. the children's tables 5. a mouse's fantasy school

… It's fun at TTS – there are no rules for mice! After lessons we can play in the **student** 1 classrooms or draw funny pictures in the Art room. **Lou** 2 pictures are crazy! The teachers have got cupboards in the room, and there are always biscuits in **Mr Swindon** 3 cupboard. But the best things are in the cafeteria. There are always chips under the **children** 4 tables. I love TTS – it's a **mouse** 5 fantasy school! CU, Tony

LANGUAGE **21**

Find the rule: *'s* or *of*?

→ WB 24/18–19 → G16–17 → KV 17

→ △133/6
△→ After …

Lösung *headings: s-genitive (for people), of-genitive (for things)*

a) *Look at the green and blue words. Copy the grid and find headings for it.*

Our tutor's name is Mr Swindon. My friend's skates are cool. Holly's bag is pink.	The name of my school is TTS. At the end of my street there is a park.

b) *Use* ***of*** *or* ***'s*** *and make more sentences.*

Lösung *1. friend's, 2. of, 3. boy's, 4. of, 5. tutor's, 6. of, 7. of, 8. student's*

1. my friend/favourite sport
2. colour/pen
3. the new boy/phone
4. first letter/word "pencil"
5. tutor/computer
6. door/recording studio
7. on the left/classroom
8. student/uniform

LANGUAGE **22**

This is our table and *that* is your table

→ WB 25/20 → G18 → Diktat- und Transfertext

→ △133/7
△→ After …

a) *Read the dialogue. What can you say about* ***this*** *and* ***that****? Copy the grid and put in* ***this*** *and* ***that****.*

	here	(over) there
	… book	… book
	… books	… books

Jay: Let's sit over there with Holly and Olivia!
Luke: No, this is our table. That's the girls' table. – Steve, this is Jay.
Jay: Hi Steve! – Luke, who's that girl with Olivia and Holly?
Luke: That's Lily. She isn't in our tutor group.

b) *Read the dialogue. What can you say about* ***these*** *and* ***those****? Put* ***these*** *and* ***those*** *in the grid.*

Lösung *here: this book, these books; (over) there: that book, those books*

Holly: I can't find my books.
Olivia: Are those your books, Holly? Over there?
Holly: No, they aren't.
Jay: Are these your books, Holly?
Holly: Yes, these books are my books. Thank you, Jay!

c) *Choose one thing in the classroom. Tell the other students what colour it is. They guess what it is. They can ask questions with* ***this*** *or* ***that****. Take turns.*

Example: It is blue. Is it this book? – No, it isn't.
Is it that bag? – Yes, it is!

How to practise correct spelling

These ideas can help you when you write texts. Do these exercises on your own, then check your answers with a partner. Are your answers right? Are your partner's answers right? Correct what is wrong.

1 Copying a text

a) *Copy lines 1–3 on page 34.*

b) *Check your partner's text. Is it correct? Is* ***your*** *text correct? Correct what is wrong.*

2 Using capital letters

Look at Tony's tips. Then write 2–3 sentences with names, places and the word "I".

Start: … is my brother / sister. We're from …

You need capital letters for:
- names of people and places
- the first word of a sentence
- the word 'I'.

3 Writing down words to learn → HA

Lösung
people: boy, partner, tutor, student, sister, brother, parents;
places: classroom, cafeteria, school, building, lake, house, flat

Find the words in the word snake. Make two lists: for people and for places.

People | Places

4 Using short forms → WB 25/21 → HA, KV 18

Lösung
I'm, She's, she's, he's, It isn't, it's

Look at Lou's tip. Write this text with short forms:

You need a ' for short forms (I'**m** / she is**n't** / …)

Hello, I am Luke. My parents are Jack and Anna. My father is English, but my mother is not. She is from Poland. Irina is my sister and she is thirteen. Jamie is my brother and he is eight. It is not always fun with Jamie, but it is always fun with my dog Sherlock.

5 Now make a spelling quiz

Copy five words from your English book.

Partner A: *Tell your partner your words.*

Partner B: *Write the words down and then spell them.*

S 1/27–31
L 1/42–46

Let's play a trick

SPEAKING

1 Before you read

→ Folie 13, KV 19

This story is about Jay's rap. What is a good rap? Can you say a line or two from a rap?

A It's a week before project day. The students in Mr Swindon's tutor group have got lots to do. The students can work in groups, in pairs, or alone. Who has got the best audio presentation? Dave and Luke can do the recordings for everyone in the TTS recording studio.

B
Dave: Great, girls. That's good. Nice poem!
Holly: Are you sure? I don't like my voice.
Olivia: Holly, no problem. And our poem is *great*!
Holly: So, who's next?
Luke: Oh, it's Mr Cute, Mr Cool. – Jay. The silly new boy.
Holly: That isn't nice! Jay isn't silly.
Olivia: Luke is jealous! Jay is the new boy and *already* so popular!
Luke: Me? Jealous?! Forget it. He's silly and his rap is silly.
Olivia: Oh, cool Luke isn't the king of our class. It's Jay! – Come on, Holly. Let's go.

C A few minutes later. Luke has got an idea …

Luke: Dave, listen: Let's play a trick on Jay!
Dave: No, Luke. Jay's cool. No tricks, OK? – Here he is! Hey Jay, I hear your rap is cool.
Jay: It's just a joke really. But thanks.
Luke: Olivia and Holly like it.
Dave: Well, we haven't got much time. Let's hear it, Jay.
Jay:
My name is Jay, you know what they say:
"He's a big star, so get out of his way[1]!"
On stage[2], on the net, on radio or TV
You see me, you hear me – you wanna[3] BE me!
So be cool, follow[4] my rules,
And maybe one day[5] YOU can be in the news[6]!

D It's project day. The students are in the classroom with Mr Swindon. Luke has got all the audio presentations on the computer.

Mr S: Great, girls. Thanks! – So now it's your turn, Jay. Luke, can we hear Jay's rap, please?
Luke: OK, here it is!

Jay's voice: *My name is Jay, you know what they say: "He's a joke, that's really great!"*
Jay: Hey Luke, that isn't my rap.
Olivia: Huh?! But that *is* your voice, Jay!
Jay's voice: *Holly is crazy, Holly is pink, Holly is* ***my*** *girl, wait and see!*
Holly: Stop it, Luke! It isn't funny. Stop it!!

E Only three or four classmates laugh. Jay is angry.

Jay: What is this, Luke? Have you got my voice on your phone?!
Luke: Uh, er, uh, yes, I have.
Jay: And the rule is 'no phones at school'!
Mr S: He's right, Luke. Please give me your phone. – Jay, are you OK?
Jay: Er, yeah, er – I think I'm OK now. And I've got a new rap! For Luke.
Mr S: For Luke? OK, let's hear it.
Jay: *My name is Jay, you know what they say:*
"Luke and his tricks, they aren't OK."
But Jay is cool, so here's a new rule:
Luke can show me his trick – and then it's cool.
– Mr Swindon, please don't make trouble for Luke. It's OK.
Mr S: Well …
Holly: That's so cool, Jay.
Luke: Really cool, Jay. Thanks. – So can I show you the trick after school?

READING

Lösung a) A week before project day – That's part A. Jealous?! – That's part B. Jay is really cool … – That's part E.

2 Headings for the story parts

→ WB 26/23 → Diktat- und Transfertext

a) *The story has got five parts. Which three parts go with these three headings?*

b) *Now write headings for the other two story parts.*

Jealous?! | Jay is really cool … | A week before project day

VOCABULARY

3 The characters

→ WB 26/24 → HA

→ ▲ 133/8
▲→ After …

Match the words to characters in the story. Give the line numbers from the story.

Example: I think Olivia is **funny**. Here's Olivia in line 15: "Cool Luke isn't the king of our class."

awful | silly | nice | cool | funny ✔ | fair | rude

Lösung EH
I think Holly is fair. Here's Holly in line 11: "That isn't nice!"

1 **Get out of his way!** [get‿aʊt‿əv‿hɪz ˈweɪ] Macht ihm doch Platz! | 2 **stage** [steɪdʒ] Bühne | 3 **wanna (= want to)** [ˈwɒnə] wollen | 4 **to follow** [ˈfɒləʊ] folgen | 5 **one day** [ˈwʌn deɪ] eines Tages | 6 **news** [nju:z] Nachrichten

Making friends[1]

VIEWING **1**

School clubs[2]

3 *Watch (0:00–1:19) and write down what clubs are in the film.*

Lösung *football club, music club, sign language club*

SPEAKING **2**

Alicia's idea → KV 20, KV 21

a) *Watch the film and find the right headings for the photos.*

Lösung *1. That's not nice. – That's photo C. 2. You aren't good at sports. – That's photo B. 3. Oh look, the football girls! – That's photo A.*

A

B

C

1. That's not nice.
2. You aren't good at sports.
3. Oh look, the football girls!

b) *The teacher and Jinsoo: Complete the dialogue with your partner. After that act the dialogue.*

Partner A: Teacher	Partner B: Jinsoo
Jinsoo, what have you got …?	Just books and …
Can I have a look[3], …?	Sure.
And what's …?	
No chewing gum[4] … You know …	It's not mine[5].

SPEAKING **3**

Talk about the characters

Lösung EH a) *Laura is popular. She has got friends because she is nice. She can play football. Alicia is alone. She hasn't got friends because she is awful. She can't play football.*

Lösung EH b) *Jinsoo a good friend. He is polite. His friend is Marley, but Laura and Emily are his friends too. Marley is Jinsoo's friend. He is different. He is cool.*

a) Start: Laura / Alicia is … | She has / hasn't got friends because …

She's | She isn't	+	alone | awful | cool | different | happy | nice | jealous | polite | popular | rude | a good friend
She can | She can't	+	play football
She's got | She hasn't got	+	friends

b) *What about Jinsoo and Marley? Talk about them. Who are their friends?*

WRITING **4**

Your school and Thomas Tallis: What's different? → HA, KV 21

Watch the film again. Write about your school and Thomas Tallis School. What have / haven't you got at your school? Look at the useful phrases on page 36.

1 **making friends** [ˌmeɪkɪŋ ˈfrendz] Freundschaft schließen | 2 **club** [klʌb] AG; Klub | 3 **to have a look** [ˌhæv‿ə‿ˈlʊk] anschauen | 4 **chewing gum** [ˈtʃuːɪŋ ˌɡʌm] Kaugummi | 5 **It's not mine!** [ɪts ˌnɒt ˈmaɪn] Mir gehört es nicht!

→ Solutions p. 272

Can you …

1. talk about what you've got? – There's a / an … | There are … | We've got …
2. talk in the classroom? – Can I use your …, please? | I've got a problem with … | Can you help …?
3. talk about rules? – We can / can't … | Don't … at school.
4. talk about a story? – I like / don't like … because … | … is polite / nice / not nice / funny / awful / rude …

LANGUAGE

1 Make one sentence → WB 27/25–26 → HA, KV 22

Example: Luke has got a dog. He is big. → Luke's dog is big.

1. Holly has got a pen. It is pink. 2. The Richardsons have got a flat. It isn't big. 3. Jay has got a school uniform. It is nice. 4. Holly has got a favourite colour. It is pink. 5. Jay has got three hobbies. They are singing, dancing and talent shows. 6. Tony has got a house. It is in TTS. 7. The Elliots have got lots of friends. They are very nice. 8. Jamie has got lots of cars. They are everywhere.

LANGUAGE

2 Mixed bag: What have they got? → WB 27/27 → HA

1. Olivia: Hi Jamie. 1 have you got there? 2. Jamie: I 2 got lots of great cars, but my 3 Luke hasn't. 3. Luke: Jamie's cars 4 everywhere! 5 are cars under the table and cars on the bed. 6 you got a brother too, Jay? 4. Jay: Yes, I 7 . 5. Luke: 8 your brother got lots of things too? 6. Jay: Yes, he 9 . But he 10 got his 11 room. Have you 12 a cat, Holly? 7. Holly: No, I 13 . Dave 14 got a cat. I've got 15 guinea pigs. 8. Jay: 16 colour are they? 9. Holly: Look, 17 is Mr Fluff and 18 is Honey. 10. Jay: They 19 cute!

SPEAKING

3 At school → WB 27/28 → KV 23

What can the students and tutors say?

WRITING

4 Your turn: Your school → HA

Write five sentences or more about your school.

⟨Revision A⟩ ist fakultativ und dient der Festigung/Wiederholung. Es werden keine neuen Sprachmittel eingeführt.

LISTENING **1**

In Dave's room

→ WB 28/1 → Folie 14

L 1/47

a) *Look at the two pictures and listen to Dave and Jay. Then say which is Dave's room.*

Voc.: In my room, Word bank (WB), p. 3

1

2

Lösung *Picture 1 is Dave's room.*

b) *Talk to a partner.*

Example: Partner A: Picture … is Dave's room because there are books.
Partner B: Yes, and Dave has got …, but …

c) *First choose a picture in a) with your partner. Then look at it for two minutes.*

Partner A: *Close your book.*
Partner B: *Describe the picture. (You can say wrong things too!)*
Can your partner say what is wrong?

WRITING **2**

Jamie's room

→ HA, KV 24

Jamie's spelling isn't so great. Find all the mistakes in his text, then write the correct text in your exercise book.

Lösung *I've got my own room now. It isn't Luke's room. He's got a room in the loft. There's a bed and a table, but I haven't got a sofa. I've got books and cars. They're on the floor. I'm very happy in my room.*

Ive got my own rom now. It isnt lukes rom.
Hees gota rom in the Loft.
Theres a ~~beb~~ deb anda ~~tadel~~ tabel, but i havnt got a sofa.
ive got booksan cars. ther'e on the flor.
Im very hapi in the rom.

Jamie

SPEAKING

3 My room

Talk to a partner about your room.
Say what you've got and where the things are.
Ask your partner questions about his/her room.

Useful phrases

I've got / I haven't got a …
There's a … on / next to / under / …
Have you got …? Is / Are there …?
Where's / Where are …?

LANGUAGE

4 Mixed bag: New friends → WB 29/2–3 → KV 25

Copy the text and put in the missing words. Then read out the dialogue with a partner.

Lösung 1. Who 2. 're/are 3. 're/are 4. What 5. boy's 6. is 7. has 8. hasn't 9. has 10. is 11. Their 12. colour 13. of 14. there 15. there 16. Whose 17. my 18. that 19. is 20. name

1. 1 are the children in the story? – They 2 Holly, Olivia, Dave, Luke and Jay. They 3 friends.
2. 4 's the new 5 name? – Jay 6 the new boy at school.
3. 7 Jay got a sister? – No, he 8 . He 9 got a brother.
4. Who 10 their tutor? – 11 tutor is Mr Swindon.
5. What 12 is the TTS uniform? – The colour 13 the TTS uniform is blue.
6. Is 14 a recording studio at TTS? – Yes, 15 is.
7. 16 guinea pigs are Mr Fluff and Honey? – They're 17 guinea pigs.
8. Is 18 Luke's dog over there? – Yes, it 19 . His 20 is Sherlock.

LISTENING

5 Sound and spelling

L 1/48

Copy the grid. Listen and put in the words.

Lösung [i:] machine, he, see, Enfield, please; [u:] cool, new, room, tutor, rule, group, Luke, school, uniform; [ʌ] but, funny, brother, under, London, colour

[i:]	[u:]	[ʌ]
machine …	cool …	but …

SPEAKING

6 Lou the supermouse → WB 29/4

Look at Lou's things. What can she do? What can't she do?

Examples: She can go cycling. She can't play basketball …

Find more online:
5cj8ih

Unit 3

I like my busy days

S1/32
L1/49

Voc.: Days of the week, p. 214

SPEAKING **1** **What's the time, please?** → WB 30/1–2 → **Folie 15, KV 26, b) HA**

→ △ 134/1
△ → After …

Voc.: The time, p. 215

Lösung a)
C: It's ten twenty.
D: It's four fifty-seven.
E: It's eleven forty-five.
F: It's six o'clock.
G: It's three fifteen.
H: It's seven fifty-five.

a) *Look at A–H. Say the time in numbers.*

Example: A: It's two thirty.
B: It's nine oh nine.

A 2:30	**B** 9:09	**C** 10:20	**D** 4:57
E 11:45	**F** 6:00	**G** 3:15	**H** 7:55

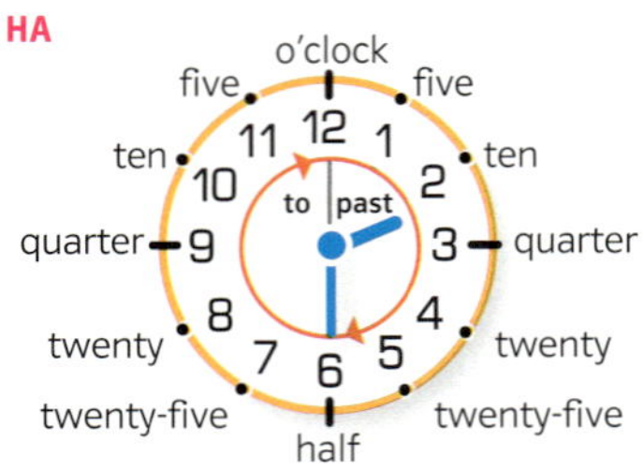

b) *Now use the phrases on the right for the times in a).*

Example: A: It's half past two.

… o'clock | quarter past / to … | half past … | twenty / five past / to … | nine minutes past … | three minutes to …

Lösung b) *B: It's nine minutes past nine. C: It's twenty minutes past ten. D: It's three minutes to five. E: It's quarter to twelve. F: It's six o'clock. G: It's quarter past three. H: It's five to eight.*

In Unit 3 lernst du
… über typische Tagesabläufe zu sprechen und zu schreiben. Dazu lernst du:
- wie man die Uhrzeit schreibt
- wie man Menschen beschreibt
- wie man sagt, dass jemand etwas regelmäßig tut *(simple present)*.

A Mum, look! I've got a surprise from Cooking Club!

B Oh no! I can't go to school by bike today!

C Sit down and have breakfast at the table, please!

D Time to get up! It's school today!

E Your things are everywhere. Come on, let's tidy your room.

F Oh, so this is how you do your homework!

G Dad – don't sleep on the sofa! Dad, go to bed. Dad?!

SPEAKING

2 Who can you see in the photos? → Folie 15

Match the speech bubbles with the right speakers. Guess who the new people are.

Across cultures

Vergleiche das, was du auf den Bildern siehst, mit deinem eigenen Alltag.

WRITING

3 Your turn: What you do every day → WB 30/3

a) *Collect phrases for what you do every day.*

b) *Now make full sentences.*
Start: I get up at 7:30. Then I …

What	When
get up	7:30
…	…

come home from school | have dinner | go to school | do my homework | have breakfast | go to bed

G19 Die einfache Form der Gegenwart
G20 Die Satzstellung in Aussagesätzen
G21 Häufigkeitsadverbien

S1/34 L1/51

I'm always busy → Folie 16

Hi Pia.
Yes, it's me!
Sorry I never write – I'm always busy.
Every morning I get up at 7 o'clock. I have breakfast with my family but there isn't always time to sit down at the table – my dad and my stepmum Claire are never happy about that! Then I go to school by bike – if my bike is OK, not like today. Lessons are from 8:40 a.m. till 3:20 p.m. After that it's Art Club on Mondays, on Tuesdays I always play netball, and on Thursdays there's my saxophone lesson at half past four. On other days I come home right away, but then I play with my little sister Lucy – and I often tidy Lucy's room. In the evenings I do my homework and I practise the sax. I sometimes help in the kitchen too. It's never easy to find time for other things. I usually read in bed, but not for long because I'm dog-tired after a busy day. But that's OK.
I'm happy – I like my busy days!
XOXO, Olivia

READING

1 Olivia's day → WB 31/4–5 → Folie 16, KV 27

Match the pictures with phrases or sentences in Olivia's e-mail to Pia.

Example: 1. "Every morning I get up at 7 o'clock."

Across cultures

Britische Schulen sind Ganztagsschulen. Sie bieten am Nachmittag oft im Rahmen von *clubs* verschiedene Aktivitäten an, z. B. Sport, Musik oder Kochen. Überlegt, wo ihr solche Dinge tun könnt.

***Lösung** 1. Every morning I get up at 7 o'clock. 2. On Tuesdays I always play netball. 3. On Thursdays there's my saxophone lesson at half past four. 4. Then I play with my little sister Lucy. 5. In the evenings I do my homework. 6. I usually read in bed.*

1

2

3

4

5

6

LANGUAGE

2 Your turn: Compare when you do things → HA → WB 32/6 → G19–21

Voc.: Prepositions, p. 216

I +	always usually often sometimes never +	get up go to bed do my homework tidy my room play / read / … +	on Mondays / … at 6:45 / … in the evenings / … before / after school …

LANGUAGE

3 Find the rule: Word order → WB 32/7 → G20–21

Lösung a) *The blue words are before the verb, but after a form of to be.*
b) *The phrases in green are at the end or at the beginning of a sentence.*

a) *Look at the sentences on the right. What can you say about the word order for the blue words? Think of 'to be' and other verbs.*

b) *What can you say about the word order for the phrases in green? Find the rule.*

How often?

I'm always busy.
I often tidy Lucy's room.
It's never easy to find time.
I usually read in bed.
I sometimes play netball.

When?

I get up at 7 o'clock.
I go to Art Club on Mondays.
On Tuesdays I always go swimming.
In the afternoons I do my homework.
At 9 o'clock I go to bed.

LANGUAGE

4 How often? → G21 → HA

→ △ 134/2
△→ After…

Lösung *2. I'm usually at home, 3. I often read, 4. I never watch, 5. I'm always happy, 6. I often play, 7. I'm never late, 8. I always have, 9. I usually play*

Add the words and write the sentences.

Example: 1. I **sometimes** go to bed late.

1. I go to bed late. (sometimes) 2. In the evenings I'm at home. (usually) 3. I read animal books. (often) 4. I watch TV in the mornings. (never) 5. I'm happy on Sundays. (always) 6. On Saturdays I play tennis. (often) 7. I'm late for school. (never) 8. I have breakfast at 7 o'clock. (always) 9. After school I play with my little brother. (usually)

MEDIATION

5 Pia's dance workshop → KV 28, HA

Lies Pias Beitrag auf der Internetseite eines deutschen Tanzvereins. Schreibe einer englischen Freundin und erzähle ihr von star4ever.

Start: They often go … | It's never easy …

Meine Freundin und ich gehen immer wieder zu star4ever, einer Tanzschule bei uns in der Nähe. Ich finde die Workshops dort immer genial.
Es ist zwar nicht einfach, am Samstag morgens um 7.00 Uhr aufzustehen, aber das vergessen wir normalerweise, weil der Workshop so Spaß macht. Oft steht vormittags Jazztanz auf dem Programm, nachmittags tanzen wir eher Hip-Hop. Ab und zu gehen wir abends in ein Musical. Sonntags tanzen wir oft in der Gruppe. Abends sind wir sehr müde, aber es lohnt sich!

Mediation skills

Don't forget! The **word order** is often different in German and English.

Example:
Montags *spiele ich immer* Fußball.
→ On Mondays *I always play* football.

Prepositions are often different in German and English.

Example:
Ich gehe *in* die Schule. → I go *to* school.

LANGUAGE

6 Where and when? → G20

Lösung 1. (After school) We look for biscuits in the cupboard (after school). 2. (In the afternoons) We draw funny pictures in the Art room (in the afternoons). 3. (At 5:15) We look for chips in the cafeteria (at 5:15). 4. (On Saturdays) We play in the classrooms (on Saturdays). 5. (In the evenings) we …

Look at the examples. Then write five sentences about Tony and Lou.

At 6:15	we	have	breakfast	in the cafeteria.	
	We	have	breakfast	in the cafeteria	at 6:15

1. after school | look for biscuits | in the cupboards
2. draw funny pictures | in the afternoons | in the Art room
3. look for chips | in the cafeteria | at 5:15
4. play | on Saturdays | in the classrooms
5. in the evenings | watch TV | in the computer room

LANGUAGE

7 Olivia's idea for Jay → WB 33/8 → KV 28

Lösung 1. We always get up at 6:45. 2. And my roommates Tyler and Steve always snore 3. But I sometimes snore too, so it's OK. 4. There are always lots of students in the cafeteria before lessons. 5. It's never boring for me here with all the new people. 6. In the mornings we usually practise a favourite song alone. 7. After lunch we never sing alone. 8. After singing it's usually time for dancing with other coaches. 9. At 6:00 we have dinner. 10. We often talk about our new dance moves. 11. On the last evening of the workshop there's a show and we always sing our favourite songs.

After Pia's post Olivia tells Jay about the dancing and singing school in Greenwich. Now it's half-term break and Jay is at the 2Cool Performing Academy for a four-day workshop. It's great! Make sentences for him.

1. We … always | at 6:45 | get up ☹
2. And my … snore | ALWAYS | roommates Tyler and Steve ☹ ☹ ☹
3. But I … snore too | so it's OK | sometimes | (But shhh! Don't tell Holly!)
4. There … before lessons | lots of students | are | in the cafeteria | always
5. We … in the mornings | practise alone | in small rooms | usually
6. After … sing | alone | never | we | lunch | (We sing in groups.)
7. It's … time for dancing | after singing | with other coaches | in the dance studio
8. We … at 6:00 | dinner | in the cafeteria | have
9. On the last … sing | a show and we | there's | evening of the workshop | always | our favourite songs | (Oh no – that's TOMORROW!!!!!)

SPEAKING

8 Role play: Let's meet

Make dialogues with a partner.

Example: A: Let's go inline skating today!
B: Sorry, I can't. I always play tennis on Mondays.
A: OK – can we go on Friday afternoon?
B: Great! Let's meet at the park at 4 o'clock.
A: Cool!

Useful phrases

Let's / We can …
practise … / play with … / meet … / go …
today / after school / tomorrow / later / in five minutes / this afternoon
always / usually …
outside the classroom / in the cafeteria
Great! / Cool! / Good!

WRITING

9 Your turn: Write about your day → HA → WB 33/9

→ △ 135/3
△ → Help with …

Choose a day and describe what you do.

My Fridays: On Fridays I always get up at 6:45, and then I have breakfast. After that …

Useful phrases

on Mondays / in the morning / evening …
always / usually …
Then / After that …
at school / in the park / …

S 1/37 L 2/1

She gets on my nerves

"Oh no – not Aunt Frances!"

It's 8 o'clock on Saturday and Dave is angry. His parents often work on Saturday mornings. Then Granny Rose usually comes and looks after Dave. But today she hasn't got time, so it's Aunt Frances.

"What's your problem with Aunt Frances?" Mrs Preston asks Dave.

"She gets on my nerves," Dave says. "She always talks – she never stops! Granny is cool. She sometimes chats, but she does other things too. She sits in the living room and reads or watches TV", he explains. "But Aunt Frances always comes into my room and talks and talks and talks! I can never play my computer games or play with Sid. She even tidies my room!"

"She's friendly and she helps," his mum says. "So be nice."

At 8:15 Mr Preston goes to work. Then at 8:45 Aunt Frances comes and Mrs Preston goes to work. (She's a vet. Lots of the neighbours take their pets to her surgery.) "A Saturday morning with my favourite boy – how nice!" she says. It isn't so nice for Dave. But what can he do?

READING **10**

Talk about Dave's problem

1. Who usually looks after Dave? 2. Who is it today? 3. Why is this a problem?

sung EH 1. Granny Rose ually looks after Dave. 2. day it's Aunt Frances. 3. She always talks and talks. Dave can never play computer games or play with Sid. She gets on his nerves.

LISTENING **11**

A nice surprise for Dave → Folie 17

L 2/2

Listen and find the right order for the pictures.

Lösung *E – A – F – B – D – C*

SPEAKING **12**

Lösung *(Picture E) 4. – That's right. (Picture A) 1. – That's wrong. Then Aunt Frances goes to the bathroom and Dave runs outside. (Picture F) 3. – That's wrong. Aunt Frances comes into the garden too, and she plays football. (Picture B) 6. – That's wrong. The ball goes into the neighbour's garden. (Picture D) 2. – That's right. (Picture C) 5. – That's right.*

Tell the story → Folie 17, HA

You know the right order for the pictures in exercise 11. Now find a sentence for every picture. But be careful: Some sentences are wrong! Find the mistakes, correct them, and then tell the story.

Start: (Picture E) Dave can't play his new computer game because …

1. Then Dave's mum goes to the bathroom and Dave runs outside.
2. Surprise! Aunt Frances and the Prestons' new neighbour are old friends.
3. But Aunt Frances comes into the garden too, and she plays with the cat.
4. Dave can't play his new computer game because Aunt Frances talks and talks.
5. After that they sit and talk, and Dave can play his computer game.
6. Oops! The ball goes into the neighbour's house.

LANGUAGE **13**

Lösung a) *I, you, we, they: work, can play, play; he, she, it: comes, tidies, looks, asks, gets, talks, stops, chats, does, sits, reads, watches TV, helps*
b) *Rule for he, she, it: infinitive + (e)s.*

Find the rule → G19

a) *Look at the text on page 55 and collect the verbs in two lists.* Start like this:

I, you, we, they	he, she, it
work …	comes tidies

Look at **G19** on page 173. What can you say about different spelling with verbs in the **he**, **she** and **it** forms?

b) *Look at the verb forms in the two lists. What's the rule for* ***he**, **she*** *and* ***it**?*

LANGUAGE **14**

→ △ 135/4
→ ▲ 135/5
△→ After …
▲→ After …

Lösung *1. lives, 2. explores, 3. goes, 4. comes, 5. looks after, 6. does, 7. works, 8. brings, 9. watches, 10. sleeps, 11. says, 12. tidies, 13. likes*

A day with the Prestons → WB 33/10–11 → HA

1. Sid the cat (live) with Dave and his parents. 2. Every day Sid (explore) Kidbrooke Gardens. 3. He (go) to other streets in Greenwich too. 4. But he always (come) home again. 5. Mrs Preston (look after) the neighbours' pets. 6. She (do) her work in a surgery. 7. She (work) on Saturdays too. 8. Holly sometimes (bring) her guinea pigs to the surgery. 9. In the evenings Mr Preston often (watch) TV in the living room. 10. But he sometimes (sleep) on the sofa. 11. Then Dave (say), "Dad, go to bed!" 12. Dave never (tidy) his room. 13. But he (like) cooking!

LANGUAGE **15**

Put in the correct verb forms
→ WB 34/12 → HA

→ △ 136/6
△ → After …

Lösung Holly: 1. loves, 2. come, 3. listen; Jay: 4. asks, 5. talk, 6. gets; Dave: 7. goes, 8. sits down, 9. see; Olivia: 10. draw, 11. talks, 12. does

Holly: listen love come
My sister Amber **1** black. Her crazy friends often **2** to our flat. They **3** to awful music in Amber's room.

Jay: talk get ask
My mother **4** lots of questions about my homework. My parents always **5** about school. It **6** on my nerves!

Dave: sit down go see
Every day our cat Sid **7** into the kitchen and **8** in front of the cupboard. Then we **9** it's time for his lunch!

Olivia: do talk draw
I often **10** pictures for my little sister – and then she **11** to the people in the pictures! She **12** lots of other funny things too.

SPEAKING **16**

Your turn: Make and play a game about your week
→ KV 29

a) *Tell your partner four things about yourself: what you often / never do, what sports / music you like, where you go after school / on Sundays, …*

b) *Make a card about your partner with the information from a). But don't write his / her name – just write 'my partner'.*

Example:

My partner never gets up late.
After school my partner plays basketball.
On Sundays my partner goes …

c) *Put the cards face down on your teacher's table. Take turns to go to the table. Take a card and read the information. The class guesses who it is.*

Is it you or your partner? Shhh! Don't tell!

LISTENING **17**

L 2/4–5

< A song: My daily routine[1] >

I wake up and I hit snooze[2]
I get up and take a shower
I get dressed[3] and go downstairs[4]
"Good morning, how are you?"

I sit down, have some toast
Drink some juice[5] to get more power
Take my schoolbag, leave the house
It's time to go to school

It's always the same but that's okay
This is how I start my day
This is how I want it to be
This is my daily routine
This is my daily routine.

Musik: T. Dorsch / P. Hoke
Text: B. Beling

1 daily routine [ˌdeɪli ruːˈtiːn] Tagesablauf | **2 I hit snooze** [aɪ ˌhɪt ˈsnuːz] Ich drücke auf den „Weiter-schlafen"-Knopf | **3 I get dressed** [aɪ ˌget ˈdrest] Ich ziehe mich an | **4 I go downstairs** [aɪ ˌgəʊ ˌdaʊnˈsteəz] Ich gehe nach unten | **5 juice** [dʒuːs] Saft

LISTENING **18**

Pets

L 2/6

Lösung *1. They're Holly, Luke and Dave. 2. They're in Mrs Preston's surgery. 3. It's about Luke's dog Sherlock and Holly's guinea pigs Honey and Mr Fluff. He often dances too.*

a) *Listen to the dialogue and answer the questions.*

1. Who are the speakers? – They're …
2. Where are the speakers? – They're in …
3. What is the dialogue about? – It's about …

Listening skills

When you listen to a dialogue, first find out the situation.
Ask: **Who? Where? What?**

Then listen again for more information.

→ △ 136/7
△ → After …

Lösung b) *Sherlock: always says hello, finds Luke's things, is a clever dog, can do lots of cool tricks; Honey: often sits in Holly's room and chats, always tidies her bed in the kitchen; Mr Fluff: never has time, is a crazy boy, runs and explores everywhere in the flat, often dances, shows he's happy*

b) *Copy the grid. Then listen to the scene again. Collect information about the pets.*

Sherlock	Honey	Mr Fluff
always says hello	often …	…

c) *Work in groups of three. Take turns to use your grids to talk about the pets. The others check the information in their grids.*

VOCABULARY **19**

Words and phrases about people

Lösung *(Smiley happy) friendly, helps everyone, always listens, funny, nice, happy, favourite, old friend, always says hello, clever, …; (Smiley unhappy) never says hello, boring, not polite, asks boring questions, always stares, plays tricks, awful, angry, gets on one's nerves, crazy, never has time, …*

Look at Unit 3 and make two lists. Use these ideas and your own ideas too.

friendly | never says hello | helps everyone
boring | not polite | always listens
asks boring questions | funny | always stares
nice | plays tricks | awful | …

🙂	☹️
friendly …	…

SPEAKING **20**

Your turn: Talk about people and pets

→ WB 35/13 → Diktat- und Transfertext

*Take turns to talk about people in your family, your neighbours or pets.
Say what you know about them and what they do.
The phrases from exercise 19 can help you too.*

Useful phrases

I've got a cool aunt / a funny …
We've got lots of … in our street.
There's a nice neighbour / boy / girl / …
She's / He's funny / friendly / …
I (don't) like our …
She / He always / never / … helps / does tricks / stares / …

There's a friendly dog in our street. He likes cats!

My sister is awful. She's into crazy music. Every day she …

How to improve your speaking

On this page you can practise good speaking.
This can help you with the Unit task.

1 Warm up with mouth jogging

L 2/7 **a)** *Listen and repeat.*

Rabba **d**abba **d**ab – **R**abba **d**ab,
Ribba **d**ibba **d**ib – **R**ibba **d**ib,
Rubba, **d**ubba **d**ub – …

b) *Make new sounds.*

Examples: Razza dazza daz – …
Puppa duppa dub – …
Linga linga ling – …

2 Rhythm and sounds → WB 36/14

L 2/8 **a)** *Stand up. First just listen to the rhythm and the words. Then clap your hands and say the words with the speaker – in a loud voice!*

1. My guinea pig is very big. – My guinea pig is very big. – …
2. Do your best in the German test. – Do your best in the German test.
3. It's a crazy day but that's OK. – It's a crazy day but that's OK.

L 2/9 **b)** *Say the sounds and then say the sentences.*

1. [d] – [t] Dave's Saturdays with his aunt aren't easy. Sid likes Dave's new T-shirt.
2. [v] – [w] We like volleyball very much. Who lives at 12 Village Way?
3. [ð] – [θ] There are three big trees there. Their brother is thirteen.
4. [s] – [z] The bags and books are on the sofa. My new friends from TTS like sweets.

3 How you speak → WB 36/15 → KV 30

You use different voices for different situations: fast, tired, angry, happy, …
For presentations you need a clear voice.
And for acting a scene? Maybe an angry or a happy voice …

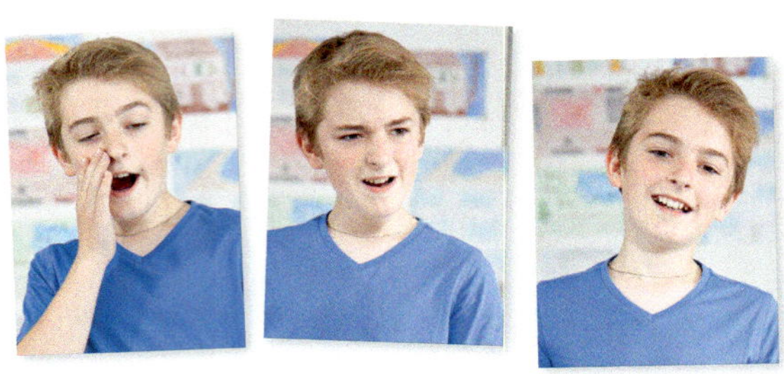

L 2/10 **a)** *Listen to different voices. What can you say about the speakers?*

Lösung a) 1. His voice is too fast. 2. Her voice is angry. 3. His voice is tired. 4. His voice is happy.

angry | too quiet | boring | (not) clear | too fast | tired | happy | …

Start: His voice is … | Her voice is …

b) *Learn three sentences from your book.*

1. Say the sentences to your partner: first in a quiet voice, then very fast.
2. Then say the sentences in a friendly voice, in an angry voice, in a tired voice.
3. Now say the sentences in a clear and friendly voice.

Scenes from a typical day

Work in groups of 4 or 5. Show students from other countries a typical day for a girl or boy in Germany. What things are interesting for them? Present 3 or 4 short scenes (1 minute!) from the day. One person presents the scenes, and the others act the characters. Here you see 3 example scenes.

Step 1

Create the main character

How to describe people: Look back at **Station 2** (pages 57–58)

Is your character a girl or a boy? Choose a name and make a mind map with information about the character.

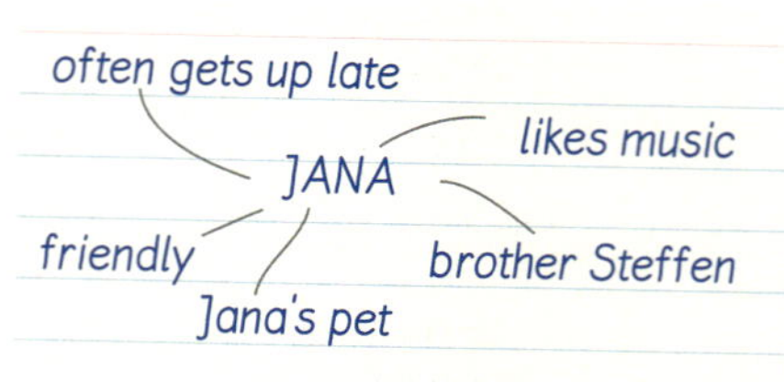

Step 2

Plan the scenes

Look at **Check-in** and **Station 1** for words / phrases about what things you can do and when you do them.

a) *Talk about what your character does every day. Collect ideas for typical scenes with roles for one or two other people too. Think: When? Where? Who? What? Funny scenes are good!*

b) *Plan three or four scenes with your best ideas from a). Write notes for the scenes in the right order.*

Scene 1:		Scene 2:		Scene 3:
In the mornings | Jana gets up late | in bed | 6:30 | mother	→	At school | lesson | Jana and best friend | never listen to tutor | tutor not happy	→	After school | plays and dances with her pet | brother thinks she's crazy

Step 3

Organise your group work

a) *Choose your roles in the scenes: the presenter, the main character, the other characters.*

b) *Make a list of other jobs.*

c) *Choose who can do the different jobs.*

Useful phrases

Who can be / act / write / … ?
Can I / you …, please?
What other jobs have we got?
Maybe I can help with …
Who can write the presenter's words / the dialogues?
Who can bring … from home?

Different people are good at different things!

Step 4

Write the texts

a) *Write the text for the presenter. He / She says what your character does on a typical day.*

b) *Write the dialogues for the scenes. Everyone in a scene has got a card with the dialogue.*

Look at **Check-in** again for help with the time. And look at the **Stations** for help with the language of typical days.

Step 5

Practise and present your scenes

a) *Learn your text by heart. Then practise your scenes in your group.*

b) *Take turns to act your scenes in class. What can you say about the other groups' characters and their days?*

Don't forget the speaking skills on the **Skills page**!

Useful phrases

She's / He's funny / …
Her / His days are crazy / …
I like / don't like …
The scene in the evening is good / …
My favourite scene is …

Remember: Always say something nice first!

S1/41–48
L2/13–20

Luke is my pet → Folie 18, KV 31

SPEAKING

1 Before you read

Say what you know about Sherlock.

A Hello. I'm Sherlock. My people are the Elliots – Jack, Anna, Irina, Luke and Jamie. I love everyone in the family, but Luke is my pet.

B Luke and I have got a nice new room in the loft. Every morning I get up and wash Luke's face. Then he gets up and washes his face again. After that he makes my breakfast. Then he has his own breakfast.

C Jack usually goes to work early. Then at twenty past eight Luke, Irina and Jamie go to school. I always help with Luke's schoolbag. At quarter to nine Anna says goodbye too. But she only works in the mornings.

D My job in the mornings is to look after the house for the family. I sometimes see cats in my garden. That's rude – it isn't their garden! So I always bark. Then they're scared and they run away.

E On Saturdays I take Luke to dog school. I like school! We have lots of fun and Luke learns lots of tricks. One trick is: I listen for the word "Sit!" But I run around and chase my tail. Then the teacher always says, "You've got a lot to learn!" Yes, Luke has got a lot to learn.

F On Sundays I sometimes take my people to Greenwich Park. It's great fun: I always see other dogs with their pets. My people like picnics. I like picnics too because there's no table. Sometimes Jamie puts his drink next to me and it falls over. Silly boy!

G In the evenings my people often sit on the sofa and watch TV. Then we play a game. I watch TV too, and they throw shoes at me. I take the shoes into my room. I like shoes!

H At 9 o'clock I take Luke to our room in the loft. He's a good pet so he can sleep in my bed. I usually fall asleep right away. After my busy day I'm dog-tired.

Lösung *2. That's right. 3. That's right. 4. That's wrong. Mrs Elliot works in the mornings. 5. That's wrong. Sherlock sometimes sees cats in the garden. 6. That's right. 7. That's wrong. The teacher says "Sit!", but Sherlock runs around and chases his tail. 8. That's wrong. Sherlock likes picnics because there are no tables in the park. 9. That's right. 10. That's wrong. Luke and Sherlock go to bed at 9 o'clock.*

READING

2 Check the information → WB 37/17–18 → HA

Voc.: Parts of the body, p. 219 / Body parts, Word bank (WB), p. 6

Is this right or wrong? Correct what's wrong.

Example: Sentence 1: That's wrong. Luke is Sherlock's pet.

1. Jamie is Sherlock's pet.
2. Luke makes Sherlock's breakfast before his own breakfast.
3. Mr Elliot usually goes to work early.
4. Mrs Elliot works in the afternoons.
5. Sherlock sometimes sees rabbits in the garden.
6. Dog school is on Saturdays.
7. The teacher says "Sit!" – and then Sherlock sits down.
8. Sherlock likes picnics because there are nice tables in the park.
9. The Elliots watch TV and throw shoes.
10. Luke and Sherlock go to bed at 9:30.

SPEAKING

3 Talk about the story

Say why you like or don't like the story.

I (don't) like … because …

I think … because …

good | funny | silly | crazy | …

WRITING

4 Work with the story → WB 37/19, 38/20 → Folie 18, HA, Diktat- und Transfertext

a) *Find headings for the pictures.* **Example:** Picture 1: Sherlock and his family

b) *What can Luke say about his dog Sherlock? Choose one part of the story. Write the text again in Luke's words.*

Who's the fastest[1]?

VIEWING

1 Headings for the film → KV 32, KV 33

4

a) *Watch (0:00–3:38). Then put the five parts in the right order and find the right headings.*

Lösung B 2. Making plans after school; E 3. A surprise for Alicia; A 5. Let's see then; D 4. Jinsoo and Marley's week; C 6. In the park

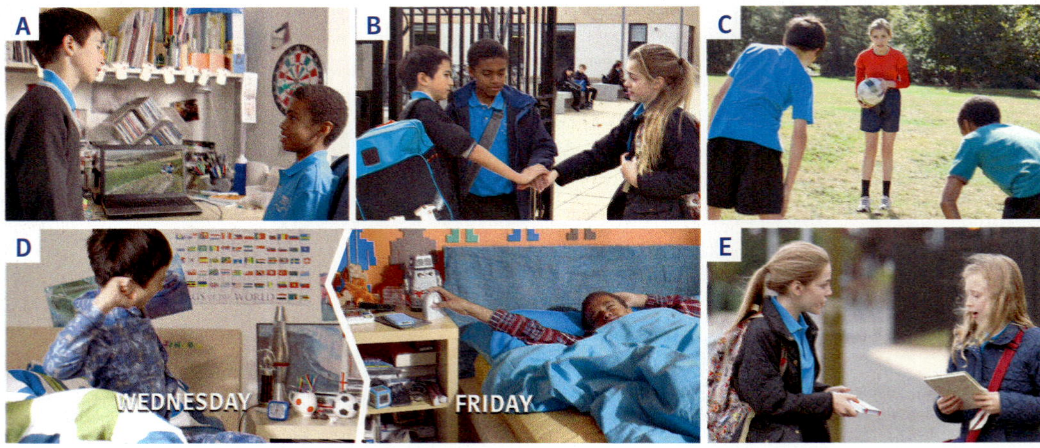

1. Laura's week
2. Making plans after school
3. A surprise for Alicia
4. Jinsoo and Marley's week
5. Let's see then
6. In the park
7. The new 3D film
8. Friends?

b) *Talk about the headings like this:*

Partner A: The heading for the first part is … | I'm not sure about the next part. | …
Partner B: I think it's … | And then it's … | The next part is … | After that it's …

SPEAKING

2 The boys' daily routine[2] → KV 32

Watch (01:27–03:06) and talk to a partner about what Jinsoo and Marley always / never / sometimes do every day.

Example: Jinsoo always gets up at 7 o'clock.

get up | play with phone | go / run to school | give pet food | do exercises | have breakfast | read a book

WRITING

3 Who's the fastest?

Lösung EH a) Jinsoo and Marley do their exercises. Laura wants to play football but the boys run in Greenwich Park. She thinks they are silly.

a) *Laura is now with Jinsoo and Marley in the park. What happens next? Write down your ideas and then watch the last part of the film (03:06–04:15).*

b) *Do you like the film's ending[3]? Explain why / why not. Write one or two sentences.*

Example: I think the ending is funny / silly / surprising / … because …

1 **the fastest** [ðə 'fɑːstɪst] der / die Schnellste | 2 **daily routine** [ˌdeɪli ruː'tin] Tagesablauf |
3 **ending** ['endɪŋ] Ende

→ Solutions p. 272

Can you …

1. say what you do every day? — I get up and … | I go to …
2. say what time it is? — It's 8 o'clock. | It's half past …
3. say how often or when you do things? — I often / never listen to … On Sundays / In the mornings …
4. describe people and what they do? — She loves … | He always talks about …

WRITING

1 What can Dave say about a typical day? → WB 39/21 → HA, KV 34

Start: I get up at … | Then I … | After that I … | I usually … | First … | Then …

WRITING

2 Write about Olivia's hobbies → HA, KV 35

Look at the things in Olivia's room.
Find out what she does.
Write five or six sentences.

Start: She reads lots of books.

draw | go | read | play | listen | make | …

LANGUAGE

3 Make sentences about the people and animals → WB 39/22–23 → HA

Be careful with the simple present forms and the word order.

Example: Sid the cat / play with Dave (often) – Sid the cat **often plays** with Dave.

1. Sherlock / chase squirrels (sometimes)
2. Dave and Jay / play computer games (often)
3. Holly / be at home in the evenings (usually)
4. Luke / go to Art Club (never)
5. Dave's parents / be busy (often)
6. The guinea pigs / get up late (usually)

Find more online: s4zm9u

How to be polite in English

When you visit a different country, it's important to know how to be polite. Can you think why? On these two pages you can learn what to say or do in an English-speaking country.

SPEAKING

1 Warm-up: Questions with 'please'

Voc: In the classroom, p. 269ff.

a) *How many polite classroom questions can you make?*

Have you got …, please? | What's …, please? | Can I / you …, please? | …, please?

Example: What's the homework, please?

b) *Everyone in the class stands up. Take turns to ask a classmate your question from a). Your classmate must give you a polite answer. Then you can sit down again and it's your classmate's turn.*

A smile and a friendly voice help you to be polite too!

VOCABULARY

2 Polite words and phrases

a) *Match pairs of phrases to make short dialogues for the speakers in the pictures.*

Lösung a)/b) *1. Is it OK to sit here, please? – Yes, of course. 2. Er, excuse me. – Huh? – Oh, sorry! 3. Here – have a sweet. – No, thanks. 4. Thank you! – You're welcome.*
EH c) 1. Ist es in Ordnung, wenn ich mich hier hinsetze? – Aber natürlich/selbstverständlich. 2. Entschuldige bitte. – Oh, tut mir leid! 3. Hier, nimm ein Bonbon/etwas Süßes. – Nein danke. 4. Danke sehr. – Gerne./Gern geschehen.

1

2

3

4

Thank you! | Excuse me. | Yes, of course. | No thanks. | Oh, sorry! | Is it OK to sit here, please? | Here – have a sweet. | You're welcome.

L2/21 **b)** *Listen and check your answers in a). Practise the dialogues with a partner.* → HA

c) *Translate the dialogues into German.*
Which German phrases have got two different translations in English?

d) *Start a list of polite words and phrases for your folder.*

VOCABULARY

3 The polite way to ask or explain → WB 40/1–2 → HA

a) *A family has got a visitor from a different country. The visitor's sentences aren't very polite. What words and phrases can help?*

Example: I want to watch TV. → Is it OK to watch TV, please? / Can I watch TV, please?

1. Help me with my bags.
2. The bathroom – where is it?
3. I need a pen.
4. No lemonade for me.
5. I want to use the computer.
6. I haven't got time to chat.

Useful phrases

Excuse me, …	Is it OK to …?
Sorry, but …	Have you got …?
Can I / you …, please?	Thank you very much.

b) *Make polite dialogues. You can use your list from exercise 2 d).*

Example: A: Excuse me. Can I look at the timetable, please?
B: Oh, am I in the way? Sorry!
A: That's OK. Thank you.

Voc.: Prepositions of place, p. 220

1. At a bus station: Person A can't see the timetable because person B is in the way.
2. In a shop: Person A has got a big box and can't open the door. Person B helps.
3. On a train: Person A wants to open the window. But it's polite to ask person B first.

VIEWING

4 How polite are people in Britain?

5

a) *Watch once and say what the film is about.*

b) *Watch again and choose the correct information.*

Lösung EH a)
In the film we see Laura. She speaks with people. Sometimes she is polite and sometimes she is not polite. Many British people like to be polite.
b) *1. b) 2. c) 3. a) 4. b)*

1. When Laura holds the door open
   a) she says "Please".
   b) the woman says "Thank you".
   c) the man is happy.
2. If you jump the queue,
   a) that's OK in Britain.
   b) you wait behind the other people.
   c) British people can't like it.
3. On an escalator
   a) you stand on the right.
   b) you stand on the left.
   c) you walk on the right.
4. People in Britain
   a) are always polite.
   b) are usually polite.
   c) aren't very polite.

SPEAKING

5 Your turn: How to be polite in your country

A visitor to your country asks what is or isn't polite where you live. What can you tell him / her?

Find more online: p9t5p8

S 1/49 L 2/22

The United Kingdom

1 Wales is a small country, but there are 600 castles there! There is a red dragon on the flag.

2 England has lots of nice beaches. But the sea is often very cold!

3 This is the Giant's Causeway in Northern Ireland. The rocks there have a very special shape.

4 Scotland has a lot of high mountains, forests, lakes and islands. It's great for hiking and canoeing.

SPEAKING

1 Four countries → WB 41/1 → Folie 19

a) *Talk about what you can see in the photos. Then say what you can do in the different countries. Take turns.*

Voc.: Geography, p. 221 / Landscape, Word bank (WB), p. 7

b) *Look at the British Isles map at the back of your book. Say where the countries are and what you can see.*

Example: Scotland is north of England. / There are a lot of sheep in Wales.

Voc.: Activities, p. 221 / Free time activities, Word bank (WB), p. 4

Useful phrases

to go surfing / hiking / canoeing / mountain biking / skiing / camping | to visit a castle / a museum

LISTENING

2 Children from the UK → WB 41/2 → KV 36, Diktat- und Transfertext

L 2/23

a) *Copy the grid. Listen and take notes. Check the spelling of the capital cities on the map.*

b) *Choose one of the countries and write a short text about it.*

Lösung a) *capital city: England: London, Wales: Cardiff, Scotland: Edinburgh, Northern Ireland: Belfast*

	England	Wales	Scotland	Northern Ireland
capital city				
other facts				

READING

3 Let's visit London!

→ Folie 20

A Buckingham Palace

B The Thames, Big Ben and the London Eye

C Madame Tussauds

Match the sentences with the photos of some of London's most famous sights.

1. This is where the British king or queen lives.
2. You can take photos with your favourite stars here.
3. This big river is in London.
4. It is a museum with models of famous people.
5. It has 775 rooms, 240 bedrooms and 78 bathrooms.
6. You can ride in it and see a lot of London from the top.

Lösung
1. Buckingham Palace
2. Madame Tussauds
3. The Thames
4. Madame Tussauds
5. Buckingham Palace
6. London Eye

VIEWING

4 What you can see on the Thames

→ WB 42/3–4 → KV 37

6

a) *Watch the film about the River Thames. Write down which sights the film talks about. Use the map of London at the back to check your answers.*

Lösung a) *Houses of Parliament, Big Ben, London Eye, The Shard, Tower Bridge, O2 Arena, Greenwich*

b) *Which sight is most interesting to you? Say why.*

Example: I'd like to go / visit / see … because it is … / I like …

arena [ə'ri:nə]: *Arena*
bridge [brɪdʒ]: *Brücke*

SPEAKING

5 Your turn: Where I live

a) *Make a poster about where you live in Bavaria or a town or city near where you live. Each group chooses one of the tasks.*

1. What people can visit.
2. What people can do.
3. Other facts: Where it is in Bavaria, what it looks like. Are there mountains / forests / lakes? Is it an old / big town or village?

b) *Find photos and write a text for the poster. Present and explain your ideas to the class.*

Useful phrases

In a town or city
church / museum / castle / park / cinema / theatre / café
to go to a concert / festival

Find more online: 28jb35

Unit 4

Let's do something fun

S 1/51 L 2/25

SPEAKING

1 Luke and Dave's tips for Jay → Folie 21, 23

Find the places in the photos on the Greenwich map. What looks fun or interesting? Why?

LISTENING

2 Jay and Shahid Shahid [ʃɑː'hiːd]

L 2/26

What does Jay tell his big brother Shahid? Listen and correct the wrong information.

Start: Jay says "Greenwich Park isn't so big." That's wrong. Greenwich Park is …

Across cultures

Greenwich Mean Time (GMT)
In Großbritannien gilt *Greenwich Mean Time* (GMT), die an der *Meridian Line* (Nullmeridian) beginnt. Die Abweichung zur GMT sagt dir, wie viel Uhr es an einem bestimmten Ort der Welt ist. In Berlin gilt GMT+1: Wenn es in London 7.00 Uhr ist, ist es in Berlin also 8.00 Uhr. Wie spät ist es um die gleiche Zeit in New York (GMT-5)?

In Unit 4 lernst du
… über Freizeitaktivitäten zu sprechen.
Dazu lernst du:

- Wortschatz für deine Freizeit
- Fragen und Antworten mit *do* und *does*
- wie man höflich mit Fremden spricht.

Greenwich Pier [ˌɡrenɪdʒ ˈpɪə]

Dave:
Greenwich Pier is a good place to watch the boats on the Thames. The Greenwich Foot Tunnel starts near the pier too. It's fun to run under the river!

Thames [temz]

Dave: Royal Observatory [ˌrɔɪəl‿əbˈzɜːvətri]
At the Royal Observatory you can stand over the Meridian Line with one foot in the east and the other in the west.

3

4

5

Dave: Mudchute Farm [ˌmʌdʃuːt ˈfɑːm]
Mudchute Farm is across the Thames from Greenwich. A farm in the city – cool. And it's free!

6

Luke:
I love the water slides at Arches Leisure Centre!

Arches Leisure Centre [ˌɑːtʃɪz ˈleʒə ˌsentə]

VOCABULARY

3 Free time activities → WB 43/1–2 → Folie 21, 23

Voc.: Free time activities, Word bank (WB), p. 4

a) *Pick-up: How many words and phrases about free time activities can you collect? Compare your lists. Which group has got more words?*

b) *Your turn: Now write down useful words for your own free time activities.*

VIEWING

4 A look at Greenwich → KV 38

7

a) *Watch the film and take notes. What places can you see and what can you do there? What looks interesting for you and why?*

→ △ 137/1
△ → Help with …

b) *Your turn: Write about where you live and what you can do there.*

G22 Entscheidungsfragen und Kurzantworten mit *do/does*

S1/52 L2/27

Well, what's your idea? → KV 39

After school on Friday …

Dave: Hey you two. Let's do something fun together at the weekend.
Jay: Great idea, Dave! But Luke: No football, OK?
Luke: OK, OK. Do you like swimming?
Jay: Yes, I do. Swimming is fun.
Luke: We can go to Arches Leisure Centre.
Dave: Not so fast! I don't like swimming and water slides.
Luke: Oh, sorry. Well, what's your idea?
Dave: What about something special? Do you know the Cutty Sark museum?
Jay: No, I don't. But is a *museum* cool?
Dave: *Very* cool – and exciting too.
Luke: Great. So where can we meet? And what time?
Dave: Let's meet at my house on Sunday. I live on the way to Cutty Sark.
Jay: Is 11 o'clock OK? In my family we don't get up very early on Sundays.
Dave: Yes, 11 o'clock at my house is fine. OK, see you on Sunday morning!

READING

1 What happens after school on Friday? → WB 44/3

→ ▲ 137/2
▲ → After …

Lösung *1. Yes, they do. 2. Yes, they do. 3. Yes, they do. 4. No, they don't. 5. No, they don't. 6. Yes, they do. 7. No, they don't.*

Example: **Do** the boys talk about Saturday? – No, they **don't**.

1. Do the boys talk about different ideas for their free time?
2. Do Jay and Luke like swimming?
3. Do they think Dave's idea is good?
4. Do the Elliots live on the way to Cutty Sark?
5. Do the Azads get up early on Sundays?
6. Do the boys say when they want to meet?
7. Do the boys talk about Holly and Olivia?

LANGUAGE

2 Find the rule for questions and short answers → WB 44/4 → G22 → KV 40

Lösung b) *Rule: questions = do + I, you, we, they + verb + rest of sentence; short answers = yes/no + I, you, we, they + do/don't*

a) *Look at the examples and find the rule.*

b) *In class, write the rule down.*

Do you play football in the park? – Yes, I do.
Do I need lots of money? – No, you don't.
Do you two like skating? – Yes, we do.
Do they often visit museums? – No, they don't.

SPEAKING

3 Your turn: Say what you like and don't like → G22–23 → KV 41

Every student in the class finds a partner. The partner pairs sit face to face in two big circles.

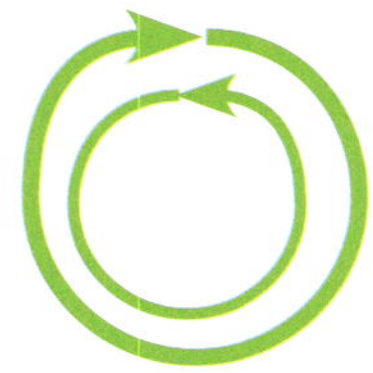

a) *Take turns to say what you like and don't like in your free time.*

Example: I like the park, but I don't like football.

→ △ 137/3
△ → After …

b) *Now everyone in the first circle moves one chair in one direction, and everyone in the second circle moves one chair in the other direction. With your new partner, take turns to ask about your free time activities.*

Do you Do you and your friends Do you and your parents Do you and your …	+	like swimming / skating / …? play football / …? go to the park / go to the …? visit museums / …?

Yes, I do.

Yes, we do.

No, I don't.

No, we don't.

LANGUAGE

4 What can we do at the weekend? → G23 → HA

Lösung 1. Sorry, I don't play badminton. 2. Let's look at the shops. They don't close till 6 o'clock. 3. Oh no, I don't like cycling in busy streets. 4. No surprise! You don't look after your money. 5. Where's that? I don't know Victoria Park. 6. Hm. They don't look big enough.

Complete the answers in the dialogues. Write the sentences down.

Example: Let's watch the boats on the river. – Good idea. We (not need money for that!)
→ Good idea. We **don't** need money for that!

1. What about a game of badminton on Sunday? – Sorry, I (not play badminton)
2. What can we do now? – Let's look at the shops. They (not close till 6 o'clock)
3. Let's go to the leisure centre on our bikes. – Oh no, I (not like cycling in busy streets)
4. I haven't got money for the museum. – No surprise! You (not look after your money)
5. Let's meet in Victoria Park. – Where's that? I (not know Victoria Park)
6. Maybe you can use my sister's skates. Here they are. – Hm. They (not look big enough)

SPEAKING

5 How to: Meet your friends → WB 45/5, 46/6 → KV 42

Make and act dialogues in groups of three or four students. These phrases can help.

Useful phrases

Do you like …? / Do you want to …?
Yes, I do. That's fun / a good idea / …
No, I don't like … / No, that's boring.
But here's a different idea …
I don't like … either. / Maybe we can … / Let's …

Where can we meet? What time?
Let's meet in the park / at my flat / …
Let's meet on Saturday / at 2:30 / …
Great! / Fine! / Bye, see you on …

S1/54
L2/29

Does the farm look nice?

"Do you spell it with S?" Olivia asks.

"No, you don't. You spell it with C," her father Desmond tells her.

At last Olivia finds the website for Mudchute Farm.

"Does the farm look nice?" Claire asks.

"Yes, it does," Olivia says. "They've got lots of animals."

"Have they got rabbits?" Olivia's half-sister Lucy asks.

"Yes, there are rabbits at Pets Corner. Look, I can show you a photo of them."

Lucy is very happy. "I love rabbits and rabbits love me!" she says.

The website gives lots of information. The farm doesn't open on Mondays, but it's open all other days of the week. It's easy to get there from Greenwich too. They can go by DLR (Docklands Light Railway).

"But does it cost lots of money?"

"No Dad, it doesn't. It's free. And we can take our own picnic," Olivia says.

The Frasers like the idea of Mudchute Farm. "What about next Sunday?" Olivia asks. "Maybe Holly can come with us."

"Yes, ask her," Claire answers. "But Sunday is often a bad day. *Lots* of people."

"Claire is right. Let's go on Saturday," Desmond says. "But we want good weather – so keep your fingers crossed!"

READING

6 Answer the questions → WB 46/7 → Folie 22, HA

→ △ 138/4
→ ▲ 138/5
△ → After ...
▲ → After ...

Example: **Does** Olivia answer everyone's questions? – Yes, she **does**.

1. Does Claire find the website?
2. Does Mudchute Farm look nice?
3. Does Lucy love rabbits?
4. Does Desmond show Lucy a photo?
5. Does the farm open on Mondays?
6. Does the DLR go there?
7. Does a visit to the farm cost lots of money?
8. Does Desmond talk about the weather?

Yes, she does. Yes, he does.
No, she doesn't. No, he doesn't.
Yes, it does.
No, it doesn't.

Lösung 1. No, she doesn't. 2. Yes, it does. 3. Yes, she does. 4. Yes, he does. 5. No, it doesn't. 6. Yes, it does. 7. No, it doesn't. 8. Yes, he does.

LANGUAGE

7 *Do* or *does*? → G22 → HA

Lösung a) Rule: do + I, you, we, they + verb + rest of sentence; does + he, she, it + verb + rest of sentence

a) *Complete the rule.*

...	+ I, you, we, they	+ verb	+ rest of sentence
...	+ he, she, it		

b) *Put in the correct forms.*

1. ... the website give lots of information?
2. ... it show photos with rabbits?
3. ... Claire and Desmond ask questions?
4. ... they think the idea of Mudchute is crazy?
5. ... lots of animals live on the farm?
6. ... Olivia like picnics?

Lösung b) 1. Does the website give lots of information? 2. Does it show photos with rabbits? 3. Do Claire and Desmond ask questions? 4. Do they think the idea of Mudchute is crazy? 5. Do lots of animals live on the farm? 6. Does Olivia like picnics?

SPEAKING

8 Your turn: Play a game about your town → WB 47/8–9

Where can you have fun in your town? Partner A thinks of a place; Partner B guesses it. You can only ask questions with yes/no answers.

Example:
Is it near our school? – Yes, it is.
Does it cost money? – No, it doesn't.
Can you go skating there? – Yes, you can.
Does it look green? – Yes, it does.
Is it the park? – Yes, it is!

LANGUAGE

9 Give the information in different words → WB 48/10 → G23 → HA

→ △ 138/6
△ → After …

Lösung
1. … Mondays. 2. … look bad. 3. … doesn't cost lots of money. 4. … doesn't close till 4 o'clock. 5. … doesn't show all the animals. 6. … doesn't go to the farm. 7. … doesn't give a phone number.

Complete the sentences and write them down. Use ***doesn't****.*

show all the animals | open on Mondays | look bad | cost lots of money | give a phone number | go to the farm | close till 4 o'clock

1. You can't visit Mudchute Farm on Mondays. → Mudchute Farm **doesn't** open on …
2. The weather for Saturday looks OK. → The weather for Saturday doesn't …
3. You don't need lots of money to visit the farm. → A visit to the farm …
4. Pets Corner is open till 4 o'clock. → Pets Corner …
5. You can't see all the animals in the photo. → The photo …
6. You can't get to the farm on the number 10 bus. → The number 10 bus …
7. There isn't a phone number on the website. → The website …

LANGUAGE

10 I've got a question for you → WB 48/11 → G24 → KV 43

Lösung 1. you 2. us 3. them 4. you 5. it 6. me 7. you 8. me 9. him 10. it 11. her

Olivia: Hi Holly. My family and I have got a question for [1]. Do you like the idea of a day at Mudchute Farm with [2]? They've got lots of animals there. You can see [3] everywhere!
Holly: Oh thanks, that's so nice of [4]. That's a great idea, I love [5]! – But you know, Mum can never give [6] much pocket money.
Olivia: Don't worry – it's free at Mudchute!
Holly: Free? That's great!
Olivia: Good! See [7] on Saturday then.
Holly: Saturday? Oh – Amber and I are with Dad on Saturday.
Olivia: Oh, please don't tell [8] you can't come! – You've got a cool dad; talk to [9] about Mudchute, OK?
Holly: Yes, maybe we can visit [10] on Sunday. And I can ask Amber too. But you know [11]. She never likes to say yes.

I	→	me
you	→	you
he	→	him
she	→	her
it	→	it
we	→	us
you	→	you
they	→	them

LISTENING **11**

People and animals on the farm

L 2/31

Lösung *2. That's right. 3. That's wrong. Bob always works on Saturdays. 4.That's right. 5. That's wrong. Olivia thinks they are funny. 6. That's wrong. They don't say hello to everyone. 7. That's right.*

On their visit to Mudchute Farm, Olivia and Holly meet Bob Green. He works on the farm. Listen and check the sentences. Are they right or wrong? Correct the wrong sentences.

Start: 1. That's wrong. Bob lives on the Isle of Dogs very near the farm.

1. Bob doesn't live near the farm.
2. He comes to work by bike.
3. He doesn't usually work on Saturdays.
4. The pigs don't have lunch.
5. Olivia doesn't like the pigs.
6. The pigs say hello to everyone.
7. Olivia and Holly help Bob with his work.
8. The pigs' breakfast looks nice.

MEDIATION **12**

Guessing new words → KV 44

8. That's wrong. The pigs' breakfast doesn't look nice, but the pigs like it.

Voc.: Farm animals, p. 224 / Animals, Word bank (WB), p. 2

WELCOME TO MUDCHUTE PARK & FARM
Mudchute Park and Farm are free for everyone. Our farm is one of the biggest inner-city farms in Europe. **Visitors** can see over 200 animals here: large farm animals in the **fields**, horses and ponies in the **Riding Centre** and small animals in Pets Corner. If you want to visit Pets Corner, have a **tasty** snack at Mudchute Kitchen or **book** a riding lesson, please check the **opening times** below.

Fun in the Riding Centre

Mudchute Park & Farm: Farm: Tuesday – Sunday 9 – 5; Park: **All day** every day
Pets Corner: Monday – Sunday 9 – 4 **Mudchute Kitchen**: Tuesday – Sunday 9 – 5
Riding Centre: Monday – Thursday 8 – 9; Friday 8 – 4:30; Saturday – Sunday 8 – 5:30
How to find us: We are on the Isle of Dogs. It is easy to get here by car, train, bus (D3, D6 or 135 bus), on foot, by bike, **river ferry** or the Docklands Light Railway (the best DLR **station** is Crossharbour).

Lösung b) 1. Auf dem Bauernhof leben mehr als 200 Tiere, z. B. Pferde und Ponys. 2. Die Farm kann man von dienstags bis sonntags von 9 bis 17 Uhr besuchen. 3. Man kann zu Fuß, mit dem Rad, mit dem Auto oder mit öffentlichen Verkehrsmitteln wie Bus und DLR hinkommen. 4. Ja, das Reitzentrum ist montags bis donnerstags von 8 bis 9, freitags von 8 bis 16:30 Uhr und am Wochenende von 8 bis 17:30 Uhr geöffnet. Man kann eine Reitstunde buchen. 5. Man kann in der Mudchute Kitchen leckere Snacks kaufen.

a) *Was bedeuten die Wörter und Ausdrücke in Blau? Erkläre, wie du diese Wörter erschließen kannst. Die grüne Box hilft dir dabei.*

Example: 'Welcome' is 'Willkommen'.
It's like the German word.

b) *Du bist mit einem deutschen Freund in London. Beantworte seine Fragen (auf Deutsch) mit Hilfe der Informationen aus dem Text.* → HA

1. Was für Tiere hat Mudchute Farm?
2. Wann kann man die Farm besuchen?
3. Wie kommt man am besten hin?
4. Ich möchte so gerne auf einem Pferd reiten! Kann man das irgendwie organisieren?
5. Gibt es ein Café oder ein Restaurant?

Mediation skills

Tips for guessing new words:
Is there a picture of the word?
Is it from a word family?
(friend – friendly; live – living room)
Is it like a German word?
Do the other words in the sentence help?

Tips for giving information:
Don't translate whole sentences.
Give the important information in your own words in German.

WRITING **13** **Mudchute Farm** → WB 48/12 → Folie 22, KV 45

A partner wants to visit Mudchute Farm. Write an e-mail to him or her about the farm. Look at pages 71, 74, 76 and the photos and the brochure on this page. Read your text again before you give it to your partner. Check the spelling, vocabulary and grammar.

→ ▲ 139/7
▲→ After …

Useful phrases

Mudchute Farm is across … | It's … | There is / are … | They've got … | You can see chickens / horses / lambs / pigs / rabbits / … | It's easy to get there by … | On the farm you can …

G25 Fragen mit Fragewörtern und *do/does*

Lösung a) *1. Where does the Greenwich Foot Tunnel go? 2. When does the Cutty Sark museum open? 3. How do we get to Greenwich Park from here? 4. How much does a visit to Mudchute Farm cost? 5. What do tourists need to see in Greenwich? Etc.*
b) *Rule: The word order in questions is question word + do/does + subject + verb.*
c) *1. It goes to the Isle of Dogs. 2. It opens at 10 o'clock. 3. Turn left and go straight on. 4. It's free. 5. Cutty Sark, the Royal Observatory, lots of places! 6. It comes in 15 minutes. 7. It's at the Royal Observatory. 8. Sorry, I can't always answer every question.*

LANGUAGE

14 Questions at the tourist information centre

→ WB 49/13–14 → G25

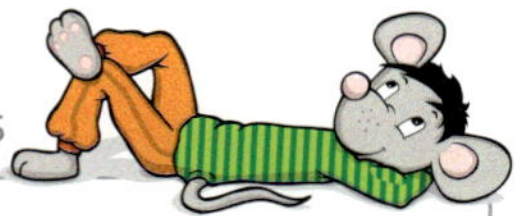

how? = wie?	**what**? = was?
where? = wo?	**when**? = wann?

a) *Match the right parts to make the questions.*

Example: Where does the Greenwich Foot Tunnel go?

Excuse me ...		
How Where What When	do does	the Greenwich Foot Tunnel go? the Cutty Sark museum open? a visit to Mudchute Farm cost? tourists need to see in Greenwich? the next boat to the centre of London come? I find the line for Greenwich Mean Time? you know the answers to everyone's questions?

b) *Find the rule for simple present questions with question words.*

c) *Take turns to ask and answer the questions from a). Here are the answers.*

It's at the Royal Observatory. | It comes in 15 minutes. | Cutty Sark, the Royal Observatory, lots of places! | It goes to the Isle of Dogs. | It opens at 10 o'clock. | It's free. | I don't know. It's my job.

WRITING

15 Your turn: Questions and answers about your town

→ Diktat- und Transfertext

→ WB 50/15, 51/16

Tourist information centres often put 'Frequently Asked Questions' (FAQ) and their answers on their website. What information do visitors to your town need? Write 6–8 questions and answers for an FAQ list.

Example: Q: How do I get to the museum?
A: The number 63 bus goes there.

museum | shops | lunch | bus | swimming | music | bad weather | market | park | river

Useful phrases

What do I need to see/visit/...?
How do I get to ...?
Where can I get information about ...?
What does ... cost?
When/What time does ... open/...?
What is the best place/day for ...?

How to talk to people in the street

1 Give friendly answers

Lösung a) 1. Yes, I do. How can I help? 2. Yes, please. How do I get to the river? 3. You're welcome. 4. I haven't got time – sorry.

a) *Match the answers. (You don't need* ***one*** *of the answers.)*

Lösung b) I'm sorry, I don't know.
Lösung EH Can you tell me the way to the station, please?

Yes, please! How do I get to the river? | You're welcome. | I haven't got time – sorry. | I'm sorry, I don't know. | Yes, I do. How can I help?

b) *Which answer* ***don't*** *you need in a)? What can the question be? Collect ideas.*

2 Use polite phrases → WB 51/17

L 2/34

Lösung a) Not in the dialogue: Can you say that again, please?; Don't worry, I can help.
c) 1. Excuse me. Can you tell me the way to the museum, please? 2. Pardon? Can you say that again, please? 3. Excuse me. Can I ask you a question, please?

a) *Look at the useful phrases. Then listen to a dialogue in a street in Greenwich. Which phrases in the box are* ***not*** *in the dialogue?*

b) *Look at exercise 1 again. Find more polite phrases. Start a list.*

c) *The people here are rude! What phrases can help them to be polite?*

1. Hey! Where's the museum?
2. What? Say that again.
3. Stop – I've got a question.

Useful phrases

Have you got a minute, please?
How can I help?
Can you say that again, please?
Can you tell me …, please?
Don't worry, I can help.
It's very nice of you to help.
That's OK – no problem.

3 Practise dialogues

Choose A ***or*** *B and make your own dialogue. Use lots of the phrases from this page.*

A: A tourist stops a person in a street in Greenwich. The tourist asks the person about interesting places.

B: For a class survey, Dave and Jay ask other people in Greenwich what they do in their free time.

S1/58–64 L2/36–42

The captain and the cabin boy → Folie 24

VOCABULARY **1**

Sea sounds, sea words

L2/35

a) *Listen to the sea sounds. What sounds do you know the words for?*

b) *Start a mind map for sea words.*

Dave, Luke and Jay go aboard Cutty Sark. They see an old sailor on the deck of the ship. He says hello to the visitors. "Ahoy, boys! I'm from a family of sailors, and I know lots of exciting stories about the sea. Tell me: Do you like stories?" "Yeah," Jay answers. "We like *good* stories," Luke says.

"Well then, listen to this story about Cutty Sark ..."

A It's 1875. Cutty Sark is on the way to England with tea from China. She's a fast ship, but it's a very long way. Lots of things can happen when there's lots of water and no land.

After only a week at sea a bad storm starts. Big waves throw the ship here and there. The captain can't hold the wheel.

"Reef the sails, everyone! Fast!" the captain shouts to his sailors. "You too!" he tells the cabin boy Ben Briggs.

B It isn't easy to climb the rigging, and in a storm it's dangerous too. Ben is fourteen. The boy does his best, but the work is new for him and he's slow. The captain doesn't like what he sees. He thinks Ben is scared.

"Cutty Sark needs brave sailors!" he shouts. "Come down, Briggs – you're in the way!"

This is awful for Ben. He really wants to be a sailor.

C The sailors climb the rigging and reef the sails. Now the captain can hold the wheel with the help of the first mate. Everyone is tired, but there's no time to sleep. The storm is very dangerous.

"Bring us something to drink, Briggs!" the captain shouts.

Ben runs and comes back to the deck with water. But he doesn't get to the wheel – because just then a monster wave hits Cutty Sark!

Lösung EH zu Aufgabe 2
1. Cutty Sark is on the way to England with tea from China. 2. The captain can't hold the wheel because a big storm throws the ship here and there. 3. The captain thinks Ben is scared because Ben is slow. 4. Ben brings the captain some water/something to drink. 5. Ben doesn't get to the wheel because just then a monster wave hits Cutty Sark. 6. The first mate falls into the sea. 7. Ben saves the first mate because he can swim. He jumps into the water and takes the lifebuoy to the first mate. 8. The captain finds out that he was wrong about Ben and that Ben is brave.

D Whoosh!!! The wave hits the wheel, and the first mate falls into the sea.

"Help!" he shouts. "I can't swim! Save me!" The captain throws a lifebuoy, but the first mate can't get to it. "Lifeboat!" the captain shouts.

Two sailors run to one of Cutty Sark's lifeboats, but Ben knows the first mate needs help right away. Ben can swim. He jumps into the water. He swims to the lifebuoy and takes it to the first mate. He stays with the first mate till the lifeboat comes.

E Well, and that's how the captain finds out he's wrong about his cabin boy. He's sorry about his angry words, and after the storm he talks to Ben.

"Brave people make good sailors," he says. "I'm very happy to have you on Cutty Sark, Briggs!"

"Wow, that's a great story. Thank you very much," Jay says. "I think the cabin boy is cool," Luke says. "How do you know his story?" Jay asks.

"Well, boys, remember: I'm from a family of sailors," the man answers.

"Wait a minute. What's your name?" Dave asks.

"Briggs," says the sailor. "My name is Briggs."

READING

2 Questions about the story → WB 52/19 → HA, Folie 24

1. Where is Cutty Sark in 1875?
2. Why can't the captain hold the wheel?
3. Why does he think Ben is scared?
4. What does Ben bring for the captain?
5. Why doesn't Ben get to the wheel?
6. What happens to the first mate?
7. How does Ben save the first mate?
8. What does the captain find out about Ben?

WRITING

3 Working with headings → WB 52/20 → Diktat- und Transfertext

→ △ 139/8
→ ▲ 139/9
△ → Help with ...
▲ → After ...

Lösung EH b)
1. A bad storm starts 2. A storm in the sea 3. The monster wave 4. The first mate needs help
5. A good sailor

a) *Read the skills box.*

b) *In your exercise book, write down important words for parts C, D and E. Then write your own headings for all five parts of the story.*

Reading skills

Why are headings useful? A heading tells the reader what is important in a part of a story. Good headings have often got action words to motivate the reader. When you can write headings, it shows that you understand what is important.

Example:
In parts A & B, you see some words in green. In Part A, it's important that the storm starts. Here are two possible headings:
1. A bad storm starts 2. A storm at sea

A trip to the country

VIEWING

1 What is geocaching[1]? → KV 46

8

a) *Look at the pictures and words. Then watch the first part of the film (00:00 – 02:34).*

A

B

C

D

need | phone | GPS device[2] | cache[3] | box with things | take something out | put something back in | write name in book

b) *In small groups write notes about each picture. Then explain geocaching to the class. What do your classmates say about it?*

SPEAKING

2 A good day for Laura and Jinsoo?

Lösung EH a) Laura wants one more coin. She says: "I need a red coin. Maybe I can find it today. I'm so excited. This is fun. Jinsoo thinks it's boring. He says: "What can we do with a first aid kit?" b) There is a red coin in the box. Laura has got four coins now. She's very happy now. Jinsoo has got a problem with his hand.

a) *Look at the pictures. What does Laura want? What does Jinsoo think?*

b) *Watch the end of the film (from 02:34). What can you say about Laura and Jinsoo now?*

WRITING

3 Your turn: Geocaching → HA, KV 47

Where would you like[5] to go geocaching? What would you[6] put in a cache? What would you like to find in a cache? What name would you write in the book? Write a short text.

Start: I'd like to go geocaching in / near … | I'd put …

1 **geocaching** ['dʒiːəʊˌkæʃɪŋ] Geocaching | 2 **GPS device** [ˌdʒiːpiː'es dɪˌvaɪs] Navigationsgerät | 3 **cache** [kæʃ] geheimes Lager | 4 **coin** [kɔɪn] Münze | 5 **would you like** ['wʊd jəˌ'laɪk] möchtest du | 6 **would you** ['wʊd jə] würdest du

→ Solutions p. 272

Can you …

1. talk about free time activities? — Do you like …? | I don't play/go …
2. ask for information about places? — Does the museum open …? | How do I get to …?
3. give information about places? — It doesn't cost … | It's near …

LANGUAGE

1 Put in the correct forms → HA

do | don't | does | doesn't

Jay: [1] you always play football in the park?
Luke: No, I [2]. I sometimes do other things too.
Jay: What about Sherlock? [3] he like the park?
Luke: Yes, he [4]. He goes skateboarding there.
Jay: Dogs [5] go skateboarding!
Luke: Yes, they [6]. Well, only special dogs like Sherlock.
Jay: Ha ha! [7] he look funny on your skateboard?
Luke: No, he [8]. He looks cool. He's very good, you know. He [9] fall over. Look, I've got a photo on my phone!

LANGUAGE

2 What do you ask? → HA, KV 48

You're at Mudchute Farm. Make questions.

1. You don't know when the farm closes.
2. You don't know how to get to Pets Corner.
3. You need to find out where the pigs live.
4. You want to know what the big rabbit eats.

how | what | do | when | where | does

LANGUAGE

3 Mixed bag: A story about Cutty Sark → WB 53/21–22 → HA, KV 49

[1] you know Cutty Sark? Cutty Sark [2] an old [3], but it is also [4] interesting museum. It's in Greenwich and it's [5] from ten [6] to five p.m. every day. There are lots [7] exciting [8] about the ship. There's one story [9] a brave cabin [10]. He works on Cutty Sark and the captain [11] like him. The captain [12] the boy is scared and [13] slow at the new work. But the captain [14] out that he is [15] about the cabin boy. There is a [16] and big waves [17] the ship. The first mate [18] into the sea. This is very dangerous [19] he can't [20]! The boy [21] slow now. He [22] wait. Before the sailors can put a [23] to sea, he [24] into the water and [25] the man. He [26] the lifebuoy to him and [27] get back to the ship together. The captain is happy and [28] thank you to the cabin boy. At [29] he thinks the boy is very [30].

⟨Revision B⟩ ist fakultativ und dient der Festigung/Wiederholung. Es werden keine neuen Sprachmittel eingeführt.

LANGUAGE

1 Tony and Lou at Cooking Club → WB 54/1–2 → HA, KV 50

Lösung EH a) *1. On Wednesdays Dave always goes to the Cooking Club. 2. Tony and Lou sometimes find sweets in Dave's bag. 3. Dave never sees Tony or Lou behind the door. 4. After school Dave often forgets biscuits on the cupboard. 5. In the afternoon Tony and Lou usually eat the biscuits.*

a) *Use the words and phrases and write five sentences. The colours can help you with the word order.*

sometimes | often | always | usually | never

Tony and Lou (2x) | Dave (3x) | goes to | find sweets | forgets biscuits

sees Tony or Lou | eat the biscuits | Cooking Club | on the cupboard

in Dave's bag | After school | behind the door | In the afternoon

Example: Tony and Lou sometimes find sweets in Dave's bag.

b) *Compare your sentences with a partner.*

LANGUAGE

2 Mixed bag: Questions for a trip to London → Folie 23, KV 51

Voc.: In town, Word bank (WB), p. 8

Lösung *1. do 2. are 3. of 4. do 5. much 6. How 7. can 8. Where 9. next 10. does 11. closes 12. do 13. them 14. When 15. from 16. do 17. go 18. museum*

1. What **1** tourists need to see in London? – The British Museum, the London Eye, the Tower of London, there **2** lots **3** interesting places.
2. What sights **4** children like? – They like Madame Tussauds or the London Dungeon very **5**.
3. **6** do we get to Buckingham Palace? – You **7** walk there from Victoria Station.
4. **8** is the London Dungeon? – It's **9** to the London Eye.
5. When **10** it close? – It usually **11** at six p.m.
6. How **12** we get tickets for the London Eye? – It's good to buy **13** on the internet.
7. **14** is Buckingham Palace open to visitors? – It's open **15** late July to late September.
8. What can you **16** when the weather is bad? – You can always **17** to a **18**, like the Museum of Natural History.

VOCABULARY

3 Sound and spelling

L 2/43

Choose four words from the box and read them to your partner. He/She writes them down. Take turns. Then listen to the CD and check the sound and the spelling with your teacher.

address | answer | boat | chocolate | circle | climb | colour | cousin | dance | early | eight | eleven | favourite | fridge | great | hobbies | jealous | know | laugh | leisure | listen | mouth | near | neighbour | nine | office | page | polite | pony | queue | slide | teacher | tidy | very | village | voice | week | world | write | wrong

LANGUAGE **4**

Free time activities

Voc.: Free time activities, Word bank (WB), p 4

Lösung EH a) I think Dave reads funny books. He doesn't play football. I think Dave plays computer games, but he doesn't go swimming. I think Holly and Olivia go inline skating. They don't skateboard. I think Holly and Olivia play with the guinea pigs, but they don't play football.

a) *Talk about the TTS students. What do they do in their free time? What don't they do?*

Example: I think Holly and Olivia go cycling. They don't play computer games.

b) *Look at the students' survey for their class. Write about their favourite free time activities.* → HA

Start: Lots of students play … / Only one girl … / Boys like … but they don't like…

Favourite activities in our class

Swimming	Basketball	Make models	Saxophone
8	13	3	3
8 students (6 girls) (2 boys)	13 students (11 boys) (2 girls)	3 students (2 girls) (1 boy)	3 students (2 boys) (1 girl)

c) *Write sentences about what you do in your free time.* → HA

Example: I play music too, but I don't like computer games.

SPEAKING **5**

An interview → WB 55/3–4 → Folie 22

Lösung a) Olivia's questions: 1. What animals do you like? 2. Can you go riding at Mudchute Farm? 3. What does a ticket cost? 4. When does the farm open? 5. How do the people come to the farm? 6. Do you meet interesting people? The woman's answers: 1. I like all animals, but I love farm animals. 2. Yes, you can. 3. The farm is free. 4. The farm is open Tuesday to Sunday from 9 a.m. to 5 p.m. 5. People can come by car, by bus, DLR and by bike. 6. Yes, you can meet a lot of interesting people at the farm.

a) *Olivia does an interview with a woman at Mudchute Farm for a text in the school magazine. Find the right information for the answers. Then act the dialogue.*

Start: What animals do you like? – I like all the animals. But I love farm animals. Can you ride the horses at Mudchute Farm? – Yes, you can.

Here are Olivia's notes:

What – animals – you – like?
You – go riding at Mudchute Farm?
What – a ticket[1] – cost?
When – the farm – open?
How – people – come to the farm?
You – meet interesting people?

And here are the woman's answers:

Riding: OK | farm animals | Tuesday to Sunday 9 – 5 | it's free | meet a lot of interesting people | by car / bus / DLR / bike

b) *Write down four more questions for Olivia.* → HA

1 **ticket** ['tɪkɪt] Eintrittskarte

Find more online: xw45he

Unit 5

Let's go shopping

S1/65 L3/1

A

B

Olivia: I like this bag. How much is it?
Woman: Yes, it's very nice. It's £25.
Olivia: Oh, that's expensive. I've only got £20.
Woman: I'm sorry. You can't have it for £20. Look – it's top quality.

Dave: Look! T-shirts: Buy One Get One Free.
Luke: Good! You buy one and I get one free.
Dave: Ha ha, very funny. – Wow! Those shoes are great.
Luke: Yes. But they aren't cheap. They cost £89.99. I can *never* buy them, forget it. You know how much pocket money I get. Or *don't* get …

Greenwich ['grenɪdʒ]

READING **1**

Shopping in Greenwich

→ Folie 25

→ ▲ 140/1
▲→ After …

a) *Where are the friends? Match photos A – D with the places on the right.*

in a clothes shop | in a snack bar | in a jewellery shop | outside a sports shop

b) *Do you think the things in the photos are expensive?*

Lösung a) *A: in a clothes shop; B: outside a sports shop; C: in a snack bar; D: in a jewellery shop*
EH b) *The bag is twenty-five pounds. I think it isn't expensive. The shoes cost eighty-nine pounds ninety-nine. That's very expensive. Etc.*

Across cultures

In Großbritannien wird in Pfund (*pounds*) gezahlt, nicht in Euro.
1 *pound* = 100 *pence* (Einzahl: 1 *penny*)
Wie viel ist ein Pfund in Euro?

Write and say prices like this:

£1	one pound
£2.50	two (pounds) fifty
99 p	ninety-nine p
€1	one euro
€3.10	three euros ten
75 c	seventy-five cents

Voc.: British money, p. 227

G26 Mengenangaben mit *of*

In Unit 5 lernst du

… wie du über das Thema Einkaufen sprechen und was du beim Kaufen und Verkaufen sagen kannst. Du lernst:

- Mengenangaben
- wie man im Englischen den Unterschied zwischen Dingen ausdrückt, die regelmäßig geschehen, und Dingen, die jetzt gerade passieren.

Woman: Hello, can I help you?
Dave: Can I have a bottle of water, please?
Woman: Sure – that's £1.10. Anything else?
Dave: Oh, yes – a can of coke and a packet of biscuits, please.
Woman: Here you are. That's £3 then.

Holly: Hello. I'm looking for a present. How much are these bracelets?
Woman: They're £3.99. But there's a special offer today – three for £12.
Holly: Excuse me, but that isn't a special offer.
Woman: Oh, sorry – four for £12. Three for £10.

LISTENING

2 What happens next? → KV 52

L 3/2

1. How much does Olivia pay for the bag?
2. Where does Luke want to go?
3. What is Dave's problem?
4. What is free for Holly?

Lösung: 2. Luke wants to go to a shop near the market. 4. Olivia's name on the bracelet is free for Holly. 3. Olivia pays £12 for the bag. 3. Dave hasn't got enough money.

SPEAKING

3 At the market → WB 56/1–3 → G26 → KV 53

Voc.: Clothes / Shops, p. 228 / Clothes, Word bank (WB), p. 9

You're at the market. Partner A wants to sell, partner B wants to buy. Together, collect phrases for A and B from the text. Make dialogues. Then swap roles.

Example: A: Good morning, can I help you?
B: Yes, I'm looking for …

£18

£12

£5.99, 2 for £10

60 p
3 for £1.50

G27 Die Verlaufsform der Gegenwart

S1/66 L3/3

Where can I get £90?

When they're in town, Dave and Luke **often go** to a café. They **sometimes meet** their friends there, and they usually have something to eat and drink.

It's 11 o'clock. Dave and Luke **are sitting** at a table outside the café **now**. Luke **is drinking** a glass of orange juice and Dave is eating a burger. They're talking about the sports shop at the moment. Luke is sad.

"I really like those shoes, but they're so expensive," Luke says. "Where can I get £90? My mum and dad *never* buy shoes like that for me."

"Don't worry," Dave answers. "Maybe you can get a job and earn some money."

"Yeah, maybe," Luke says.

"Look," Dave says. "It's Holly and Olivia. What are they doing here? – Hey!" he shouts. "Where are you going?"

"Hi you two. We're just coming back from South Street," Olivia tells them. "There's a flea market in the community centre next Saturday and we want to get a table."

"The community centre organises a flea market every year," Holly adds. "People sell things and make money. Some of the money

always goes to charity, but you usually make twenty or thirty pounds. We want to sell clothes, toys, DVDs and other things. Look, here's a flyer."

Luke looks at Dave. "Are you thinking what I'm thinking? My dad is clearing out the garage [ɑː] today." He feels hopeful again.

"Yeah, maybe you can sell some things and buy that pair of shoes," Dave says.

"Can we get a table with you?" Luke asks.

"Why not?" Olivia answers. "We can sell our things together."

"Wait a minute," Luke says. "My phone is ringing."

READING

1 What's in the text? → HA

Match the sentence parts. Write the sentences.

Lösung 1. c) 2. e) 3. f) 4. g) 5. a) 6. b) 7. d)

1. Dave and Luke often go to a café
2. Luke is drinking orange juice and
3. Luke doesn't know where
4. Luke never gets
5. Holly and Olivia are coming back from
6. The girls want to get a table
7. Maybe Luke can make some money and

a) the community centre in South Street.
b) at the flea market next Saturday.
c) when they're in town.
d) buy those shoes.
e) Dave is eating a burger.
f) he can get £90.
g) expensive shoes from his parents.

SPEAKING

2 Your turn: How can you earn money? → HA

What do you think about Luke's idea? How can you make money?

help a neighbour | go shopping for your granny | work in the garden | …

Lösung 1. Right. 2. Right. 3. Wrong. Luke's dad is clearing out the garage. 4. Wrong. The garage is full of things from Luke's room. 5. Wrong. Luke needs some of the things. 6. Right. 7. Wrong. Luke's dad thinks that the shoes are very expensive. 8. Wrong. Luke is coming home now.

LISTENING

3 Luke is on the phone → WB 57/4

L 3/4

Right or wrong? Correct the wrong sentences.

1. Luke is talking to his dad.
2. The four friends are sitting in the café.
3. Luke's dad is clearing out the loft.
4. The garage is full of things from the loft.
5. Luke's dad is throwing things away.
6. Luke wants to make some money with the things.
7. Luke's dad thinks it's a good idea to buy the shoes.
8. Luke doesn't want to come home now.

LANGUAGE

4 Find the rule: What is happening? → G27

→ △ 140/2

△ → After ...

Lösung a) *blue sentences: often go, sometimes meet = simple present; green sentences: are sitting now, is drinking (now) = is/are + verb + -ing (present progressive)* **c)** *signal words for the simple present: often, sometimes, usually, never, always, every year; signal words for the present progressive: 11 o'clock, now, at the moment, just, today*

a) *Some of the words in the text on page 88 are blue and some are green. In the boxes below you can see the full sentences from the text. What is the difference between the blue and the green sentences? Find the rule.*

Dave and Luke often go to a café. They sometimes meet their friends there.

Dave and Luke are sitting at a table outside the café now. Luke is drinking a glass of orange juice.

b) *In your exercise book, start a grid with the blue and green sentences in 4a). We call the form in the blue sentences the simple present; the form in the green sentences is the present progressive. Find more examples of these forms in the text and add them to your grid.* → HA

c) *What signal words (e.g. 'often') are part of your rule? How many can you find in the text on page 88? Add signal words for the simple present and the present progressive to your grid.*

LANGUAGE

5 What is everyone doing? → WB 57/5 → G27 → Folie 26, KV 54

→ ▲ 141/3

△ → After ...

Ask and answer questions about what the people in the picture are doing.

Example:

A: What's the man in the red T-shirt doing?
B: He's drinking coffee.

Lösung EH
A girl is running after a dog. Two men are sitting outside a café. A boy is asking the way. Two people are telling the boy the way. Two women are talking (to each other). A woman is reading a magazine. Etc.

G19 Die einfache Form der Gegenwart

LANGUAGE

→ ▲ 141/4
▲→ After ...

6 Everyone is busy → HA, KV 55

a) *Pia's family hasn't got time for her. So what is she doing (picture F)?*
To find out, first write down what everyone is doing in pictures A–E. Then use letters 2+3 from the verb in A, letter 4 from B, letter 3 from C, letters 1+2+3 from D and letter 4 from E.

Lösung a) *A: Pia's mum is shopping. B: Pia's brother Lukas is swimming. C: Pia's dog Bella is sleeping. D: Pia's dad is working. E: Pia's brother David is talking on his phone. Letters 2+3 (A), 4 (B), 3 (C), 1+2+3 (D), 4 (E) = homework. F: Pia is doing her homework.*
EH b) dabei sein, etwas zu tun; am/beim ... sein; gerade etwas tun

A

B

C

A. mum | **B.** brother Lukas | **C.** dog Bella | **D.** dad | **E.** brother David | **F.** Pia

D

E

F

b) *There's no progressive form in German. Think: Which phrases can you use in German to show that something is happening at the moment?*

LANGUAGE

→ △ 142/5
△→ After ...

7 At the charity shop with Mum → WB 58/6 → G19, 27 → HA, KV 56

Simple present or present progressive? Put in the right forms. The signal words can help you.

Today, Holly and her mum (1 go) shopping. They (2 look) for clothes for Holly and her sister. When they need something, Holly and her mum often (3 go) to a charity shop. They always (4 find) interesting things there – and cheap too! They sometimes (5 see) nice things in other shops, but Holly's mum never (6 buy) expensive clothes. Holly (7 stand) outside a charity shop at the moment. Have they got any nice things today?

Lösung *1. are going 2. are looking 3. go 4. find 5. see 6. buys 7. is standing*

Across cultures

In Großbritannien gibt es viele günstige *charity shops* – das sind Gebrauchtwarenläden, die gespendete Bücher, Kleider oder CDs verkaufen, und deren Einnahmen für wohltätige Zwecke gespendet werden. Gibt es solche Läden auch in Deutschland? Was kann man dort kaufen?

SPEAKING

8 I'm sorry, I'm busy → WB 58/7

Sit back to back. Use the ideas in the box to make telephone dialogues.

A: Hey, let's go ... today!
B: I'm sorry, I can't come with you. I'm just ...
A: Oh, too bad. Can't you do that tomorrow?
B: No, I can't. I always ... on Mondays / Tuesdays / ...

swimming | to the museum | shopping | to the park | to Mudchute Farm | to the cinema | do my homework | tidy my room | play football | go to my dad's house | help in the kitchen | walk the dog

S1/68 L3/6

That's what friends are for

The friends are now at Luke's house. They're helping to clear out the garage. Jay is helping too.

Olivia: Hey, look at this bike. It's really cute. The wheels are so small!

Luke: It's my first bike.

Dave: That must be worth a few pounds.

Luke: Let's keep our fingers crossed. Here are some nice clothes. They're too small for me or Jamie now, but they're good quality.

Olivia: How many bags have we got?

Holly: Not many – about six or seven. But we can put all the clothes in them. Have you got any stuff to sell, Olivia?

Olivia: Well, I haven't got any old clothes. My sister always gets them. But maybe I can find some other things.

Jay: I've got some old things too. We can put all our stuff together and sell it to help Luke.

Holly: Hey, good idea!

Luke: Thanks, that's cool.

Dave: That's what friends are for!

Dad: Here are some old skates. And there are a few toys here. You don't play with these.

Dave: I've got a lot of old toys in my bedroom. And some shoes.

Olivia: Have you got any books or DVDs or computer games?

Luke: No, there are no books or DVDs here.

Jay: I haven't got any old computer games. But I've got a football and a couple of posters – and lots of books.

Dad: Well, Luke, you've got a lot of stuff. How much do you want for everything? You can't ask for *too* much money. People come to flea markets to find a bargain, they don't want to spend much money on things.

Holly: I can bring some cards. We can write the prices on them.

Dad: OK. I've got a little time on Saturday; I can take all your stuff to the community centre in the car.

Luke: Thanks Dad!

Dad: That's what parents are for!

***Lösung** 1. There are six people at Luke's house (Luke, Luke's dad, Jay, Olivia, Dave, Holly). 2. They are clearing out the garage. 3. Yes, there is a lot of stuff in the garage (a bike, some clothes, a few toys, some old skates). 4. Jay says that they can put all their stuff together and sell it to help Luke. 5. They have got about six or seven bags. 6. Olivia hasn't got any old clothes to sell because her sister always gets them. 7. Jay has got some old things, Dave has got a lot of old toys and some shoes and Jay has got a football, a couple of posters and lots of books. 8. They can't ask for too much money because people come to flea markets to find a bargain. 9. I think Jay's idea is great because they all work together to help Luke. 10. Luke is happy at the end because his dad can take all his stuff to the community centre in the car on Saturday.*

READING **9**

Working with the text

→ WB 59/8 → HA

Answer the questions.

1. How many people are at Luke's house?
2. What are they doing?
3. Is there a lot of stuff in the garage?
4. What is Jay's idea?
5. How many bags have they got?
6. Has Olivia got any clothes to sell?
7. What have the other children got?
8. How much money can they ask for?
9. What do you think of Jay's idea?
10. Is Luke happy at the end? Why?

G28 Die Mengenwörter *some, any* und *no*
G29 Zusammensetzungen mit *some, any, every* und *no*
G30 Die Mengenwörter *much, many* und *a lot of*
G31 Die Mengenwörter *a few, a little* und *a couple of*

LANGUAGE **10**

→ △ 142/6
→ ▲ 143/7

△→ After …
▲→ After …

Lösung a) *1. any 2. some 3. any 4. any 5. some 6. any*

Find the rule: Some or any, much or many? → WB 59/9–10, 60/11–13 → G28–30 → KV 57, KV 58

a) *Look for* ***some*** *and* ***any*** *in the text on page 91 and find translations for the sentences. Then say where you use* ***some*** *and where you use* ***any****. Write down the rule.*

1. Have you got … computer games?
2. Yes, I've got … computer games.
3. No, I haven't got … computer games.
4. Have you got … money?
5. Yes, I've got … money.
6. No, I haven't got … money.

b) *Look at the box and complete the dialogue with the right words.*

Lösung b) *1. many 2. lots of 3. many 4. much 5. a lot of 6. much*

A: Have you got something / anything to sell?
B: No, I've got something / nothing to sell. But Dad has got something / anything. He's got a lot of old books.
A: We need a bag. Has anybody / somebody got a bag? Anybody / Somebody must have a bag.
B: I'm sorry. Anybody / Nobody has got a bag.

somebody | anybody | nobody | someone | anyone | no one | something | anything | nothing

c) *Now find examples of* ***much****,* ***many*** *and* ***lots of / a lot of*** *in the text. Then say where you use* ***much****, where you use* ***many*** *and where you use* ***lots of / a lot of****. Write the rule.* → HA

1. How … people can you see?
2. There are … things here.
3. There aren't … books here.
4. How … money have we got?
5. Luke drinks … orange juice.
6. There isn't … coke in the fridge.

SPEAKING **11**

A class survey → WB 61/14 → G28–31

Ask questions in your class and talk about what you find out.

Example: Has anybody got a hamster?
Is there anybody with two brothers?
Can anyone play the guitar?
…

Nobody has got four brothers.
Six students have got a dog.
Some people play the guitar.
…

SPEAKING **12**

A game: Who am I? → WB 62/15, 63/16 → Diktat- und Transfertext

B is one of the friends – A asks questions to find out who B is. Use the grid.

Example: A: Have you got any shoes? → B: Yes, I have. / No, I haven't. But I've got some …
A: Are you Luke?

	clothes	shoes	toys	books	DVDs	skates	posters
Luke	✔	✘	✔	✘	✘	✔	✘
Dave	✘	✔	✔	✘	✘	✘	✘
Jay	✔	✘	✘	✔	✘	✘	✔
Olivia	✘	✘	✔	✘	✘	✔	✘

How to use the telephone

1 Answering machines

→ WB 63/17

L 3/8 → 143/8 ▲→ After …

a) *Listen to the messages on three answering machines A, B and C, and find out:*

1. Who is speaking?
2. Does it say when you can call again?
3. Can you leave a message?

L 3/9

b) *Now listen to four callers: Which messages match answering machines A, B and C?*

When you listen, you don't always need to understand every word. Just try to answer these questions first: Who? Where? When? What?

2 A phone call

L 3/11

Listen to the dialogue. Right or wrong? Correct the wrong sentences.

1. Holly is calling the community centre.
2. Olivia wants to speak to Alicia Walker.
3. Alicia Walker answers the phone.
4. Mr Walker is putting Olivia through.
5. There aren't any places left.
6. The table is £8 for the day.

Lösung 1. Wrong. Olivia is calling the community centre. 2. Wrong. Olivia wants to speak to Alicia Baines. 3. Wrong. Andrew Walker answers the phone. 4. Right. 5. Wrong. There are a few places left. 6. Wrong. The table is £3 for the day.

3 Role play: Make your own dialogues

Choose A, B or C.

A. Olivia wants to talk to Holly. She isn't there. Amber answers the phone.
B. Luke wants to ask Dave to come to the park. Aunt Frances answers the phone.
C. Holly calls Olivia. Lucy answers the phone.

Useful phrases

Hello! | Hi! | Good evening!
This is … | I'm …
Can I speak to …? | I'd like to …
Sorry, … Can I take a message?
Please tell her / him to call me back.
Just a minute she's / he's …
I'll get her / him.

4 < A song: Ring, ring, ring >

L 3/12

Listen to the first part of a song. Match parts 1–7 with the headings a)–g).

Lösung 1. f) 2. a) 3. c) 4. g) 5. d) 6. e) 7. b)

1. Yes, this is Miss Renee King from Philadelphia.
2. I want you to please give me a call[1]
   On area code[2] 215 222 4209.
3. And I'm calling in reference to the music business.[3]
4. Thank you.
5. Hey, how you doin'?
6. Sorry you can't get through.
7. Why don't you leave your name and your number?
   And I'll get back to you.

a) my phone number
b) Please leave me a message.
c) why I'm calling
d) hello
e) I'm not here at the moment.
f) my name
g) thanks

Text: De La Soul
© Warner-tamerlane

1 **give me a call** [ˌɡɪv mi_ə 'kɔ:l] Rufen Sie mich an | 2 **area code** ['eəriə ˌkəʊd] Vorwahl | 3 **in reference to the music business** [ɪn ˌrefrns tə ðə 'mju:zɪk ˌbɪznɪs] bezüglich des Musikgeschäftes

Our great flea market game

After pages 86–93, you can say how many things you've got and talk about them. You know what to say when you want to buy or sell something. You know how to talk about prices. Now you can organise your own flea market in the classroom. Work in groups of three.

Step 1

Prepare for the flea market

a) *Bring three small things from home to sell. (Don't worry, you can have everything back after the end of the game! But don't bring expensive things.)*

b) *Think about how you want to set up the tables to show your things.*

c) *Now look at all your things together and put them in groups: toys, books, school things, clothes … Make a mind map for each group with the words for the things.*

d) *Talk about what you want to sell and why. Decide how much money you want for the things and make price cards.*

Useful phrases

This is a … | It's old / small, but …
You can … it. | You can … with it.
I'm selling it because …
I like it / I don't like it because …
I think … is a good price.

You can find help on how to say prices in **Check-in**, and you can practise how to talk about prices in **Station 2**.
You can use a dictionary to find out what your things are in English.

Useful phrases

Selling:
Can I help you?
There's a special offer today: …
I've got some really nice …
This is a great … | You can … with it.
You can't have it for …
It's worth …

Buying:
I'm looking for …
Have you got any …
How much is / are …?
I like the … because …
No, that's too much. I can give you …

Step 2

Collect language for buyers and sellers

In the unit there are a lot of useful words and phrases for buyers and sellers. Collect them in two lists. Can you think of more things to say?

Step 3

Now buy and sell

Half of the groups are sellers. They can set up their tables and sell things to the other half. Swap roles after ten minutes.

You can play different games with different goals too:

A Buyers: Buy lots of things but don't spend much money.
Sellers: Sell all your things.
B Try to sell your things for lots of money.
C Each group writes a task on a card, like "Buy only red things", "Spend only £10" or "Try to make £20". Put all the cards in a bag. Then each group takes one and tries to do what it says.

Step 4

Talk about the flea market

Do you like the game? Is it fun? Why? / Why not?
Who is a good buyer / seller and why?
Talk about it.

S 2/2–7
L 3/13–18

Lucky Luke? → Folie 27

A It's Saturday morning and the friends are standing with Sherlock behind their table at the flea market. Luke's dad is helping with their things. At the next table an old man is selling a lot of stuff: books and wine glasses, tables and chairs. The flea market is very busy and people are walking from table to table. Many of them are looking for bargains.

B There is always a raffle at the flea market and the prizes usually come from different shops in Greenwich.

"Are there any good prizes?" Holly asks.

"They don't want to say what the prizes are before the raffle starts," Luke's dad says. "But the tickets cost £2 each."

"I haven't got any money for the raffle just now," Olivia says.

"I have!" Dave answers. "Let's hope we're lucky." He takes his money and buys a ticket.

C It's 4 o'clock now and Holly is checking how much money they've got.

"You've got £16, Luke," she says. "Olivia and I have got £21. Dave has got £10, and Jay £15. That's not too bad."

"But it isn't enough," says Luke. "I need £90 for the shoes. Then some money goes to charity and the table costs £3. I don't think I can make so much money today."

"Wait and see," says the old man at the next table. "It's still early."

D "Who can look after Sherlock?" Luke's dad asks. "He's barking."

"I can take him," Luke answers. "I want to look at the other tables." Luke goes to the other tables with Sherlock, but Sherlock just barks and barks. "Stop it!" Luke says.

He's just looking at a model of Cutty Sark when Sherlock sees a small dog and pulls – and the table falls over. Now the model is in pieces.

"Oh no!" Luke says. "I'm really sorry!"

"That's an expensive model," the woman says. "I hope you can pay for it."

"How much does it cost?" Luke asks.

The woman shows Luke the price. "It's £15," she says. She gives him the broken model in a bag. Luke is horrified but takes the bag and gives her the money.

"Now I've got one pound and a bag full of rubbish," he says. "This is awful. What can I do?"

He goes back to his friends and tells them the story.

Stop and think:
What can Luke do?
How can the story go on?

E "Oh Sherlock," Jay says. "Look at Cutty Sark now! Awful. – But wait, what's that? There's something in the bag with the pieces of the model. What is it?"

It's a coin. It looks very old, as old as Cutty Sark.

"It isn't a pound coin," Luke says. "I can't buy anything with it."

"But Luke," his dad says. "Maybe it's worth more than just a pound."

They go and ask the old man at the next table.

The man looks at the coin and says, "Hm, this is a half sovereign[1]. It's 150 years old. It's got a picture of Queen Victoria's[2] head on it. There are still a few of them, but it's made of gold[3] so it's worth a lot. Do you want to sell it? Let's say £110?"

"What?" Luke asks. "That old thing? I can't believe it!" He hugs Sherlock.

F Olivia has a big smile on her face. "You're really lucky, Luke. Now you can get your shoes, we can give some money to charity and go for a big pizza together. What do you think? But wait, where's Dave?"

Just then Dave comes back to the table. He's got a pink school bag with a pony on it. He looks disappointed.

"Look at my prize from the raffle," he says. The friends all laugh. "But wait a minute – Holly, don't *you* love ponies?"

1 **sovereign** ['sɒvrɪn] britische Goldmünze | 2 **Queen Victoria** [ˌkwi:n vɪk'tɔ:riə] Königin Victoria (1819–1901) | 3 **made of gold** [ˌmeɪd‿əv 'gəʊld] aus Gold

READING **1**

Understanding the story → WB 64/19

Lösung EH
1. … an old man. 2. … the raffle. 3. … the shoes cost £90. 4. … the model is in pieces. 5. … in the bag with the pieces of the model. 6. … that the coin is worth a lot. 7. … he gets £110 for the coin. 8. … he has got a pink school bag with a pony on it from the raffle.

Complete the sentences. Sometimes more than one answer is possible.

1. Next to the friends' table there's …
2. Luke's dad talks about …
3. £62 isn't enough because …
4. Luke gives the woman £15 because …
5. Jay sees something …
6. The old man says …
7. Luke is lucky because …
8. Dave isn't happy because …

2

The people in the story

Go through the text and read what the people do or say. Then look at the words on the right. Which people can you use the words for? Explain when the people feel like this, and why.

☺	nice | friendly | helpful | happy | lucky | hopeful | thankful | excited
☹	angry | helpless | sad | disappointed | horrified

READING **3**

Retell the story → WB 64/20 → Folie 27, Diktat- und Transfertext

→ △ 143/9
△ → Instead of …

a) *Find the important information in the six parts of the story (A–F).*

b) *Write down key words and ideas for each part.*

c) *Then use these words and ideas to retell the story in your own words. Try not to use too many sentences from the text.* → HA

Out and about[1] in Greenwich

SPEAKING

1 What do you think? → KV 59

a) *Look at the pictures and the words. Which go together?*

Lösung a) A: home, parcel B: phone shop, cool smart phones C: bag of popcorn D: Greenwich Market E: gift shop, gift F: post office

post office[2] | phone shop | home | Greenwich Market | gift[3] shop | bag of popcorn | cool smart phones | gift | parcel[4]

b) *Now talk about what you think happens in the film.*

Example: I think Marley's mum … / Maybe Marley and Jinsoo …

buy | look at / for | run | remember | closes at 5:30 p.m. | walk | get to

VIEWING

2 The main idea of the story → KV 60

9

a) *Watch the film, then look at these sentences. Which one is the main idea of the story?*

Lösung a) Sentence 2 is the main idea of the story.

1. Marley and Jinsoo buy lots of things and haven't got enough money for the post office.
2. The boys are having lots of fun, but they're late for the post office and must run.
3. The boys are looking for a gift for Marley's mum.

b) *Now retell the story in four or five sentences. Write them down.*

SPEAKING

3 Oops! I always forget …

What things do you sometimes / often / always forget to do for your mum, dad or teachers? Tell the class.

1 out and about [ˌaʊt ənd əˈbaʊt] unterwegs | **2 post office** [ˈpəʊst ˌɒfɪs] Postamt | **3 gift** [gɪft] Geschenk | **4 parcel** [ˈpɑːsəl] Päckchen

→ Solutions p. 272

Can you ...

1. say what never / often / always / ... happens? — Usually / When I'm in town, I ...
2. say what is happening at the moment? — The teacher / My friend ... | I'm ...
3. say how much you've got of something? — I've got some / a lot of / a packet of ...
4. say how many things you've got? — I've got some / a few / a lot of / two ...
5. say what you haven't got? — I haven't got any ...

LANGUAGE

1 A busy restaurant → HA, KV 61

a) *Copy the text about Jay's aunt and uncle's restaurant and put in the right forms.*

It's Saturday morning and Mr Azad (1 chat) to a woman at the market. Mr Azad (2 go) to the market every morning. He always (3 buy) everything for the restaurant there. He usually (4 stop) and (5 talk) to the people. Aunt Seeta is in the restaurant. Jay and his brother (6 work) in the kitchen with her because there are lots of things to do. They often (7 help) in the restaurant when it's busy. Then they (8 get) some extra pocket money, and they (9 have) a nice dinner. Aunt Seeta (10 stand) in front of the cooker at the moment, and Jay and his brother Shahid (11 make) a nice curry.

b) *Now read the dialogue and put in* ***some*** *or* ***any****.*

Jay: Shahid, can you see 1 tomatoes?
Shahid: No, sorry, there aren't 2 tomatoes here. Aunt Seeta, have we got 3 tomatoes?
Seeta: Look, there are 4 bags on the table. Are the tomatoes there?
Shahid: Oh, yes – thanks!
Jay: Oh, and we haven't got 5 cheese.
Seeta: Yes, we have – you can find 6 cheese in the fridge.
Jay: Mmm, and there's 7 nice mango yoghurt too!

LANGUAGE

2 Olivia is looking for a present → WB 65/21–22 → HA, KV 62

Complete the text with ***something***, ***anything***, ***everything*** *or* ***nothing****.*

Olivia wants to give her mum 1 nice on her next visit, so she is going shopping with Holly. They look at 2 in the shops in Greenwich, but they can't find 3. "How much do you want to spend?" Holly asks. "Well, I can't buy 4 expensive, I haven't got much money. But I need 5 special – maybe there's 6 in this little shop?" Olivia answers. "I don't think so. Look at the prices! There's 7 nice and cheap here," Holly says. "Let's go to Greenwich Market! Or maybe you can find 8 at the charity shop. 9 is very expensive there."

Find more online: hj2ek3

Food in the UK

Food is an important part of every culture. Of course not everyone in the UK eats the same things. But on these two pages you can find out what is popular with many people there.

VOCABULARY **1**

Warm-up: A quick class contest

Close your books. Who can write down the most food words in one minute? (Keep your list – it can help you with exercise 3.)

LISTENING **2**

Food in British homes → WB 66/1 → KV 63

L3/19

a) *Listen and find the right photos for the conversations.*

Lösung a) Conversation 1 goes with photo 5. Conversation 2 goes with photo 1. Conversation 3 goes with photo 6. Conversation 4 goes with photo 3. Conversation 5 goes with photo 2. Conversation 6 goes with photo 4. b) Photo 1: It's bacon and egg. Photo 2: It's a cheese sandwich. Photo 3: It's a steak pie. Photo 4: It's fish and chips. Photo 5: It's a chicken curry. Photo 6: It's a fruit cake. EH c) 1. I'd like to try the chicken curry. 2. I like bacon and egg. It's my favourite breakfast. 3. We eat fruit cake in Germany too. 4. Our cheese sandwich is the same. 5. I don't like the steak pie. It looks strange. 6. Fish and chips are great.

b) *Listen again for the correct phrases for the food in the photos. The words on the right can help.*

bacon | bread | cake | cheese | chicken | chips | curry | egg | fish | fruit | pie | sandwich | steak

c) *Talk about the food in the photos. The useful phrases can help you.*

Examples:

1. The steak pie looks strange!
2. I'm not sure about steak pies, but steaks are great!

Useful phrases

The … looks good / strange / …
… are great / are my favourite food.
I (don't) like …
I'd like to try the …
We eat … in Germany too.
Our … is / isn't the same.

Voc.: Drinks / Food, Word bank (WB), pp. 10–11

VOCABULARY

3 Word groups

→ WB 66/2 → HA, KV 64

Lösung a) *Breakfast: cereal, egg, toast; Snacks: biscuit, crisps, nuts; Sweet food: biscuit, cake, chocolate; Healthy food: apple, tomato, nuts, fish, cereal*

a) *Collect words for the headings below. Use the words in the box and your own words too. Some words go with different headings.*

apple | biscuit | butter | cake | cereal | chocolate | crisps | egg | fish | ham | nuts | plum | strawberry | toast | tomato | …

Breakfast   Snacks   Sweet food   Healthy food   Cold food   Hot food

b) *What is your favourite food? Add new words to your personal vocabulary.*

VIEWING

4 Shopping for food

→ WB 66/3

10

Lösung a) *Laura and bananas, oranges, bread, ready meals and fruit salad go together. The man and pasta go together. The old woman and the apples and pies go together. The young woman and the baked beans and toast go together.*
b) *1. Wrong. – The woman needs apples. 2. Wrong. – Laura loves apple pie but not for dinner. 3. Wrong. – The woman loves baked beans on toast. 4. Right. 5. Wrong. – Chicken Tikka Masala is very popular. 6. Wrong. – Laura's father needs milk for his coffee. 7. Wrong. – The young woman likes baked beans on toast./ The young man likes pasta. 8. Right.*

a) *Watch the film about a supermarket in Greenwich. While you watch: Match the people with the food words.*

Start: Laura and … go together. | The man and … go together.

apples
baked beans
bananas
oranges   bread
ready meals
fruit salad   pies
toast   pasta

b) *Are the sentences right or wrong? Correct the wrong information.* → HA

1. The woman needs bananas.
2. Laura likes apple pie for dinner.
3. The man loves baked beans on toast.
4. The supermarket has got Indian food.
5. Chicken tikka masala isn't so popular.
6. Laura's dad needs milk for his tea.
7. The young woman likes pasta.
8. You can buy bread in bags.

chicken tikka masala [ˌtʃɪkɪn ˌtɪkə məˈsɑːlə]

c) *Watch again. Then compare this supermarket with supermarkets where you live.*

SPEAKING

5 Your turn: Your food

→ HA, KV 65

A British friend asks: What do people eat in Germany? Collect ideas in class. Give examples of popular food.

Useful phrases

Lots of people eat / like …
… is / are very popular.
We often have … for lunch / for …

Find more online: 7ke4vb

English around the world → Folie 28

Many people in different countries around the world speak English. Learn about where and why, and listen to some different kinds of English.

SPEAKING

1 Which countries speak English? → KV 66

a) *Which countries do you know where the people speak English? Check your answers with the world map at the back.*

b) *Think of situations when German people speak English. Where are they and who do they speak to? The phrases can help.*

Useful phrases

German people often / sometimes speak English …
in a hotel | on the beach | on video chat | …
with…
friends | people in their family | tourists | people from …
when they are …
on holiday | at home | at work | in another country | in town | …

VIEWING

2 Speaking English

11

a) *Watch the film. What is it about?*

Lösung EH a) *The film is about the use of English in different countries. It shows that the English people speak in different countries is not exactly the same. The British and the Americans use some different words, for example. English also helps people from two different countries to talk to each other.*
b) *United States of America, Australia, New Zealand, Canada, India, Rwanda*

b) *Does Marley talk about any of the countries in your answers to exercise 1? Which?*

c) *Look at the pictures and say what happens in the two scenes.*

A

B

d) *Watch the film again. Say which sentences are right. Correct the wrong sentences.*

1. The American man is working in England.
2. American English is not the same as British English.
3. You can see English on posters in China, India and in some other countries.
4. The South Korean[1] man can't help the Romanian[2] woman.

Lösung d) *1. wrong: He is on holiday. 2. right 3. right 4. wrong: He can show her where the supermarket is.*

e) *With a partner, act out one of these scenes:*

1. You're on holiday and make a new friend from another country.
2. You help an English-speaking person in your town.

Hi! / Hello! | How are you? | I'm … from … | Where are you from? | Are you here on holiday? | I'm looking for … | Can you …?

1 **South Korean** [ˌsaʊθ kəˈriːən] südkoreanisch | 2 **Romanian** [rʊˈmeɪniən] **rumänisch**

READING

3 Why English is a world language → WB 67/1–2 → KV 67

Lösung EH a) Many people in the world speak English because of the English sailors in history and because American culture is very important in many countries today.

a) *Think before you read: Why do many people in the world speak English?*

b) *Read the text. Then match the sentences about the English language today.*

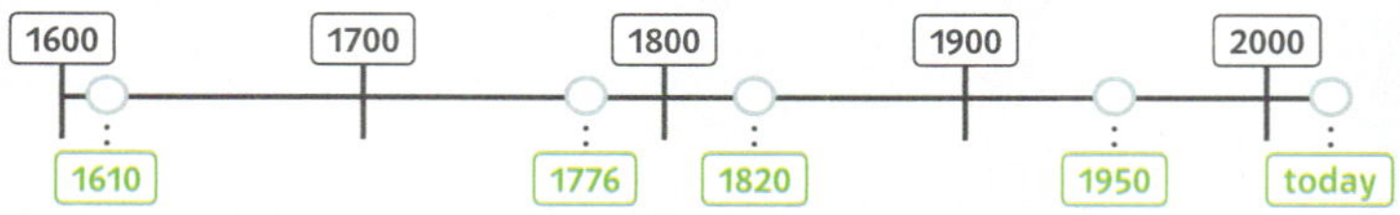

From about 1600: British sailors go to other countries, e.g. to America and India, to buy and sell things. They take the English language with them.
1610: The first people from Britain go to live in America.
1776: America is now independent from Britain, but most Americans still speak English.
About 1820–1900: Many countries are under British government, like Canada, Australia, India and South Africa. Their official language is English.
From 1950: People all around the world learn English because they love American music and Hollywood films.

Today:

Lösung b) 1. d) 2. c) 3. b) 4. a)

1. More than 400 million people in the world today speak English as their first language,
2. English is still an official language in a lot of countries
3. A lot of people still like American culture,
4. We use new technology from America (the internet, the e-mail)

a) to communicate with people all around the world in English.
b) so they often watch films and listen to songs in English.
c) although they are not under British government any more.
d) and more than 600 million speak English as a second or official language.

LISTENING

4 Where are we from? → KV 68, Diktat- und Transfertext

L 3/20

Lösung a) Speaker 1: Scotland, Speaker 2: Australia, Speaker 3: USA, Speaker 4: Ireland b) Scotland: lad and lasses, wee, loch; Australia: sunnies, G'day; the USA: cookie, candy, movie; Ireland: I'm grand, What's the craic? c) They talk about famous cities in their country, the landscape and animals, for example.

a) *Listen to four people from different English-speaking countries. Which place does each person come from?*

Australia | Scotland | the USA | Ireland

cookie | arvo | wee | loch | lads and lasses | I'm grand! | G'day! | candy | movie | What's the craic?

b) *Listen again. In which country can you hear these words? What do they mean?*

c) *What else do the four people talk about?*

VOCABULARY

5 Your turn: English in your language → WB 67/3, 68/4 → Folie 29, KV 67

Which German words are like words in English? Put them into the grid.

Clothes	Technology	Food	Sport	...
T-shirt				

Find more online: fc3we8

Unit 6

It's my party!

S2/8 L3/21

Who's this? Oh, it's Holly, Olivia, Luke, Jay and Dave – they're having fun at a costume party. Who gets the prize for the best costume?

Where can you have fun with your friends and eat pizza at the same time, like these teenagers? That's right – at the bowling alley!

SPEAKING

1 Talking about the photos → Folie 30

Which parties in the photos look fun? Why?

Across cultures

Vergleiche, wie die Personen auf den Bildern und du und die Kinder in deiner Klasse Geburtstag feiern.
Wie sagt man „Happy Birthday" in deiner Sprache?

LISTENING

2 Which party?

Listen to some of the people in the photos.

1. Which party are they at (photos A–E)?
2. Which of the conversations are about food, people, activities? Explain.

Lösung 1. dialogue 1 – D; dialogue 2 – E; dialogue 3 – C; dialogue 4 – A; dialogue 5 – B;
2. dialogue 1: boy, ice rink; dialogue 2: cake, girl, candles; dialogue 3: girl, bumps; dialogue 4: muffins, Holly, costumes; dialogue 5: cheese, pizza, burger, chips, bowling

VOCABULARY

3 Party mind maps → WB 69/1 → HA

Start three mind maps and add more ideas as you work through this unit:

1. kinds of parties
2. what you can do at parties
3. what you need for a party

In Unit 6 lernst du

… über Geburtstage und Feiern zu sprechen und zu schreiben. Du lernst:

- Wortschatz zum Thema Feiern
- zu sagen, was erlaubt, erforderlich oder verboten ist (*can / can't, must / needn't, mustn't*)
- über die Vergangenheit zu sprechen

These boys are giving a friend 'the bumps' for her birthday!

C

Why not celebrate your birthday at the ice rink? You can skate to good music with your friends.

D

E

When you blow out the candles on your birthday cake, you can make a wish. One, two, three – blow!

SPEAKING **4** **Birthdays: Saying the date** → WB 69/2

→ ▲ 144/1

▲ → After …

Voc.: Ordinal numbers / Months, p. 234

a) *Say the dates on the right. (Look at page 234 for help.)*

Example: **The** first **of** January …

1st January ✔ | 2nd March | 3rd June
4th August | 5th October | 6th December

b) *Stand up and make a line of your birthdays through the year. Then say all your birthdays along the line. Here are some phrases for organising your line.*

A: When is your birthday?
B: It's on 13th February.
A: Oh, my birthday is in April, so I'm after you. It's on 23rd April.

WRITING **5** **Your turn: Your birthday ideas** → HA

→ △ 144/2

△ → Help with …

Is your birthday in the spring / summer / autumn / winter? Write about your ideas for a birthday party.

Lou's birthday is **in** June. It's **on** 2nd June.

S 2/10 L 3/24

I can't wait!

Monday 16th May at the Richardsons' house …

Holly: Only four more days. – I can't wait!

Amber: Are you really planning a sleepover? That's so boring!

Holly: Sleepovers aren't boring!

Amber: Maybe when you're twelve …

Mum: Amber, you mustn't talk to Holly like that. It's *her* birthday. Holly, who's coming on Friday?

Holly: Olivia, of course. She says she's got a surprise present for me! And Pia, and –

Mum: Pia? Isn't she in Cologne?

Holly: No, they've got school holidays this week so she's here with her parents.

Amber: Please tell me that some of your friends listen to cool music and don't always wear pink.

Holly: My friends are *very* cool!

Amber: Cool? In pink?! *Please*. Have a party with a *black* theme. I've got lots of black decorations so you needn't buy any new stuff.

Holly: Black?! Never! The theme of my party is PINK!

Amber: Oh no – please don't invite me!

Mum: Stop it, girls. Amber, you can't make the rules! You can go and buy some new decorations, Holly – but you mustn't spend a lot of money! And you must tidy your room before you decorate it.

Holly: OK. Can we make a trifle and a cake?

Mum: Yes, of course we can. But you needn't buy candles, I've got some.

Holly: Cool! Now, what else? I need ice cream, music and a DVD – we can watch films all night!

Mum: That's fun! But just remember, you mustn't eat too many sweets. And your friends can't stay late on Saturday morning because we want to go to Granny's house for lunch.

Holly: OK, OK, no more rules! Where's my phone? I must talk to Olivia!

READING

1 Sleepovers

a) *Answer the questions.*

1. What does Holly want for her birthday party?
2. What does Amber think of Holly's idea? Why?
3. What do you think about Amber and the way the sisters talk together?

b) *Your turn: Talk about sleepovers*

1. What happens at a sleepover?
2. How often do you have one?
3. Do you like sleepovers? Why / why not?

READING

2 Rules for Holly's sleepover → HA

Lösung 1. Amber can't make the rules. 2. Holly needn't buy candles. 3. Holly and her friends can watch a film. 4. Holly must tidy her room. 5. Holly and her friends mustn't eat too many sweets. 6. Holly's friends can't stay late on Saturday.

Make sentences with these words.

1. … can't make the rules.
2. … needn't buy candles
3. … can watch a film.
4. … must tidy her room
5. … mustn't eat too many sweets.
6. … can't stay late on Saturday.

Holly and her friends
Amber
Holly's friends
Holly

LANGUAGE

3 Find the rule → WB 70/3–4 → G32–33 → HA

*Copy the list. Find more examples of **can, can't, must, mustn't** and **needn't** in the text. What are the sentences in German? Compare English and German.*

Lösung Du darfst/kannst fünf Leute einladen. Ihr dürft/könnt nicht die ganze Nacht fernsehen. Du musst eine DVD holen. Du darfst nicht zu viel Süßes essen. Du brauchst keinen Kuchen zu kaufen.

English	German
You can invite five people. **You can't** watch TV all night. **You must** get a DVD. **You mustn't** eat too many sweets. **You needn't** buy a cake.	Du darfst … …

LANGUAGE

4 Holly calls Olivia → HA

→ △ 144/3
△ → After …

What does Holly say to Olivia about the sleepover? Make sentences with these words. Use your list from exercise 3 to check and talk about your answers with a partner.

I You We	can can't must mustn't	come early so we can do our hair together! tell the boys. They think sleepovers are silly! bring some music if you like. meet today – I'm making my cake with Mum. help me decorate my room if you have time. call Pia now!

LISTENING

5 Holly's Friday night sleepover

L 3/25

Listen to the girls and answer the questions.

1. What do the girls do? Name five things.
2. Why can't some people come to the party?
3. How does Holly feel when she talks to her mum, Amber and Jay?
4. What do you think about Holly's rules?
5. Imagine you have a sleepover: Who can/can't come? Why?

LANGUAGE **6**

Lösung *1. You needn't take food and drinks. 2. You mustn't run on the ice. 3. You needn't have your own skates. 4. You mustn't skate with your bag. 5. You can skate alone. 6. You mustn't eat on the ice. 7. You can put your phone and money in a locker. 8. You must wear gloves.*

A skating party → HA, KV 69

*Amber gets an invitation to a skating party. Look at the poster and say what you **can**, **must**, **needn't** or **mustn't** do at the ice rink.*

Example: You **needn't** take food or drinks.

take food and drinks ✔ | run on the ice | have your own skates | skate with your bags | skate alone | eat on the ice | put your phone and money in a locker | wear gloves

+ + + ALEXANDRA PALACE + + ICE RINK + + + +

We have:

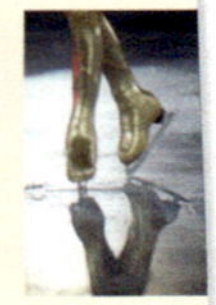

Party food and drinks
Skates in all sizes
Lockers for your bags
Teachers to help you

But remember:

Please don't
- run on the ice!
- eat on the ice!
- skate without gloves!

SPEAKING **7**

Your turn: Rules at home, rules at school → G33 → HA

*Make a grid about what you **must**, **mustn't** and **needn't** do at home and at school. Talk about your ideas with your partner.*

→ △ 145/4
△→ Help with …

Start: At home, I must make my bed every day. What about you?

SPEAKING **8**

Placemat activity: Birthday presents

a) *First work on your own: Think of birthday present ideas. Describe the things and put them in groups in **your** part of the placemat. Are they useful, funny, …? Can you eat them? …*

b) *In your group, discuss what is good for boys or for girls, for young or for old people, and why. Decide what you would like to give to Holly, Olivia, Dave, Jay and Luke for their birthdays. Write the things in the **middle** of your placemat.*

LISTENING **9**

L 3/26–27

‹ A song: Hey you! › → KV 70

a) *Listen to the song "Hey you!". Answer these questions.*

1. What kind of text is it?
2. What does the speaker want to do?

b) *Sing the song.*

LANGUAGE **10**

Lösung *1. must 2. needn't 3. can 4. must 5. mustn't 6. can't*

Complete the instructions for a party game → WB 71/5 → KV 71

can | can't | must | mustn't | needn't

1. You ___ dance when you hear the music.
2. You ___ dance alone. Dance with a friend if you like!
3. You ___ make funny faces or do silly moves – it's more fun.
4. When the music stops, you ___ stop.
5. Stand very still: You ___ move at all!
6. Don't move before the music starts again, or you're out – you ___ play any more! The last person in the game wins a prize.

MEDIATION 11 A very special birthday party

→ WB 71/6 → HA

→ ▲ 145/5
▲→ After …

Ein Freund aus England ist mit seinen Eltern bei euch zu Besuch. Nächste Woche willst du deinen Geburtstag mit Freunden und Familie feiern. Du findest dieses Angebot im Internet. Dein Freund möchte wissen, was Favorite *ist und was man dort machen kann. Er fragt auch, was es kostet und ob seine Eltern mitkommen können. Was antwortest du ihm?*

Mediation skills

First find out **what information in the text is important** for the other person. Don't tell him / her anything else.

If you don't know how to translate a word, try to **explain** what it means:
- *Prinz* = the child of …
- *Freizeit, Schule, Mahlzeiten* = typical …

If you don't understand everything in a list of things, **use examples**: You can choose …, e.g. / like …

Lösung EH
Favorite is an old castle. They organise birthday parties for children there. The castle is like a time machine. It sounds great! We can have a lot of fun there. We can dance, wear costumes and act out roles. We can bring our food and drinks and have a picnic in the garden after the tour. The tour costs 120 euros for 20 children and four parents. So your parents can come too.

KINDERGEBURTSTAG IN SCHLOSS FAVORITE

Ein Kindergeburtstag in Schloss Favorite ist eine Reise in der Zeitmaschine! Lassen Sie Ihr Kind und seine Freunde erleben, womit sich Prinzen und Prinzessinnen die Zeit vertrieben, was sie lernten und aßen. […] Die barocke Umgebung bietet viel Überraschendes! Basteln, Tanzen, Rollenspiel, Kostümierung – die Bausteine können Sie frei zusammenstellen. Bringen Sie die Geburtstagsverpflegung mit, die Sie möchten. Wie wäre es mit einem Picknick im Schlossgarten?

Konditionen

Altersklasse:	5 bis 14 Jahre
Gruppengröße:	maximal 20 Kinder
Begleitperson:	notwendig
Preis:	120,00 €; vier Begleitpersonen frei
Hinweis:	auch in englischer und französischer Sprache buchbar
Essen und Trinken:	kann mitgebracht werden für Picknick im Garten im Anschluss an die Führung

READING 12 How do you make a trifle?

→ ▲ 146/6

a) *Read how to make a trifle. Does it sound good? Explain.*

b) *Your turn: What is your favourite party food? Talk about it.*

Across cultures

In Großbritannien sind *trifles* beliebte Party-Desserts. Was esst ihr in eurer Familie gerne zum Nachtisch?

For a trifle you need:
1 sponge cake or 1 packet of sponge fingers
1 packet of jelly, water
1 packet of custard, milk
500 g of fresh or tinned fruit
250 ml of cream

Break small pieces of cake into a big glass bowl. Slice the fruit and put it on top. Prepare the jelly, leave it to cool and pour it over the cake and fruit. Put the bowl in the fridge. Prepare the custard and pour it on the jelly. Leave it to cool. Whip the cream and put it on top.

G34 Die einfache Form der Vergangenheit

S 2/12–14
L 3/29–31

No problem!

Dave has got a new friend on the internet, Emily from the USA. He's writing an e-mail to her to tell her about his last birthday.

Hi Em,
You wanted to know about my twelfth birthday and what I did. Well, some things went wrong, but it was OK in the end. When I got up, I tripped over Sid and hurt my foot. But no problem, the morning was cool because I had breakfast with my parents. That doesn't happen very often because they always work a lot. They gave me a new computer and a new pair of shoes – they were the wrong size! But no problem, I can take them back to the shop. My granny made a cake for me, but she only put eleven candles on it. So I ran to the shop to get one more. But no problem, the cake was yummy! Sid tried some of it and was sick[1] on the floor. But no problem, I cleaned the floor and he was OK again later.
Dave

Dear Dave – you REALLY had some bad luck there! But you always see the positive side[2] of things. I like that!
Em

Well, my birthday party wasn't so bad: On Saturday I had a big party. I invited all my friends. Luke and Jay and the girls came in the afternoon, and we played with my new computer. For dinner, my parents bought pizza, and my mum made a big salad. After dinner we ate my trifle – mmm. Then we all watched a fantasy film and really liked it!
Bye, Dave

READING **13**

What happened? → HA

a) *Are the sentences right or wrong? Correct the wrong sentences.*

Example: 1. Dave tripped over Sherlock. – That's wrong, Dave tripped over **Sid**.

1. Dave tripped over Sherlock. ✔
2. Dave's parents gave him a football.
3. They gave him a pair of shoes too.
4. The shoes were the right size.
5. Dave's granny made a cake with twelve candles.
6. The cake was great.
7. Sid was sick on the bed.

b) *What do you think about Dave's last birthday?*

Lösung a) 1. That's wrong. Dave tripped over Sid. 2. That's wrong. Dave's parents gave him shoes and a computer. 3. That's right. 4. That's wrong. The shoes were the wrong size. 5. That's wrong. Dave's granny made a cake with eleven candles. 6. That's right. 7. That's wrong. Sid was sick on the floor.

1 **to be sick** [bi ˈsɪk] sich erbrechen | 2 **to see the positive side (of sth)** [ˌsiː ðə ˈpɒzətɪv ˌsaɪd] das Gute an einer Sache sehen

LANGUAGE **14**

***Lösung b)/c)** Rules for spelling and pronunciation of regular forms: regular forms = infinitive + ed; spelling: consonant + y = ied; short verbs = two consonants; pronunciation: [d], [t] or [ɪd]. Irregular: did, went, got up, hurt, had, gave, were, made, put, ran, came, bought, ate; Regular: wanted, cleaned, invited, played, watched, liked, acted, barked, closed, danced, matched, talked; Regular with different spelling: tripped, tried, chatted, copied, rapped, stopped*

Find the rule → WB 72/7–8 → G34

a) *Find the infinitives for all the simple past forms in the text.*

wanted | did | went | was | got up | tripped | hurt | had | gave | were | made | put | ran | tried | cleaned | invited | came | played | bought | watched | liked | ate

b) *Write the simple past forms in a grid like this. What rules are there for spelling regular forms? And for their pronunciation?* → HA

Irregular	Regular	Regular with different spelling
did	wanted	tripped
…	…	…

There are no rules for irregular forms: You must learn them by heart!

c) *Can you put these verbs into the simple past? Write the forms in the right place in the grid:*

act | bark | chat | close | copy | dance | match | rap | stop | talk

LANGUAGE **15**

→ △ 146/7
△ → After …

Lösung 1. I went to the flea market last year. 2. Yesterday Sid had a mouse for dinner. 3. My mum came home late last night. 4. At 8 o'clock yesterday Sherlock got up with Luke. Etc.

Make sentences about the past → HA

Example: 1. I go to the flea market every year. → I **went** to the flea market **last year**.

1. I go to the flea market every year. → last year ✔
2. Sid sometimes has a mouse for dinner. → yesterday
3. My mum often comes home late. → last night
4. Sherlock gets up with Luke every morning. → at 8 o'clock yesterday
5. Holly and her mum go shopping together. → last Saturday
6. You're always really funny. → at the party last week
7. I always put a lot of cream on my cake. → last Sunday

When you see these signal words, use the past tense:
last week / month / year
two days **ago**
yesterday

WRITING **16**

Your turn: Your last birthday → WB 73/9–10 → HA, KV 72, KV 73

Write about your last birthday. Collect your ideas in a mind map first and find the simple past forms of the verbs (look at pages 191 and 275). Put your text in your folder. You can add photos too.

You can start like this:

My last birthday was on … | I wanted … | I got … | My mum … / I … / We … | It was …

Writing skills

Always go through your texts again and correct any mistakes before you show them to someone. Check:

- Is the **spelling** correct?
- Did I choose the **right words**?
- Did I use the correct **verb forms**?
- Is it **clear** what I want to say?

G35 Fragen in der einfachen Vergangenheit
G36 Die Verneinung in der einfachen Vergangenheit

S 2/17
L 3/34

An American party → Folie 31

Emily and her brother Ryan are having a video chat with Dave and Luke.

Emily: Did you get my postcard from New York, Dave?
Dave: Yes, I did. Thanks, Emily. The Statue of Liberty looks really cool! Were you sad to go home again?
Emily: Yes, I was! But I was happy to see Sunny when we came home.
Ryan: At least we didn't have school!
Luke: Why didn't you have school?
Emily: It's our summer vacation now. – Hey, did you know? Yesterday was the Fourth of July. That's Independence Day here!
Dave: Cool! What happened?
Ryan: We had a Fourth of July party with a barbecue and then we went to the park and watched the fireworks. They were awesome!
Dave: Was Sunny scared of the fireworks?
Emily: No, she wasn't because she didn't go with us. She stayed at home and slept.
Luke: Dogs always do that! What did you do in the morning?
Ryan: First we had breakfast. Dad made Fourth of July pancakes. They weren't normal – they were red, white and blue! After that, we put the flag outside our house. Then Emily and I decorated the yard.
Luke: Sorry, what did you decorate? Did you say 'yard'?
Dave: It's the American word for 'garden'.
Luke: And I thought we all spoke English! Did your Mum make any special food?
Emily: Yes, she did. She made my favourite chocolate cookies with flags on top. Mom makes great cookies!
Luke: Mmmm. Sounds good. What other food was there?
Emily: Hot dogs, burgers, fries –
Ryan: – And lots of candy! Sorry, I'm going now – I've got a baseball game this afternoon. It was great to talk to you guys. Bye!
Dave: See you! Hey Luke, look! It's Sunny. I think she wants you to get Sherlock. Maybe they want to talk too.

READING **17**

Talk about Emily and Ryan's vacation → WB 74/11–12a) → G34–36

a) *What did Emily and Ryan do in their summer vacation?*

b) *Ask and answer questions about the dialogue.*

1. Was Emily's postcard from New York?
2. Were Emily and Ryan at school on 4th July?
3. Did Ryan like the fireworks at the park?
4. Was Sunny at the fireworks?
5. Were the pancakes red, white and blue?
6. Did Emily and Ryan make the cookies?

Yes,	he she it they	was. were. did.
No,		wasn't. weren't. didn't.

c) *Ask and answer more questions on the text.*

Lösung EH a) *Emily and Ryan went to New York on their summer vacation. They had a Fourth of July party with lots of food and watched the fireworks in the park.*
b) 1. Yes, it was. 2. No, they weren't. 3. Yes, he did. 4. No, she wasn't. 5. Yes, they were. 6. No, they didn't.

LANGUAGE **18**

Find the rule: Differences between past and present → WB 75/12b) → G35–36 → KV 74

Lösung EH
In questions and negative sentences in the simple present you use does/doesn't in the third person singular and do/don't for all the other persons.
In questions and negative sentences in the simple past you use did/didn't for all persons.

Look at the sentences in the present and the past.
What are the differences for ***questions*** *and* ***negative sentences****?*
Write down the rule.

Simple present	Simple past
Do you like the fireworks?	Did you like the fireworks?
Does Dave like the postcard?	Did Dave like the postcard?
What does Luke ask?	What did Luke ask?
Luke doesn't understand the word 'yard'.	Luke didn't understand the word 'yard'.
Emily and Ryan don't go to school on 4th July.	Emily and Ryan didn't go to school on 4th July.

WRITING **19**

→ ▲ 147/8
▲→ After …

That isn't right → WB 75/13 → HA, KV 75

Lösung 1. didn't send, sent a postcard from New York 2. didn't have, had a barbecue 3. didn't like, stayed at home and slept 4. didn't make, Ryan's dad made 5. didn't decorate, Emily and Ryan decorated 6. didn't eat, ate hot dogs, burgers and fries

Correct the sentences.

Example: Emily wrote a postcard to Luke.
→ Emily didn't write a postcard to Luke. She wrote a postcard to Dave.

1. Emily sent a postcard from Washington.
2. Emily's family had a picnic on 4th July.
3. Sunny liked the fireworks.
4. Ryan made pancakes for breakfast.
5. Ryan's parents decorated the yard.
6. They ate sandwiches at the party.

VOCABULARY **20**

Talk like an American

Lösung EH I love summer vacation and I love Independence Day. This year my mom made cookies for our party in the yard. We had burgers too, and fries, and all the candy was red, white and blue like the American flag.

Voc.: American English, p. 238

Correct the text: Use the American word instead of the British English word.

fries | yard | vacation
candy | cookies | mom

I love the summer holidays and I love Independence Day. This year my mum made biscuits for our party in the garden. We had burgers too, and chips, and all the sweets were red, white and blue like the American flag.

SPEAKING **21**

Your turn: Special days

Think about what you did last Christmas, last Easter or on New Year's Eve. Take turns to ask and answer questions. Remember the word order!

have a special dinner | go to church | look for Easter eggs | stay up till midnight | watch fireworks | sleep late

LANGUAGE **22**

What was special? → G34, 36

Lösung a) *1. But two days ago he ate pancakes because it was the Fourth of July. 2. But last Tuesday she went to school by car because she got up too late. 3. But last year he didn't play baseball because he broke his arm. 4. But last Thursday she didn't play soccer because she went to a pizza restaurant. 5. But last night they didn't do any homework because it was the first day of vacation.*

a) *Make sentences about Emily and Ryan. Use the simple past.*

Example: Emily usually takes Sunny to the park after school.
But yesterday they went in the morning **because** it was Sunday.

1. Ryan often eats cereal for breakfast.
(two days ago / eat pancakes / Fourth of July)
2. Emily usually goes to school on the school bus.
(last Tuesday / go to school by car / get up too late)
3. In the summer Ryan often plays baseball after school.
(last year / not play baseball / break (*past:* broke) his arm)
4. Emily plays soccer after school on Thursdays.
(last Thursday / not play soccer / go to a pizza restaurant)
5. In the evenings, Emily and Ryan do their homework after dinner. (last night / not do any homework / first day of the vacation)

b) *Say what you usually do. Then say what you did on a special day and why.*

MEDIATION **23**

What's different in the US? → Diktat- und Transfertext

Lösung EH *Dear Holly, Alina told me many interesting things about America and what is different there. Strangers are always very friendly and start to talk. They all want to know how you are. And when Alina goes out with other girls, she and the girls say nice things, for example, how nice they look. Waiters in American restaurants are always very friendly too. They tell the people their first name and bring water for free. People in America go everywhere by car. There aren't many busses and trains. American teenagers usually don't go to school or the city centre by bike. It's different in Germany. That's all for now. Love, Pia*

Pias Cousine Alina ist als Austauschschülerin in den USA. Sie schreibt Pia oft und Pia erzählt Holly davon. Holly möchte wissen, über welche Unterschiede zwischen Deutschland und den USA Alina berichtet.

fremde Menschen: strangers | *Kellner:* waiter | *Vorname:* first name

Lies zunächst Alinas E-Mail an Pia. Dann schreibe Pias Antwort an Holly.

Liebe Pia,
mir gefällt's hier bei meiner Gastfamilie richtig gut! Die Stadt ist nicht groß, aber es gibt dort alles, was man braucht. Die Schule ist echt interessant und Sarah, meine Austauschpartnerin, ist supernett. Überhaupt sind alle sehr freundlich zu mir. Aber anders als bei uns sind auch fremde Leute immer total nett und plaudern sofort drauflos. Alle wollen wissen, wie es einem geht. Und wenn ich mit anderen Mädchen ausgehe, sagen wir uns immer nette Sachen, wie toll wir aussehen und so 🙂.
Als wir neulich in einem Restaurant essen waren (übrigens sehr lecker!), hat uns der Kellner superfreundlich begrüßt und uns gleich seinen Vornamen gesagt. Das passiert bei uns in Deutschland nicht! Danach hat er uns sofort ungefragt Wasser gebracht, für das wir nicht mal bezahlen mussten. Sarah sagt, das sei normal hier. Vieles ist hier wirklich ganz ungewohnt.
Sarah hat schon eine ganze Weile den Führerschein. Hier auf dem Land kommst du sonst auch nirgends hin. Die Leute in Amerika fahren fast überallhin mit dem Auto. Es gibt kaum Busse und Bahnen, und anders als die deutschen Jugendlichen fahren die jungen Leute normalerweise nicht mit dem Fahrrad zur Schule oder in die Stadt. Wir machen oft schöne Ausflüge mit dem Auto, und Sarahs Eltern sind auch froh, wenn sie mal nicht fahren müssen! Im Anhang sind ein paar Fotos.
Übrigens, schickst du mir noch die Fotos von deiner Geburtstagsfeier?
Bis bald, Alina

1 **student exchange** ['stju:dnt‿ɪksˌtʃeɪndʒ] Schüleraustausch

How to write and reply to party invitations

1 Writing an invitation card → WB 76/14 → HA, KV 76

Lösung a) *1. b) 2. f) 3. d) 4. a) 5. c) 6. g) 7. e) 8. h)*

a) *Match the words and phrases on the right with the different parts of the invitation card.*

1. Dear Tina,
2. Please come to my pizza party
3. on Saturday 17th March
4. at 1:30 p.m.
5. My address is 16 Rosendale Road.
6. Let me know if you can come.
7. Love, Lara
8. P.S. You must wear a silly hat!

a) time
b) greeting
c) place
d) date
e) ending
f) theme of party
g) asking for a reply
h) extra information

Lösung EH b) *Dear Pia, Please come to my pirate party on Saturday 29th of August at 2:30 p.m. My address is Kornblumenweg 12. Please let me know if you can come! And wear a costume! Love, Anna*

b) *Choose a theme for a party and write an invitation card for it. Give it to your partner.* → HA

Writing skills

When you write your invitation, remember:
- who is it for?
- what is the invitation about?
- when does the party take place?
- where does it take place?
- do you want to ask the person to do or bring something?
- use a nice greeting and ending

→ ▲ 147/9
▲ → After …

Lösung EH c) *Dear Anna, Thank you very much for your invitation. I would love to come to your party! See you on Saturday! Love, Pia*

c) *Write a reply to your partner's invitation.* → HA

Useful phrases

Dear …,
Thank you for …
I would love to … | See you on …
I'm sorry, but I can't … | I hope you have a nice party.
Love, …

Say thank you.
Say if you can come or not.
Say you're sorry if you can't come.
Use a nice greeting and ending.

2 Other forms of invitation

Lösung *Birthday party at my house next Saturday! Can you come? Let me know! See you, Tony*

Can you read Tony's text? Write it. → HA

Across cultures

In englischsprachigen Ländern ist es Tradition, sich handgeschriebene Grußkarten zu schicken. Was haltet ihr davon? Bekommt oder schreibt ihr auch welche? Gibt es einen Unterschied zwischen E-Mails, SMS, usw. und handgeschriebenen Briefen?

WRITING

1 Pre-reading: Jay and his friends

Who is close / not so close to Jay? Draw a diagram with Jay, Dave, Luke, Holly and Olivia.

S 2/20–24
L 3/37–41

Don't they like me any more? → Folie 32, KV 77

A "That's strange," Jay thinks. "Where is everyone?" Jay is at school and it's only three days till his birthday. He's very excited and he's got some fun ideas for a birthday party with his friends. But where are they ? … Ah, there they are.

"Hey Luke, hey Dave!" Luke and Dave are talking and laughing, but they suddenly stop when they see Jay.

"Hi," he says. "You know it's my birthday on Saturday. Do you want to come to my house? No girls! Just boys' games and burgers!"

"Er – sorry, Jay, I can't," Luke answers.

"Cool idea, but I'm busy too," Dave says, and they walk away. Jay can't believe that they don't want to celebrate with him.

B Jay is disappointed. But then he sees Holly and Olivia.

"Hm, if the boys don't want me, I can ask the girls. I'm sure I can count on Holly." The girls are whispering, but Jay can hear them.

"But that isn't very nice. I can't –"

"Oh come on Holly, don't be a baby. He – " Olivia sees Jay: "Oh, hi Jay, how are you?" Jay is smiling.

"Hi girls. Great! How about a film and pizza night on Saturday? It's my birthday."

Holly doesn't know what to say: "Er …" Olivia suddenly talks very fast. "Yes, we know, but we can't come on Saturday because it's Holly's birthday sleepover that evening. Sorry!"

Holly looks at Jay, and the girls hurry away. Jay is alone. Again.

C On Saturday afternoon, Jay is at home. It's his birthday today, but he feels lonely and bored. He tries to call his friends on the phone, but they don't answer. What's wrong? Don't they like him any more?

"I'm very unlucky," he thinks. "Other people have fun on their birthdays and see their friends, open presents, play games … But I'm just sitting here alone and nothing is happening."

His mum is on the phone, but he can't hear what she's saying. After the phone call she asks Jay, "Why are you looking so sad? Don't worry! Come out with Dad and me to Hamid and Seeta's restaurant. You can have carrot pudding and a mango lassi, and then we can go to the cinema."

"Thanks Mum," Jay says. But he really wants to be with his friends, not his family.

D At 5 o'clock, Jay and his parents get into the family car and go into Greenwich. Jay is hungry and is feeling better when his mum suddenly stops the car. "Oh no!"

"What's wrong?" asks Jay.

"I haven't got my bag with me – have you got any money?" she asks Jay's dad.

"No, it's at home," he answers.

"Well, we must go back and get it." Jay can't believe it! "How unlucky am I?" he thinks. "Everything is going wrong! I just want to go to bed and forget it's my birthday."

Fifteen minutes later, they're back at home. Jay's mum stops the car. "Jay, can you run inside and get my bag, please?"

E Jay doesn't run – he isn't happy or excited about this evening. He needn't hurry. He walks to the door and opens it.

"Surprise!!!" everyone shouts.

There are lots of nice decorations and all his friends are wearing costumes, Sherlock too! He looks *very* funny.

"What ...?"

"Happy birthday!" they all shout. Then they sing 'For he's a jolly good fellow'. There are presents, party food, a cake, and the best thing is the alien costume for Jay. "Wow!" he says. "I can't believe it! You're all *really* cool, and Mum and Dad too. I'm so lucky. It's a great birthday after all! Let's have fun!"

READING

2 Think about the story → WB 77/16–17 → G37 → HA, Folie 32

a) *Use these words to say how Jay feels in each part of the story. Say why.*

excited · sad · happy · bored · lucky · thankful · disappointed · unlucky · lonely · hopeful

Example: In part A Jay feels excited because it's three days till his birthday.

b) *Tell the story again. First work on your own. Then swap texts with a partner.*

→ △ 147/10
△→ Help with ...

1. Find headings for each part of the story.
2. Look for key words and make notes about the most important things.
3. Write down what happens in each part.
4. Read your partner's text and correct the mistakes.

Example:

A: Jay talks to Dave and Luke at school
Jay wants to invite Dave and Luke to his birthday party, but they're busy. Jay feels disappointed.

c) *The text says what **Jay** feels. What about the other people? Can you guess what their feelings are?*

d) *What are Olivia and Holly talking about in B? Imagine Jay isn't there, and write their dialogue.* → HA

e) *Talk about the ending of the story. What do you think about it?*

Don't forget to use linking words like *and, but, because, so, when, that, then.* → G37

SPEAKING

3 The people in the story → WB 77/18 → Diktat- und Transfertext

*Talk with a partner: Do you like surprises or not? Say why. Why don't **you** plan a surprise party for a friend?*

The sleepover

VIEWING

1 Film scenes → KV 78

Lösung a) *4. – 3. – 1. – 5. – 6. – 2.*

a) *Here are six scenes from the film. Watch the film and put the scenes in the right order.*

1. It's a mistake
2. The pillow fight[1]
3. A surprise guest[2]
4. Nathan must stay in
5. Sleepover games + poor Nathan
6. Back in the house

b) *Talk about who is in each scene, where they are and what happens.*

SPEAKING

2 Nathan and the girls → KV 78, KV 79

Lösung EH a)
Group 1: A: Laura, Emily, Parule at front door; Alicia comes to sleepover; surprise; B: Laura's mobile; Alicia and Alice on friends list, invitation to Alicia, not Alice, mistake; C: Laura, Alicia and Parule playing "Sleeping Beauty" with Emily, Alicia is fun, Alicia and Laura now friends?
Group 2: A: Nathan can't go out with friends, always comes home late, must stay at home, unhappy; B: girls having fun with sleepover, Nathan tries to go out; C: Nathan's mum comes home, must go back in the house.

a) *A film can tell two stories. Make two groups. Then look at the pictures for your group and watch the film again. Make notes for each picture.*

Group 1:

A

B
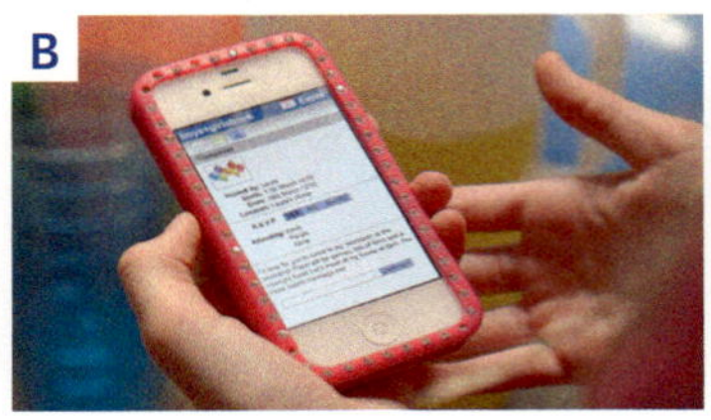

C

Group 2:

D

E

F

b) *Make pairs with one student from group 1 and one student from group 2. In your pairs, use your notes to answer these questions and tell your story. Then talk about your ideas in class.*

Group 1: Is it a 'lucky mistake'?

Group 2: What's Nathan's problem?

SPEAKING

3 Your turn: Your sleepover

a) *Tell a partner what happens at a sleepover –* ***your*** *sleepover!*

Or:

b) *Plan a sleepover with a partner. Say what your friends can/can't, must/needn't, mustn't do.*

1 **pillow fight** [ˈpɪləʊ ˌfaɪt] Kissenschlacht | 2 **guest** [gest] Gast

→ Solutions p. 272

Can you …

1. talk about birthdays and parties? — My birthday is on … | Happy birthday! We can play … | My mum always makes a … We need … | Let's go …
2. talk about rules and instructions? — You must … / needn't … / mustn't …
3. write an invitation card? — Dear …, | Please come … on … at …, Love, …
4. talk about the past? — Yesterday | Last year … | Did you …

LANGUAGE

1 Put in *can, can't, must, mustn't* or *needn't* → HA, KV 80

It's 4:30 p.m. The friends are outside a small shop for party things.

Dave: Look – only four people [1] go in.
Luke: I'm staying outside with Sherlock. He [2] go in. It says "no animals".
Olivia: And it says we [3] eat or drink in the shop, so eat your sandwich, Jay!
Holly: Come on, we [4] go in before it's too late. The shop closes at 5:00.
Dave: You [5] try this costume, Jay!
Jay: It's cool. But I [6] get the hat. I've got a nice hat at home.

Holly: Dave, you [7] only think about Jay! You haven't got a costume!
Olivia: It's OK. We [8] buy it today. The party is next week.

LANGUAGE

2 Mixed bag: My sister's birthday → WB 78/19 → HA, KV 81

It [1] my sister's 4th birthday last Sunday. When she [2] up, we gave her the [3]. That was fun! My parents and I [4] her a lot of presents and a cake. First she [5] out the candles on the [6] and [7] a wish. Then she [8] her presents. She [9] really happy [10] them. Then we played a [11] together.

Later we [12] lunch at our granny's house. Then we [13] to the zoo. We [14] at all the animals, but we [15] the horses for a long time. My sister [16] them! The pigs [17] funny too. I [18] them best. In the evening we had an Indian curry for [19].

LANGUAGE

3 Make questions and answers → WB 78/20 → HA, KV 82

1. What / you / do / last Saturday? – cinema
2. Where / you / go / holiday / last summer? – Scotland
3. When / Emily and Ryan / watch / fireworks? – 4th July
4. What / Emily and Ryan / eat / 4th July? – red, white and blue things
5. Sunny / see / fireworks too? – no
6. She / sleep? – yes

Find more online: wx9m2s

Special days, special events

Holidays, festivals and traditions are a part of every culture. Learn about different special days in the UK and compare them with special days where you live.

SPEAKING **1** **Warm-up: What are special days?** → KV 85

What kind of special days are there?
What special days do you like? Why?
The box on the right can help you.

Useful phrases

We celebrate … | I like … | My favourite special days are …
religious / national holidays | weddings | birthdays | family events | sports events | village / town festivals | …

VIEWING **2** **Special days in Britain (1)** → KV 83

13

Watch the film about three special days.
While you watch: Make notes about the names of the special days, and when they take place.

Voc.: Special days, Word bank (WB), p. 12

Lösung EH
1. Shrove Tuesday/ Pancake Day: Tuesday before people start to fast until Easter; 2. Guy Fawkes Night/Bonfire Night: 5th November; 3. Notting Hill Carnival: every August

1

2

3

LISTENING **3** **Special days in Britain (2)** → KV 84

L4/1

Now listen to people as they talk about three more special days. Make notes while you listen.

Lösung EH
1. two young men are talking about Wimbledon: tickets cost a lot, Centre Court, tradition, strawberries
2. man and woman are talking about Kate: Kate/Catherine, supermarket, jeans and T-shirt, Buckingham Palace, balcony, wedding, dress
3. two boys are talking about Mother's Day: something for his mum, mum is cool, something special, make something for her, breakfast

1

2

3

SPEAKING

4 What do you think? → WB 79/1–2 → HA

Lösung a) 1. g)
2. b) 3. e) 4. c) 5. h)
6. a) 7. d) 8. f)

a) *First match the sentence parts below about the special days on page 120.*

1. Guy Fawkes Night 's
2. People celebrate a historical event
3. Shrove Tuesday is
4. Pancake Day has got
5. Big events in the British royal family
6. A family event like
7. It isn't a holiday or a festival,
8. The Notting Hill Carnival takes place

a) Mother's Day isn't big, but it can be very special.
b) on Guy Fawkes Night. People all over the country celebrate with bonfires and fireworks.
c) a religious background. And food plays a role too!
d) but Wimbledon is an event with a very long tradition in the UK. And it's famous all over the world!
e) another name for Pancake Day.
f) every August and it's a fun day for thousands of Londoners.
g) on 5th November.
h) can often bring the whole country together. A royal wedding is a good example.

b) *What do you think about the six different special days? Explain.*

c) *Which scenes from the film and which dialogues from the recording do you like best? Why?*

Useful phrases

I like … because traditions are important. | There's something like it where I live / where my parents are from / … | It looks like fun!

for the family | for everyone | British | international | fun | serious | colourful | sports

WRITING

5 Your turn: More special days → WB 79/3 → HA, KV 85

*Write the names of the events and traditions on page 120 in a list. Think of **more** special days. What is interesting about them? The ideas below can help you. Then add these days to your list. Look on the internet for information and dates.*

The most important Christian holidays: Christmas | Easter | Whitsun (Pentecost)

Other special days: Diwali | Eid | Hanukkah | Halloween | name day | Thanksgiving | Valentine's Day | …

WRITING

6 Around the year: A time line → HA, KV 86

Make a time line with the months of the year. Then put all the festivals and special days from the film, the recording and from exercise 5 in the right place on your line. Write a short text (2–3 sentences) for each special day / festival / event.

Find more online: rc5867

A first look at the US

→ Folie 33

S 2/26
L 4/2

★★★ What I like about the US ★★★

We Americans love baseball! My favourite team plays in this stadium, they're the Washington Nationals. Look at that flag in the shape of the US!

Here we are rafting down the Grand Canyon. It is 277 miles (446 km) long and up to 1.1 miles (1.8 km) from the top to the bottom!

We watched this alligator in the Everglades in Florida. The Native Americans called the area Pa-hay-okee, that means 'grassy[1] waters' in English. It became a national park in 1947.

I go to the State Fair of Texas every year. It's so much fun! You can try special food, see different farm animals like cows and horses, and watch a rodeo. You can also ride the big wheel, the Texas Star.

SPEAKING

1 So much to see or do

→ Folie 33

a) *Talk about the posts on the pinboard[2]. Say what you would like to visit, see or do in the US, and why.*

b) *In class, talk about what else you know about the US.*

WRITING

2 A quiz

Look at the US map at the back of the book. Write six quiz questions about the US for your partner.

Voc.: A US map, p. 241

Examples: Where is …? Where do polar bears live? What do people grow / make / produce in …?

Useful phrases

in the northeast / on the west coast / …
to grow corn / wheat / cotton
to produce oil / …

1 **grassy** ['grɑːsi] grasig |
2 **pinboard** ['pɪnbɔːd] Pinnwand

READING 3 Washington and New York → WB 80/1 → Folie 34, KV 87

L 4/3

a) *Read the texts about Washington and New York and use them to explain which sights are in the pictures.*

b) *Choose one of the sights. You were there. Tell your partner about it. He / She can ask questions. Take turns.*

Lösung a) *A: The White House*
B: The Statue of Liberty
C: Central Park
D: The National Air and Space Museum

A

B

Washington D.C. is the capital city of the US. It is named after the first President of the US, George Washington. The government meets in the Capitol. The President lives in the White House, but a lot of people work there too. Washington is famous for its monuments and museums. One of the most famous is the National Air and Space Museum. About 9 million people visit it every year – it's very popular. You can look at a rock from the moon there and watch 3D films about space.

C

New York, or the Big Apple, is the most famous city in the US. People from all around the world live there.
There are five different areas: Brooklyn, the Bronx, Queens, Staten Island and Manhattan. Manhattan is a small island so there are a lot of skyscrapers there. Central Park is in the middle of Manhattan. You can do lots of fun things there like ice-skating and climbing on rocks, or you can go to the zoo. But one of the most famous sights in New York is the Statue of Liberty. The French gave it to America as a present in 1886. It is now a symbol of freedom everywhere in the world.

D

LISTENING 4 A trip to Washington → WB 81/2–3 → KV 88

L 4/5

Emily and Ryan are talking. Make a list of what they did in Washington and say if they enjoyed it or not. → Diktat- und Transfertext

WRITING 5 Your turn: A famous place in Germany → HA

Write a short text like the texts in exercise 3 about a famous town or city in Germany.

Revision C

⟨Revision C⟩ ist fakultativ und dient der Festigung/Wiederholung. Es werden keine neuen Sprachmittel eingeführt.

LISTENING

1 Phone calls → Folie 30, KV 89

L4/6

Listen to four phone calls. Match the calls with the notes. (There isn't a call for one note.)

Lösung phone call 1 – note E; phone call 2 – note A; phone call 3 – note C; phone call 4 – note B; no phone call – note D

A	B	C	D	E
JUNE	JUNE	JUNE	JUNE	JUNE
26 SATURDAY	26 SATURDAY	26 SATURDAY	26 SATURDAY	26 SATURDAY
Costume party here	Ice rink	Sleepover	Pizza at Alfredo's	My room or garden?

LANGUAGE

2 Olivia wants to earn some money → WB 82/1 → HA

What do Olivia and Claire say? Copy the text and put in the right verbs.

can | must | needn't | mustn't | can't

Lösung 1. can 2. needn't 3. can't 4. can 5. must 6. can't 7. can 8. can't/mustn't 9. needn't 10. can 11. must

Olivia: How **1** I earn some money, Claire? Have you got any ideas?
Claire: You **2** earn money. We give you pocket money.
Olivia: But I **3** buy DVDs with my pocket money. They're too expensive.
Claire: Well, you **4** help Mrs Wilson. She **5** get up because she's ill[1].
Olivia: Oh, so she **6** go shopping. That's a job for me! I **7** walk her dog too.
Claire: OK, but you **8** bring that dog into our house. He's crazy!
You've got a busy day today, Olivia! But you **9** tidy your room.
You **10** do that tomorrow. But remember –
Olivia: Yes, Claire, I know. I **11** do my homework first!

SPEAKING

3 Things for a party → WB 82/2

Look at the picture of the kitchen cupboard.
With a partner, ask each other about what you've got – or haven't got – for a party.

Example:

A: Have we got **any** biscuits?
B: Yes, we've got **a few packets of** biscuits. But have we got **any** lemonade?
A: No, we haven't. But we've got **some** …

1 **ill** [ɪl] krank

LANGUAGE

4 At the flea market → WB 82/3 → HA

Lösung 1. go 2. is wearing 3. is looking 4. gives 5. is showing 6. wears 7. are listening 8. buy

Simple present or present progressive? Put in the right forms.

Mario and Dan are at the flea market. They (1 go) there every Saturday. It's a nice day and Dan (2 wear) his new T-shirt. Mario (3 look) for a present for his sister. He always (4 give) her something for her birthday. At the moment Dan (5 show) Mario a bracelet. "My sister never (6 wear) jewellery," Mario says.
A man and a woman behind the table (7 listen) to the boys. "What about this bag?" the man asks. "It's top quality! Girls often (8 buy) things like this. It's only £10."

LANGUAGE

5 When? → HA

Lösung 1. b) 2. d) 3. a) 4. c)

Match the sentences with the phrases on the right.

1. Luke plays football
2. Amber is writing an e-mail
3. Jay went to the music shop
4. Sherlock goes for a walk

a) yesterday.
b) on Tuesdays.
c) every day.
d) at the moment.

SPEAKING

6 A lot of things happened → WB 83/4 → HA, KV 90

Lösung Did Amy get ...? – Yes, she did. Did Amy go ...? – No, she didn't. Did she make ...? – Yes, she did. Did she start ...? – Yes, she did. Did she go ...? – Yes, she did. Did Jack get ...? – No, he didn't. Did he go ...? – Yes, he did. Did he make ...? Yes, he did. Did he start ...? – Yes, he did. Did he get ...? – Yes, he did. Did he go ...? – Yes, he did.

Look at the grid.
What happened to these children last year? Ask and answer questions.

	get new baby brother / sister	go to new school	make new friends	start new sport	get birthday presents	go on holiday
Amy	Lily	–	Sophie Jack	football	bicycle	summer: camping France
Jack	–	Thomas Tallis	Harry Amy	basketball	sports shoes	winter: skiing Scotland

WRITING

7 Around the year → WB 83/5 → HA

What happened to you last year? How did you feel? Use ideas from exercise 6 and the phrases from the box to write a text about your year. You can start like this:

Last year was an exciting year ...

Useful phrases

in the spring / summer / autumn / winter
in January / February / March / ...
... weeks ago
on my last birthday

MEDIATION **8**

Let's go to the car boot sale!

Lösung EH
1. Öffnungszeiten: 9 Uhr für Verkäufer, 10:30 bis 14:30 für Käufer; Eintrittspreise: 50 Pence für Käufer, unter 16 frei;
2. Anmeldung: per E-Mail oder Telefon; Gebühren: 5 Pfund das Auto für Verkäufer;
3. Anfahrt: Landkarte mit Anfahrtsbeschreibung vorhanden;
4. Regeln und Ausschlüsse: Hund an der Leine OK, aber kein Essensverkauf.
Wir können unseren Hund zu dem Flohmarkt mitnehmen und Papa kann sich anmelden und seine Schuhe verkaufen. Mama braucht keinen Kuchen zu backen, da kein Essen verkauft werden darf. Das Auto kostet 5 Pfund und für Verkäufer öffnet der Flohmarkt schon um 9 Uhr. Besucher kosten 50 Pence und sie können ab 10:30 Uhr hinein. Eine Anfahrtsbeschreibung ist in der Anzeige dabei.

Du bist mit deinen Eltern und eurem Hund in England. Eure englischen Freunde möchten nächsten Samstag zu einem „Car boot sale" gehen (eine Art Flohmarkt) und zeigen euch Informationsmaterial. Deine Familie mag Flohmärkte und will mit dem Auto dorthin fahren. Dein Vater möchte ein Paar zu kleine Schuhe verkaufen und deine Mutter selbst gebackene Kuchen. Welche Informationen sind für deine Familie wichtig?

Deine Eltern interessiert besonders:
1. Öffnungszeiten, Eintrittspreise
2. Anmeldung, Gebühren
3. Anfahrt
4. Regeln und Ausschlüsse

Car boot sale

at Bunbury Common, Tarporley CW6 9QE
POSTED ON: 22/06

Location	Map
Occurrence	Regular
Held On	Saturday
Start Date	25th August
End Date	25th August
Seller Start Time	9am
Buyer Entry Time	10:30am – 2:30pm
Seller Pitch Fee	£5 – car, £8 – van, £2 – trailer £15 – professional sellers, all pitches
Buyer Entry Fee	50p per person, U16's free, £1 – on site parking
Refreshments	Yes
Toilets	Yes
Organiser(s) Name	Debbie Andrews
Telephone	07731 7649
Email	Dand@acbprovi.com
Website	
Additional Info	New and second-hand items for sale. Come and browse, come and buy! In aid of Help Club, registered charity. Dogs on leads are welcome. No livestock or food sales. Free raffle ticket for all sellers with a cash prize on offer to the winning ticket.

MEDIATION

9 An Easter tradition

a) *Vorübung: Lies den Artikel und übertrage folgende Formulierungen sinngemäß ins Englische.*

1. der besonderen Art
2. im Herzen der Stadt
3. es ist eine Augenweide
4. es fand zum ersten Mal statt
5. es werden immer neue Muster entworfen
6. zur Eröffnung
7. Leckereien zur Osterzeit
8. die kleinen Künstler

b) *Du wohnst in Bad Reichenhall. Dein Freund Jack aus Großbritannien muss für die Schule eine Präsentation über eine deutsche Tradition erstellen. Er findet folgenden Artikel im Internet. Ihm gefallen die Fotos und er bittet dich ihm zu erklären, um welche Tradition es sich handelt. Schreibe ihm eine E-Mail.*

Brunnen: fountain | *Kunsthandwerk:* arts and crafts

Lösung EH a) 1. very special 2. in the city centre 3. it looks great/awesome/very nice 4. it took place for the first time 5. there are always new ideas how to decorate it 6. on the first day/when the fountain opens 7. special Easter food/yummy food 8. children
b) Hello Jack, How are you? Of course I can tell you something about our very special Easter tradition here in Bad Reichenhall. Every two years, people decorate a fountain with colourful Easter egss in the city centre of Bad Reichenhall. It is made up of 4,000 real eggs. Visitors love to look at it! The event took place in 2001 for the first time, but there are always new ideas how to decorate the fountain. We usually have got an Easter market when it opens on Sunday, March 22nd from 11–5 p.m. You can eat yummy food there or look at and buy arts and crafts. Children can paint colourful Easter eggs too. I hope this helps you for your presentation. Bye, …

Osterbrunnen und Kunsthandwerk in Bad Reichenhall

Ein Osterschmuck der besonderen Art entsteht alle zwei Jahre in Bad Reichenhall. Der Brunnen am Florianiplatz im Herzen der Altstadt wird wieder aus 4000 echten, handbemalten Eiern errichtet und von der Initiative Altstadt, einer Einrichtung im Gewerbeverein, gemeinsam mit vielen Helfern, mit Tausenden echten Eiern, Girlanden und Frischblumen prachtvoll verziert. Das wunderschöne Zusammenspiel der Farben ist eine Augenweide und gibt dem Florianiplatz österliches Flair. In monatelanger Vorbereitung werden die zerbrechlichen Unikate bemalt, damit das Gesamtkunstwerk entstehen kann.

2001 wurde der erste Brunnen gestaltet. Mittlerweile wächst die Zahl der Eier. Die Eiermalleidenschaft hat einige Helfer erfasst und so werden immer neue Muster entworfen. Die Krone ist jedes Mal andersfarbig und die Zusammenstellung immer eine Überraschung für die zahlreichen Besucher, die sich alle zwei Jahre über dieses Schmuckstück freuen.

Zur Eröffnung findet traditionell am verkaufsoffenen Sonntag von 11–17 Uhr der beliebte Palmbesenmarkt mit Kunsthandwerk fürs Osternest, Palmbesen und -buschen sowie Dekorationen und Leckereien zur bevorstehenden Osterzeit um den Brunnen statt. Am Tiroler Tor kann beim Flohmarkt des Sozialpsychiatrischen Zentrums wieder nach Herzenslust gestöbert werden. Den kulinarischen Teil übernimmt die ansässige Gastronomie sowie in diesem Jahr das Sozialpsychiatrische Zentrum mit Kaffee, Kuchen und frisch gebackenen Krapfen. Auch die kleinen Künstler können wieder bunte Eier gestalten.

Der Osterbrunnen wird immer zwei Wochen vor dem Ostersonntag eröffnet und bleibt drei Wochen lang geschmückt.

Legende

Diese Symbole und Erklärungen zeigen dir, wie du mit den Hilfen, Aufgaben und Aktivitäten auf den *Practice pool*-Seiten arbeiten kannst.

△ Hilfe zur Unit-Aufgabe | oder eine leichtere Aufgabe | oder eine zusätzliche Aufgabe

▲ eine zusätzliche Herausforderung

Unit 1

▲ 1 A game: Who am I? → After Station 1, p. 17/3

Take turns to guess the people and animals from Brook Lane.

Example:

That's easy – you're Irina!

Luke is my brother. I'm not eight.

△ 2 Complete the sentences → After Station 1, p. 17/5

Lösung 1. We 2. It 3. I 4. They 5. She 6. He 7. you

1. Here are our family photos. ___'re the Elliots.
2. Our house is in Brook Lane. ___'s a small house.
3. My name is Luke. ___'m eleven.
4. Jack and Anna are my parents. ___'re OK.
5. Irina is my sister. ___'s always in the bathroom!
6. Jamie is my brother. ___'s eight.
7. Look, Sherlock, ___'re in the family too. Here's your photo!

▲ 3 Things in the bedroom → After Station 2, p. 19/10b)

a) *Look at the picture on page 19 again.*

Partner A: *Write down six things in the bedroom. Show your list to your partner.*

Examples: cars, wardrobe, …

Partner B: *Make a grid and put your partner's words into the correct list.*

Examples:

There is	There are
wardrobe	cars
…	…

b) *Write sentences with your ideas from a).*

Example: There's a wardrobe next to the bed.

△ 4 Prepositions → After Station 2, p. 19/10b)

Put in the correct prepositions.

Lösung 1. in 2. on 3. on 4. of 5. behind 6. in 7. in 8. from 9. on 10. in 11. with 12. from 13. at 14. in 15. with

1. What can you see [1] the picture?
2. [2] the left there's a dog. – Hey, it's Sherlock. He can't sit [3] the bed!
3. The mouse is scared [4] the cat. Where is the mouse?
4. It's [5] the door. So you can't see it.
5. I can see a red car [6] the street. It's [7] front of our house.
6. Is Pia [8] England? No, she isn't. She's [9] holiday [10] London.
7. Who is in London [11] Pia? Her parents. They're [12] Germany.
8. Is Luke [13] home? No, he isn't. He's [14] the park [15] Sherlock.

Lou

▲ 5 What's in the picture? → After Station 2, p. 19/11

Describe what you can see in the picture and where it is.

Lösung EH Sherlock is in the middle of the room. There are two footballs in the picture. There's a wardrobe on the right. There are six pens in front of the wardrobe. On the left there's a bed. There's a shoe and a football on the bed. There's a red clock next to the bed. There's a lamp behind the bed on the floor. There's a football in the middle on the floor. There are two books and two T-shirts on the floor. There are pictures on the wall. Etc.

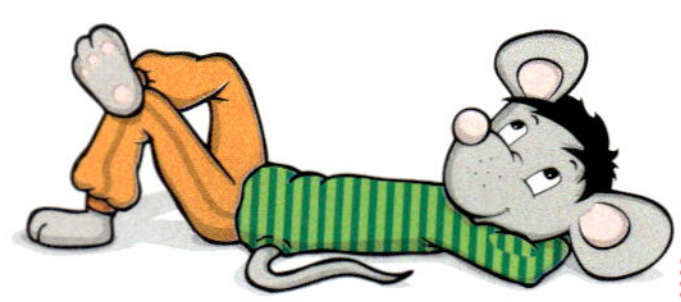

Tony

△ 6 Numbers → Help with Station 2, p. 20/12b)

Choose a group of three numbers. You say the numbers and your partner writes them down. Take turns to say the numbers and to write.

4-14-40	67-6-16	41-47-49	13-3-34
8-80-18	55-15-5	65-62-69	79-7-17
9-19-95	12-2-28	21-24-22	33-36-31

△ 7 Questions for Sherlock → After Station 2, p. 21/17 b)

Sherlock is in Greenwich Park with a new friend, Danny.
Copy the dialogue and put in the right forms.

Lösung 1. Is 2. is 3. Are 4. aren't 5. Is 6. is 7. are 8. are 9. Is 10. isn't

is | isn't | are | aren't

Danny: Tell me about your house, Sherlock. **1** there a garden?
Sherlock: Yes, there **2** . It's great for crazy games with Luke and Jamie.
Danny: **3** there only boys in your family?
Sherlock: No, there **4** . There's a girl too – Irina. But she isn't so crazy.
Danny: Is the living room in the house nice? **5** there a big sofa?
Sherlock: Yes, there **6** . It's fun on the sofa in front of the TV.
Danny: Cool! And **7** there good things in the cupboards in the kitchen?
Sherlock: Oh yes, there **8** . My favourite biscuits are in the cupboards.
Danny: Your house is great for a dog. **9** there a cat in the family too?
Sherlock: A cat?! No, there **10** . My house isn't for cats!

△ 8 A game: Where's my mouse? → Instead of[1] Station 2, p. 22/18 a)

Choose a mouse in the picture. Write down where it is. Can your partner guess?

in the bathroom / living room / loft / …

under / on / in / …

the table / bed / toilet / …

Example:

It's in the bedroom, behind the wardrobe.

A: Is your mouse in the kitchen?
B: No, it isn't.
A: Is it in the bedroom?
B: Yes, it is. But where?
A: Is it under the bed?
B: No, it isn't. Guess again.

1 **instead of** [ɪn'sted‿əv] (an)statt; anstelle von

Unit 2

▲ 1 School words
→ After Check-In, p. 33/3 → HA

Lösung EH *There are crazy pictures in the Art room. The students come to the cafeteria for lunch. The school rules are in the planner. The school uniform at TTS is blue.*

Match a word from A with a word from B. Write sentences about Thomas Tallis School with the word pairs. (You can write sentences with your own words too.)

Example: recording studio – music → The students can make music in the recording studio.

A pictures | blue | lunch | music | school rules

B recording studio | school | uniform | Art room | planner | cafeteria

△ 2 Who has got what?
→ After Station 1, p. 35/4 → HA, Folie 10

Lösung *1. Olivia and Holly have got TTS planners. 2. Dave has bot an orange pencil-case. 3. Mr Swindon has got books for everyone. 4. Luke and Jay have got rulers. 5. Holly has got sweets. 6. Dave and Olivia have got blue schoolbags. 7. Jay and Mr Swindon have got red pens. 8. Luke has got a ball.*

a) *Look at the picture and complete the sentences with the correct words. Use **has got** or **have got**.*

1. Olivia and Holly **have got** …
2. Dave **has got** …
3. Mr Swindon …
4. Luke and Jay …
5. Holly …
6. Dave and Olivia …
7. Jay and Mr Swindon …
8. Luke …

… books for everyone. | … red pens. | … blue schoolbags. | … TTS planners. | … a ball. | … sweets. | … an orange pencil-case. | … rulers.

b) *Write more sentences about the picture.*

△ 3 Make two lists
→ Help with Station 1, p. 36/7 a) → HA

What has Thomas Tallis School got? What have you got at your school? Collect information in two lists like this. Your ideas can help you to talk about the two schools in exercise 7a).

Thomas Tallis	Our school
recording studio	computers
uniform	school rules
school rules	Art room
…	…

△ 4 Questions and question words → After Station 1, p. 37/12

Lösung a) 1. Who's 2. What 3. What/Who 4. What's 5. What's 6. What's 7. Whose 8. What 9. Whose 10. Who's/What's
b) 1. What's your name? 2. What's your name? 3. How are you? 4. Who can you see in the picture? 5. What can you see on the right? 6. Whose car is this? 7. Who are your friends? 8. Who's your best friend? Etc.

a) *Where can you use **who** or **what** or **whose**?*

1. ___'s your tutor ?
2. ___ has Luke got?
3. ___ can you see in the picture?
4. ___'s your name?
5. ___'s in your pencil-case?
6. ___'s your favourite colour?
7. ___ dog is Sherlock?
8. ___ colour is your bike?
9. ___ pencil is this?
10. ___'s in the car?

b) *Say it in English.*

1. Wie heißen Sie?
2. Wie heißt du?
3. Wie geht es dir?
4. Wen kannst du auf dem Foto sehen?
5. Was kannst du auf der rechten Seite sehen?
6. Wem gehört dieses Auto?
7. Wer sind deine Freunde?
8. Wer ist dein bester Freund?
9. Was hast du in der Mitte deines Zimmers?
10. Welche Farbe hat dein Mäppchen?
11. Wo ist deine Schule?
12. Wessen Lehrer ist Mr Swindon?

▲ 5 A class game: Guess the rule → After Station 2, p. 40/17 c)

a) *First work alone for three minutes. Think of school rules that you can draw in pictures (rules at TTS, rules at your school – or your own ideas for funny rules).*

b) *Now make two big groups and play the game. In your group, take turns to draw pictures for school rules and to guess the rules. Draw and guess for ten minutes. Which group has got more rules?*

△ 6 Find the correct forms of the words → After Station 2, p. 42/21

Lösung a) 1. The Elliots 2. Luke Elliot's 3. Luke's brother's 4. The Elliots' 5. Luke's 6. Luke's 7. Luke's mother's 8. The Zajacs' 9. Jn Zajac's 10. Luke and Jamie's b) 1. Holly's 2. Jay's 3. The name of 4. The colour of the Elliots' 5. of my room 6. Holly's 7. of the alphabet 8. Prestons' cat 9. The door of 10. My friend's 11. of the street 12. Holly and Amber's

a) *Is it **s**, **'s** or **s'**?*

1. The (Elliot) live in Greenwich.
2. Luke (Elliot) father is English.
3. (Luke) (brother) name is Jamie.
4. The (Elliot) (dog) name is Sherlock.
5. (Luke) dad is an only child.
6. (Luke) mother is from Poland.
7. (Luke) (mother) family are the (Zajac).
8. The (Zajac) home is in Cracow.
9. Mila is Jan (Zajac) mother.
10. Filip Zajac is Luke and (Jamie) grandad.

b) *Is it **'s**, **s'** or **of**? Make sentences.*

1. Holly | lucky charm | pink
2. Jay | new school | in Greenwich
3. The name | the school | Thomas Tallis
4. The colour | the Elliots | car | blue
5. The table | in the middle | my room
6. Mr Fluff and Honey / Holly/ guinea pigs
7. "A" | first letter | alphabet
8. Sid | the Prestons | cat
9. The door | our school building | green
10. My friend | house | big
11. Our house | at the end | street
12. Holly and Amber | parents | Sally and Steve

Example: Holly's lucky charm is pink.

△ 7 I want to buy these, please! → After Station 2, p. 42/22

Lösung 1. This 2. that 3. that 4. These 5. those 6. these 7. these 8. this 9. this 10. those

*Jay and Dave are in the school shop. Write the sentences with **this**, **that**, **these** or **those**.*

Jay: Hello, Mrs White. I want to buy a new pencil case, please.
Dave: 1 pencil case here? It's pink!
Jay: No, 2 's Holly's favourite colour! I want 3 blue pencil case there, on the left.
Dave: And coloured pencils? 4 here are nice.
Jay: No, not these twelve pencils, but I want two of 5 yellow pencils, please. And an exercise book. One of 6 blue books here.
Mrs White: So you want 7 things: 8 pencil case, 9 exercise book and two of 10 pencils?
Jay: That's right. Thank you!

▲ 8 Luke's 'phone rap' → After Story, p. 45/3

Luke's 'phone rap' has got Jay's voice from different parts of Unit 2.
*Can you find **all** the words / lines from the rap in the unit?*

Unit 3

△ 1 Say what time it is → After Check-in, p. 50/1

a) *Use **past**: 7:05, 8:11, 9:20, 11:15, 12:28, 1:07, 2:30, 3:09, 5:16, 6:25*

Example: It's five past seven.

b) *Use **to**: 5:45, 6:35, 7:38, 9:50, 10:49, 10:59, 12:31, 1:40, 2:36*

c) *Is it **past** or **to**? 7:09, 8:15, 9:30, 10:32, 11:45, 12:01, 1:05, 4:18, 5:42, 6:40*

d) *Now write the time in numbers:*

1. It's twenty to seven.
2. It's eleven minutes past nine.
3. It's half past one.
4. It's six minutes past eight.
5. It's eleven minutes to twelve.
6. It's quarter to three.

Lösung d) *1. 6:40 2. 9:11 3. 1:30 4. 8:06 5. 11:49 6. 2:45*

△ 2 A game: Whispers[1] → After Station 1, p. 53/4

1. *Work in groups of 5–6. Sit in a circle[2]. Take turns to make a sentence for your group. Think how often you do something. The ideas below can help you. Write your sentence on a card.*

   Example: I often read in bed.

always | often | usually | never | sometimes	play | watch | read | go | do | make | …	skateboarding | magazines | TV | DVDs | things on the internet | computer games | with my friends | cycling | basketball | …

2. *Whisper your sentence to the person next to you. Then that person whispers the sentence to the person next to him/her.*

3. *The words go from person to person till the sentence comes back to you. If it's correct, make a tick (✔) on the card. (And if it **isn't** correct, maybe it's funny!)*

4. *Now a different student can think of a new sentence. Which group can collect the most correct sentences in 5 minutes?*

1 **whisper** ['wɪspə] Geflüster; Flüstern | 2 **circle** ['sɜːkl] Kreis; Ring

△ 3 Word order → Help with Station 1, p. 54/9

Before you write your text in exercise 9, collect ideas in a time line like this. Then you've got the right order for your ideas.

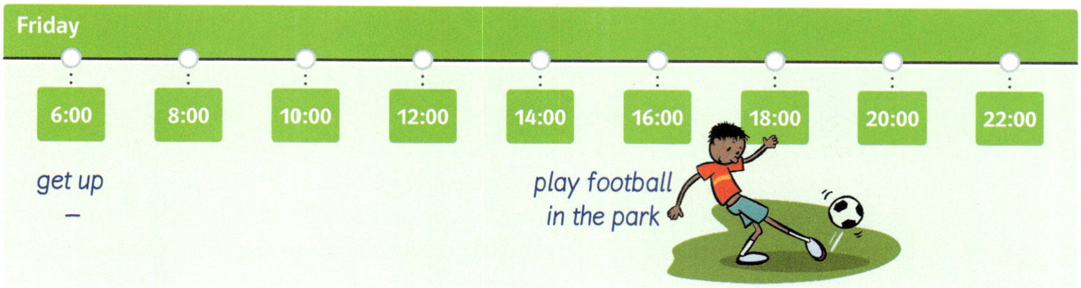

△ 4 At home with Sid → After Station 2, p. 56/14 → HA

Write the sentences with the correct verb forms.

Lösung *1. gets up 2. sleeps 3. explores 4. finds 5. likes 6. play 7. plays 8. watches 9. like 10. likes 11. wants 12. brings*

1. Every morning Dave (get up) early for school.
2. But Sid (sleep) till late. It's too early for him!
3. Sid always (explore) the house and garden.
4. He sometimes (find) a mouse. Yummy!
5. Sid (like) Dave.
6. After school Sid and Dave (play) computer games together.
7. Well, Dave (play) games. Not Sid.
8. Sid (watch) Dave and his games.
9. Holly and Olivia (like) Sid.
10. Sid (like) the girls too.
11. He (want) to play with Mr Fluff and Honey!
12. But Holly *never* (bring) her guinea pigs to Dave's house.

▲ 5 Write about your pet → After Station 2, p. 56/14 → HA

Think of your pet. (You haven't got a pet? What animal can be a good pet for you?) Look for information about it. Then find vocabulary in the alphabetical word list (p. 242) or a dictionary to describe:

- where it lives
- what it eats
- what it likes
- what it does in the morning / afternoon / evening
- how you take care of it
- why you like it.

△ 6 Make group sentences → After Station 2, p. 57/15

a) *Everyone in the class makes four or five cards.*
Write down a different word or phrase on every card. You can choose:

- words for people or things → **Examples:** my granny | she | they | school
- different verb forms → **Examples:** goes | ask | likes
- words to say how often / when / where / … → **Examples:** never | always

b) *Put all the cards face down on a table. Choose one card. Then find two or more partners with words. Can their words make a sentence with the word on* ***your*** *card? Show your cards in the right order so everyone can see your sentence.*

c) *Repeat with a different card and different partners.*

△ 7 Words and phrases → Help with Station 2, p. 58/18 b)

You can hear these words and phrases in the listening text on page 58.
You can use them for the grid in exercise 18 b).

crazy
boring
happy
cool
great

he / she runs and explores
he / she finds things
he / she hasn't got time
he / she often dances
he / she always tidies his / her bed

Unit 4

△ 1 Write about where you live → Help with Check-in, p. 71/4 b)

These words and phrases can help you to write about where you live.

Useful phrases

It's nice / cool / fun / … where I live.
… is / are great / fun / cool!
The park / leisure centre / … is my favourite place.
The park / farm / city / museum / … has got …
You can see / do / …
It costs money to go to …
The museum / park / … is free!

Places:
boat | ship | lake | river | park | street | leisure centre | museum | shop

▲ 2 Give the correct answers and explain → After Station 1, p. 72/1 → HA

Look at exercise 1 on page 72 again.
First, write down the correct answers,
then give more information. Be creative!

Examples:
Do the boys talk about different ideas for their free time?
– Yes, they do. Luke talks about …
And Dave talks about …

△ 3 A chat with a new friend → After Station 1, p. 73/3 b)

Partner A is Tony, partner B is Tony's new friend, Alex.
Look at the two grids and write more little dialogues for the friends.

Example: Tony: **Do** you like football?
Alex: Yes, I **do**. I often play football. **Do** you …?

1	play football	play tennis	go swimming	go skating	visit museums
Tony	often	sometimes	sometimes	often	never
Alex	often	often	never	sometimes	sometimes

2	read books	get up late	eat cheese	visit friends	play with cats
Tony	often	sometimes	often	often	never
Alex	sometimes	often	often	sometimes	never

△ 4 Free time for Holly and Luke → After Station 2, p. 74/6

Ask and answer questions about Holly and Luke. Use the information in the grid.

	Holly	Luke
do fun things with friends	✔	✔
play football	✘	✔
skate in Greenwich Park	✔	✘
visit lots of museums	✘	✘
often go swimming	✘	✔

Examples:

1. Does Holly do fun things with friends?
   – Yes, she does.
2. Does Luke skate in Greenwich Park?
   – No, he doesn't.

▲ 5 Does Dave like swimming? → After Station 2, p. 74/6

What do you know about the characters and their free time activities? Take turns to ask and answer questions. If your English book doesn't give the information, say "I don't know".

Examples: Does Dave like swimming? – No, he doesn't.
Does Olivia visit museums? – I don't know.

HA

△ 6 Tony, can you help, please? → After Station 2, p. 75/9 → HA

Lösung *Tony doesn't tidy his bedroom. He tidies the living room. Tony doesn't wash his T-shirt. He washes Lou's T-shirt. Tony doesn't buy sweets. He buys biscuits. Tony doesn't look for Lou's skates. He looks for his skateboard.*

There's a note for Tony from Lou. But Tony doesn't do the right things. Write down what Tony does and what he doesn't do.

Example: Tony doesn't get up at 6:30.
He gets up at 7:30.

7:30 ✔ | living room | Lou's T-shirt | biscuits | Tony's skateboard

- get up at 6:30
- tidy your bedroom
- wash your T-shirt
- buy sweets
- look for my skates

▲ 7 At home on the farm → After Station 2, p. 77/13 → HA

Choose one of the animals in the photos on page 77. Write a short text for the animal. (Funny texts are good too!) Lou's questions can give you some ideas.

Example:
I'm a pig and I live on Mudchute Farm. I like it here because …

- What animal are you? (chicken / horse / lamb / pig / rabbit?)
- Is Mudchute Farm a good place to live? Why / Why not?
- Who are your friends on the farm?
- What can you say about the visitors to the farm?

△ 8 Which heading is better? → Help with Story, p. 81/3

a) *Which heading (1 or 2) do you like better?*

b) *Which heading tells a very short version of the story?*

Lösung b) *D2: Ben saves the first mate*

A

1. The captain talks to a boy
2. A storm starts

B

1. The captain thinks Ben is scared
2. There is a lot of water

C

1. A monster wave hits Cutty Sark
2. Ben brings the water

D

1. Ben jumps into the water
2. Ben saves the first mate

E

1. The captain is happy with Ben
2. The captain talks to Ben

▲ 9 Ben's thought bubbles → After Story, p. 81/3

What do you think Ben thinks in the five parts of the story? Look at the pictures and write a thought bubble for Ben for parts A–E.

This is dangerous! Can I help?

…

Unit 5

▲ 1 Shops → After Check-in, p. 86/1 → HA

Work in groups of four. You can use a dictionary for more vocabulary.

a) *What other things can you buy in the places in the photos on pages 86–87? Write them down.*

b) *What other shops do you know?*

c) *Your turn: What shops do you like? Talk about where you buy things, what shops you like / don't like, what your favourite shops are and why.*

△ 2 In town → After Station 1, p. 89/4 → HA

Lösung a) 1. is reading 2. is looking 3. is talking 4. is selling 5. is eating 6. are listening 7. is writing

a) *Imagine[1] you're looking at some photos. Say what you can see.*

Start: In photo one, Holly and Olivia are …

1. Holly and Olivia (read) a fashion magazine.
2. Holly (look) at a nice T-shirt.
3. Olivia (talk) to Holly.
4. A woman (sell) oranges.
5. Olivia (eat) an orange.
6. Holly and Olivia (listen) to music.
7. Holly (write) a text message.

Lösung b) 1. Are you working 2. I always work 3. are you doing 4. Are you doing 5. We're looking 6. She's looking 7. Is she buying 8. She usually wears 9. She doesn't always wear 10. She sometimes wears 11. she's calling

b) *Olivia's phone is ringing. It's her mum, Janet. (Olivia doesn't live with her, but she often visits her at the weekend, and they often chat.) Complete the sentences with the correct forms and write them down. Sometimes there are signal words to help you.*

Mum: Hey Liv, how are you?
Olivia: Hi Mum, fine, and how are you? (1 you, work) at the moment?
Mum: No, my dear[2], (2 I, always, work) in the mornings. And what about you? What (3 you, do)? (4 you, do) your homework?
Olivia: No, Mum. I'm in town with Holly. (5 we, look) at some clothes. (6 she, look) at a blue T-shirt just now.
Mum: (7 she, buy) a blue T-shirt? (8 she, usually, wear) pink clothes!
Olivia: (9 she, not, always, wear) pink, (10 she, sometimes, wear) other colours too. – Oh, (11 she, call) me, Mum. So it's goodbye now.
Mum: Can you come on Sunday?
Olivia: Yeah, cool. See you then. Bye!
Mum: Bye Liv.

Olivia

1 **to imagine** [ɪ'mædʒɪn] sich etwas vorstellen | 2 **my dear** [maɪ 'dɪə] (mein) Liebling

▲ 3 Describing pictures → After Station 1, p. 89/5

a) Partner A: *Look for a picture or photo in this book. Don't show it to your partner. Describe what the people / animals in the picture are doing.*
Partner B: *Listen, and find the right picture.*

b) Partner A: *Think of a verb in the present progressive and act it out for your partner.*
Partner B: *Guess what your partner is doing. You can ask yes / no questions.*

c) *Look for funny photos or cartoons. Write down what is happening in them. Read your texts to the class and let them choose their favourite picture. After the class does this with other students' pictures, make a class display with everyone's favourites.* → HA

▲ 4 Role play: A chat → After Station 1, p. 90/6

Olivia often talks to her mum on the phone.
Now sit back to back and chat to your partner in English.
Don't translate every word. The signal words can help you.

A	B
Du begrüßt Partner B und fragst, wie es ihm/ihr geht.	Du sagst, dass es dir gut geht, bedankst dich und fragst zurück.
Du sagst, dass es dir auch gut geht, und fragst, wo er/sie ist.	Du sagst, dass du mit deiner kleinen Schwester im Garten bist. Sie spielt mit der Nachbarskatze.
Du sagst, dass du gerade bei deiner Oma zu Besuch bist. Du gehst oft zu ihr.	Du sagst, dass das prima ist und dass du deine Oma auch gerne magst. Dann erzählst du, dass du gerade ein Buch liest und auf deine Schwester aufpasst.
Du sagst, dass du gerade deiner Oma in der Küche hilfst.	Du sagst, dass das toll ist, und fragst, was sie kocht.
Du entschuldigst dich und sagst, dass du es nicht weißt und dass du jetzt einkaufen gehst, weil deine Oma ein paar Karotten braucht.	Du sagst, dass ihr euch bald wieder seht.
Du verabschiedest dich.	Du verabschiedest dich.

△ 5 Today is different → After Station 1, p. 90/7 → HA

a) *Choose the right verb form and write the sentences.*

Lösung a) 1. walks 2. is playing 3. practises 4. is visiting 5. help 6. is staying 7. is going 8. comes 9. is looking

1. Luke (1 walks / is walking) around Brook Lane with Sherlock every evening. But today Luke can't do that because he (2 plays / is playing) football with his friends.
2. Olivia (3 practises / is practising) the saxophone every day. But today she hasn't got time. She (4 visits / is visiting) Mudchute Farm with her family and Holly.
3. Holly and Amber usually (5 help / are helping) their mum, but today Amber (6 stays / is staying) at home and Holly (7 goes / is going) shopping with her mum.
4. Granny Rose usually (8 comes / is coming) to the Prestons' house when they're busy, but today Aunt Frances (9 looks / is looking) after Dave.

b) *Now write these sentences.* → HA

Lösung b) 1. Holly usually buys pink clothes. But today she is looking at a white T-shirt. 2. Luke takes the dog out every day. But today his dad is taking Sherlock to the park. 3. Amber always wears black clothes. But today she is wearing blue jeans. Etc.

1. Holly usually (buy) pink clothes. But today she (look at) a white T-shirt.
2. Luke (take) the dog out every day. But today his dad (take) Sherlock to the park.
3. Amber always (wear) black clothes. But today she (wear) blue jeans.
4. Jay usually (have) breakfast at 7 o'clock. But today he (have) breakfast at 10 o'clock.
5. Dave's parents (work) long hours. But today they (come) home early.
6. Dave and Luke often (play) computer games. But today they (go) swimming.

△ 6 What have we got? → After Station 2, p. 92/10 → HA

a) *Write the sentences with **some** or **any**.*

Lösung a) 1. any 2. any 3. some, any, some 4. some, any

1. Have you got 1 carrots? – Yes, I have.
2. Have you got 2 cheese? – No, I haven't.
3. I need 3 apples. – Sorry, I haven't got 4 apples. But I've got 5 oranges.
4. We need 6 bags. – Sorry, we haven't got 7 bags.

b) *Put in **much**, **many** or **lots of/a lot of**.* → HA

Lösung b) 1. much 2. much 3. many 4. lots of/a lot of 5. many 6. much 7. a lot of 8. many 9. much 10. much 11. many

1. Tony: How 1 food is there in the fridge?
   Lou: Not 2, I'm sorry.
2. Tony: How 3 carrots have we got?
   Lou: I've got 4 carrots.
3. Tony: There aren't 5 carrots in my bag.
   Lou: OK, I can give you some.
4. Tony: How 6 water have we got?
   Lou: I've got 7 water.
5. Tony: I can't see 8 bottles in your bag.
   Lou: Look, they're here.
6. Tony: There isn't 9 cheese in the fridge.
   Lou: No, but it's here in my bag.
7. Tony: A holiday is so 10 fun!
   Lou: Yes, but please don't ask so 11 questions!

▲ 7 In the skater shop → After Station 2, p. 92/10

*Put in **some / any** or **something / anything / everything**.*

Lösung *1. anything 2. Everything 3. some 4. something 5. any 6. everything 7. something 8. some 9. Some 10. any 11. any 12. some 13. something*

Dave: Is there **1** interesting here?
Jay: Oh yes, I know this shop! **2** is so cool here. I'm sure they have **3** really cool T-shirts. I need a present for Shahid
Dave: OK, maybe we can find **4**. But I don't think there are **5** cheap clothes here. **6** is expensive.
Man: Hi you two. Can I do **7** for you?
Jay: Hi. Yes, can you show us **8** really cool skater T-shirts, please?
Man: What about these? **9** of them are brand new.
Jay: Yes, but haven't you got **10** blue T-shirts?
Man: I'm sorry, I haven't got **11** of these in blue. But those over there are last year's shirts, and **12** of them are blue. And I can make a special price for them just for you.
Jay: Great! So at last I've got **13** cool and not too expensive!

▲ 8 Answering machines → After Skills, p. 93/1 → HA

Write your own answering machine messages in English. They can be useful. They can be funny!

△ 9 Retell the story → Instead of Story, p. 97/3 → HA

a) *Write answers to the questions for each part of the story.*

A
1. Where are the friends?
2. Who is there too?
3. What is he doing?
4. How many people are there?
5. What are they doing?

B
1. What can you say about the raffle?
2. How much are the raffle tickets?
3. Who buys a raffle ticket?

C
1. How much money have the friends got at 4 o'clock?
2. Why is Luke sad?

D
1. What happens when Luke is looking at the Cutty Sark model?
2. What does Luke do?
3. How does he feel?

E
1. What does Jay find?
2. Who gives the friends some information about it?
3. What is it worth?

F
1. Why is Luke happy?
2. What can the friends do now?
3. What is Dave's prize?
4. What does he do with it?

b) *Look at your answers from a). Which of them tell you the most important things in each part? Which of them are not so important? Use the important answers in exercise 3c) on page 97.*

Unit 6

▲ 1 Birthdays in your family → After Check-in, p. 105/4

Work with a partner. Talk about birthdays in your family and take notes.

Example: A: When is your mum's birthday?
B: It's **in** June. It's **on** 1st June.
A: Have you got any brothers or sisters?
B: Yes, my brother's name is Marco.
A: When is Marco's birthday?
A: His birthday is **on** 2nd August.

Now write down the information about your partner's family and give the text to your partner. Correct your partner's text.

Leo's birthday is on 7th May.
Leo's mum's birthday is in June.
His brother's birthday is on 2nd August.
...

△ 2 Your birthday ideas → Help with Check-in, p. 105/5

You can use these words and phrases to write about your birthday ideas.

Example: I'd like to … on my birthday because my birthday is in the … I want to be with my family / friends and …

celebrate | go | have fun | meet | see | visit | watch

bowling alley | cinema | farm | home | ice rink | park | pizza restaurant

△ 3 Family talk → After Station 1, p. 107/4

a) *What is right: **must** or **needn't**? Write the sentences.* → HA

Lösung a) *1. We must buy some. 2. Great. So we needn't buy any. 3. You needn't look at the map. 4. You must watch it. 5. We must run.*

1. I want to make an apple pie, but there aren't any apples. → We ___ buy some.
2. We've got lots of chocolate cake. → Great. So we ___ buy any.
3. I know how to get to the bus station. → You ___ look at the map.
4. The film is great! → You ___ watch it.
5. The film starts at seven thirty. It's only six thirty. → We ___ run.

b) *Complete the dialogue in your exercise book with **can**, **can't**, **must** or **mustn't**.* → HA

Lösung b) *1. can 2. can 3. can 4. Can 5. can't 6. can 7. must 8. can 9. must/can 10. must 11. mustn't 12. can 13. can't/mustn't 14. can't*

Luke: Mum, [1] I invite some friends here on Saturday?
Mum: Yes, you [2]. You [3] invite four or five friends.
Irina: [4] I come too?
Luke: No, you [5]. Girls [6] come to my loft. I want to be with my friends.
Mum: Your room looks awful. You [7] tidy it before your friends [8] come.
Irina: Good idea, and you [9] tidy my room too.
Luke: You [10] be crazy!
Mum: Luke, you [11] talk to your sister like that!
Luke: But she's so silly. She always thinks she [12] make the rules.
Irina: Mum! He [13] call me silly!
Mum: Please stop it now, you two, or you [14] have any ice cream!

△ 4 Your turn: Rules at home, rules at school

→ Help with Station 1, p. 108/7 → HA

Match the phrases with the right verbs and use them to do exercise 7 on page 108.

Lösung At home: tidy my room, watch TV till late, practise/play the guitar/piano/…, help in the kitchen, do my homework, clean the house, play computer games every day; At school: wear uniform, shout in the classroom, bring skates to school

At home

tidy	in the kitchen
watch	my room
practise/play	my homework
help	the guitar/piano/…
do	computer games every day
clean	TV till late
play	the house

At school

wear	in the classroom
shout	skates to school
bring	uniform

guitar

piano

skates

uniform

▲ 5 Mediation: A visit to a castle

→ After Station 1, p. 109/11 → HA

Du bist im Urlaub in England zusammen mit deinen Eltern, deinen Großeltern und deinem kleinen Bruder. Ihr möchtet das Schloss Durham besuchen. Dein Opa ist 70 und nicht bei bester Gesundheit. Deine Oma ist 68 und versteht kein Englisch. Beantworte ihre Fragen.

1. Wie wird das Schloss heute genutzt?
2. Kann man es jederzeit besichtigen?
3. Kann Opa mit? Er ist so schlecht zu Fuß.
4. Was kostet es dann für uns alle?

Lösung EH
Das Schloss ist heute ein Teil der Durham Universität und ein Museum. Es wohnen über 100 Studenten dort. Man kann es nur mit einer Führung besichtigen. Das Schloss ist nicht geeignet für Rollstuhlfahrer und da man bei der Führung viele Treppen steigen muss, kann Opa leider nicht mitkommen. Wir können für uns ein Familienticket für 12 Pfund nehmen und für dich ein Seniorenticket zu 3,50 Pfund, d.h. es kostet für uns alle dann 15,50 Pfund.

PUBLIC GUIDED[1] TOURS OF THE CASTLE

The castle is now home to the students of University College, part of Durham University. Durham Castle is a registered museum as well as a vibrant living and working community. It is the home of University College, the founding College of Durham University, and over 100 students are resident during term. Visits to Durham Castle are by guided tour only. Tours are led by our guides, who explain the history of this iconic building and tell you what it's like to live in it today.

Tour Prices
- Adult £5
- Concessions: (senior citizens, students, children up to 16): £3.50
- Family ticket (2 adults plus 1–4 children) £12

Accessibility[2]
The nature and layout of the castle means that the majority of the building is inaccessible to wheelchair users. The tour route involves[3] many steps and staircases, some of which are uneven. Unfortunately due to these reasons we cannot offer guided tours to visitors who have difficulties using stairs.

1 **guided** ['gaɪdɪd] geführt | 2 **accessibility** [əkˌsesə'bɪləti] Zugänglichkeit, Barrierefreiheit | 3 **to involve** [ɪn'vɒlv] beinhalten

▲ 6 How do you make party pizza rolls?[1] → After Station 1, p. 109/12

Use the pictures and information to explain how to make the pizza rolls. You can prepare them for your next party.

What you need:

8 breakfast rolls
1 can of tomatoes, chopped[2]
200 g of salami, chopped
200 g of mushrooms[3], chopped
200 g of grated[4] cheese
salt[5], pepper[6], oregano[7]

Useful phrases

to cut in half[8] | baking tray[9] | to mix[10] | to bake[11] | oven[12] | degrees[13]

△ 7 A birthday party in London → After Station 2, p. 111/15 → HA

Copy the text and put in the right past tense forms.

Lösung 1. invited 2. went 3. was 4. was 5. got 6. stayed 7. had 8. played 9. tripped 10. hurt 11. wasn't 12. put 13. listened 14. made 15. watched 16. was

Last week John (1 invite) us to his birthday party. We (2 go) to see him in London. It (3 be) a nice day. There (4 be) four boys and two girls at the party. John (5 get) a lot of presents. First we (6 stay) in the house and (7 have) some really nice cake. Then we (8 play) football outside.

One boy (9 trip) over the ball and (10 hurt) his hand, but it wasn't so bad after all because John's mum (11 put) some ice on it. Later we (12 listen) to some music in John's room. John's sister (13 make) a pizza for us and after that we (14 watch) a film. It (15 be) a great party!

1 **roll** [rəʊl] Brötchen | 2 **chopped** [tʃɒpt] gewürfelt | 3 **mushroom** ['mʌʃrʊm] Pilz | 4 **grated** ['greɪtɪd] gerieben | 5 **salt** [sɔ:lt] Salz | 6 **pepper** ['pepə] Pfeffer | 7 **oregano** [ˌɒrɪ'gɑ:nəʊ] Oregano | 8 **to cut in half** [ˌkʌt‿ɪn 'hɑ:f] halbieren | 9 **baking tray** ['beɪkɪŋ ˌtreɪ] Backblech | 10 **to mix** [mɪks] vermischen | 11 **to bake** [beɪk] backen | 12 **oven** ['ʌvən] Backofen | 13 **degree** [dɪ'gri:] Grad

▲ 8 What they didn't do and what they did → After Station 3, p. 113/19

Tony was tired last week, but Lou wasn't – so they didn't do things together. What didn't they do? What did they do? Take turns!

Example:
You: Tony didn't go swimming with Lou, he read a book.
Your partner: Lou didn't read a book, she went swimming in the boating lake.

swim in the boating lake | go skating in the park | read a book | watch TV
play tennis with a friend | buy cheese at the market | sleep on the sofa | listen to music
prepare dinner for her friends | play a computer game

▲ 9 What's different? → After Skills, p. 115/1c) → HA

a) *Compare the two texts. Which invitation is more formal[1]? What about the address and date? Collect some useful phrases for formal and informal[2] invitations.*

b) *Invite your teacher to an English Day in your classroom. Write a formal invitation.*

Room 24, TTS
8th June

Dear Mr Parker,

We would like to invite you to our End of School Year party. It's in Room 24 on Friday 18th June at 2:00 p.m. We hope to see you there.

Yours sincerely[3]
Class 7a

Hi Sam

I'm having a winter party at my house on Sunday 10th December at 6:00. I hope you can come. Let me know!

Love, Zoe

△ 10 Useful words → Help with Story, p. 117/2b) → HA

Lösung 1. Jay invites his friends to his party but they can't come. 2. Jay is disappointed because they can't come. 3. Jay is sad, so his parents take him out. 4. Jay thinks it's an awful birthday, but it isn't. 5. In the end, there is a party and Jay is happy.

*Use **and**, **but**, **so** or **because** to make one sentence from two. Write the sentences.*

1. Jay invites his friends to his party. They can't come.
2. Jay is disappointed. They can't come.
3. Jay is sad. His parents take him out.
4. Jay thinks it's an awful birthday. It isn't.
5. In the end, there's a party. Jay is happy.

1 **formal** ['fɔːml] formell | 2 **informal** [ɪn'fɔːml] informell | 3 **Yours sincerely** [ˌjɔːz sɪn'sɪəli] Mit freundlichen Grüßen

S 2/28 L 4/7

Merry Christmas[1]

In the weeks before Christmas, we write Christmas cards, sing Christmas carols[2] and eat lots of hot mince pies. Yummy!

1

2

On 24th December it is Christmas Eve[3]. In the evening I put my stocking in the living room. (It's a special long one for lots of presents!) Father Christmas comes in the night with his reindeer and puts presents into our stockings.

3

4

The next day is Christmas Day. In the morning, we open our presents. Then my cousins come for a big dinner at 2 o'clock. There are Christmas crackers on the table. In the paper[4] crackers there are silly jokes, paper hats and small presents.

5

1 Christmas in Britain → KV 91

a) *Ask and answer questions about Isabella's Christmas.*

b) *Find the answers to these cracker joke questions.*

1. What has got four legs but can't walk?
2. Why isn't Cinderella[6] good at football?
3. What's orange and sounds like a parrot[5]?
4. When is it not lucky to see a black cat?

Answers: 1. A table 2. Because she runs away from the ball. 3. A carrot 4. When you're a mouse.

L 4/8 c) *Sing the song "We wish you a Merry Christmas".*

1 **Merry Christmas!** [ˌmeri ˈkrɪsməs] Frohe Weihnachten! | 2 **carols** [ˈkærəlz] Weihnachtslieder | 3 **Christmas Eve** [ˌkrɪsməs‿ˈiːv] Heiligabend | 4 **paper** [ˈpeɪpə] Papier | 5 **parrot** [ˈpærət] Papagei | 6 **Cinderella** [ˌsɪndrˈelə] Aschenputtel

Rhymes and activities

1 Rhymes

S 2/29–30 L 4/9–10

a) *Find the rhyme words in Lou's rhyme. Then make new short rhymes with different words.*

Rain, rain, go away,
Come again another day.

Example: Dave, Dave, here's a book,
Come here now and take a look.

b) *In rhymes like this one, many words start with the same letter, or the sounds in the middle of the words are the same. Who can say this best?*

Three **gr**ey **g**eese[1] crossed over[2] a **gr**een river;
Grey were the **g**eese and **gr**een was the river.

c) *Collect rhyme words, words with the same first letter, or words with the same sounds. Then write a rhyme or a poem with your words.*

2 A funny nursery rhyme[3]

Hey diddle diddle, the cat and the fiddle,
The cow jumped over the moon,
The little dog laughed to see such[4] fun
And the dish[5] ran away[6] with the spoon[7].

S 2/31 L 4/11

a) *Sing the song. Why is it funny?*

b) *Now write your own funny rhyme or story. For example, match animals to silly activities.*

3 How many days are in August?

Thirty days in September,
April, June and November.
All the rest have thirty-one,
except[8] February, which[9] has twenty-eight.

S 2/32 L 4/12

a) *Many children learn this rhyme about months in the UK. Ask and answer questions:*
How many days are in May? / … your birthday month? / …?

b) *How do you know the number of days in different months in German?*

1 **geese** [gi:s] Gänse | 2 **crossed over** [krɒst‿ˈəʊvə] überquerten | 3 **nursery rhyme** [ˈnɜ:sri ˌraɪm] kurzes Kinderlied | 4 **such** [sʌtʃ] solche | 5 **dish** [dɪʃ] Schale | 6 **ran away** [ræn‿əˈweɪ] lief weg | 7 **spoon** [spu:n] Löffel | 8 **except** [ɪkˈsept] außer | 9 **which** [wɪtʃ] welcher/der

The end of world time ist eine fakultative Fortsetzungsgeschichte in vier Teilen. Der neue Wortschatz ist rezeptiv und unter dem Text annotiert.

S 2/33–37
L 4/13–17

The end of world time[1] Chapter 1

→ Folie 35, KV 92, KV 93

"Wow – is this really it, the start of world time? What a great place!"

Lucy, Sandy and Asim are very good friends. Today, they're visiting the Royal Observatory in Greenwich and its special sight, the Meridian Line. It's great fun to stand over the Line, with one foot in the east and one foot in the west.

"Yes, it's so cool," Asim says. "Let's stand over the Meridian Line at 1 o'clock when the red ball falls. Look, it's already going all the way to the top. Hurry up!"

The three friends race each other to the Meridian Line to see where time starts.

"Whew, here we are! Hurry up, Sandy! Ten, nine, eight, seven, …" Asim shouts.

"Hey, let's all jump when the red ball falls," Lucy laughs. "Three, two, one – jump!"

When they jump up together at exactly 1 p.m., they still think it's great fun. But something is wrong[2] – very wrong!

"Awesome! I feel like I was up in the air for a long time. What about you, Asim?"

"I don't know, I feel a bit funny. Like – like my head is under water. Sandy, what are you looking at?"

"Not looking, silly – listening. Can you hear anything[3]? It's very quiet here. I can't hear the birds. And what about all the people, the cars, and all the other London noises[4]? I don't like this at all."

"You two watch too many horror films," Lucy says. "Everything is OK. Let's go to the Planetarium. Remember, we've got tickets for the show."

The Greenwich Planetarium is famous for its shows. There's a huge projector which brings you the night sky and pictures of our solar system, the galaxy and the universe. The friends take out their tickets and feed them into the machine. There's no-one there.

"Hey, it's so quiet here too. And are we the only visitors?" Sandy asks.

Inside, they sit down. Then the lights flicker[5] – one, two, three.

"It's starting. Wow, we really *are* the only visitors," Asim says. "I feel like a VIP!"

"Shhh, Asim, listen to the music. I think I know this song, but it sounds so weird. It's going backwards[6], isn't it?" Sandy says.

Suddenly, the friends hear a strange, scary voice. But they can't see anyone.

"WELCOME TO MY VERY SPECIAL SHOW! I am the Time Lord[7], and I am as old as the Earth[8]. Let me tell you about my plan: I am fed up with[9] you humans[10]. You are ruining[11] your beautiful planet Earth. All around us there is only death[12] and war[13] and destruction. Your parents and

1 **world time** ['wɜːld taɪm] Weltzeit | 2 **something is wrong** [ˌsʌmθɪŋ‿ɪz 'rɒŋ] etwas stimmt nicht | 3 **anything** ['eniθɪŋ] irgendetwas | 4 **noise** [nɔɪz] Geräusch | 5 **the lights flicker** [ðə ˌlaɪts 'flɪkə] das Licht flackert | 6 **backwards** ['bækwədz] rückwärts | 7 **Time Lord** ['taɪm lɔːd] Herrscher über die Zeit | 8 **the Earth** [ɜːθ] die Erde | 9 **I am fed up with** [aɪ‿æm fed‿'ʌp wɪð] ich habe die Nase voll von | 10 **humans** ['hjuːmənz] die Menschen | 11 **to ruin** ['ruːɪn] zerstören | 12 **death** [deθ] Tod | 13 **war** [wɔː] Krieg

your grandparents never listen. So today, at 1 o'clock exactly, I stopped all the clocks in the world. There is no more[14] time for you. The clocks are running backwards now, and they will run faster and faster. Every human will become younger[15] and younger. Soon there will only be babies, and I hope that tomorrow at 1 o'clock, the Earth will be free of you! You silly children jumped across the Meridian Line at the wrong moment, so you escaped[16]. But when World Time stops tomorrow, you will die[17] too! – However, there is one last[18] chance for you. Let me tell you about my rival, the Time Fairy[19]. She, too, is as old as the Earth. She thinks young people are good people, so she wants to give you one last chance: Bring us – not one, not two, no – THREE *really* convincing[20] stories of children who have *really* made a difference[21] to life[22] on Earth! Tell us your stories, and then Lord and Lady Time will decide[23]: Will humans get more time – or not? This is your only chance to help the human race. You have got until 1 o'clock tomorrow!"

"Very funny," Lucy says. "I think this is just a silly trick. I don't believe a word."

"A silly trick?" the Time Lord laughs. "Ha, ha, ha, just look at *this*, you silly girl!"

The lights in the Planetarium flicker again, and on the huge screen, Lucy, Sandy and Asim can see pictures of Greenwich – and it already looks very different. There aren't many old people any more, and children are looking down at clothes that are too big for them.

Then they hear the scary voice again.

"So, children. The future[24] of the human race lies in your hands. See this hourglass[25]

here? When the sand is through, your time will be up[26]. And the sand will fall faster and faster!"

Before they can say a word, the lights flicker again – one, two, three – and they feel a cold wind. Now the children are really scared.

"What can we do? Where can we find three really good stories? And how do we know that the Time Lord will like them?"

But then they hear a new voice.

"Hello children. I'm the Time Fairy. What the Time Lord says is true[27]. But don't be afraid, I can help you – a little. Listen: Maybe someone in your family knows a good story. They're getting younger, but they can still remember things. Go now, and hurry! Call me when you need more help. Good luck!"

"Hey, my granny knows a lot of stories," Asim says. "Let's call her!"

The friends go outside. It's still very quiet. Asim calls his family.

"Hi Mum, it's me, Asim. Can I speak to Gran? – What? It's you, Gran? You sound so different!"

"She's getting younger too!" Sandy says. "Er, Gran, we need your help." …

14 **no more** ['nəʊ mɔː] keine mehr | 15 **young** [jʌŋ] jung | 16 **to escape** [ɪ'skeɪp] entkommen | 17 **to die** [daɪ] sterben | 18 **last** [lɑːst] letzte | 19 **Time Fairy** ['taɪm ˌfeəri] Zeitfee | 20 **convincing** [kən'vɪnsɪŋ] überzeugend | 21 **to make a difference** [ˌmeɪk‿ə 'dɪfrns] etw. verändern | 22 **life** [laɪf] Leben | 23 **to decide** [dɪ'saɪd] entscheiden | 24 **future** ['fjuːtʃə] Zukunft | 25 **hourglass** ['aʊəglɑːs] Sanduhr | 26 **time will be up** [ˌtaɪm wɪl bɪ‿'ʌp] die Zeit ist abgelaufen | 27 **true** [truː] wahr

S 2/38–42
L 4/18–22

The end of world time

Chapter 2

→ Folie 35, KV 92, KV 94, KV 95

"I really hope the Time Lord likes my granny's story!" Asim whispers.

The children are back inside the Planetarium. Again, they hear the strange[1] music. It *is* backwards, and it's faster this time. They can see the hourglass too, and the sand is running faster than before.

The lights in the Planetarium flicker – one, two, three. Then they hear the Time Lord's voice.

"Ah, there you are, children. Before you tell me your first story, take a good look[2] at the world outside. You can see that I really can change time!"

On the big screen inside the Planetarium, the Time Lord shows the children Sandy's garden. It looks like a film going backwards. All the leaves[3] are getting smaller, and the flowers are going back into the earth. Then they can see inside Lucy's house. Her family is much younger – and much shorter[4]. They see them standing on boxes in the kitchen so they can get things out of the cupboards. Lucy's guinea pigs are much smaller too – almost babies.

"That's why my granny sounds so young on the phone. We really must stop this before our families are all babies!" Asim says.

Suddenly, the Time Lord's voice booms out[5] and stops the children.

Tick, tock, one two three,
Take a look and you can see
How the Time Lord ends World Time,
Faster, faster, hear the chime[6]!

Humans[7] no longer grow old[8],
Soon their hearts[9] will be stone cold[10]
Then the Earth will be free of them,
Ending all this great mayhem[11]!

"So, you can see what I can do! There are no old people now. Everybody is much younger, and everybody thinks this is wonderful. But they do not know that they cannot stop this. Ha, ha, ha! No-one can stop this, unless[12] – let us hear your first story and see how 'wonderful' young people are. Which of you wants to go first?"

"I'd like to go first," Asim says.

1 **strange** [streɪndʒ] seltsam | 2 **take a good look** [ˌteɪk‿ə ˌgʊd 'lʊk] schaut genau hin | 3 **leaves** [li:vz] Blätter | 4 **short** [ʃɔ:t] klein | 5 **to boom out** [bu:m‿'aʊt] dröhnen | 6 **chime** [tʃaɪm] Glockengeläut | 7 **humans** ['hju:mənz] die Menschen | 8 **to grow old** [grəʊ‿'əʊld] alt werden | 9 **heart** [hɑ:t] Herz | 10 **stone cold** [stəʊn 'kəʊld] kalt wie Stein | 11 **mayhem** ['meɪhem] Chaos | 12 **unless** [ən'les] es sei denn

"This is the true story of Baruani Ndume from the Congo in Africa. When he's only seven years old, Baruani and his parents have to run away from the war in the Congo. Baruani ends up in a camp for refugees[13] in Tanzania. On the way there, he loses[14] his parents. There are over 60,000 refugees in the camp[15], and he can't find his mum and dad. But he isn't the only child with no parents. Baruani now works to help other children. He starts a radio programme in which he talks about the refugee children and their problems. The best thing about Baruani's programme is that he helps children to find their parents, or he helps parents to find their children. You can now hear the programme in Tanzania, Burundi, Rwanda and in the Congo. For this work, Baruani Ndume gets the *International Children's Peace Prize*."

"Thank you for the first story, Asim. Very interesting – but you know that we need *three* stories, and it is getting more and more difficult[16] to find them. Your grandparents cannot help you now, they are already too young! Ha, ha, ha!"

And with a cold wind, the Time Lord is gone[17].

"I really like your story," Sandy says. "It shows that young people can make a difference, even in war. Let's hope we can stop the Time Lord before he stops us!"

"Do you think the Time Fairy can help us this time?" Asim asks. "But how can we call[18] her?"

"Yes, that's clever to say 'when you need more help, call me', but not to tell us *how* we can call her!" Lucy answers. "Let's try shouting 'Lady Time'."

The children call the Time Fairy's name, and the lights flicker – one, two, three – but they only hear the music again.

"We haven't got much time! What can we do?" Sandy says.

"Hey, look!" Asim shouts. "There are some words on the wall[19] here! Let's all try and call her together."

Tick, tock, one two three,
Come and help us, Time Fairy!
Stop the Time Lord, give us time,
Speak to us after this rhyme.

"You want to speak to me, children?" the kind[20] voice says. "I think Asim's story is really good. Try and find another story like that, maybe a story about a girl who helps other children. Use the internet for this – here, you can do this inside the Planetarium. I can change the walls into computer screens[21]. Use your hands to write and look for a story that way[22]."

Lucy thinks she's in a dream.

"Cool! Look at these huge screens!" she cries. "Maybe I can play my favourite computer game first? I mean, now that my parents can't stop me."

"No way, Lucy!" Sandy says. "We have to save the world[23] first – and then you can play as long as you like[24]. So let's all work together! I want to go next." …

13 refugee [ˌrefjʊ'dʒi] Flüchtling | **14 to lose** [luːz] verlieren | **15 camp** [kæmp] Flüchtlingslager | **16 difficult** ['dɪfɪklt] schwierig | **17 is gone** [ɪz 'gɒn] ist verschwunden | **18 call** [kɔːl] rufen | **19 wall** [wɔːl] Wand | **20 kind** [kaɪnd] freundlich | **21 screen** [skriːn] Bildschirm | **22 that way** ['ðæt weɪ] so; auf diese Art und Weise | **23 to save the world** [ˌseɪv ðə 'wɜːld] die Welt retten | **24 as long as you like** [əz ˌlɒŋ‿əz jə'laɪk] solange du willst

S 2/43–47 L 4/23–27

The end of world time

Chapter 3

→ Folie 35, KV 92, KV 96, KV 97

"There's so much to read, and time is running out[1]!" Sandy says.

It isn't so easy to find a good true story on the internet, but then Sandy thinks she's got one. Suddenly, the computers disappear[2], and the children hear the music again. It's really fast this time! The lights flicker – one, two, three – and the Time Lord's voice booms out again:

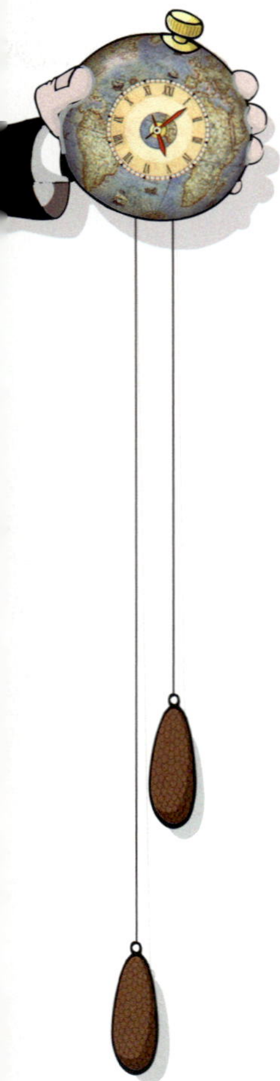

Tick, tock, one two three,
Take a look and you can see
How the Time Lord ends World Time,
Faster, faster, hear the chime!

Humans no longer grow old,
Soon their hearts will be stone cold
Then the Earth will be free of them,
Ending all this great mayhem!

"Take a good look at the world out there," the Time Lord says. "Do you find it funny?"

"Oh, look, Asim, your mum is trying to use the car," Lucy laughs. "But she's too small! Can you see how many cushions[3] she's got on her seat[4]? Ha ha! She looks like the princess on the pea!"

The streets of Greenwich are really quiet. Not many people can drive a car.

"I really like Greenwich like this," Asim says. "It looks like a great place – no cars, only young people, everybody is into sports – see how many joggers there are!"

Sandy isn't so happy. "I don't like it at all. Where are our friends? They're all little babies! And can't you see that the Time Lord and his trick are changing Greenwich? Look! It's dirty, and all the shops are closed!"

The Time Lord laughs out loud. "Oh, you are a clever girl! See what I can do? Everyone is under 20 now, and people are beginning to see that this is not so wonderful. People do not want to work hard – or they do not know how. No-one cleans[5] the streets or works in the hospitals[6]. Who can help when there is an accident[7]? Who can stop crime[8]? There are no schools. There is no money in the banks. And no-one can stop me! Well, maybe *you* can – let us have your second story and see how 'wonderful' young people can be. Who is next?"

Sandy is nervous, but starts to tell her story.

"This is the story of Alexandra Scott. Her friends call her Alex. Alex is one year old when the doctors find out that the little girl has got cancer[9]. When Alex is four years old, she tells her mother that she wants to start a lemonade stand[10]. Alex wants to sell lemonade and give the money to the doctors so they can 'help other kids, like they help me.' She works very hard and, in the end, she gives $2,000 to the doctors. Then other people open more and more lemonade stands. When she's only eight years old, Alex dies. That's very sad. But in

1 time is running out [ˌtaɪm ɪz ˌrʌnɪŋ ˈaʊt] die Zeit wird knapp | **2 to disappear** [dɪsəˈpɪə] verschwinden | **3 cushion** [ˈkʊʃn] Kissen | **4 seat** [siːt] Sitz | **5 to clean** [kliːn] sauber machen | **6 hospital** [ˈhɒspɪtl] Krankenhaus | **7 accident** [ˈæksɪdnt] Unfall | **8 crime** [kraɪm] Kriminalität | **9 cancer** [ˈkænsə] Krebs | **10 lemonade stand** [ˌleməˈneɪd ˌstænd] Limonadenstand

only four years, the doctors get over $1 million. In 2005, Alex's parents start *Alex's Lemonade Stand Foundation*. Today, America has got a special weekend[11] every June that's called Lemonade Days. More than 10,000 people work at more than 2,000 lemonade stands, and they all give money to help children with cancer."

"Thank you for your story, Sandy," the Time Lord says, and the children think they can hear a tear[12] in his voice. "You found it on the internet? You were just in time, because the internet is no longer running – there is no-one to look after it now, everybody is too young and they do not know how things work. Hm – cancer is a terrible[13] thing, but soon you will all be babies, and that will be the end of cancer too!" And with a cool wind, the Time Lord is gone.

"I don't think he likes our stories," Sandy says. "We need more help from the Time Fairy. Let's call her again. Do you remember what we have to say?"

"Of course – let's say this all together:"

Tick, tock, one two three,
Come and help us, Time Fairy!
Stop the Time Lord, give us time,
Speak to us after this rhyme.

"You want to speak to me again, children?"

"Yes, we don't think our stories are good enough," Sandy says. "And we've only got one more chance now."

"Don't worry, the Time Lord is always like this. Of course, he's still angry because I always win[14] our battles[15]. But I know him – Sandy, your story is great. Remember, I can see the Time Lord. And I

can see the tears in his eyes. So how can I help you this time?"

"Well, maybe you can tell us what books we can use to find a story. You know the internet is down[16], and we can't ask our grandparents or parents – they're all too young and don't remember a thing."

"Lucy, it's your story next. My old rival[17] is very fond of[18] stories where people with a good life see that other people on Earth have got a very difficult life – and how they try and help. I can't give you books, but look here …"

Suddenly, there's a warm wind, and the Planetarium is filled with sheets of paper[19]. They're everywhere in the air[20]. Asim jumps up and catches[21] one.

"Hey, there are stories on these!" he shouts.

"But there are hundreds[22] of them!" Lucy answers. "How can we find the right one?"

"You must work together!" the kind voice says.

"What? Oh, I understand!" Lucy shouts. "Let's all do this together. Ready? One, two, three – jump!" …

11 **weekend** [ˌwiːk'end] Wochenende | 12 **tear** [tɪə] Träne | 13 **terrible** ['terəbl] schlimm; furchtbar | 14 **to win** [wɪn] gewinnen | 15 **battle** ['bætl] Kampf | 16 **is down** [ɪz 'daʊn] ist außer Betrieb | 17 **rival** ['raɪvl] Rivale | 18 **is fond of** [ɪz 'fɒnd‿ɒv] mag gerne | 19 **a sheet of paper** [ˌʃiːt‿ɒv 'peɪpə] ein Blatt Papier | 20 **air** [eə] Luft | 21 **to catch** [kætʃ] fangen | 22 **hundreds** ['hʌndrədz] hunderte

S 2/48–51
L 4/28–31

The end of world time

Chapter 4 → Folie 35, KV 98, KV 99

"Quick, put the sheets away, or the Time Lord will see that we got help from Lady Time."

Lucy, Sandy and Asim are inside the Planetarium. On the wall, they can see the hourglass, and to their horror[1] there's very little sand left[2]. Then the lights flicker – one, two, three. Once again, they hear the music, and the Time Lord's voice booms out:

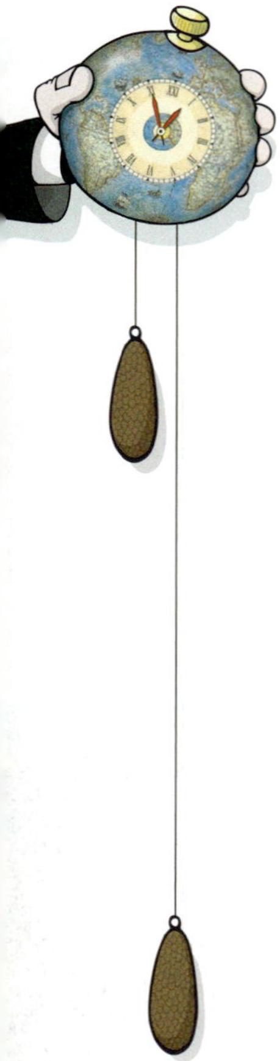

Tick, tock, one two three,
Take a look and you can see
How the Time Lord ends World Time,
Faster, faster, hear the chime!

Everybody now is young,
And your silly song is sung.
War and wickedness[3] will cease[4],
Bringing me and World Time peace[5]!

"You can see what I can do," the Time Lord says. "My clock is running faster and faster. Take a good look at the world out there. Everybody eats baby food! Before all the babies fall asleep and never wake up[6] again, let us have your last story about how 'wonderful' young people can be. OK, I am listening. Remember, this is your last chance!"

Lucy is shaking when she starts to tell her story.

"This is the story of Ryan Hreljac from America. When Ryan is only six years old, his teacher talks to the class about water in Africa. Ryan learns that children there have to walk many miles[7] every day just to get water. This is new to him. 'So not everyone lives like me?' he thinks. 'I have to do something about this.' Ryan starts to work and earn money so that people can build[8] a well[9] for a village[10] in Africa. He does jobs around the house, and he speaks in front of people about clean[11] water. He earns $70 and thinks this is enough to build a well. But then he learns that the well costs $2,000. So he works harder. When Ryan is only seven years old, he's got enough money to help

build a well at a primary school in Uganda. Ryan then starts the *Ryan's Well Foundation*. His foundation organises about 700 projects in 16 countries. Almost one million people have now got clean water because Ryan and his foundation helped them. Ryan says that water is very important to all life. He also says that anyone can change the world. You need to find something you're passionate[12] about. Then you take one step, and then another."

"That's the end of my story. And now – now I just hope it's not the end of the human race," Lucy says quietly.

There's a long pause.

"Thank you for your stories," the Time Lord says at last. "They were really very

1 **to their horror** [tə ðeə 'hɒrə] zu ihrem Entsetzen | 2 **left** [left] übrig | 3 **wickedness** ['wɪkɪdnəs] Bosheit; Schlechtigkeit | 4 **to cease** [si:s] aufhören | 5 **peace** [pi:s] Frieden | 6 **to wake up** [weɪk_'ʌp] aufwachen | 7 **mile** [maɪl] Meile (= 1,609 km) | 8 **to build** [bɪld] bauen | 9 **well** [wel] Brunnen | 10 **village** ['vɪlɪdʒ] Dorf | 11 **clean** [kli:n] sauber | 12 **passionate** ['pæʃnət] leidenschaftlich

interesting. What do you think, Time Fairy?"

"Well, do you remember the dinosaurs? I think that was the last time that you were the winner[13] of our battle. And that was a long time ago!" The Time Fairy laughs. "I think the stories are very promising[14]. With more children like this, the world really can be a different place. Of course, there are still a lot of problems, but children *can* make a difference!"

There is another long pause. It's suddenly very quiet in the Planetarium. The huge screen is dark. The children can see the hourglass, and the last grains[15] of sand slowly fall – and then stop. They hear the Time Lord's voice again, but now it sounds very old and tired:

Oh, I hate[16] it, but it is true,
There is nothing I can do.
Your three stories – a breakthrough[17]
For all humans, I undo[18]
My clever spell[19] – and time can tick,
Ending Time Lord's biggest trick.

Tick, tock, one two three,
Take a look and you can see:
World Time now begins once more[20]
Out, you three, run through that door!

You will see things are okay,
Greenwich has a normal day.
You three really saved World Time,
Turn around and hear my chime!

The children run out through the door of the Planetarium. Outside, it's very noisy[21] – typical everyday Greenwich noises. They can hear the music again, but this time, it's playing forwards[22], and they know exactly what it is: '*London Bridge is falling down*'!

"Wow, I can't believe it, we did it! We really saved the world today. Let's go home!"

Suddenly, their three phones start ringing. The children answer them at the same time. They feel a warm wind on their faces.

"Hello, it's me, the Time Fairy. I want to thank you for helping me. Humans have got another 100 years now, and then my battle with the Time Lord will start again. Thank you – and good-bye!"

The three children look down at their smartphones. On the screens, they can see everything in 3D – the phones are like crystal balls[23]. They laugh out loud when they see and hear their parents.

"Yuck! Why am I eating baby food? And look – it's all over my T-shirt! Sandy, where are you?"

"Why are all these boxes in the kitchen? Lucy, was that you?"

"Who on earth put all these cushions in the car? Asim, this isn't funny!"

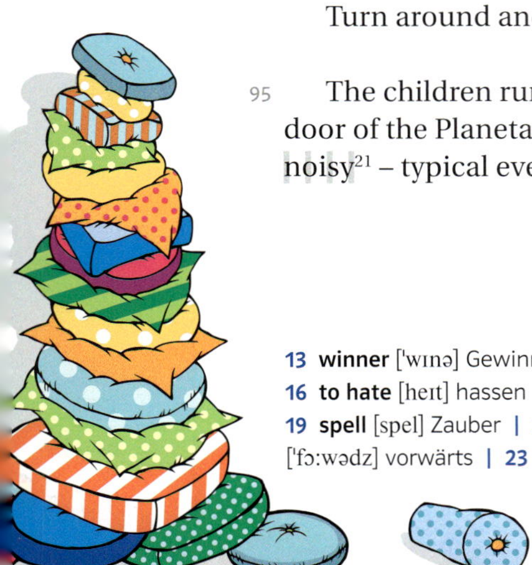

13 winner ['wɪnə] Gewinner | **14 promising** ['prɒmɪsɪŋ] vielversprechend | **15 grain** [greɪn] Körnchen | **16 to hate** [heɪt] hassen | **17 breakthrough** ['breɪkθru:] Durchbruch | **18 to undo** [ʌn'du:] rückgängig machen | **19 spell** [spel] Zauber | **20 once more** [wʌns 'mɔ:] wieder; noch einmal | **21 noisy** ['nɔɪzi] laut | **22 forwards** ['fɔ:wədz] vorwärts | **23 crystal ball** [ˌkrɪstl 'bɔ:l] Kristallkugel

Grammar

Liebe Schülerin, lieber Schüler,
jede Sprache besteht aus bestimmten Bausteinen und funktioniert nach bestimmten Regeln. Die Bausteine sind z. B. einzelne Wörter (Vokabeln). Die Regeln für ihre Zusammensetzung nennt man Grammatik. Für deine Muttersprache brauchst du die Regeln nicht auswendig zu lernen: Die meisten wendest du automatisch richtig an. Wenn du aber weitere Sprachen lernst, musst du außer den Vokabeln auch die wichtigsten Grammatikregeln lernen, um dich zu verständigen und Missverständnisse zu vermeiden.

Diese ***Grammar*** soll dir zeigen, wie du die Bausteine der englischen Sprache richtig kombinieren kannst.

Jedes Grammatikkapitel (**G**) in dieser *Grammar* behandelt Themen, die auf bestimmten Seiten vorne in den *Units* vorkommen (z. B. Seiten 16–18). Erklärungen, Regeln, Bilder und Übersichtstabellen helfen dir, die Grammatik zu verstehen. Ein Ausrufezeichen (**!**) bedeutet: Hier musst du ganz besonders aufpassen. Mit kleinen **Aufgaben** kannst du überprüfen, ob du alles verstanden hast. Die Lösungen findest du ab S. 273.

Grammatical terms

English term		Example	*Deutsche Bezeichnung*
adverb of frequency	G21	I **never** write.	*Häufigkeitsadverb*
definite article	G9	**The** black and white dog is Sherlock.	*bestimmter Artikel*
demonstrative pronoun	G18	**This** is Pia. **That** is her mum. **These** pens are red, and **those** are blue.	*Demonstrativpronomen*
expressions of quantity with *of*	G26	Can I have **a bottle of** water, please?	*Mengenangaben mit* of
imperative	G15	**Be** polite. **Don't bring** your phone to school.	*Imperativ, Befehlsform*
indefinite article	G8	I've got **a** blue pen and **an** orange pen.	*unbestimmter Artikel*
indefinite pronoun (compounds with **some**, **any**, **every**, and **no**)	G29	There's **something** here for **everyone**.	*Indefinitpronomen (Zusammensetzungen mit* some, any, every, *und* no*)*
infinitive	G15	be, go, play	*Infinitiv, Grundform*
long form	G2 G10	I **am** Luke. We **have got** a pet.	*Langform*
main clause	G37	**I like my friend.**	*Hauptsatz*
modal auxiliary	G14 G32 G33	**can**, **can't** **can**, **can't**, **mustn't** **must**, **needn't**	*Modalverb, modales Hilfsverb*

English term		Example	*Deutsche Bezeichnung*
negative (form)	G3 G11 G23 G36	I**'m not** English. I **haven't got** my lucky charm. We **don't** get up early on Sundays. I **didn't** decorate the yard.	*Verneinung*
noun	G1	boy, dog, family, street	*Nomen, Substantiv, Hauptwort*
object	G20	Dave plays **computer games** after school.	*Objekt*
object form of personal pronouns	G24	me, you, him, her, it, us, you, them	*Objektform der Personalpronomen*
personal pronoun	G2	I, you, he, she, it, we, you, they	*Personalpronomen, persönliches Fürwort*
plural	G1	two girl**s**, three cat**s**, five house**s**, two **mice**	*Plural, Mehrzahl*
possessive determiner	G6	my, your, his, her, its, our, your, their	*Possessivbegleiter*
possessive form with *of*	G17	I live at the end **of** the street.	*Besitzform mit* of
present progressive	G27	They **are sitting** at a table outside a café.	*Verlaufsform der Gegenwart*
quantifier	G28 G30 G31	**some**, **any**, **no** **much**, **many**, **a lot of** **a few**, **a little**, **a couple of**	*Mengenwort*
question with question word	G5 G13 G25	**Who** are you? **What** can you see? **When** does the farm open?	*Frage mit Fragewort*
s-genitive	G16	This is Luke**'s** house.	s-*Genitiv*
short answer	G4 G7 G12 G22	Yes, I am. / No, I'm not. Yes, there is. / No, there isn't. Yes, I have. / No, I haven't. Yes, we do. / No, we don't.	*Kurzantwort*
short form	G2 G11	I**'m** Luke. We **haven't got** a pet.	*Kurzform*
simple past	G34	You **wanted** to know about my 12th birthday.	*einfache Vergangenheit*
simple present	G19	Olivia **plays** netball on Tuesdays.	*einfache Gegenwart*
singular	G1	a flat, one brother, an exercise book	*Singular, Einzahl*
subject	G20	**Dave** plays computer games after school.	*Subjekt, Satzgegenstand*
subordinate clause	G37	I like my friend **because she is nice**.	*Nebensatz*
verb	G2 G10 G19	be have got go, play	*Verb, Tätigkeitswort*
word order	G20	I – do – my homework – in the evenings.	*Satzstellung*
Yes/No question	G4 G7 G12 G22 G35	**Are** you from Greenwich? **Is** there a book on the table? **Have** you **got** a uniform? **Do** you know the Cutty Sark museum? **Did** you like the party?	*Entscheidungsfrage, Frage ohne Fragewort*

Unit 1

G1 *Nomen im Singular und Plural*
Seite 16 Nouns in the singular and plural

FUNKTION

Den Singular benutzt du für ***eine*** *Person oder Sache:*
a boy, a photo.

Den Plural benutzt du für ***mehrere*** *Personen oder Sachen:*
a boy – two boy**s**
a door – three door**s**.

REGEL

- *Du bildest den Plural von fast allen englischen Nomen durch Anhängen des Buchstabens* **s***:* a dog – two dog**s**.
- *Bei der Aussprache musst du allerdings aufpassen. Die Endung des Wortes im Singular bestimmt, wie der Plural ausgesprochen wird:*

[s]	[z]	[ɪz]
nach harten (stimmlosen) Konsonanten	nach weichen (stimmhaften) Konsonanten und nach Vokalen	nach Zischlauten
a park – two park**s** a flat – two flat**s** a biscuit – two biscuit**s**	a boy – two boy**s** a bed – two bed**s** a tree – two tree**s**	a house – two hous**es** a sentence – two sentenc**es** a fridge – two fridg**es**

❗ *Es gibt auch Ausnahmen bei der Schreibung, z. B.*
a family – two famil**ies**, a hobby – two hobb**ies**.
Später lernst du weitere unregelmäßige Formen.

AUFGABE *Bilde den Plural folgender Wörter und lasse deine Aussprache von einer anderen Person kontrollieren:*

1. home
2. squirrel
3. house
4. street
5. clock
6. school
7. wardrobe
8. flat

G2 *Die Personalpronomen und die Formen von* be

Seiten 16–17 The personal pronouns and the forms of *be*

FUNKTION

*Mit den Personalpronomen (*I, you, he *usw.) und der passenden Form von* be *drückst du aus, wer oder was jemand oder eine Sache ist.*

Singular			*Plural*
I	you	he she it	we you they
			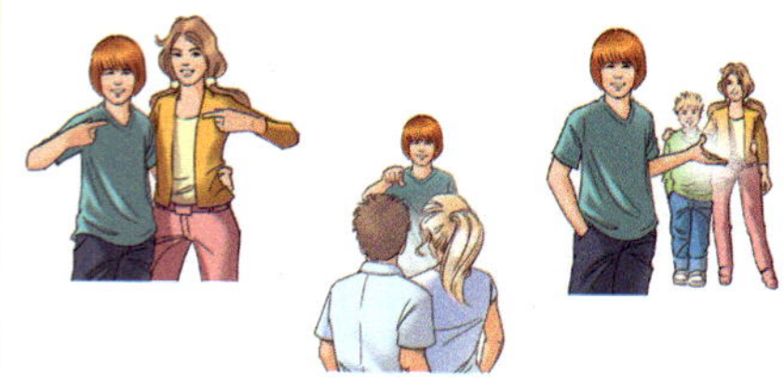
am	**are**	**is**	**are**

❗ *Sachen und Tiere werden mit* it *bezeichnet. Kennst du die Tiere jedoch persönlich bzw. beim Namen, verwendest du die entsprechende weibliche oder männliche Form:* This is Sherlock. **He**'s a nice dog.

❗ **I** *wird immer großgeschrieben.* **You** *kann* ***du***, ***Sie*** *(Höflichkeitsform) oder* ***ihr*** *heißen:* **You** are nice. *(Du bist nett./Ihr seid nett./Sie sind nett.)*

REGEL

- *Mit den Personalpronomen werden meist die Kurzformen von* be *verwendet, weil sie sich flüssiger sprechen oder lesen lassen. Hier siehst du eine Übersicht:*

	Langformen (long forms)			*So entsteht die Kurzform*			*Kurzformen (short forms)*	
Singular	I	**am**	Luke.	I	am	Luke.	**I'm**	Luke.
	You	**are**	cool.	You	are	cool.	**You're**	cool.
	He	**is**	my brother.	He	is	my brother.	**He's**	my brother.
	She	**is**	twelve.	She	is	twelve.	**She's**	twelve.
	It	**is**	a big house.	It	is	a big house.	**It's**	a big house.
Plural	We	**are**	from Greenwich.	We	are	from Greenwich.	**We're**	from Greenwich.
	You	**are**	cool.	You	are	cool.	**You're**	cool.
	They	**are**	good friends.	They	are	good friends.	**They're**	good friends.

- *Im gesprochenen Englisch verwendest du mit den Personalpronomen immer die Kurzformen, auch wenn du gesprochene Sprache aufschreibst (Dialoge). Die Langformen kommen nur noch manchmal in schriftlichen Texten oder zur Betonung vor.*

AUFGABE *Überprüfe, ob du die Formen von* be *richtig verwenden kannst.*

1. *Sage, wer du bist und wie alt du bist.*
2. *Sage, woher du kommst.*
3. *Sage zu der Person neben dir, dass sie nett ist.*
4. *Zeige auf ein Foto im Buch, das eine Person zeigt, und sage der Person neben dir, dass sie/er nett ist.*

G3 *Die Verneinung von* be

Seite 18

The negative forms of *be*

FUNKTION

Mit den Personalpronomen und der passenden Form von be *und* not *drückst du aus, was jemand oder eine Sache* **nicht** *ist. Meistens benutzt du die Verneinung, wenn du etwas richtigstellen willst:* This **isn't** Mr Fluff – it's Honey.

– *Beim Sprechen werden die verneinten Formen zu* **Kurzformen** *zusammengezogen:*

	Langformen (long forms)			*Kurzformen* (short forms)		
Singular	**I am**	**not**	English.	**I'm**	**not**	English.
	You are	**not**	fourteen.	**You**	**aren't**	fourteen.
	He is	**not**	quiet.	**He**	**isn't**	quiet.
	She is	**not**	here.	**She**	**isn't**	here.
	It is	**not**	a big garden.	**It**	**isn't**	a big garden.
Plural	**We are**	**not**	from Greenwich.	**We**	**aren't**	from Greenwich.
	You are	**not**	crazy.	**You**	**aren't**	crazy.
	They are	**not**	good friends.	**They**	**aren't**	good friends.

– *Bei den Formen mit* are *und* is *wird* not *zu* **n't** *verkürzt.*

– *Bei* am *geht das nicht.* I *und* am *werden zur Kurzform* **I'm** *zusammengezogen und* not *bleibt stehen:* I'm **not** English.

AUFGABE *Überprüfe, ob du die Formen von* be *richtig verneinen kannst.*

1. *Sage, dass du nicht acht Jahre alt bist.* (I …)
2. *Sage, dass du und dein Freund/deine Freundin nicht aus London kommen.* (We …)
3. *Sage, dass deine Wohnung nicht groß ist.* (It …)
4. *Sage, dass deine Freunde nicht verrückt sind.* (They …)

G4 *Entscheidungsfragen und Kurzantworten mit* be

Seiten 19, 21 Yes/No questions and short answers with *be*

FUNKTION

Entscheidungsfragen mit be *verwendest du, um zu fragen, ob etwas stimmt oder nicht. Im Englischen beantwortet man solche Fragen mit Kurzantworten.*

REGEL – *In Entscheidungsfragen mit* be *tauschen das Subjekt und das Verb einfach die Plätze, genau wie im Deutschen:*

Luke is	from Greenwich.	**Luke ist**	*aus Greenwich.*
Is Luke	from Greenwich?	**Ist Luke**	*aus Greenwich?*

– *So bildest du die Kurzantworten:*

Ein einfaches „yes" oder „no" klingt unhöflich. Deshalb solltest du immer die Kurzantworten verwenden!

REGEL – *Wenn du mit „***yes***" antwortest, verwendest du in der Kurzantwort die* **Langform** *von* be. *Nur bei Antworten mit „***no***" ist die* **Kurzform** *richtig.*

Frage	*Kurzantwort* +	*Kurzantwort* –
Are you eleven?	**Yes**, **I am**.	**No**, **I'm not**.
Is he from Greenwich?	**Yes**, **he is**.	**No**, **he isn't**.
Is she your sister?	**Yes**, **she is**.	**No**, **she isn't**.
Is it in the bedroom?	**Yes**, **it is**.	**No**, **it isn't**.
Are we in Brook Lane?	**Yes**, **we are**.	**No**, **we aren't**.
Are you English?	**Yes**, **we are**./**Yes**, **I am**.	**No**, **we aren't**./**No**, **I'm not**.
Are they your friends?	**Yes**, **they are**.	**No**, **they aren't**.

AUFGABE *Überprüft, ob ihr Entscheidungsfragen und Kurzantworten richtig bilden könnt. Stellt euch gegenseitig Fragen und beantwortet sie.*

1. *Frage die Person neben dir, ob sie aus [Name deiner Stadt] kommt.*
2. *Frage dann die Personen, die am Nebentisch sitzen, ob sie aus [Name deiner Stadt] kommen.*
3. *Frage eine Person, ob ihre Freunde nett sind.*
4. *Frage eine Person, ob Tony ein Meerschweinchen ist.*
5. *Frage eine Person, ob ihr zu Hause seid.*

G5 *Fragen mit Fragewörtern*

Seite 22 Questions with question words

FUNKTION

Wenn du nach bestimmten Informationen fragst, brauchst du die passenden Fragewörter – Wer? Was? Wo? Wann? usw.

REGEL – *Hier siehst du Beispiele für Fragewörter, die du schon kennst:*

Frage	*Antwort*	*Wonach wird gefragt?*
Where are you, Irina?	I'm in the bath.	*Wo …?*
Where are you **from**?	I'm from Greenwich.	*Woher …?*
Who is always quiet?	Tony is always quiet.	*Wer …?*
What is this, Tony?	It's a biscuit.	*Was …?*
How old are you, Dave?	I'm eleven.	*Wie alt …?*

– *Nach einem Fragewort wird* is *oft verkürzt:* Where**'s** …?, Who**'s** …?, What**'s** …?, How**'s** …?
Where's Sherlock? – He's in the living room.
Who's that? – It's Mrs Elliot.
What's this? – It's a biscuit.

AUFGABE *Überprüft, ob ihr Fragen und Antworten richtig bilden könnt. Stellt euch gegenseitig Fragen und beantwortet sie.*

1. *Frage die Person neben dir, wer sie ist.*
2. *Frage die Person, was ihre Lieblingsfarbe ist.*
3. *Frage die Person, wo sie herkommt.*
4. *Frage die Person, wie alt sie ist.*
5. *Frage die Person, was in ihrem Zimmer ist.*

G6 *Die Possessivbegleiter*

Seiten 16, 21 Possessive determiners

FUNKTION *Possessivbegleiter verwendest du, um auszudrücken, zu wem etwas oder jemand gehört.*

REGEL – *Possessivbegleiter stehen entweder direkt vor einem Nomen* (I live with **my parents**.) *oder vor einem Adjektiv + Nomen* (I live with **my little brother**.)

Jeder Possessivbegleiter hat im Englischen nur eine Form: **my** sister – **my** brother – **my** parents.

Personalpronomen		*Possessivbegleiter*		
I	'm from Greenwich.	**My**	name is Luke.	*Mein Name …*
You	're on holiday in London.	**Your**	room is nice.	*Dein Zimmer …*
He	's my friend.	**His**	name is Dave.	*Sein Name …*
She	's from Germany.	**Her**	name is Pia.	*Ihr Name …*
It	's a nice house.	**Its**	door is green.	*Seine Tür …*
We	're in the house.	**Our**	house is small.	*Unser Haus …*
You	're a family.	**Your**	family is big.	*Eure/Ihre Familie …*
They	're cool parents.	**Their**	names are Anna and Jack.	*Ihre Namen …*

! *Pronomen und Begleiter kannst du nicht immer direkt ins Englische übertragen. Vergleiche:*
*Das Mädchen ist nett. **Es** kommt aus Köln. **Seine** Familie ist in London im Urlaub.*
The girl is nice. **She**'s from Cologne. **Her** family is on holiday in London.

! **Your** *kann **dein**, **euer** oder **Ihr** heißen. Deshalb musst du den Zusammenhang beachten:*

Sherlock is **your** dog. — *Sherlock ist **dein** …*
Sherlock is **your** dog, Luke and Jamie. — *Sherlock ist **euer** …*
Is this **your** dog, Mr Elliot? — *Ist das **Ihr** …*

! *Verwechsle nicht* **you're** *mit* **your** *und* **it's** *mit* **its**!

You're (= You are) a nice dog. — ***Du bist** ein lieber Hund.*
Your dog is nice. — ***Dein/Euer/Ihr** Hund ist lieb.*
It's (= It is) a nice house. — ***Es ist** ein schönes Haus.*
Its door is green. — ***Seine** Tür ist grün.*

AUFGABE *Überprüfe, ob du die Possessivbegleiter richtig verwenden kannst.*

1. *Sage, dass dein Zimmer klein ist.*
2. *Sage, dass euer Wohnzimmer groß ist. Seine Wände sind weiß.*
3. *Sage, dass deine große Schwester nett ist.*
4. *Sage, dass Lou und ihre Familie in Greenwich wohnen. Ihre Wohnung ist toll für Mäuse.*
5. *Tony wohnt bei den Elliots. Sage, dass seine Wohnung auf dem Dachboden ist. Sie befindet sich in Brook Lane.*

G7 *Aussagesätze, Fragen und Kurzantworten mit* there is/there are

Seiten 21–22 Statements, questions and short answers with *there is/there are*

FUNKTION

Wenn du sagen möchtest, dass sich Personen, Tiere oder Sachen irgendwo befinden, kannst du das mit **there is** *oder* **there are** *tun.*

Singular	**There is** a mouse under the chair. **Is there** a mouse under the chair?	**Yes, there is. / No, there isn't.**
Plural	**There are** two mice. **Are there** two mice under the chair?	**Yes, there are. / No, there aren't.**

REGEL

- **There is** *(Singular) /* **there are** *(Plural) entspricht dem deutschen* ***es gibt …, da ist/ da sind …, es liegen …*** *oder* ***es stehen …*** **There is** *wird meist zu* **there's** *verkürzt.*
- *Bei der Frage tauschen* **there** *und die Form von* **be** *einfach die Plätze:* **Is there …? / Are there …?** *Die Kurzantwort nimmt das* **there** *wieder auf:* **Yes, there is. / No, there isn't.** *Und im Plural:* **Yes, there are. / No, there aren't.**

AUFGABE

Überprüft, ob ihr Aussagesätze mit there is/there are *bilden und Fragen stellen und beantworten könnt.*

1. *Sage, wie viele Autos auf dem Tisch stehen.*
2. *Frage, ob ein Fußball unter dem Stuhl ist.*
3. *Frage, ob zwei Kekse unter dem Bett sind.*
4. *Frage, ob es einen Keks auf dem Stuhl gibt.*
5. *Sage, dass eine Uhr auf dem Tisch steht.*

Unit 2

G8 *Der unbestimmte Artikel*

Seiten 34–35 The indefinite article

FUNKTION

Den unbestimmten Artikel verwendest du mit einem Nomen, das etwas noch nicht näher Bekanntes bezeichnet.

REGEL *Du verwendest* **a** *vor Konsonanten und* **an** *vor Vokalen. Dabei zählt die Aussprache des folgenden Wortes, nicht die Schreibung!*

a [ə]		an [ən]	
a	problem [ə 'prɔbləm]	an	interview [ən‿'ɪntəvju:]
a	uniform [ə 'ju:nɪfɔ:m]	an	uncle [ən‿'ʌŋkl]
a	new boy [ə 'nju: ˌbɔɪ]	an	English test [ən‿'ɪŋglɪʃ ˌtest]

AUFGABE *Wie lautet der unbestimmte Artikel bei* cousin, aunt, fridge, idea, answer, loft, address?

G9 *Der bestimmte Artikel*

Seiten 34–35 The definite article

FUNKTION

> *Den bestimmten Artikel verwendest du mit einem Nomen, das etwas bereits Bekanntes bezeichnet.*

REGEL *Im Englischen verwendest du nur eine Form des Artikels für Lebewesen oder Sachen im Singular oder im Plural:* **the**. *Die Schreibung bleibt gleich, aber die Aussprache ändert sich: Du sprichst* [ðə] *vor Konsonanten und* [ði] *vor Vokalen. Dabei zählt wieder die Aussprache, nicht die Schreibung des folgenden Wortes!*

the [ðə]		the [ði]	
the	problem [ðə 'prɔbləm]	the	interview [ði‿'ɪntəvju:]
the	uniform [ðə 'ju:nɪfɔ:m]	the	uncle [ði‿'ʌŋkl]
the	new boy [ðə 'nju: ˌbɔɪ]	the	English test [ði‿'ɪŋglɪʃ ˌtest]

AUFGABE *Wie lautet der bestimmte Artikel bei dog, house, Art room, exercise book, ending?*

G10 *Besitz und Zugehörigkeit mit* have got *ausdrücken*

Seiten 34–35 Expressing possession and affiliation with *have got*

FUNKTION

> *Mit* **have got** *bzw.* **has got** *kannst du ausdrücken, dass jemand etwas hat.*

REGEL – *Alle Formen werden gleich gebildet (*have got*), außer in der 3. Person Singular –* he, she, it. *Da benutzt du* has got*:* **He/She/It has got ...**

– *Auch hier gibt es wieder Langformen für die Schriftsprache und Kurzformen für die gesprochene Sprache:*

Langform		
Singular		
I	**have got**	a cat.
You	**have got**	a cat.
He	**has got**	a cat.
She	**has got**	a cat.
It	**has got**	a nice colour.
Plural		
We	**have got**	a cat.
You	**have got**	a cat.
They	**have got**	a cat.

Kurzform	
Singular	
I**'ve got**	a cat.
You**'ve got**	a cat.
He**'s got**	a cat.
She**'s got**	a cat.
It**'s got**	a nice colour.
Plural	
We**'ve got**	a cat.
You**'ve got**	a cat.
They**'ve got**	a cat.

AUFGABE *Überprüfe, ob du die Formen von* have got *richtig verwenden kannst.*

1. *Sage, dass du eine Frage hast.*
2. *Sage, dass deine Lehrerin/dein Lehrer eine große Tasche hat.*
3. *Sage, dass ihr einen Computerraum habt.*
4. *Sage, dass der Computerraum zehn Computer hat.*

G11 *Die Verneinung von* have got

Seiten 34–35

The negative form of *have got*

FUNKTION

Mit **haven't got** *bzw.* **hasn't got** *kannst du ausdrücken, dass jemand etwas* ***nicht*** *hat.*

REGEL – Have got *ist ein zweiteiliges Verb. In der Verneinung steht das* **not** *zwischen* **have** *und* **got**.

– *Für* **he**, **she**, **it** *verwendest du* **hasn't got** *statt* **haven't got**: Holly **hasn't got** her lucky charm.

! *Vorsicht bei den Kurzformen! Du kannst nicht sagen:* We'~~ven't~~ got a pet.
Richtig ist: We **haven't got** a pet.

AUFGABE *Überprüft, ob ihr auch die verneinten Formen von* have got *richtig verwenden könnt. Erzählt euch gegenseitig, was ihr in eurer Schultasche habt oder nicht habt.*

G12 *Entscheidungsfragen und Kurzantworten mit* have got

Seiten 34, 36

Yes/No questions and short answers with *have got*

FUNKTION

Entscheidungsfragen mit **have got/has got** *verwendest du, um zu fragen, ob jemand etwas hat. Die Kurzantwort bildest du mit* **have/has** *oder* **haven't/hasn't**.

REGEL

She **has got** a blue school uniform.

Has **she** **got** a blue school uniform? – Yes, **she has**.

Frage	*Kurzantwort* +	*Kurzantwort* −
Have you got a pen?	Yes, **I have**.	No, **I haven't**.
Has he got a brother?	Yes, **he has**.	No, **he hasn't**.
Has she got green pens?	Yes, **she has**.	No, **she hasn't**.
Have you got a recording studio?	Yes, **we have**.	No, **we haven't**.
Have they got a big house?	Yes, **they have**.	No, **they haven't**.

AUFGABE

Überprüft, ob ihr Entscheidungsfragen und Antworten mit have got *richtig bilden könnt. Stellt euch gegenseitig Fragen und beantwortet sie.*

1. *Frage deine Partnerin/deinen Partner, ob sie/er ein Haustier/einen Bruder / eine Schwester/ein großes Zimmer/einen Bleistift hat.*
2. *Denke an eine Person, die ihr beide kennt. Deine Partnerin/dein Partner muss erraten, wen du meinst, indem sie/er Entscheidungsfragen stellt. Antworte mit Kurzantworten.*

G13 *Die Fragewörter* who, what *und* whose

Seite 37

The question words *who, what* and *whose*

FUNKTION

Mit **who** *fragst du nach Personen.*
Mit **what** *fragst du nach Sachen.*
Mit **whose** *fragst du, wem etwas gehört.*

REGEL

– **Who** *oder* **what** *können Subjekt oder Objekt des Fragesatzes sein.*

Frage	*Wonach wird gefragt?*
Who's your tutor? **Who** has got a pen?	*Wer …? (Subjekt)*
Who can you see?	*Wen/Wem …? (Objekt)*
What's in your bag?	*Was …? (Subjekt)*
What have you got in your bag?	*Was …? (Objekt)*
Whose picture is this?	*Wessen …?*

AUFGABE *Überprüfe den Gebrauch der Fragewörter, indem du diese Fragen ins Englische übersetzt.*

1. *Was ist in deinem Zimmer?*
2. *Wen kannst du im Haus sehen?*
3. *Was hat Luke in seinem Zimmer?*
4. *Wessen Schuluniform ist blau?*
5. *Wer hat ein Meerschweinchen?*
6. *Wem gehört dieser Hund?*

G14 *Die Modalverben* can *und* can't

The modal auxiliaries *can* and *can't*

Seiten 32–33
39–41

FUNKTION

*Mit **can** sagst du, dass jemand etwas kann, und mit **can't** sagst du, dass jemand etwas nicht kann.*

***Can** und **can't** verwendest du auch, um zu sagen, was erlaubt oder verboten ist.*

Dave: Here's your TTS planner, Jay. You **can** read the school rules in it.
Jay: Thanks. **Can** we use phones at school?
Dave: No, we **can't**. – Look, here's the recording studio. I like music. And you? **Can** you sing?
Jay: Yes, I **can**.
Dave: Great!

REGEL

– *Das kennst du schon aus Pick-up B: Mit* can *und* can't *drückst du aus, dass jemand etwas kann oder nicht kann:*

Holly **can** skate fast.	*Holly **kann** schnell skaten.*
Dave **can't** meet Luke.	*Dave **kann** sich **nicht** mit Luke treffen.*

– *Mit **can** kannst du aber auch eine **Erlaubnis** und mit **can't** ein **Verbot** ausdrücken. Im Deutschen benutzt du dafür die Verben **können** oder **dürfen**.*

You **can** call me Jay.	*Du **kannst/darfst** Jay zu mir sagen.*
We **can't** use phones at school.	*Wir **dürfen** in der Schule **keine** Handys benutzen.*

– Can *und* can't *sind **in allen Personen gleich**:*

I	**can** / **can't**	show Jay the school.	*Ich kann …*
You		pay here.	*Du kannst …*
He/She/It		go fast.	*Er/Sie/Es kann …*
We		use computers in the break.	*Wir dürfen/können …*
You		go into the Art room now.	*Ihr dürft/könnt … / Sie dürfen/können …*
They		buy sweets at school.	*Sie können …*

– **Can** *kannst du auch in* ***Entscheidungsfragen*** *verwenden. Damit bittest du um Erlaubnis oder fragst, ob jemand etwas kann. Meist werden sie mit einer Kurzantwort beantwortet.*

Can I go into the computer room alone?	– Yes, you **can**./No, you **can't**.
Kann/Darf *ich allein in den Computerraum gehen?*	– ***Ja***./***Nein***.
Can Jay sing?	– Yes, he **can**./No, he **can't**.
Kann *Jay singen?*	– ***Ja***./***Nein***.

AUFGABE **a)** *Überprüfe, ob du* can *und* can't *richtig verwenden kannst.*

1. *Sage, dass ihr in der Cafeteria Süßigkeiten kaufen könnt.*
2. *Sage, dass ihr im Klassenzimmer nicht essen dürft.*
3. *Sage, dass ihr keine Haustiere mit in die Schule bringen dürft.*
4. *Sage, dass du Badminton spielen kannst.*

b) *Überprüft, ob ihr Entscheidungsfragen richtig stellen und mit Kurzantworten beantworten könnt. Wechselt euch ab.*

1. *Frage, ob dir deine Partnerin/dein Partner die Cafeteria zeigen kann.*
2. *Frage, ob du ihr/sein Lineal benutzen kannst.*
3. *Frage, ob deine Freundin/dein Freund das Handy deiner Partnerin/deines Partners benutzen kann.*
4. *Frage, ob deine Partnerin/dein Partner skaten kann.*

G15 *Der Imperativ*

Seiten 39–40 **The imperative**

FUNKTION

> *Mit dem Imperativ kannst du jemanden auffordern, etwas zu tun oder nicht zu tun.*

REGEL

– *Der Imperativ sieht immer gleich aus, nämlich wie die Grundform (Infinitiv) eines Verbs:* **Look** at this! **Come** here. **Be** polite.

– *Der verneinte Imperativ besteht aus* **Don't** *und dem Infinitiv des Verbs und sieht immer gleich aus, egal, wie viele Personen du ansprichst:*
Don't forget your planner. **Don't bring** your phone to school, please.

> *Bei Verboten – sei ganz Ohr – setz einfach ein* don't *davor.*

AUFGABE *Überprüfe, ob du den Imperativ und den verneinten Imperativ richtig bilden kannst.*

1. *Sage einer Person, dass sie ihren Namen aufschreiben soll.*
2. *Sage deinen beiden Klassenkameraden hinter oder vor dir, dass sie ihre Hausaufgaben nicht vergessen sollen.*
3. *Sage einer Person, dass sie nicht unhöflich sein soll.*

G16 *Die Besitzform bei Nomen und Namen (Der s-Genitiv)*

Seite 41 The possessive form of nouns and names (The s-genitive)

FUNKTION

> *Die Besitzform bei Nomen und Namen zeigt an, dass etwas zu jemandem gehört.*

This is **Luke's** room.

This is the **Elliots'** house.

REGEL

- *Du bildest die Besitzform von Nomen oder Namen im Singular, die Personen oder Tiere bezeichnen, durch Anhängen von* **'s** *(Apostroph + s):*
  Luke**'s** house, Olivia**'s** house, the girl**'s** house, the teacher**'s** house.
- *Endet das Nomen oder der Name auf* **-s** *(wenn es z. B. eine Pluralform ist), bildest du die Besitzform durch Anhängen von* **'** *(Apostroph):*
  The Elliots**'** house, the girls**'** house, James**'** house.

! *Wenn mehrere Namen stehen, wird das* **'s** *nur an den letzten angehängt:*
Mr Swindon is Luke and Dave**'s** teacher.

AUFGABE *Überprüfe, ob du die Besitzform richtig schreiben kannst.*

1. This is the (Elliots) house.
2. Sherlock is (Luke) dog.
3. Olivia is (Holly) friend.
4. Don't sit at the (girls) table, Jay!
5. Mr Swindon is (Holly and Olivia) teacher.

G17 *Die Besitzform mit of*

Seite 42 The possessive form with *of*

FUNKTION

> *Die Besitzform mit* **of** *zeigt an, dass etwas zu einer Sache gehört.*

REGEL

- *Zugehörigkeit zu Personen oder Tieren wird in der Regel mit dem s-Genitiv (→ G14) ausgedrückt, Zugehörigkeit zu Sachen dagegen meist mit* **of**.

AUFGABE *Bilde Sätze. Entscheide, ob du die Besitzform mit of oder den s-Genitiv verwenden musst:*

1. this / is / end / lesson
2. Z / is / last letter / alphabet
3. dog / Luke / is / black and white
4. house / Elliots / is / small
5. colour / door / is / green
6. name / street / is / Brook Lane

G18 *Die Demonstrativpronomen* this / that *und* these / those

Seite 42 The demonstrative pronouns *this / that* and *these / those*

FUNKTION *Um auf Personen oder Dinge hinzuweisen, benutzt du* **this / that** *bzw.* **these / those**.

REGEL

- *Um auf eine Person oder Sache in der Nähe hinzuweisen, benutzt du* this.
  Um auf eine weiter entfernte Person oder Sache hinzuweisen, benutzt du that.
  That *wird oft mit der Kurzform verwendet:*
  This is our table. **That's** the boys' table over there.
- *Wenn du zwei Personen oder Dinge einander gegenüberstellen willst, benutzt du bei der ersten Person oder Sache* this, *bei der zweiten* that:
  This is Honey, and **that** is Mr Fluff.
- *Der Plural von* this *ist* these, *und der Plural von* that *ist* those:
  These books are new, but **those** books are old.
- *Die Demonstrativpronomen* this, that, these *und* those *können entweder alleine stehen (anstelle eines Nomens oder Pronomens) oder als Begleiter vor einem Nomen:* **This** is Pia. **This** girl is nice.

AUFGABE *Überprüfe, ob du weißt, wann du welche Form verwenden musst.*

1. *[1] is my new friend Holly. [2] girl over there is Amber, her sister.*
2. *[3] pen is blue, and [4] pen is green.*
3. *[5] are my skates. Is [6] your new skateboard?*
4. *Who's [7] new boy at Luke and Dave's table?*
5. *I like [8] house. [9] houses at the end of the street aren't nice.*
6. *What's on [10] photo? Can I look at it?*

Unit 3

G19 *Die einfache Form der Gegenwart*

Seiten 52–57 The simple present

FUNKTION

Du verwendest das simple present, *um …*

- *auszudrücken, dass jemand etwas regelmäßig, aus Gewohnheit, oft, manchmal oder nie macht:* I (always) **go** to school by bike.
- *allgemeingültige Aussagen bzw. Aussagen über Zustände zu machen:* Cats **like** mice. I'**m** a student.
- *zu erzählen, was der Reihe nach passiert, z. B. in einer Geschichte:*
- Dave is at home alone today. He **plays** computer games. Then he **hears** something outside. What can it be? He **goes** to the door and **listens**.

Hi,
My name is Dave. I'm eleven. I **go** to Thomas Tallis School. I always **go** to school by bike. Luke is my friend. He usually **goes** to school by bus,

REGEL

- *Bei* I, you, we *und* they *gleicht das Verb der Grundform (Infinitiv).*
- *Nur bei* **he**, **she** *und* **it** *(3. Person Singular) wird an den Infinitiv des Verbs ein* **s** *angehängt.*

I You	play	netball on Tuesdays.
He/She/It	play**s**	with mice.
We You They	play	netball on Tuesdays.

He, she it, *das „s" muss mit.*

Das Verb be *hat mehr als zwei Formen:* am/is/are *(→ G2). Die Formen von* have *lauten* have/has *(→ G8).*

! *Bei einigen Verben musst du bei der 3. Person Singular* **-es** *anhängen:* go – he/she/it go**es**. *Das gilt auch für Verben, die auf Zischlaut enden:* watch – he/she/it watch**es**.

! *Wenn das Verb auf Konsonant +* **-y** *endet, schreibst du es in der 3. Person Singular mit* **ie** *und hängst dann das* **s** *an:* tidy – he/she/it tid**ies**. *Das* y *wird aber nicht ersetzt, wenn es nach einem Vokal steht:* play – he/she/it pl**ay**s.

AUFGABE *Überprüfe, ob du das* simple present *richtig bilden kannst.*

1. *Sage, dass du deine Freunde täglich triffst.*
2. *Sage, dass du dienstags in den Fußballverein gehst.*
3. *Sage, dass deine Freundin/dein Freund Saxofon spielt.*
4. *Sage, dass deine Freundin/dein Freund abends fernsieht.*
5. *Sage, dass du und deine Schwester freitags euer Zimmer aufräumt.*

G20 *Die Satzstellung in Aussagesätzen*

Seiten 52–54

Word order in statements

FUNKTION

Die Wortstellung in englischen Aussagesätzen ist strikt festgelegt, um Missverständnisse zu vermeiden.

REGEL

- *Im Aussagesatz steht zuerst das Subjekt, dann folgt die Verbform und oft auch noch ein Objekt.*
- *Du kannst eine Orts- oder Zeitangabe ergänzen. Diese steht meist am Satzende.*
- *Enthält der Satz eine Orts- und eine Zeitangabe, steht zuerst der Ort und dann die Zeit – genau wie im Alphabet:* **O** *vor* **Z***:*
  I meet my friends **in the park** **on Sundays**.
- *Für Richtungsangaben gilt dasselbe wie für Ortsangaben.*
- *Zeitangaben können aber auch am Satzanfang stehen, oft zur Betonung.*

Zeit	*Subjekt*	*Verb*	*Objekt*	*Ort*	*Zeit*
	Dave	plays	computer games		**after school.**
	Luke	listens to	music	**on the bus**	**in the mornings.**
On Sundays	I	meet	my friends	**in the park.**	

❗ *Orts- oder Zeitangaben stehen im Englischen niemals zwischen Verb und Objekt.*
Vergleiche: Olivia always **plays netball** **on Tuesdays**.
Olivia ***spielt*** ***dienstags*** *immer* ***Korbball***.

AUFGABE *Überprüfe, ob du die Regeln zur Satzstellung richtig verstanden hast.*

1. *Sage, dass du jeden Morgen um 7 Uhr aufstehst.*
2. *Sage, dass du in der Küche frühstückst.*
3. *Sage, dass du den Bus um 7:45 Uhr nimmst.*
4. *Sage, dass du nach der Schule zum Fußballverein gehst.*
5. *Sage, dass du abends hundemüde bist.*

G21 *Häufigkeitsadverbien*

Seiten 52–54 Adverbs of frequency

FUNKTION

Die Wörter **always, usually, often, sometimes** *und* **never** *nennt man Häufigkeitsadverbien. Mit ihnen kannst du ausdrücken, wie oft etwas passiert.*

REGEL

– *Häufigkeitsadverbien stehen vor dem Vollverb:*

Subjekt	*Häufigkeitsadverb*	*Vollverb*	
I	**always**	go	to school by bike.
She	**usually**	goes	
We	**never**	go	
They	**sometimes**	go	

– *Das Häufigkeitsadverb steht nach dem Verb* be *bzw. nach einem Hilfsverb wie* can:

Subjekt	*be / Hilfsverb*	*Häufigkeitsadverb*	*Vollverb*	
Olivia and Holly	are	**never**		***late for school.***
They	can	**usually**	eat	***lunch at school.***
They	can't	**always**	go	***outside at break.***

– *Bei* have got *steht das Häufigkeitsadverb zwischen* have *und* got*:* Olivia **has never got** time.

– *In verneinten Sätzen steht* sometimes *immer vor* be *bzw. dem Hilfsverb:*
Sherlock **sometimes isn't** very nice to cats.
Jay **sometimes can't** go out on Saturday.

! *Häufigkeitsadverbien stehen im Englischen niemals zwischen Verb und Objekt.*
Vergleiche: Olivia always **plays netball on Tuesdays**.
*Olivia **spielt** dienstags **immer Korbball**.*

AUFGABE *Überprüfe, ob du die Häufigkeitsadverbien richtig verwenden kannst. Erzähle vom Alltag der Katze Sid.*

1. *Sage, dass Sid immer sein Frühstück mag.*
2. *Sage, dass er normalerweise im Haus ist.*
3. *Sage, dass er manchmal draußen spielt.*
4. *Sage, dass er abends oft rausgeht.*

Unit 4

G22 *Entscheidungsfragen und Kurzantworten mit* do/does

Seiten 72–75

Yes/No questions and short answers with *do/does*

Dave: **Do you know** the Cutty Sark museum?
Jay: **No, I don't. Does it** open on Sundays?
Dave: **Yes, it does.** Let's go there together!

FUNKTION

Entscheidungsfragen mit **do** *oder* **does** *verwendest du, um zu fragen,* ***ob*** *jemand etwas tut. Im Deutschen beantwortest du solche Fragen mit „ja" oder „nein". Im Englischen klingen „yes" und „no" allein unhöflich. Deshalb ist es besser, sie mit einem kurzen Satz (= Kurzantwort) zu beantworten.*

REGEL

- *Entscheidungsfragen und Kurzantworten mit* be, can *und* have got *kennst du schon:*
  Are you from England? – Yes, **I am**. / No, **I'm not**.
  Can you help me? – Yes, **I can**. / No, **I can't**.
  Has he **got** a bike? – Yes, **he has**. / No, **he hasn't**.
- *Um Entscheidungsfragen und Kurzantworten mit anderen Verben zu bilden, verwendest du das Hilfsverb* do. *Die Entscheidungsfrage beginnt mit dem* ***Hilfsverb****. Danach folgen* ***Subjekt*** – ***Vollverb*** *und, falls vorhanden, Objekt – Ort – Zeit.*
- *Die Kurzantwort wird mit dem Hilfsverb am Anfang der Frage gebildet, hier also* do *bzw.* don't*:*

Entscheidungsfrage				*Kurzantwort*	
Hilfsverb	*Subjekt*	*Vollverb im Infinitiv*		+	–
Do	**you**	**like**	water slides?	Yes, **I do**. Yes, **we do**.	No, **I don't**. No, **we don't**.
Does	**Dave**	**eat**	sweets?	Yes, **he does**.	No, **he doesn't**.
Do	**they**	**live**	in Greenwich?	Yes, **they do**.	No, **they don't**.

❗ *Achte auch hier wieder auf die 3. Person Singular.*

❗ *Verwende niemals* do/does *in Fragen mit einer Form von* be *oder einem Hilfsverb wie* can*!*
Nicht: ~~Do you be~~ in the kitchen?,
sondern: **Are** you in the kitchen?
Nicht: ~~Does she can~~ play tennis?,
sondern: **Can** she play tennis?

AUFGABE *Überprüft, ob ihr Entscheidungsfragen richtig stellen und beantworten könnt. Stellt euch gegenseitig folgende Fragen und beantwortet sie.*

1. *Frage deine Partnerin/deinen Partner, ob sie/er Greenwich Park kennt.*
2. *Frage, ob sie/er Inliner mag.*
3. *Frage, ob ihr/sein Vater/Bruder Museen mag.*
4. *Frage, ob ihre/seine Freunde Fußball spielen.*
5. *Frage, ob ihre/seine Mutter aus England kommt.*
6. *Frage, ob sie/er Badminton spielen kann.*

G23 *Verneinte Aussagesätze in der einfachen Gegenwart*

Seiten 72–75

Negative statements in the simple present

FUNKTION

Mit **don't** *oder* **doesn't** *kannst du sagen, dass jemand etwas* ***nicht*** *tut oder dass etwas* ***nicht*** *geschieht.*

We **don't** get up very early on Sundays.

REGEL

- *Diese Verneinungen durch angehängtes* not *(bzw.* n't*) kennst du schon:*

+	−
I **can** dance. She**'s** English. We**'re** at Thomas Tallis School. They**'ve got** time.	I **can't** dance. She **isn't** English. We **aren't** at Thomas Tallis School. They **haven't got** time.

- *Wenn ein Satz kein Hilfsverb (z.B.* can*) und keine Form von* be *oder* have got *enthält, musst du eine Form von* **do** *und* **not** *und den* ***Infinitv des Verbs*** *verwenden, um ihn zu verneinen. Dabei musst du wieder bei der 3. Person Singular aufpassen, denn das* **s** *wandert vom Vollverb zum Hilfsverb:*

Subjekt	*Hilfsverb + not*	*Vollverb im Infinitiv*	*Objekt*
I	don't	like	dogs.
You	don't	like	dogs.
He/She/It	**doesn't**	like	dogs.
We	don't	like	dogs.
You	don't	like	dogs.
They	don't	like	dogs.

- **Do** *wird manchmal* ***als Vollverb*** *verwendet. Das erkennst du daran, dass im Satz kein weiteres Vollverb vorkommt. In diesem Fall wird* do *auch mit* don't/doesn't *verneint:*
  I **don't do** my homework alone.
- *Denke daran, dass du* don't/doesn't ***nicht*** *zur Verneinung brauchst, wenn im Satz …*
  - *eine Form von* be *steht:* I**'m not** in the museum. / She **isn't** in the museum. / We **aren't** in the museum. *(Nicht:* I ~~don't be~~ in the museum.*)*
  - *ein Hilfsverb wie* can *steht:* I **can't play** football. *(Nicht:* I ~~don't can~~ play football.*)*

Vorsicht bei have got *und bei* have *als Vollverb:*
Have you **got** time?
– I **haven't got** time.
Do you **have** lunch at school?
– I **don't have** lunch at school.

AUFGABE *Überprüfe, ob du Aussagen richtig verneinen kannst.*

1. *Sage, dass du nicht mit dem Fahrrad zur Schule fährst.*
2. *Sage, dass dein Bruder dir nicht bei den Hausaufgaben helfen kann.*
3. *Sage, dass du nicht jeden Tag Sport machst.*
4. *Sage, dass du kein Haustier hast.*
5. *Sage, dass deine Freundin/dein Freund keine Katzen mag.*
6. *Sage, dass Mudchute Farm nicht in Greenwich ist.*

G24 *Objektformen der Personalpronomen*

Seiten 74–75

The object forms of personal pronouns

FUNKTION

*Die Subjektformen der Personalpronomen (*I, you, he, …*) kennst du schon (→ G2). Die Objektformen benötigst du, wenn das Pronomen Objekt (Wem?/Wen oder was?) des Satzes ist.*

REGEL

- *Personalpronomen gibt es als Subjekt des Satzes (***I** love rabbits.*)* *oder als Objekt des Satzes (*Rabbits love **me**.*).*
- **It** *und* **you** *können Subjekt oder Objekt des Satzes sein. Alle anderen Pronomen haben eine Subjekt- und eine Objektform.*

Subjektform	*Objektform*
I love rabbits.	Rabbits love **me**.
Can **you** do your homework?	I can help **you**.
He is a nice boy.	I like **him**.
Where is **she**?	Can I talk to **her**?
Where is Greenwich? – **It**'s in England.	You spell **it** with a 'w'.
We want to go to Mudchute Farm.	Holly can come with **us**.
Do **you** want to go swimming, Jay and Luke?	I can take **you** in the car.
They like the park.	You can see **them** in the park.

– *Im Gegensatz zum Deutschen gibt es im Englischen nur eine Objektform des Personalpronomens:*
Can you help **me**? *Kannst du* ***mir*** *helfen?*
Look at **me**. *Schau* ***mich*** *an!*

! *Beachte die verschiedenen Entsprechungen für das deutsche „sie" bzw. „Sie":*

a) *Personalpronomen weiblich/Singular:*
This is Lucy. **She** likes animals. ***Sie*** *mag … = Lucy*

b) *Nomen ist im Deutschen weiblich:*
This is a cat. **It** is black. ***Sie*** *ist … = die Katze*

c) *3. Person Singular, als Objekt:*
Olivia knows the way. You can ask ***her***. *Du kannst* ***sie*** *…*

d) *2. Person Plural, Höflichkeitsform als Objekt:*
I can't hear **you**, Mr Swindon. *Ich kann* ***Sie*** *…*

e) *3. Person Plural, als Objekt:*
I can ask **them** later. *Ich kann* ***sie*** *…*

AUFGABE *Überprüfe, ob du die Objektpronomen richtig verwenden kannst. Vervollständige diese Sätze.*

1. Holly: I've got two guinea pigs at home. I like (*sie*) and they like (*mich*).
2. Luke: I don't usually like museums – but Cutty Sark is different. Do you know (*es*)?
3. Dave: Greenwich is great! I love (*es*). There are lots of boats. You can watch (*sie*) on the Thames.
4. Jay: Where's Dave? I want to talk to (*ihm*) about Sunday.
   Dave: I'm here. But I haven't got time now. Can I call (*dich*) later?
5. Olivia: Mudchute Farm is great! You can sometimes help with the animals there. You can play with (*sie*). I want to go there with my family. Lucy likes animals and they like (*sie*).
6. Lucy and Olivia: Can you take a photo of (*uns*), please?
   Claire: OK, girls. Look at (*mich*). Cheese …

G25 *Fragen mit Fragewörtern und* do/does

Seite 78 Questions with question words and *do/does*

FUNKTION

Mit Fragewörtern wie **who, what, when, where, why** *und* **how** *fragst du nach bestimmten Informationen.*

FAQs MUDCHUTE PARK & FARM

Q: How do you get to Mudchute Farm?
A: You can get there by DLR, by bike or on foot.

Q: What does it cost?
A: It's free to visit.

Q: When does the farm open?
A: It opens at 8:00 a.m. every day.

REGEL

- *Fragen mit* be, can *und* have got *kennst du schon:*
  Where is your house?
  When can we meet?
  What have you **got** in your bag?
- *Wenn du Fragen mit anderen Verben als* be, have got *oder* can *stellen möchtest, brauchst du nach dem Fragewort das Hilfsverb* do.

Die Wortstellung nach dem Fragewort entspricht der von Entscheidungsfragen (→ G20).

Fragewort	*Hilfsverb*	*Subjekt*	*Vollverb*
What	**do**	**Luke and Jay**	**like**?
They like **swimming**.			
When	**does**	**Olivia**	**go** to sax lessons?
She goes to sax lessons **on Thursdays**.			
Where	**does**	**Luke**	usually **play** football?
He usually plays football **in Greenwich Park**.			
Why	**does**	**Sherlock**	**like** Greenwich Park?
He likes Greenwich Park **because he can meet other dogs there**.			
How	**do**	**I**	**get** to the Cutty Sark museum?
You can go **by bus** or **by boat**.			

- **Do** *wird manchmal* ***als Vollverb*** *verwendet:*
  What **does** Luke **do** on Sundays? – He goes to Greenwich Park with Sherlock.
- *Fragen mit Fragewörtern funktionieren nur dann wie im Deutschen, wenn nach dem* ***Subjekt*** *gefragt wird:* **Who likes** pizza? **What looks** like a ship and is a museum? (Siehe auch → G11.)
  Pass daher auf bei:

Who likes you?	**Who do** you **like**?
Wer (Subjekt) mag *dich?*	***Wen (Objekt) magst*** *du?*

AUFGABE *Überprüfe, ob du Fragen richtig stellen kannst. Stelle dir vor, du bist als Tourist in Greenwich. Stelle einem Einheimischen folgende Fragen und ordne seine Antworten zu.*

1. *Frage, wo der See ist, auf dem du Boot fahren kannst.*
2. *Frage, wie du zum Greenwich Park kommst.*
3. *Frage, was du in Greenwich Park machen kannst.*
4. *Frage, wann das Royal Observatory samstags öffnet.*
5. *Frage, wer das ist.*
6. *Frage, warum er in Greenwich wohnt.*

It's in Greenwich Park. — *Oh, that's my dog. Her name is Molly.* — *It opens at 10 o'clock.* — *You can walk there. It's over there.* — *Because it's a nice part of London. I work here.* — *You can go to the boating lake, play football or visit the Royal Observatory.*

Unit 5

G26 *Mengenangaben mit of*

Seiten 87–88

Expressions of quantity with *of*

FUNKTION *Viele Lebensmittel werden in Verpackungseinheiten verkauft, z. B. eine* ***Flasche*** *Wasser, eine* ***Packung*** *Kekse. Um solche Verpackungseinheiten im Englischen wiederzugeben, brauchst du das Wort* **of**.

zählbare Dinge	
I've got **two** **biscuits** for Sherlock.	*zwei Kekse*
Jay and his brother sometimes eat **a packet of** **biscuits** after school.	*eine Packung Kekse*
Olivia never eats **two bags of** **sweets**.	*zwei Tüten Bonbons*
nicht zählbare Dinge	
Olivia usually has **a bottle of** **water** with her lunch.	*eine Flasche Wasser*
Luke always drinks **two glasses of** **orange juice** in the morning.	*zwei Gläser Orangensaft*

REGEL – *Du kannst die genaue Menge von* ***zählbaren Dingen*** *durch eine Zahl angeben, z. B.:* **two** **biscuits**.

- ***Bei* nicht zählbaren Dingen** *wie Wasser brauchst du* ***immer ein Mengenwort****,*
  d. h. ein Behältnis, eine Verpackung, eine Maßangabe oder ein Gewicht.
  Danach folgt *im Englischen das Wort* **of**, *z. B.:* a bottle of **water**.
- *Die Mengenwörter kannst du auch vor zählbaren Dingen benutzen, z. B.:*
  They eat **a packet of biscuits** after school.

In Cafés und Restaurants wirst du manchmal auch hören:
Two cokes, please. (*Statt:* Two cans of coke, please.)
Two orange juices, please. (*Statt:* Two glasses of orange juice, please.)

! *Beachte folgenden Unterschied:* *zwei Kilogramm Zucker* — two kilogram**s** of sugar
drei Stück Kuchen — three piece**s** of cake

AUFGABE *Überprüfe, ob du die Mengenangaben richtig verwenden kannst. Sage, was Lukes Mutter alles im Einkaufswagen hat.*

G27 *Die Verlaufsform der Gegenwart*

Seiten 88–90 The present progressive

FUNKTION

Das present progressive *verwendest du, um zu sagen, was* ***jetzt gerade*** *passiert. Die Handlung ist* ***im Verlauf****, also zum Zeitpunkt des Sprechens* ***noch nicht abgeschlossen****. Zur Erinnerung: das* simple present *verwendest du, um zu sagen, was immer, manchmal, oft oder nie passiert, oder um über aufeinanderfolgende Handlungen zu sprechen (→ G17).*

Hi Mum.

Hi Dave.
Where are you?
What **are** you **doing**?

I'**m sitting** outside a café with Luke, Olivia and Holly.

REGEL – *Du bildest das* present progressive *aus einer* ***Form von*** **be** ***+ ing-Form des Verbs****.*
Die ing*-Form bildest du aus dem Infinitiv durch Anhängen von* -ing.

I	**'m** walk**ing**	to the café.
You	**'re** walk**ing**	
He/She/It	**'s** walk**ing**	
We/You/ They	**'re** walk**ing**	

Wenn du im deutschen Satz die Wörter jetzt (now), *jetzt gerade* (just) *oder momentan/im Augenblick* (at the moment) *benutzt, benutzt du im englischen Satz für andauernde Handlungen oder Vorgänge das* present progressive.

❗ *Wenn ein Verb auf ein stummes* **e** *endet, entfällt das* **e**, *z. B.:*
come → coming, have → having, organise → organising, write → writing.

❗ *Endet ein Verb auf kurzen Vokal + Konsonant, so wird der Konsonant verdoppelt, z. B.:*
get → getting, put → putting, run → running, sit → sitting, swim → swimming.

REGEL

– *Die* ***verneinte Form*** *des* present progressive *bildest du aus einer* ***Form von be + not + ing-Form des Verbs***:
I**'m not reading** a book, I'm reading a magazine.
He/She/It **isn't playing** in the garden.
You/We/They **aren't sitting** in a café.

Im Deutschen gibst du die Verlaufsform oft wieder durch:
– dabei sein, etwas zu tun,
– gerade etwas tun,
– am / beim … sein.

– ***Entscheidungsfragen*** *beginnst du im* present progressive *mit der* ***Form von be***.
Danach folgt das ***Subjekt*** *und die* **ing-Form** *des Verbs:*
Is she drinking a glass of orange juice? – Yes, she is. / No, she isn't.
Are you eating burgers? – Yes, I am. / No, I'm not.
– Yes, we are. / No, we aren't.

– *In* ***Fragen mit Fragewort*** *steht zuerst das Fragewort. Danach verwendest du dieselbe Wortstellung wie in Entscheidungsfragen:*
What **is your dad doing** today? – He's clearing out the garage.
What **are you drinking**? – I'm drinking a glass of water.

AUFGABE **a)** *Überprüfe, ob du das* present progressive *richtig anwenden kannst. Es ist Mittwochabend. Was machen die Leute gerade bzw. was machen sie nicht?*

1. *Sage, dass Olivia gerade Saxofon spielt.*
2. *Sage, dass Jay gerade singt und tanzt.*
3. *Sage, dass Holly und Amber gerade ihre Hausaufgaben machen.*
4. *Sage, dass Luke und Jamie momentan nicht im Garten Fußball spielen.*
5. *Sage, dass Dave im Augenblick nicht Computer spielt.*

b) *Was machen die Leute auf dem Flohmarkt gerade? Schaut euch das Bild an. Stellt euch gegenseitig Fragen und beantwortet sie. Zum Beispiel:*

A: Is Holly talking to Jay?
B: No, she isn't. She's holding a yellow T-shirt.

G28 *Die Mengenwörter* some, any *und* no

Seiten 91–92 The quantifiers *some, any* and *no*

FUNKTION

> **Some** *und* **any** *verwendest du, wenn du keine genauen Mengenangaben machen kannst.*
>
> *Mit* **not … any** *oder* **no** *drückst du aus, dass nichts vorhanden ist. Im Deutschen benutzt du dafür „kein / keine".*

REGEL

- Some, (not …) any *und* no *kannst du vor zählbaren Nomen im Plural (z. B.* toys, books*) und vor nicht zählbaren Nomen (z. B.* money, clothes*) verwenden.*
- **Some** *benutzt du, um zu sagen, dass etwas vorhanden ist:*
  There are **some** old toys in Dave's bedroom. *In Daves Zimmer sind* ***einige*** *…*
  Luke needs **some** money for shoes. *Luke braucht* ***etwas/ein wenig*** *…*
- **Some** *kannst du auch in höflichen Bitten, Angeboten oder Vorschlägen benutzen, wenn du eine positive Antwort erwartest:*

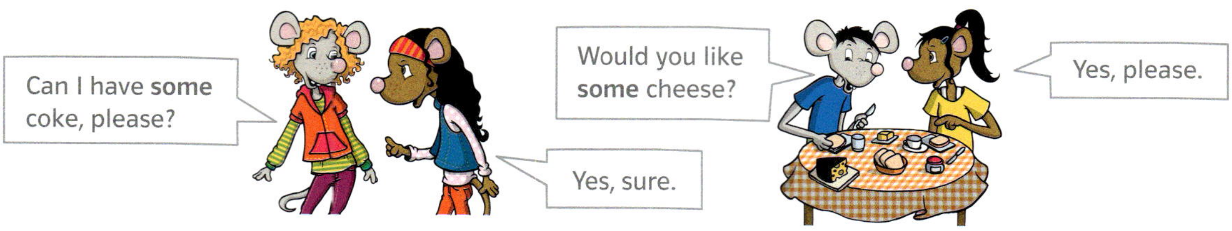

- **Any** *benutzt du in Fragen und zur Verneinung:*
  Luke: Have you got **any** DVDs or books to sell? *Hast du (****ein paar****) DVDs …*
  Jay: No, I have**n't** got **any** old DVDs or books. *Nein, ich habe* ***keine*** *…*
  Luke has**n't** got **any** money for new shoes. *Luke hat* ***kein*** *…*
- *Statt* not … any, *kannst du auch* no *verwenden:*
  There are**n't any** skates here. = There are **no** skates here.
- *Im Deutschen haben Sätze mit* some *und* any *oft eine Entsprechung ohne Mengenangabe.*
  Vergleiche: I need **some** money. *Ich brauche Geld.*
  Have you got **any** DVDs? *Haben Sie DVDs?*

AUFGABE *Vervollständige den Dialog mit den Mengenwörtern* some *und* any.

Peter: Have you got 1 plans for the weekend?
Joe: There's a flea market on Sunday. I'd like to sell 2 toys and books there to earn 3 extra pocket money.
Peter: That's a good idea. like flea markets. Would you like 4 help?
Joe: Oh, that's nice of you. Have you got 5 things to sell?
Peter: Well, not really. But my parents have got 6 old glasses and pictures. They want to sell them. Let's get a table together. Maybe my parents can help us.

G29 *Zusammensetzungen mit* some, any, every *und* no

Seite 92 Compounds with *some, any, every* and *no*

FUNKTION

Mit Zusammensetzungen von **some, any, every** *und* **no** *bezeichnest du nicht genauer bestimmte Personen oder Dinge.*

REGEL

- *Wie* **some** *und* **any** *werden auch ihre Zusammensetzungen verwendet (→ G26):*

Aussage	*Frage*	*Verneinte Aussage*
There is always **somebody** / **someone** there.	Does **anybody / anyone** want to buy these shoes?	I do**n't** want to ask **anybody** / **anyone**.
I want **something** cheap.	Is there **anything** on the table?	I ca**n't** see **anything**.

- *Zusammensetzungen mit* some *können in höflichen Bitten, Antworten und Vorschlägen verwendet werden, auf die eine positive Antwort erwartet wird:* Would you like **something** to eat?

***Bedeutung der Zusammensetzungen mit* some, any, every *und* no:**	
somebody / someone, anybody / anyone	*(irgend)jemand*
something, anything	*(irgend)etwas*
everybody / everyone	*jeder, alle*
everything	*alles*
nobody / no one	*niemand, keiner*
nothing	*nichts*

! *Wenn Zusammensetzungen mit* any *verneint werden, ändert sich die Übersetzung:* I do**n't** want to ask **anybody** *(= niemanden).*

! *Verwechsle* **any** *(= jede/-r/-s beliebige) nicht mit* **every** *(= jede/-r/-s ohne Ausnahme):*
Anyone can do that! *Das kann doch jeder (beliebige Mensch)!*
Everyone gets a role card. *Jeder bekommt (= alle bekommen) ein Rollenkärtchen.*

AUFGABE *Überprüfe, ob du die zusammengesetzten Formen richtig verwenden kannst.*

1. *Sage, dass alles in Ordnung ist.*
2. *Sage, dass gerade nichts passiert.*
3. *Frage, ob irgendjemand ein Spiel verkaufen will.*
4. *Frage eine Person, ob sie jemanden hier kennt.*
5. *Sage, dass du vielleicht auf dem Flohmarkt etwas finden kannst.*

G30 *Die Mengenwörter* much, many *und* a lot of

Seiten 91–92 The quantifiers *much, many* and *a lot of*

FUNKTION

Mit **a lot of, (not) many** *und* **(not) much** *drückst du aus, dass viel oder wenig von etwas vorhanden ist.*

Um zu fragen, wie viel von etwas vorhanden ist, verwendest du **how much** *oder* **how many**.

Cool! There are **a lot of** toys on the table.

There aren't **many** things on the table.

How much money have we got?

REGEL

- **A lot of** *verwendest du, um zu sagen, dass* **viel von etwas vorhanden** *ist. Du kannst es* **vor allen Nomen** *benutzen, egal ob sie in einem Aussagesatz oder in einer Frage stehen:*
  - We drink **a lot of orange juice** at home.
    Wir trinken zu Hause ***viel*** *Orangensaft.*
  - My friend does**n't** get **a lot of pocket money**.
    Mein Freund bekommt ***nicht viel*** *Taschengeld.*
  - Has your brother got **a lot of books**?
    Hat dein Bruder ***viele/eine Menge*** *Bücher?*

A lot of *und* lots of *sind bedeutungsgleich.*

- **Much** *oder* **many** *benutzt du hauptsächlich* ***in Fragen oder zur Verneinung***.
  - **Much** *verwendest du* ***vor nicht zählbaren Nomen im Singular***:
    Peter: **How much money** do you want for that bike?
    Joe: I do**n't** want **much money**.
  - **Many** *verwendest du* ***vor zählbaren Nomen im Plural***:
    Peter: **How many DVDs** have you got?
    Joe: I have**n't** got **many DVDs**.
- *Nach* a lot of, not much *und* not many *kannst du das Nomen in der Antwort weglassen.*
  How many books have you got?
  - **Not many.** *(Statt:* I haven't got many books.*)*
  - **A lot./Lots.** *(Statt:* I've got a lot of books.*)*

  How much money have you got?
  - **Not much.** *(Statt:* I haven't got much money.*)*
  - **A lot./Lots.** *(Statt:* I've got a lot of money.*)*

Oft wirst du die Kombinationen **too much** *(zu viel) und* **so much** *(so viel) sehen.*

In verkürzten Antworten entfällt **of** *in* a lot of *und* lots of.

AUFGABE *Überprüft, ob ihr* much *und* many *richtig verwenden könnt. Stellt euch gegenseitig folgende Fragen. Wählt eine passende Antwort:* A lot. Not much. Not many.

Fragt euch gegenseitig, …
… wie viel Taschengeld ihr bekommt.
… wie viele Hausaufgaben ihr bekommt.
… wie viel Freizeit ihr habt.
… wie viele Bücher ihr habt.
… wie viele Freunde ihr habt.

G31 *Die Mengenwörter* a few, a little *und* a couple of

Seiten 91–92 The quantifiers *a few, a little* and *a couple of*

FUNKTION

Mit den Mengenwörtern **a few, a couple of** *und* **a little** *kannst du ausdrücken, dass „einige", „ein paar" oder „ein bisschen" von etwas vorhanden sind.*

REGEL

- **A few** *und* **a couple of** *haben fast die gleiche Bedeutung.*
  Du verwendest sie ***vor zählbaren Dingen oder Personen im Plural***:
  - Mr Elliott: There are **a few** toy**s** here. *… **ein paar** Spielsachen.*
    Luke: They must be worth **a couple of** pound**s**. *… **ein paar** Pfund.*
  - I'm at the flea market with **a few** friend**s**. *… **ein paar** Freunden.*
- **A little** *verwendest du* ***vor nicht zählbaren Nomen im Singular***:
  - Jay has got **a little time**. *… **ein bisschen** Zeit.*
  - They have got **a little money** in their money box. *… **etwas** Geld.*
- *Nach* a few, a couple of *und* a little *kannst du das Nomen in der Antwort weglassen.*
  Have you got any **toys** at home?
  - Yes, I've got **a few.** *(Statt:* … a few toys at home.*)*
  - Yes, I've got **a couple.** *(Statt:* … a couple of toys at home.*)*
  How much time have you got?
  - **A little.** *(Statt:* … a little time.*)*

AUFGABE *Überprüfe, ob du* a few, a couple of *und* a little *richtig verwenden kannst. Vervollständige diese Sätze.*

1. My dad is clearing out the garage with … friends.
2. I get just … pocket money.
3. It's raining. There are only … people at the flea market.
4. There are … boys and girls at the table. They're looking at the toys.
5. My parents work a lot. But they've got … free time in the evenings.
6. Let's wait … minutes.

Unit 6

G32 *Die Modalverben* can, can't *und* mustn't

Seiten 106–109 The modal auxiliaries *can, can't* and *mustn't*

FUNKTION

Mit **can** *kannst du eine Erlaubnis einholen oder erteilen.*
Mit **Can you ...?** *kannst du jemanden bitten etwas zu tun.*
Mit **can't** *oder* **mustn't** *drückst du ein* **Verbot** *aus.*

Holly: **Can** we watch a film?
Mum: Yes, you can. But you **can't** watch films all night. And you **mustn't** eat too many sweets.
Holly: OK. **Can** you give me some money for new decorations, please?
Mum: Yes, I **can**. Here you are.

REGEL

- *Dass du mit* can *sowohl eine Fähigkeit als auch eine Erlaubnis ausdrücken kannst, hast du schon in* → G12 *gelernt.*
- *Um ein* ***Verbot*** *auszudrücken, kannst du statt* can't *auch* **mustn't** *verwenden:*
  You **mustn't** talk to Holly like that. *Du* ***darfst*** *mit Holly* ***nicht*** *so reden.*
- *Mit der* ***Frage*** **Can you ...?** *leitest du eine höfliche Bitte ein. Du erkennst sie auch am Wort* please. *Solche Fragen werden oft mit einer Kurzantwort beantwortet.*
  Holly: **Can you** make a cake, please? ***Kannst du*** *bitte einen Kuchen backen?*
  Mum: **Yes, I can./No, I can't.** ***Ja./Nein.***
- *Die Modalverben* can, can't *und* mustn't *sind* ***in allen Personen gleich. Du verwendest sie nur für die Gegenwart.***
- *Dem* ***Modalverb*** *folgt immer ein* ***Vollverb*** *im Infinitiv (außer in der Kurzantwort):*
  Holly **can invite** her friends.

Mustn't *bedeutet also nicht „nicht müssen", sondern* ***„nicht dürfen"***.

AUFGABE *Kannst du die Modalverben can, can't und mustn't richtig verwenden? Setze sie ein.*

1. 1 *I invite all my friends, please?*
2. *Four or five* 2 *come, but not all of them.*
3. *I* 3 *make a cake, but I* 4 *prepare dinner because I haven't got much time.*
4. *You* 5 *always be so loud! The neighbours* 6 *sleep.*
5. *You* 7 *spend too much money on sweets, but you* 8 *buy some decorations.*

G33 *Die Modalverben* must *und* needn't

Seiten 106–109 The modal auxiliaries *must* and *needn't*

INVITATION

Dear Pia,

Please come to my pink birthday party.
(You **must** wear something pink!)
It's on Friday 20th May at 5 p.m.

My address is 127 Brook Lane.
Let me know if you can come.

Love, Holly

PS: You **needn't** bring a sleeping bag
but you **must** bring your pyjamas.

FUNKTION

Das Modalverb **needn't** *benutzt du, um zu sagen, dass etwas* ***nicht notwendig*** *ist.*

Das Modalverb **must** *benutzt du, um zu sagen, dass etwas aus Sicht des Sprechers* ***notwendig*** *ist. Damit werden oft Regeln formuliert.*

REGEL – *Genau wie die Modalverben* can, can't *und* mustn't *sind auch* must *und* needn't ***in allen Personen gleich. Du verwendest sie nur für die Gegenwart.***

must	Holly, you **must** tidy your room before the party!	*Holly, du* ***musst*** *dein Zimmer vor der Party aufräumen!*
	Where's my phone? I **must** talk to Olivia.	*… Ich* ***muss*** *(unbedingt) mit Olivia sprechen.*
	You **must** listen to this new song.	*Du* ***musst*** *dir dieses neue Lied anhören.*
needn't	You **needn't** buy candles. I've got some.	*Du* ***brauchst keine*** *Kerzen zu kaufen …*

❗ *Nicht verwechseln!*

I **must** talk to Olivia. — *Ich* ***muss*** *… (Nicht: I* ~~need~~ *talk to Olivia.)*
I **mustn't** talk to Olivia. — *Ich* ***darf nicht*** *…*
I **needn't** talk to Olivia. — *Ich* ***brauche nicht*** *…*

❗ *Im Englischen kann ein Modalverb nicht ohne Vollverb vorkommen (außer in der Kurzantwort).*
Vergleiche: Ich ***muss*** *in die Stadt, um ein Geschenk zu kaufen.*
I **must go** into town to buy a present.

AUFGABE *Überprüfe, ob du die Modalverben* must, mustn't *und* needn't *richtig verwenden kannst. Was sagen die Eltern ihrem Sohn? Vervollständige die Sätze.*

G34 *Die einfache Form der Vergangenheit*

Seiten 110–111 The simple past

FUNKTION

Das simple past *verwendest du, um über Handlungen oder Ereignisse zu sprechen, die zu einer bestimmten Zeit in der Vergangenheit stattgefunden haben und abgeschlossen sind.*

Hi!
You **wanted** to know about my 12th birthday. It **was** great and very pink! I **had** a sleepover party. My friend **gave** me a beautiful T-shirt. My mum **made** a trifle and a cake. GREAT!!!

REGEL

- *Bei der Bildung des* simple past *musst du zwischen regelmäßigen Verben und unregelmäßigen Verben unterscheiden. Die Form ist jedoch in allen Personen gleich.*
- ***Regelmäßige Verben*** *bilden das* simple past *aus dem* ***Infinitiv des Verbs + ed****, z. B.:*

clean	– cleaned	[d]
happen	– happened	[d]
invite	– invited	[ɪd]
like	– liked	[t]
listen	– listened	[d]
order	– ordered	[d]

play	– played	[d]
trip	– tripped	[t]
stay	– stayed	[d]
want	– wanted	[ɪd]
watch	– watched	[t]
work	– worked	[t]

Zeitangaben wie yesterday, last week/month/year, on my last birthday *können dir den Gebrauch des* simple past *signalisieren.*

Beachte die Aussprache von -ed:
- *Sprich* [d] *nach Vokalen gefolgt von stimmhaften Konsonanten.*
- *Sprich* [t] *nach stimmlosen Konsonanten.*
- *Sprich* [ɪd] *nach* [t] *oder* [d].

❗ *Das stumme* **e** *fällt am Ende weg:* like – liked, invite – invited. *(Nicht:* likeed!*)*
Bei kurzem betontem Vokal wird ein einfacher Konsonant am Wortende verdoppelt: trip – tri**pp**ed.
Bei Konsonant + -y *wird das* y *zu* ie*:* try – tr**ie**d.

- *Bei* ***unregelmäßigen Verben*** *musst du die Formen des* simple past ***auswendig lernen****.*
  Hier sind einige unregelmäßige Verben:

come	– came	[keɪm]
do	– did	[dɪd]
go	– went	[went]
get	– got	[gɒt]
give	– gave	[geɪv]

have	– had	[hæd]
hurt	– hurt	[hɜːt]
make	– made	[meɪd]
put	– put	[pʊt]
run	– ran	[ræn]
say	– said	[sed]

- *Nur das Verb* be *hat im* simple past *zwei Formen:* I/He/She/It **was** … [wɒz] *(Singular)*
  We/You/They **were** … [wɜː] *(Plural)*
  Die verneinten Formen lauten **wasn't** *und* **weren't**.

❗ *Das* simple past *kannst du im Deutschen mit dem Präteritum (z. B. er spielte, er ging) wiedergeben. Oft benutzt man aber das Perfekt (z. B. er hat gespielt, er ist gegangen). Umgekehrt heißt das, dass deutsche Sätze im Perfekt im Englischen mit dem* simple past *wiedergegeben werden müssen, wenn die beschriebenen Handlungen bzw. Ereignisse zu einer bestimmten Zeit in der Vergangenheit stattgefunden haben.*
Vergleiche: Gestern ***hat*** *er eine E-Mail* ***bekommen****.* Yesterday he **got** an e-mail.

AUFGABE *Überprüfe, ob du das* simple past *richtig bilden kannst. Vervollständige die E-Mail, indem du die Verben ins* simple past *setzt.*

> Dear Aunt Sally,
> Thank you for your birthday card. I (like) it a lot. You (want) to know about my birthday party. I (invite) six friends to our house. They (give) me a cake and a new football. In the afternoon we (play) some funny games and in the evening we (do) karaoke. Mum (make) pizza for everyone. We (go) to bed very late, so we (be) all tired the next day. But it (be) a great party!
> Love, Joe

G35 *Fragen in der einfachen Vergangenheit*
Questions in the simple past

Seiten 112–113

FUNKTION

> *Mit* **did, was / were** *kannst du nach Handlungen oder Ereignissen fragen, die zu einer bestimmten Zeit in der Vergangenheit stattgefunden haben und abgeschlossen sind.*

REGEL

- *Fragen mit be und die entsprechenden Kurzantworten werden in der einfachen Vergangenheit mit* was *oder* were *gebildet:*
  Was Sunny scared? – No, she **wasn't**.
  Were the pancakes good? – Yes, they **were**.
- *Du weißt schon, wie man Fragen in der einfachen Gegenwart bildet, wenn kein Hilfsverb vorhanden ist: mit dem Hilfsverb* do / does *(→ G20, G23).*
  Fragen in der einfachen Vergangenheit bildet man mit did.
  Anders als im simple present *sind die Formen für alle Personen gleich.*

Fragewort	*Hilfsverb*	*Subjekt*	*Vollverb (Infinitiv)*	
	Did	you	**like**	the party?
	Did	Sunny	**sleep?**	
What	**did**	Emily and Ryan	**do**	in the morning?
What	**did**	Ryan's dad	**make**	for breakfast?

- *Entscheidungsfragen mit* did *werden mit Kurzantworten beantwortet:*
  Did you get my postcard? – Yes, I **did**. / No, I **didn't**.

! *Verwende* did *nicht in Fragen mit Fragewörtern, wenn du nach dem Subjekt fragst:*
What happened? **Who** went to see the fireworks? *Nicht:* ~~What did happen?~~ ...

AUFGABE *Überprüft, ob ihr Fragen in der einfachen Vergangenheit richtig bilden und beantworten könnt. Stellt euch gegenseitig Fragen und beantwortet sie.*

1. *Frage deine Partnerin / deinen Partner, ob sie / er am Sonntag zu Hause war.*
2. *Frage, ob sie / er ferngesehen hat.*
3. *Frage, was sie / er gestern gemacht hat.*
4. *Frage, ob es ihr / ihm gefallen hat.*
5. *Frage, wann sie / er ins Bett gegangen ist.*

G36 *Die Verneinung in der einfachen Vergangenheit*

Seiten 112–114 **Negative statements and questions in the simple past**

FUNKTION

> *Mit* **didn't, wasn't / weren't** *kannst du sagen, dass jemand etwas* ***nicht*** *getan hat oder etwas* ***nicht*** *geschehen ist. Oft benutzt man verneinte Aussagesätze, um etwas richtigzustellen.*

Sunny did**n't go** with us.

REGEL
- *Die Verneinung von Aussagen mit* be *bildest du in der einfachen Vergangenheit mit* was / were + not*:* We **weren't** at home in the evening. Sunny **wasn't** scared.
- *Du weißt schon, wie man verneinte Aussagesätze in der einfachen Gegenwart bildet, wenn kein Hilfsverb vorhanden ist: mit dem Hilfsverb* do / does + not *(→ G21). Verneinte Aussagesätze in der einfachen Vergangenheit bildet man mit* didn't. *Anders als im* simple present *sind die Formen für alle Personen gleich.*

Subjekt	*Hilfsverb*	*Vollverb (Infinitiv)*	
I	**didn't**	**decorate**	the yard.
Emily	**didn't**	**go**	to school last week.

> *Für verneinte Fragen schließt du einfach ein ‚not' an* did*, was* *oder* were *an:*
> Why weren't you at home?
> Why didn't you go home after the film?

AUFGABE *Überprüfe, ob du die Verneinung in der einfachen Vergangenheit richtig bilden kannst. Verneine die folgenden Aussagen und korrigiere sie mit Hilfe der Information in Klammern.*

1. *I went to the skater park on Monday. (Tuesday)*
2. *My teacher gave us a lot of homework last Thursday. (Wednesday)*
3. *I liked the football game yesterday. (last week)*
4. *We were at home on Saturday evening. (bowling alley)*
5. *The girls had a sleepover last week. (skater party)*
6. *Dave was in New York three weeks ago. (London)*

G37 *Haupt- und Nebensätze*

Seite 117 Main clauses and subordinate clauses

FUNKTION

Um Aussagen inhaltlich miteinander zu verbinden, kannst du Satzgefüge aus Haupt- und Nebensätzen bilden.

REGEL

- *Beiordnende Konjunktionen wie* **and** *und* **but** *können zwei Hauptsätze verbinden:*
  Holly lives in Greenwich, **and** she's at TTS. It's Jay's birthday, **but** he isn't happy.
- *Unterordnende Konjunktionen können Hauptsätze mit Nebensätzen verbinden. Wenn du ihre Bedeutung lernst, kannst du verschiedene logische Verknüpfungen ausdrücken.*

! *Anders als im Deutschen gibt es im Englischen keinen Unterschied zwischen der Satzstellung im Hauptsatz und der Satzstellung im Nebensatz. Im Deutschen werden Haupt- und Nebensätze immer durch Komma getrennt. Wenn der Hauptsatz vor dem Nebensatz steht, wird im Englischen kein Komma gesetzt.*

because	Jay is disappointed **because** nobody calls him.	*... weil ihn niemand anruft.*
when	Jay is surprised **when** he opens the door.	*... als er die Tür öffnet.*
that	Jay thinks **that** nobody likes him any more.	*... dass ihn niemand mehr mag.*

AUFGABE *Überprüfe, ob du Sätze sinnvoll verknüpfen kannst. Welche Konjunktionen passen hier?*

1. *He had lots of fun ... He was at his friend's sleepover.*
2. *He knows ... I'm his friend.*
3. *He tripped over Jamie's car ... He didn't hurt his foot.*

Vocabulary

Im ***Vocabulary*** findest du alle wichtigen englischen Wörter und Redewendungen aus Green Line 1 in der Reihenfolge, in der sie im Buch vorkommen. Diese musst du lernen und anwenden können. Das *Vocabulary* ist in drei Spalten aufgeteilt:

- Links stehen die englischen Wörter und Sätze. Die Lautschrift in Klammern zeigt dir, wie du das Wort oder den Satz aussprichst (siehe unten).
- In der Mitte steht die deutsche Übersetzung.
- Rechts findest du Beispielsätze, Erklärungen, Bilder oder Hinweise auf Besonderheiten.

Die **grün** gedruckten Wörter in den Kästen im *Vocabulary* sind ein Zusatzangebot. Du kannst sie verwenden, um über bestimmte Themen zu sprechen, musst sie aber nicht lernen.

Anderen nützlichen Wortschatz für den Unterricht, den du **verstehen** musst, findest du ab S. 269. Die Worterklärungen in den Fußnoten bei manchen Texten musst du nicht lernen.

Auf das *Vocabulary* folgt das ***Dictionary (English – German, German – English)***. Falls du ein Wort vergessen hast, kannst du in diesen alphabetischen Wortlisten nachsehen.

Englische Begriffe wie *e-mail, cool* oder *cornflakes*, die du auch im Deutschen verwendest, stehen nicht im *Vocabulary*. Du kannst ihre Aussprache und Übersetzung aber im *Dictionary* nachschlagen. Das gilt auch für Wörter, die auf Englisch und Deutsch fast gleich geschrieben und ausgesprochen werden, wie z. B. *park* oder *partner*.

Abkürzungen und Zeichen

pl	Mehrzahl (Plural)
sg	Einzahl (Singular)
ugs.	umgangssprachlich
5	In dieser Übung kommen die Wörter vor.
!	Achtung!
•	Diese Wörter kennst du wahrscheinlich aus der Grundschule.
*	unregelmäßiges Verb (siehe Liste *Irregular verbs* im Anhang)
=	entspricht
↔	ist das Gegenteil von
→	ist verwandt mit
Fr./Lat.	verwandte Wörter in anderen Fremdsprachen
AE	*American English*
BE	*British English*

Englische Laute

Mitlaute (Konsonanten)

[b]	**b**ed	[p]	**p**icture
[d]	**d**ay	[r]	**r**ed
[ð]	**th**e	[s]	**s**ix
[f]	**f**amily	[ʃ]	**sh**e
[g]	**g**o	[t]	**t**en
[ŋ]	morni**ng**	[tʃ]	**ch**air
[h]	**h**ouse	[v]	**v**ideo
[j]	**y**ou	[w]	**w**e, **o**ne
[k]	**c**an, mil**k**	[z]	ea**s**y
[l]	**l**etter	[ʒ]	revi**s**ion
[m]	**m**an	[dʒ]	pa**g**e
[n]	**n**o	[θ]	**th**ank you

Selbstlaute (Vokale)

[ɑː]	c**ar**	[i]	happ**y**
[æ]	**a**pple	[iː]	t**ea**cher
[e]	p**e**n	[ɒ]	d**o**g
[ə]	**a**gain	[ɔː]	b**a**ll
[ɜː]	g**ir**l	[ʊ]	b**oo**k
[ʌ]	b**u**t	[u]	Jan**u**ary
[ɪ]	**i**t	[uː]	t**oo**, tw**o**

Doppellaute

[aɪ]	**I**, m**y**
[aʊ]	n**ow**, m**ou**se
[eɪ]	n**a**me, th**ey**
[eə]	th**ere**, p**air**
[ɪə]	h**ere**, id**ea**
[əʊ]	hell**o**
[ɔɪ]	b**oy**
[ʊə]	s**ure**

[ː]	der vorangehende Laut ist lang, z. B. *you* [juː]
[‿]	der Bindebogen zeigt, dass zwei Wörter in der Aussprache verbunden werden
[ˈ]	die folgende Silbe trägt den Hauptakzent
[ˌ]	die folgende Silbe trägt den Nebenakzent

Vocabulary skills

Es gibt viele Tipps und Tricks, die dir das Vokabellernen erleichtern können.
Hier findest du einige davon zum Ausprobieren.

Ein fester Arbeitsplatz

Richte dir zu Hause einen festen Arbeitsplatz ein, an dem du alles greifbar hast, was du zum Lernen brauchst: Schreibzeug, Hefte, Bücher etc. Dort kannst du in Ruhe deine Hausaufgaben machen, dich auf Tests und Klassenarbeiten vorbereiten – und auch Vokabeln lernen.

Umgang mit der Wortliste

Schau dir in der Wortliste die englischen Wörter, die deutsche Übersetzung und die Sätze und Bilder in der rechten Spalte genau an, am besten mehrmals hintereinander. Um dir die neuen Wörter besser einprägen zu können, kannst du sie abschreiben oder dir unterschiedlich vorsagen, z. B. laut, leise oder singend.

Kleine Lernpakete

Mehrere kleine, leichte Pakete sind nacheinander leichter zu heben als ein großes, schweres! Für das Vokabellernen bedeutet das, dass du neue Wörter am besten in kleinen Paketen von 10 bis 15 Vokabeln lernst. Außerdem behältst du neue Wörter besser, wenn du sie erst einmal fünf Minuten lang lernst, sie nach einer halben Stunde wiederholst und sie am Ende deiner Hausaufgaben oder vor dem Einschlafen noch einmal überprüfst.

Klebezettel

Schau dich z. B. in deinem Zimmer um und überlege dir, für welche Gegenstände du schon die Wörter auf Englisch kennst. Schreibe jeweils das englische Wort auf einen selbstklebenden Zettel und klebe ihn an den entsprechenden Gegenstand (an deine Uhr, an deinen Tisch usw.). So übst du jedes Mal, wenn du den Gegenstand benutzt, das englische Wort.

Bildwörter

Um dir Wörter besser einzuprägen, kannst du sie auch bildlich darstellen. Suche dir aus der Wortliste zwei oder drei Wörter aus und versuche, sie bildlich darzustellen.

Mind maps

Neue Wörter kannst du dir besser merken, wenn du sie zusammen mit anderen Wörtern zum gleichen Thema lernst. Fertige dazu ein *mind map* an:

1. Zeichne einen Kreis und schreibe das Thema in die Mitte.
2. Zeichne Linien an den Kreis und schreibe ans Ende jeder Linie ein Wort, das zum Thema passt.

Mind maps können auch mehr als zwei Ebenen haben, z. B.: *house – kitchen – fridge*. Du kannst sie um Bilder oder Hinweise zur Aussprache erweitern, wenn es dir hilft, dir die Wörter einzuprägen. Nun kannst du z. B. *mind maps* zum Thema *pets, schoolbag* oder *hobbies* anfertigen.

Körperbewegungen

Vielleicht fällt dir das Vokabellernen leichter, wenn du nicht nur im Sitzen lernst. Manche Wörter lassen sich gut mit einem Gesichtsausdruck oder einer Körperbewegung verbinden. Suche dir fünf Wörter aus der Wortliste aus und stelle sie pantomimisch dar. Deine Partnerin/dein Partner versucht, sie zu erraten. Tauscht dann die Rollen. (Du kannst natürlich auch mit deinen Eltern oder Geschwistern lernen.)

Wörter aufnehmen

Je öfter du eine Vokabel hörst, desto leichter kannst du sie dir merken. Nimm hierfür neue Wörter auf dein Handy oder mit dem Mikrofon auf deinen Computer auf. Sprich zuerst das englische Wort, mache dann eine kurze Sprechpause und sage schließlich die deutsche Bedeutung. In einem zweiten Durchlauf kannst du die gleichen Wörter in umgekehrter Reihenfolge aufnehmen, also zuerst die deutsche Bedeutung, dann eine kurze Sprechpause und zum Schluss das englische Wort. (Du kannst auch eine andere Reihenfolge als die im Buch nehmen.)

Hör dir deine Aufnahme immer mal wieder an. Übe die Wörter, indem du dir während der Sprechpause die englische bzw. deutsche Bedeutung überlegst und vor dich hin sagst.

Vokabelheft

Manchmal wirst du Wörter benötigen, die nicht in der Wortliste stehen. Wahrscheinlich bittest du dann deine Lehrerin/deinen Lehrer um Hilfe. Die zusätzlichen neuen Wörter kannst du in einem Vokabelheft notieren. Dein Vokabelheft sollte drei Spalten haben: In die erste Spalte schreibst du das englische Wort, in die zweite die deutsche Übersetzung und in die dritte Spalte kannst du einen Beispielsatz schreiben. Wenn du möchtest, kannst du dein Vokabelheft um Bildwörter und *mind maps* erweitern.

Vokabelkartei

Vokabeln kannst du gut mit Hilfe einer Vokabelkartei lernen. Dazu brauchst du Karteikarten und einen Karton mit fünf Fächern. Schreibe das englische Wort auf die Vorderseite der Karteikarte und die deutsche Bedeutung auf die Rückseite. Als Merkhilfe kannst du zusätzlich zum englischen Wort auch ein Bild malen oder einen Beispielsatz aus dem Buch aufschreiben.

Stelle alle Karten ins erste Fach. Übe jeden Tag 5 bis 10 Minuten, und zwar so: Nimm eine Karte nach der anderen heraus und überprüfe, ob du die Übersetzung weißt (deutsch – englisch, englisch – deutsch). Wenn ja, stellst du die Karte ins zweite Fach. Mache so lange weiter, bis das erste Fach leer ist. Das zweite Fach bearbeitest du dann genauso, allerdings nicht jeden Tag, sondern nur einmal in der Woche, das dritte Fach alle zwei Wochen usw.

Beziehungen zwischen Wörtern

Lerne möglichst nicht nur einzelne Wörter! Am besten merkst du dir Wörter zusammen mit anderen Wörtern, z. B.:

bike	go by bike
party	have a party, go to a party
mum	mum ↔ dad
white	white ↔ black
friendly	friendly → friend

Solche Beziehungen kannst du dir z. B. in deinem Vokabelheft oder in deiner Vokabelkartei notieren.

Andere Sprachen

Manche englischen Wörter kannst du dir vielleicht leichter merken, weil sie in einer anderen Sprache ähnlich sind, z. B.:

Englisch:	hungry	geography
Deutsch:	hungrig	Geografie
Englisch:	a table	a question
Französisch:	une table	une question
Englisch:	parents	colour
Französisch:	les parents	couleur
Latein:	parentes	color

Auch solche Ähnlichkeiten kannst du dir in deinem Vokabelheft oder in deiner Vokabelkartei notieren.

Pick-up A I'm from Greenwich

I'm from Greenwich. [ˌaɪm frɒm ˈɡrenɪdʒ]	Ich bin aus Greenwich.	*I'm from* Germany. ! Achtung Aussprache.
Look! [lʊk]	Schau/Schaut mal!	
two boys and a dog [tuː ˌbɔɪz‿ənd‿ə ˈdɒɡ]	zwei Jungen und ein Hund	Look, a *boy* and a *dog*!
in Greenwich Park [ˌɪn ˌɡrenɪdʒ ˈpɑːk]	im Greenwich-Park	Look! Two boys and a dog *in Greenwich Park*.
Dogs are my friends, but not cats. [ˌdɒɡz‿ə maɪ ˌfrendz bʌt nɒt ˈkæts]	Hunde sind meine Freunde, aber Katzen nicht.	! Wenn man *are* nicht betont, spricht man es [ə]. 
I'm a mouse. [ˌaɪm‿ə ˈmaʊs]	Ich bin eine Maus.	
• **mouse** *(sg)* [maʊs], **mice** *(pl)* [maɪs]	Maus, Mäuse *(Pl.)*	one *mouse* – two *mice*
Here's your ball. [ˌhɪəz jə ˈbɔːl]	Hier ist dein Ball.	*Here's* Luke.
• **Hello.** [helˈəʊ]	Hallo.	
I'm Pia. [aɪm ˈpiːə]	Ich heiße Pia.; Ich bin Pia.	Hello, *I'm Pia*.
You're a nice dog. [jɔːr‿e ˈnaɪs ˌdɒɡ]	Du bist ein lieber Hund.	*You're a nice dog*, Sherlock. 
What's your name? [ˌwɒts jə ˈneɪm]	Wie heißt du?; Wie heißen Sie?	*What's your name?* – I'm Olivia.
• **Sorry!** [ˈsɒri]	Entschuldigung!; Tut mir leid!	
My dog is crazy. [maɪ ˌdɒɡ‿ɪz ˈkreɪzi]	Mein Hund ist verrückt.	My dog is nice, but *crazy*!
My name is Luke. [ˌmaɪ ˌneɪm‿ɪz ˈluːk]	Ich heiße Luke.	
We're from Greenwich. [ˌwɪə frəm ˈɡrenɪdʒ]	Wir sind aus Greenwich.	Luke *is from* Greenwich.
Where are you from? [ˌweər‿ə ju ˈfrɒm]	Woher kommst du?; Woher kommt ihr?; Woher kommen Sie?	*Where are you from?* – We're from Greenwich.
Are you on holiday? [ɑː ju‿ɒn ˈhɒlədeɪ]	Sind Sie im Urlaub?; Seid ihr im Urlaub?; Bist du im Urlaub?	Pia is *on holiday* in London.
• **yes** [jes]	ja	
I'm here with my parents. [aɪm ˌhɪə wɪð maɪ ˈpeərənts]	Ich bin mit meinen Eltern hier.	***Fr.*** parents *(m)*; ***Lat.*** parentes *(m)*
How old are you? [haʊ‿ˈəʊld‿ə ˌjuː]	Wie alt bist du?; Wie alt sind Sie?	! Achte auf die Verbindung zwischen den Wörtern beim Sprechen.
You too? [juː ˈtuː]	Du auch?	! Satzstellung: Are you ten *too*, Luke?
• **no** [nəʊ]	nein	*no* ↔ yes

3 •	**German** ['dʒɜːmən]	deutsch; Deutsch; aus Deutschland; Deutsche/-r	Are you *German*? – Yes, I'm from Cologne. 
4	**different** ['dɪfrnt]	anders; unterschiedlich; verschieden	Dogs and cats are *different*. ***Fr.*** différent/-e; ***Lat.*** differens
5	**I'm English.** [aɪm‿'ɪŋglɪʃ]	Ich bin Engländer/-in.	Are you *English*? – No, I'm German.

Numbers 1–12

1 **one** [wʌn]	4 **four** [fɔː]	7 **seven** ['sevn]	10 **ten** [ten]
2 **two** [tuː]	5 **five** [faɪv]	8 **eight** [eɪt]	11 **eleven** [ɪ'levn]
3 **three** [θriː]	6 **six** [sɪks]	9 **nine** [naɪn]	12 **twelve** [twelv]

	I love dogs. [aɪ 'lʌv ˌdɒgz]	Ich liebe Hunde.; Ich mag Hunde total gern.	
	Dogs love squirrels. [ˌdɒgz ˌlʌv 'skwɪrəlz]	Hunde lieben Eichhörnchen.	Look, a squirrel! *I love squirrels.*
	That was close! [ˌðæt wəz 'kləʊs]	Das war knapp!	
	animal ['ænɪməl]	Tier	Cats and dogs are *animals*. ***Fr.*** animal *(m)*; ***Lat.*** animal *(nt)*
•	**Thank you.** ['θæŋk ju]	Danke.	Here's your ball. – Oh, *thank you*.
	This is Pia. [ˌðɪs‿ɪz 'piːə]	Das (hier) ist Pia.	
	a girl from Germany [ə ˌgɜːl frəm 'dʒɜːməni]	ein Mädchen aus Deutschland	Is Olivia *a girl from Germany*? – No, Olivia is from Greenwich.
•	**school** [skuːl]	Schule	Pia is a girl from *school*. – No, Pia is a girl from Germany.
	Greenwich Park is big. [ˌgrenɪdʒ ˌpɑːk‿ɪz 'bɪg]	Der Greenwich-Park ist groß.	Sherlock is a *big* dog.
	It's great for cycling. [ɪts ˌgreɪt fə 'saɪklɪŋ]	Er ist super zum Radfahren.	*Cycling* is *great* in Greenwich Park.
	I don't like cycling. [aɪ ˌdəʊnt ˌlaɪk 'saɪklɪŋ]	Ich fahre nicht gern Rad.	*I don't like* cats, but I like Luke!
	My favourite sport is football. [maɪ ˌfeɪvrɪt ˌspɔːt‿ɪz 'fʊtbɔːl]	Mein Lieblingssport ist Fußball.	*My favourite* animals are dogs.
	I like the boating lake. [aɪ ˌlaɪk ðə 'bəʊtɪŋ ˌleɪk]	Ich mag den See mit den Booten.; Mir gefällt der See mit den Booten.	
	What's that? [wɒts 'ðæt]	Was ist das?	A squirrel? *What's that?*
	Let's go! [lets 'gəʊ]	Lass/Lasst uns hingehen!; Los, gehen wir hin!	A boating lake? Great, *let's go*!
	It's fun. [ɪts 'fʌn]	Es macht Spaß.	Football *is fun*! – Cycling too.
7	**puzzle** ['pʌzl]	Rätsel	Here's a *puzzle* about Greenwich.

	rat [ræt]	Ratte	I don't like *rats*. ***Fr.*** rat *(m)*
	I'm not scared of dogs. [aɪm ˌnɒt ˌskeəd‿əv 'dɒgz]	Ich habe keine Angst vor Hunden.	Are you *scared of* rats? *I'm not.*
	I'm scared of cats. [aɪm ˌskeəd‿əv 'kæts]	Ich habe Angst vor Katzen.	
	Worms are OK. [ˌwɜːmz‿ɑːr‿əʊ'keɪ]	Würmer sind o.k.	Football is *OK*.
	Rabbits are nice. [ˌræbɪts‿ɑː 'naɪs]	Kaninchen sind nett.	
	They're my friends. [ˌðeə maɪ 'frendz]	Sie sind meine Freunde.	Are Olivia and Dave OK? – Yes, *they're my friends*!
	They don't eat mice. [ðeɪ ˌdəʊnt‿iːt 'maɪs]	Sie essen keine Mäuse.	
8	**word** [wɜːd]	Wort	'Squirrel' is the English *word* for 'Eichhörnchen'.

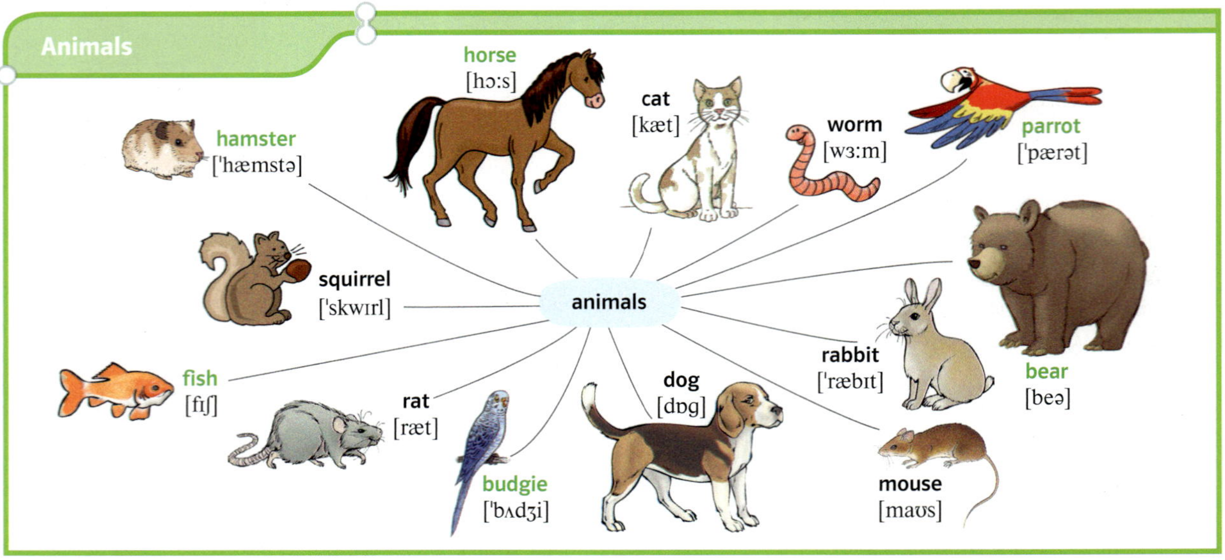

9	**Inline skating is great.** [ˌɪnlaɪn ˌskeɪtɪŋ‿ɪz 'greɪt]	Inlineskatesfahren ist toll.	Let's go *inline skating* in the park.
	Volleyball is a great sport. [ˌvɒlibɔːl‿ɪz‿ə 'greɪt ˌspɔːt]	Volleyball ist ein toller Sport.	Football *is a great sport* too!
10	**the same** [ðə 'seɪm]	der-/die-/dasselbe; der/die/das gleiche	*the same* ↔ different
11•	**colour** ['kʌlə]	Farbe	***Fr.*** couleur *(f)*; ***Lat.*** color *(m)*
	correct [kə'rekt]	richtig; korrekt	Pia is from Stuttgart. Is that *correct*?
	What's your favourite colour? [ˌwɒts jə ˌfeɪvrɪt 'kʌlə]	Was ist deine Lieblingsfarbe?	

Colours

black [blæk]	schwarz	grey [greɪ]	grau	red [red]	rot
blue [blu:]	blau	orange ['ɒrɪndʒ]	orange	white [waɪt]	weiß
brown [braʊn]	braun	pink [pɪŋk]	pink; rosa	yellow ['jeləʊ]	gelb
green [gri:n]	grün	purple ['pɜ:pl]	lila; violett		

12	**picture** ['pɪktʃə]	Bild; Foto	! My dog is <u>in</u> the *picture*. (not: on)
	people *(pl)* ['pi:pl]	Leute; Menschen	*People* like dogs and cats, but not rats!
13	**thing** [θɪŋ]	Ding; Sache	Talk about the *things* in the picture.
	number ['nʌmbə]	Zahl; Nummer	What's your favourite *number*, Luke? *Lat.* numerus *(m)*
	Boat number eight is pink. [ˌbəʊt nʌmbər‿eɪt‿ɪz 'pɪŋk]	Boot Nummer acht ist rosa.	
	I can see Sherlock. [ˌaɪ kən ˌsi: 'ʃɜ:lɒk]	Ich kann Sherlock sehen.; Ich sehe Sherlock.	*I can see* Luke too.
14	**Roll two dice.** [ˌrəʊl ˌtu: 'daɪs]	Würfle/Würfelt mit zwei Würfeln.	
	Four and six is ten. [ˌfɔ:r‿ənd ˌsɪks‿ɪz 'ten]	Vier plus sechs ist zehn.	
	please [pli:z]	bitte	*Please* listen. Thank you.
	Can you name four sports? [ˌkæn jʊ ˌneɪm ˌfɔ: 'spɔ:ts]	Kannst du vier Sportarten nennen?	
	Say your phone number. [ˌseɪ jɔ: 'fəʊn ˌnʌmbə]	Sage deine Telefonnummer.	*Say* your name.
	What colour is Sherlock? [ˌwɒt ˌkʌlər‿ɪz 'ʃɜ:lɒk]	Welche Farbe hat Sherlock?	*What colour is* your English book?
15	**alphabet** ['ælfəbet]	Alphabet	The *alphabet*: A, B, C, … *Fr.* alphabet *(m)*
	Rap like me. [ˌræp laɪk 'mi:]	Rappe/Rappt wie ich.	
	I love you. [aɪ 'lʌv ju]	Ich liebe dich.; Ich mag dich.	

The alphabet

a [eɪ]	**e** [i:]	**i** [aɪ]	**m** [em]	**q** [kju:]	**u** [ju:]	**y** [waɪ]
b [bi:]	**f** [ef]	**j** [dʒeɪ]	**n** [en]	**r** [ɑ:]	**v** [vi:]	**z** [zed]
c [si:]	**g** [dʒi:]	**k** [keɪ]	**o** [əʊ]	**s** [es]	**w** ['dʌblju:]	
d [di:]	**h** [eɪtʃ]	**l** [el]	**p** [pi:]	**t** [ti:]	**x** [eks]	

Unit 1 It's fun at home

Check-in

at home [ət 'həʊm]	zu Hause	Luke is *at home*.
• **family** ['fæmli]	Familie	Pia and her parents are a *family*. ***Fr.*** famille *(f)*; ***Lat.*** familia *(f)*
to **live** [lɪv]	wohnen; leben	We *live* in Greenwich.
flat [flæt]	Wohnung	Pia's *flat* is in Cologne.
in the street [ˌɪn ðə 'stri:t]	in der Straße; auf der Straße	Sherlock is *in the street*.
• **house** [haʊs]	Haus	Luke's *house* is in Greenwich.
door [dɔ:]	Tür	That's his house – with the green *door*.
TV *(= television)* [ˌti:'vi: ('telɪvɪʒn)]	Fernsehen; Fernseher	
• **chair** [tʃeə]	Stuhl; Sessel	
table ['teɪbl]	Tisch	Can you see a *table* in the picture? ***Fr.*** table *(f)*
shower ['ʃaʊə]	Dusche	
bath [bɑ:θ]	Bad; Badewanne	It's fun for Sherlock in the *bath* and in the shower too!
toilet ['tɔɪlət]	Toilette	Where's the *toilet*, please? ***Fr.*** toilettes *(pl)*
bed [bed]	Bett	I love my *bed*.
clock [klɒk]	Uhr	That's a nice *clock*!
wardrobe ['wɔ:drəʊb]	Kleiderschrank	Look! A mouse! – Where? – In the *wardrobe*!
cupboard ['kʌbəd]	Küchenschrank; Schrank	! Das „p" wird nicht gesprochen.
cooker ['kʊkə]	Herd	

Rooms at home

1 **living room** ['lɪvɪŋ rʊm]	Wohnzimmer	The TV is in the *living room*.
bedroom ['bedrʊm]	Schlafzimmer	Luke's wardrobe is in his *bedroom*.
kitchen ['kɪtʃɪn]	Küche	The cooker is in the *kitchen*.
bathroom ['bɑ:θrʊm]	Bad; Badezimmer	! im Bad = in the *bathroom* in der Badewanne = in the bath
• **good** [gʊd]	gut	Luke and Sherlock are *good* friends.
biscuit ['bɪskɪt]	Keks	Here's a *biscuit* for you, Sherlock. – Woof!
• **under** ['ʌndə]	unter	Sherlock! Your ball is *under* the table.
2 • to **help** [help]	helfen	Can you *help* me, please?
to **collect** [kə'lekt]	sammeln	Let's *collect* words for 'at home'.
new [nju:]	neu	I'm *new* in London.
3 • **small** [smɔ:l]	klein	**BIG** small

Station 1: This is my family

• **sister** ['sɪstə]	Schwester	Is Holly Luke's *sister*? – No, Holly is a girl from school.
• **little** ['lɪtl]	klein	Jamie is Luke's *little* brother. *little* sister ↔ big sister
• **brother** ['brʌðə]	Bruder	*brother* ↔ sister
• **father** ['fɑ:ðə]	Vater	Luke's *father* is English.
• **mother** ['mʌðə]	Mutter	Your *mother* and your father are your parents.
cousin ['kʌzn]	Cousin/Cousine	Jan is Luke's *cousin* in Cracow. *Fr.* cousin *(m)*, cousine *(f)*
an [ən]	ein/-e	! Vor a, e, i, o, u wird *a* zu *an*: a cat, a dog ABER: *an* animal, *an* idea
only child ['əʊnli ˌtʃaɪld]	Einzelkind	
dad [dæd]	Papa	
she's [ʃi:z]	sie ist	Irina is Luke's big sister. *She's* (= she is) OK.
isn't *(= is not)* [ɪznt]	ist nicht	Luke's mother *isn't* English.
always ['ɔ:lweɪz]	immer; ständig	Let's go to the boating lake. That's *always* fun!
easy ['i:zi]	einfach; leicht	English is *easy* for me! I'm English.
he's [hi:z]	er ist	Jamie is Luke's brother. *He's* eight.
mum [mʌm]	Mama	! *Mum* und Dad werden nur als Name groß geschrieben: Hello, *Mum*! ABER: Where's Luke's *mum*?
uncle ['ʌŋkl]	Onkel	! Alle Familienbezeichnungen werden als Name groß geschrieben, z. B.: *Uncle* Jack, *Grandma* Carol. *Fr.* oncle *(m)*
aunt [ɑ:nt]	Tante	Luke's *Aunt* Mila is his cousin's mum. *aunt* ↔ uncle

	grandad ['grændæd]	Opa	
	grandma ['grænmɑ:]	Oma	Your mother's or your father's mother.
1	**family tree** ['fæmli ˌtri:]	Stammbaum	
3	**Tell me about ...** ['tel mi‿əˌbaʊt]	Erzähle mir von ...	

Adjectives

nice	[naɪs]	nett	**crazy**	['kreɪzi]	verrückt	**clever**	['klevə]	schlau
cool	[ku:l]	cool	**quiet**	[kwaɪət]	ruhig	**silly**	['sɪli]	albern, dumm
great	[greɪt]	großartig	**small**	[smɔ:l]	klein	**noisy**	['nɔɪsi]	laut
fun	[fʌn]	witzig	**tall**	[tɔ:l]	groß	**short**	[ʃɔ:t]	klein
OK	[əʊ'keɪ]	in Ordnung	**friendly**	['frendli]	freundlich			

4	**guinea pig** ['gɪni: ˌpɪg]	Meerschweinchen	
	quiet [kwaɪət]	still; ruhig; leise	Mice and rabbits are *quiet* animals. *Lat.* quietus
5	**language** ['læŋgwɪdʒ]	Sprache	English is a *language*. *Fr.* langue *(f)*, langage *(m)*; *Lat.* lingua *(f)*
	only ['əʊnli]	erst; bloß; nur	
6	**wrong** [rɒŋ]	falsch	! Das „w" wird nicht gesprochen. *wrong* ↔ right
8 •	**Thanks.** [θæŋks]	Danke.	! *Thanks.* = Thank you.
•	**very** ['veri]	sehr	Your house is *very* nice.
	some [sʌm; səm]	einige; ein paar; etwas	Here are *some* holiday photos.
	of [ɒv; əv]	von	Look! This is a photo *of* Pia.
	to **say hello (to)** [ˌseɪ hel'əʊ tə]	grüßen; Grüße ausrichten (an)	Please *say hello to* your parents from me.
•	**to** [tʊ; tə]	zu; nach; auf; in	Let's go *to* the boating lake. Let's go *to* London. ! Wenn man *to* nicht betont, spricht man es [tə].

Station 2: What's the problem?

	problem ['prɒbləm]	Problem; Schwierigkeit	Cats in the house? That's a big *problem* for Tony! *Fr.* problème *(m)*
	there is/are [ðər‿'ɪz/'ɑ:]	da ist/sind; es gibt	*There's* a dog. And *there are* two cats. 
•	**there** [ðeə]	da; dort; dahin; dorthin	*there* ↔ here
	garden ['gɑ:dn]	Garten	Luke and his family live in a house with a *garden*.
•	**behind** [bɪ'haɪnd]	hinter	Is there a garden *behind* your house?

	Mr ['mɪstə]	Herr *(Anrede)*	*Mr* Elliot is Luke's father.
	Mrs ['mɪsɪz]	Frau *(Anrede)*	! Achtung Aussprache.
	now [naʊ]	jetzt; nun	Your friends are here, Luke. – Great! *Now* we can go to the park.
	car [kɑː]	Auto	
	everywhere ['evriweə]	überall; überallhin	The park is great for rabbits. They're *everywhere*.
	again [ə'gen]	wieder; noch einmal; noch mal	What? Can you say that *again*, please?
	floor [flɔː]	Fußboden	Look at your room! Your things are everywhere on the *floor*!
•	**next to** ['nekst tə]	neben	I love this picture! That's Lou *next to* me.
•	**in front of** [ɪn 'frʌnt‿əv]	vor	There's a car *in front of* the house. *in front of* ↔ behind
	to **listen (to)** ['lɪsn]	zuhören; anhören	! Achtung Aussprache: Das „t" in *listen* wird nicht gesprochen.
	idea [aɪ'dɪə]	Idee; Einfall	Let's go to the park with Sherlock. – Great *idea*! *Fr.* idée *(f)*
	loft [lɒft]	Dachboden	Where's your new bedroom? – In the *loft*.
	own [əʊn]	eigene/-r/-s	! *own* verwendet man immer mit ‚my', ‚your', ‚his', ‚her', etc.: This is my *own* room.
10	**in the middle (of)** [ɪn ðə 'mɪdl‿əv]	in der Mitte (von); mitten in	I live *in the middle of* London.
	on the right [ɒn ðə 'raɪt]	auf der rechten Seite; rechts	
	on the left [ɒn ðə 'left]	auf der linken Seite; links	

Prepositions

Where's Sherlock? He's . . .

on the bed.

under a tree.

at home with Luke.

in front of Luke and Dave.

behind Pia.

in the bath.

next to Luke.

Things in my room

wardrobe	['wɔ:drəʊb]	Kleiderschrank	shelf, shelves *(pl)*	[ʃelf, ʃelvz]	Regal	toy	[tɔɪ]	Spielzeug
bed	[bed]	Bett	rug	[rʌg]	Teppich, Vorleger	cuddly toy	['kʌdli ˌtɔɪ]	Stofftier
table	['teɪbl]	Tisch	guitar	[gi'tɑ:]	Gitarre	computer	[ˌkəm'pju:tə]	Computer
chair	[tʃeə]	Stuhl	**skateboard**	['skeɪtbɔ:d]	Skateboard			
lamp	[læmp]	Lampe	poster	['pəʊstə]	Poster			
mirror	['mɪrə]	Spiegel						

12	**from ... to** [frəm ... tə]	von ... bis	Say the numbers *from* 13 *to* 20.

Numbers 13 – 100

thirteen [ˌθɜ:'ti:n]	dreizehn	**nineteen** [ˌnaɪn'ti:n]	neunzehn	**sixty** ['sɪksti]	sechzig
fourteen [fɔ:'ti:n]	vierzehn	**twenty** ['twenti]	zwanzig	**seventy** ['sevnti]	siebzig
fifteen [ˌfɪf'ti:n]	fünfzehn	**twenty-one** [ˌtwenti'wʌn]	einundzwanzig	**eighty** ['eɪti]	achtzig
sixteen [ˌsɪk'sti:n]	sechzehn	**thirty** ['θɜ:ti]	dreißig	**ninety** ['naɪnti]	neunzig
seventeen [ˌsevn'ti:n]	siebzehn	**forty** ['fɔ:ti]	vierzig	**a/one hundred** [ə 'hʌndrəd] [ˌwʌn 'hʌndrəd]	hundert/ einhundert
eighteen [ˌeɪ'ti:n]	achtzehn	**fifty** ['fɪfti]	fünfzig		

13	**answer** ['ɑ:nsə]	Antwort	! Das „w" wird nicht gesprochen.
	wall [wɔ:l]	Wand; Mauer	What colour are the *walls* in your room? 
	fridge [frɪdʒ]	Kühlschrank	There's only a small *fridge* in our kitchen. *Fr.* frigo *(m)*
14	**address** [ə'dres]	Adresse	! Achte auf die Schreibung. *Fr.* adresse *(f)*
15	**its** [ɪts]	sein/-e; ihr/-e	! Achtung Rechtschreibung: *It's* a good school. = Es ist ... What's *its* name? = sein

Pronouns

Personalpronomen			Possessivbegleiter		
I	[aɪ]	ich	my	[maɪ]	mein / -e
you	[ju:]	du	your	[jɔ:]	dein / -e
he	[hi:]	er	his	[hɪz]	sein / -e
she	[ʃi:]	sie	her	[hɜ:]	ihr / -e
it	[ɪt]	es	its	[ɪts]	sein / -e
we	[wi:]	wir	our	[aʊə]	unser / -e
you	[ju:]	ihr / Sie	your	[jɔ:]	euer / eure
they	[ðeɪ]	sie	their	[ðeə]	ihr / -e

17	to **remember** [rɪ'membə]	sich erinnern (an); sich merken; denken an	Do you *remember* the cabin boy's name?
	or [ɔ:]	oder	Who is English? Pia *or* Olivia?
	more [mɔ:]	mehr; weitere	Tony: *More* dogs are great – but not *more* cats.

Unit task: My fantasy house

fantasy ['fæntəsi]	Fantasie; Traum-	Is this a picture of your own house? – No, it's a *fantasy* house. *Fr.* fantaisie *(f)*
to **draw** [drɔ:]	zeichnen	Let's *draw* a picture.
step [step]	Stufe; Schritt	

My house

roof	[ru:f]	Dach	hall	[hɔ:l]	Flur	garage	[gæ'rɑ:ʒ]	Garage
door	[dɔ:]	Tür	cellar	['selə]	Keller	shed	[ʃed]	Schuppen
window	['wɪndəʊ]	Fenster	terrace	['terɪs]	Terrasse	garden	['gɑ:dn]	Garten
loft	[lɔft]	Dachboden	balcony	['bælkəni]	Balkon			

Story: Where's Mr Fluff?!

	busy ['bɪzi]	belebt; beschäftigt	Let's go to Luke's house. – Not now. I'm *busy*. Sorry! ! Achtung Aussprache.
	Who … for? [ˌhu: 'fɔ:]	Für wen …?	A new bedroom! *Who* is it *for*: Luke or Jamie?
•	**who** [hu:]	wer; wem; wen	
	to **explore** [ɪk'splɔ:]	auf Entdeckungsreise gehen; sich umschauen; erkunden; erforschen	A new park? Great! Let's go and *explore*! *Fr.* explorer; *Lat.* explorare
	best [best]	beste/-r/-s	Olivia is Holly's *best* friend.
	bag [bæg]	Tasche; Tüte	What's in Olivia's *bag*? 
	maybe ['meɪbi]	vielleicht	Ding-dong! Who's that? – *Maybe* it's Olivia. Yes, it is.
	after ['ɑ:ftə]	nach *(zeitlich)*	Let's go to the park *after* school.
	visit ['vɪzɪt]	Besuch	After Olivia's *visit* Holly can only find one guinea pig. *Fr.* visite *(f)*
	outside [ˌaʊt'saɪd]	nach draußen; draußen; außerhalb (von)	Where's Sherlock? – He's *outside* in the garden.
	awful ['ɔ:fl]	schrecklich; furchtbar	A mouse in the house? Oh no! This is *awful*!
	Don't worry! [ˌdəʊnt 'wʌri]	Keine Sorge!	It's OK. *Don't worry!*
1	**sentence** ['sentəns]	Satz	There are two or more words in a *sentence*.
2	**right** [raɪt]	richtig; korrekt	Is Luke eleven? – Yes, that's *right*.
4	**ending** ['endɪŋ]	Ende; Schluss *(einer Geschichte)*	

Check-out

to **talk about** ['tɔ:k‿əbaʊt]	sprechen über; erzählen von	*Talk about* your family.

Pick-up B This is fun!

	day [deɪ]	Tag	It's a nice *day* for the boating lake. – OK, let's go to the park.
	• **happy** ['hæpi]	glücklich; froh; fröhlich	Lou is *happy*.
	• **can't** [kɑːnt]	kann nicht; können nicht	Where's Mr Fluff? I *can't* see him. ! Achtung Aussprache: can [æ] ↔ *can't* [ɑː]
	to **meet** [miːt]	treffen; sich treffen	Where can I *meet* you? – Let's *meet* in the park.
	to **show** [ʃəʊ]	zeigen	Please *show* me your new skates.
	game [geɪm]	Spiel	
	to **want (to)** ['wɒnt tə]	wollen; mögen	I *want to* play a game.
	• to **play** [pleɪ]	spielen	Let's *play* football. – No, let's *play* a different game.
	boring ['bɔːrɪŋ]	langweilig	That's *boring*! ↔ That's fun!
	You're into sports. [ˌjɔːr‿ˌɪntə 'spɔːts]	Du magst doch Sport.; Du stehst doch auf Sport.	*You're into* computer games? *I'm into* inline skating.
	Try skating! [ˌtraɪ 'skeɪtɪŋ]	Versuch es mal mit Inlineskating.; Probier mal Inlineskating.	
	fast [fɑːst]	schnell	Not so *fast*, Olivia! Skating isn't easy.
	so [səʊ]	so; also	I like rabbits. They're *so* quiet.
	I'm sorry! [ˌaɪm 'sɒri]	Tut mir leid!	
	I'm fine. [ˌaɪm 'faɪn]	Mir geht's gut.	*I'm fine.* = I'm OK.
	cute [kjuːt]	niedlich; süß	I like Lou. She's so *cute*!
	lucky charm [ˌlʌki 'tʃɑːm]	Glücksbringer; Talisman	Holly's *lucky charm* is pink.
1	**text (message)** ['tekst ˌmesɪdʒ]	SMS; Kurznachricht	! Du kannst *text message* sagen oder einfach *text*.
4	**reading** ['riːdɪŋ]	Lesen	*reading* → to read
	music ['mjuːzɪk]	Musik	! Achtung Aussprache. ***Fr.*** musique *(f)*; ***Lat.*** musica *(f)*
5	to **paint** [peɪnt]	anmalen; malen	
	to **go swimming** [ˌgəʊ 'swɪmɪŋ]	Schwimmen gehen	Let's *go swimming*. Swimming is fun. – I like it too.
	to **read** [riːd]	lesen	This text is in English. Can you *read* it?
	• **book** [bʊk]	Buch	
	to **take photos** [ˌteɪk 'fəʊtəʊz]	fotografieren; Fotos machen	Please *take a photo* of me!
	to **watch** [wɒtʃ]	beobachten; (sich) ansehen; zuschauen	! Beachte den Unterschied: Help! I can see a mouse! = sehen Let's look at your photos. = anschauen Hey, Olivia, I can skate! Watch! = zuschauen

card [kɑ:d]	Karte; Spielkarte	Let's play *cards*. *Fr.* carte *(f)*
magazine [ˌmægəˈzi:n]	Zeitschrift	*Fr.* magazine *(m)*
to **watch TV** [ˌwɒtʃ ti:ˈvi:]	fernsehen	Let's *watch TV*.
DVD [ˌdi:vi:ˈdi:]	DVD	
Me too. [ˌmi: ˈtu:]	Ich auch.	I love reading. – *Me too.*
7 • **bike** [baɪk]	Fahrrad	My *bike* is red. 
silly [ˈsɪli]	dumm; doof; albern	That's a *silly* game!

Hobbies

play … 	**badminton** **basketball** **football** **volleyball** **tennis** **handball**	play … 	**(computer) games** with **animals / cars** in the **garden / park** **outside** **at home**	go … 	**boating** **cycling** **(inline) skating** **swimming** **horse-riding** **skiing** **snowboarding**	make … 	**music** **models**

Unit 2 I'm new at TTS

Check-in

rule [ru:l]	Regel	In Tony's home there's only one *rule*: NO CATS!
planner [ˈplænə]	Handbuch; Kalender	
lunch [lʌnʃ]	Mittagessen	
cafeteria [ˌkæfəˈtɪəriə]	Cafeteria	Lunch at school is in the *cafeteria*. *Fr.* cafétéria *(f)*
money [ˈmʌni]	Geld	
machine [məˈʃi:n]	Automat; Maschine; Apparat; Gerät	In our street there's a *machine* for sweets. *Fr.* machine *(f)*
to **pay (for)** [peɪ]	bezahlen	*Fr.* payer
finger [ˈfɪŋgə]	Finger	! Achtung Aussprache: Das „g" wird mitgesprochen!
Art [ɑ:t]	Kunstunterricht	I love the pictures in the *Art* room. ! Schulfächer werden im Englischen groß geschrieben. *Fr.* art *(f)*; *Lat.* ars *(f)* 
to **buy** [baɪ]	kaufen	Let's *buy* a new planner.
• **sweets** *(pl)* [swi:ts]	Süßigkeiten; Bonbons	No, Sherlock! *Sweets* aren't good for dogs.
shop [ʃɒp]	Geschäft; Laden	Is there a *shop* at your school?

• **pen** [pen]	Füller	
• **pencil** ['pensl]	Bleistift; Buntstift	
pencil-case ['pensl ˌkeɪs]	Federmäppchen; Mäppchen	My *pencil-case* is green.
exercise book ['eksəsaɪz ˌbʊk]	Übungsheft	*exercise book* → book
ruler ['ru:lə]	Lineal	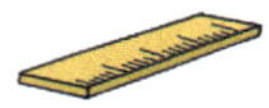
• **rubber** ['rʌbə]	Radiergummi	
uniform ['ju:nɪfɔ:m]	Uniform	The *uniform* at Thomas Tallis School is blue.
recording studio [rɪ'kɔ:dɪŋ ˌstju:diəʊ]	Aufnahmestudio; Tonstudio	A *recording studio* at a school? Wow!
1 **tutor** ['tju:tə]	Klassenlehrer/-in	Who is your *tutor*?
3 • **classroom** ['klɑ:srʊm]	Klassenzimmer	*classroom* → class
classmate ['klɑ:smeɪt]	Klassenkamerad/-in; Mitschüler/-in	

Station 1: Have you got questions for Jay?

• to **have got** [hæv 'gɒt]	besitzen; haben	Luke *has got* a dog. The Elliots *have got* a nice house.
question ['kwestʃən]	Frage	*Question*: How old are you? *Fr.* question *(f)*
today [tə'deɪ]	heute	*today* → day
• **schoolbag** ['sku:lbæg]	Schultasche	*schoolbag* → bag 
tutor group ['tju:tə ˌgru:p]	Klasse *(in einer englischen Schule)*	Jay is new in Luke and Dave's *tutor group*.
Good morning. [ˌgʊd 'mɔ:nɪŋ]	Guten Morgen.	
everyone ['evriwʌn]	jeder; alle	Hello! Is *everyone* here today?
student ['stju:dnt]	Schüler/-in; Student/-in	Luke and Dave are *students* at TTS.
to **call** [kɔ:l]	nennen	My name is Jahangir, but you can *call* me Jay.
him [hɪm]	ihn; ihm	Tell Mr Swindon your name. Tell *him* your name.
no [nəʊ]	kein/-e	*No* problem!
I like singing and dancing. [ˌaɪ laɪk ˌsɪŋɪŋ‿ənd 'dɑ:nsɪŋ]	Ich singe und tanze gern.	
to **sing** [sɪŋ]	singen	Let's *sing* a song.
to **dance** [dɑ:ns]	tanzen	The music is great – let's *dance*. *Fr.* danser
project ['prɒdʒekt]	Projekt	! Achte auf die Betonung: Die erste Silbe wird betont. *Fr.* un projet
well [wel]	tja; nun	Are you happy with a school uniform? – *Well*, not always!
something ['sʌmθɪŋ]	etwas	
Wait and see! [ˌweɪt‿ənd 'si:]	Warte ab!	What has Jay got? – *Wait and see!*

5 •	**teacher** ['tiːtʃə]	Lehrer/-in	! Du kannst *tutor* oder *teacher* sagen.
6 •	**board** [bɔːd]	Tafel	The *board* in your classroom can be a blackboard or a whiteboard.
7	**group** [gruːp]	Gruppe; Klasse	*Fr.* groupe *(m)* 
	lots (of) ['lɒts‿əv]	viel/-e; jede Menge	
8	**office** ['ɒfɪs]	Büro	
	grandparents *(pl)* ['græn‚peərənts]	Großeltern	*grandparents* = grandpa and grandma *Fr.* grandparents *(m)*
	talent show ['tælənt ‚ʃəʊ]	Talentwettbewerb	
	to **send** [send]	schicken; senden	Can I *send* you an e-mail?
	food [fuːd]	Essen; Lebensmittel	There's no *food* in my schoolbag.
	carrot ['kærət]	Karotte; Möhre	*Fr.* carotte *(f)* 
	pudding ['pʊdɪŋ]	Pudding; Nachtisch	
	restaurant ['restrɒnt]	Restaurant; Gaststätte	*Fr.* restaurant *(m)*
	pocket money ['pɒkɪt ‚mʌni]	Taschengeld	You can buy things with your *pocket money*.
9	to **use** [juːz]	benutzen; verwenden; gebrauchen	Can I *use* your skates?
	Here you are. [‚hɪə ju‿'ɑː]	Bitte schön.	Have you got my rubber? – Oh, yes. Sorry! *Here you are.*
	Be polite. [‚biː pə'laɪt]	Sei/Seid höflich.	*Be polite* with words like 'please' and 'thank you'.
11	**whose** [huːz]	wessen	
13	**German students are lucky.** [‚dʒɜːmən ‚stjuːdənts‿ə 'lʌki]	Deutsche Schüler haben Glück.	! *I'm lucky.* = Ich habe Glück. I'm happy. = Ich bin glücklich.
	lesson ['lesn]	Unterrichtsstunde; Schulstunde; Unterricht	We've got an English *lesson* today. *Fr.* leçon *(f)*
	building ['bɪldɪŋ]	Gebäude	Our classroom is in the new *building*. The Art room is in the old *building*.

School subjects

Art	[ɑːt]	Kunst
English	['ɪŋglɪʃ]	Englisch
German	['dʒɜːmən]	Deutsch
Geography	[dʒi'ɒgrəfi]	Erdkunde
Maths	[mæθs]	Mathematik
Science	[saɪəns]	Naturwissenschaften
Music	['mjuːzɪk]	Musik
Latin	['lætɪn]	Latein
French	[frenʃ]	Französisch
History	['hɪstri]	Geschichte
PE (Physical Education)	[‚piː'iː]	Sport
RE (Religious Education)	[‚ɑːr‿'iː]	Religion

Station 2: Don't stare! It's rude.

to **stare** [steə]	starren; anstarren	to see – to look – to watch – *to stare*
rude [ruːd]	unhöflich; unverschämt	*rude* ↔ polite

	funny ['fʌni]	lustig; witzig	Let's draw *funny* pictures of animals!
	to **sit** [sɪt]	sitzen	Where can we *sit*? – Let's *sit* at this table here, OK?
	lunch break ['lʌnʃbreɪk]	Mittagspause	We can go to the cafeteria in the *lunch break*.
	them [ðem]	sie *(Pl.)*; ihnen	
	to **forget** [fə'get]	vergessen	Don't *forget* the photos!
16•	to **do** [du:]	machen; tun	It's a nice day. What can we *do*? – We can play football.
	fun [fʌn]	lustig; witzig; fröhlich	You can do *fun* things with a dog!
	into ['ɪntə]	in; in … hinein	Please don't go *into* my bedroom.
	alone [ə'ləʊn]	allein; ohne fremde Hilfe	Look, Olivia! I can skate *alone* now.
	to **bring** [brɪŋ]	bringen; mitbringen	Holly can't *bring* her guinea pigs to school.
17	to **be late** [bi 'leɪt]	zu spät dran sein; zu spät kommen	Don't *be late*! 
•	to **be** [bi:]	sein	
	to **wear** [weə]	anhaben; tragen *(Kleidung)*	*Wear* your uniform. That's a school rule!
	to **run** [rʌn]	rennen; laufen	We're late! – Oh no! Let's *run*!
	homework ['həʊmwɜ:k]	Hausaufgabe(n)	! *homework* steht immer im Singular: Our *homework* today is easy. 
18	to **look at** ['lʊk‿ət]	anschauen; ansehen	*Look at* that picture in your book.
20•	**when** [wen]	wenn; wann; als	Be polite *when* you talk to people.
	already [ɔ:l'redi]	schon; bereits	Have you got this book? – Yes, I've *already* got it.
	to **add** [æd]	hinzufügen; ergänzen	Make a list of the old words. Then *add* the new words.
•	**chips** *(pl) (BE)* [tʃɪps]	Pommes frites	
21	**end** [end]	Ende; Schluss	
22	**over there** [ˌəʊvə 'ðeə]	da drüben; dort drüben	
	these [ði:z]	diese (hier)	This car is Jamie's. – Yes, and *these* cars are Jamie's too.
	those [ðəʊz]	diese dort; jene	! this → these that → *those*
	to **find** [faɪnd]	finden; herausfinden	*Find* your ball, Sherlock!

Skills: How to practise correct spelling

	to **practise** ['præktɪs]	üben; trainieren	First *practise* the dialogue, then present it.
	spelling ['spelɪŋ]	Rechtschreibung	
2	to **need** [ni:d]	brauchen; benötigen	Let's make dialogues. – OK, but I *need* a partner.
	place [pleɪs]	Ort; Stelle; Platz	Greenwich is a *place* in England. *Fr.* place *(f)*
	first [fɜ:st]	erste/-r/-s	Today is my *first* day at the new school.
3	to **learn** [lɜ:n]	lernen	You *learn* lots of things at school.

Story: Let's play a trick

to **play a trick (on)** [ˌpleɪ‿ə ˈtrɪk‿ɒn]	einen Streich spielen	The students want to *play a trick on* their teacher.
week [wiːk]	Woche	There are seven days in a *week*.
before [bɪˈfɔː]	vor *(zeitlich)*; bevor	We've got English *before* lunch. And after lunch we've got German.
to **work** [wɜːk]	arbeiten	Let's *work* in the garden!
pair [peə]	Paar	Two things (or two people) are a *pair*. 
presentation [ˌpreznˈteɪʃn]	Präsentation; Vortrag	
recording [rɪˈkɔːdɪŋ]	Aufnahme; Aufzeichnung	*recording* → recording studio
poem [ˈpəʊɪm]	Gedicht	text – story – song – rhyme – *poem* *Fr.* poème *(m)*
sure [ʃʊə; ʃɔː]	sicher	Where is the book? – I'm *sure* it's in your bag.
voice [vɔɪs]	Stimme	Sing that song again! You've got a nice *voice*.
next [nekst]	nächste/-r/-s; der/die Nächste(n)	You're *next*, Jay!
to **be jealous (of)** [bi ˈdʒeləs]	eifersüchtig sein (auf); neidisch sein (auf)	Is Luke *jealous of* Jay? *Fr.* jaloux/jalouse
popular [ˈpɒpjələ]	beliebt; populär	The students and teachers like Jay. He's *popular*. *Fr.* populaire
king [kɪŋ]	König	
• **class** [klɑːs]	Klasse; Schulklasse	
Come on! [ˌkʌm‿ˈɒn]	Komm schon!; Komm jetzt!	*Come on*! Let's go!
A few minutes later. [ə ˌfjuː ˌmɪnɪts ˈleɪtə]	Ein paar Minuten später.	
I hear ... [aɪ ˈhɪə]	Ich habe gehört, dass ...	*I hear* you're in Mr Swindon's tutor group. – Yes, that's right.
just [dʒʌst]	gerade; nur; einfach	
joke [dʒəʊk]	Witz	
really [ˈrɪəli]	wirklich	It's very good. I *really* like it.
• **much** [mʌtʃ]	viel	I haven't got *much* time.
• **time** [taɪm]	Zeit	How much *time* have we got?
• to **know** [nəʊ]	kennen; wissen	I *know* Luke. He's the funny boy with the nice dog. ! Achtung Aussprache: Bei Wörtern mit „kn" wird das „k" nicht ausgesprochen.
It's your turn. [ˌɪts ˈjɔː tɜːn]	Du bist dran.	
Stop it! [ˈstɒp‿ɪt]	Mach/Macht das aus!; Hör/Hört auf!	That music is awful. *Stop it!*
to **laugh** [lɑːf]	lachen	Don't *laugh* at me!

angry ['æŋgri]	wütend; zornig; verärgert; böse	The teacher is *angry* with the students. They're late again.
He's right. [ˌhi:z 'raɪt]	Er hat recht.	Greenwich is in London. – Yes, you*'re right*.
• to **give** [gɪv]	geben; schenken	Can you *give* me a biscuit, please?
to **think** [θɪŋk]	denken; nachdenken	A problem? First stop and *think*! There's always an answer.
to **make trouble** [ˌmeɪk 'trʌbl]	Ärger machen; in Schwierigkeiten bringen	

Check-out

story, stories *(pl)* ['stɔ:ri; 'stɔ:riz]	Story; Geschichte; Erzählung	Holly thinks *stories* about animals are great.
because [bɪ'kɒz]	weil; da	I like Lou *because* she's so cute! ! Im Deutschen steht das Verb im Nebensatz am Ende: … weil sie so süß ist.

Unit 3 I like my busy days

Check-in

• **cheese** [tʃi:z]	Käse	Mice love *cheese*. 

Days of the week

Monday ['mʌndeɪ]	Montag	**Friday** ['fraɪdeɪ]	Freitag
Tuesday ['tju:zdeɪ]	Dienstag	**Saturday** ['sætədeɪ]	Samstag/Sonnabend
Wednesday ['wenzdeɪ]	Mittwoch	**Sunday** ['sʌndeɪ]	Sonntag
Thursday ['θɜ:zdeɪ]	Donnerstag		

a.m. [ˌeɪ'em]	vormittags *(Uhrzeit)*	
p.m. [ˌpi:'em]	nachmittags *(Uhrzeit)*; abends *(Uhrzeit)*	
surprise [sə'praɪz]	Überraschung	I've got a *surprise* for you! *Fr.* surprise *(f)*
Cooking Club ['kʊkɪŋ ˌklʌb]	Koch-AG	
club [klʌb]	Klub; Verein; AG	
by *(bike)* [baɪ]	mit *(dem Fahrrad)*	Let's go *by* car.
to **sit down** [ˌsɪt 'daʊn]	sich hinsetzen; sich setzen	It's time for lunch. *Sit down*, please, everyone.
to **have breakfast** [ˌhæv 'brekfəst]	frühstücken	! *Have* bedeutet hier „essen".
Time to get up! [ˌtaɪm tə ˌget‿'ʌp]	Es ist Zeit aufzustehen!	It's *time to get up*, Dave!

	to **tidy** *(a room)* ['taɪdi]	aufräumen; in Ordnung bringen	Can you *tidy* your room, please, Olivia?
	this is how you (do) ... ['ðɪs‿ɪz haʊ jʊ ˌduː]	so machst du ...	*This is how you do* this exercise.
	to **sleep** [sliːp]	schlafen	
	to **go to bed** [ˌɡəʊ tə 'bed]	ins Bett gehen	I sometimes *go to bed* late. *to go to bed* ↔ to get up
1	**What's the time?** [ˌwɒts ðə 'taɪm]	Wie spät ist es?; Wie viel Uhr ist es?	*What's the time*, please?

The time

It's ten **o'clock**.	Es ist zehn Uhr.	(Zeitangabe bei vollen Stunden)
It's five **past** ten.	Es ist fünf nach zehn.	
It's ten **oh** six.	Es ist sechs nach zehn.	
It's quarter **past** ten.	Es ist viertel nach zehn.	
It's **half past** ten.	Es ist halb elf.	(! half past ten = halb elf)
It's quarter **to** eleven.	Es ist viertel vor elf.	
It's nine **minutes to** eleven.	Es ist neun (Minuten) vor elf.	
It's one o'clock **a.m.**	Es ist ein Uhr.	(! Ab 13 Uhr fängt man im Englischen wieder bei 1 an. Vormittags- und Nachmittagsstunden werden mit a.m. und p.m. unterschieden.)
It's one o'clock **p.m.**	Es ist 13 Uhr.	

3	**every** ['evri]	jede/-r/-s	I play football *every* day.
•	to **come** [kʌm]	kommen	Can you *come* to my house now?
	home [həʊm]	nach Hause	Let's go *home* now!
	dinner ['dɪnə]	Abendessen	breakfast - lunch - *dinner* *Fr.* dîner *(m)*
	at 7:30 [ət ˌsevn‿'θɜːti]	um halb acht	I get up *at 7:30*.
	then [ðen]	dann; danach	First read the text. *Then* we can talk about it.

Station 1: I'm always busy

	never ['nevə]	nie; niemals	*never* ↔ always
•	**morning** ['mɔːnɪŋ]	Morgen; Vormittag	I have breakfast in the kitchen every *morning*.
	stepmum ['stepmʌm]	Stiefmutter	
	if [ɪf]	wenn; falls; ob	*If* it's a nice day, we can go to the park.
	till [tɪl]	bis	My English lesson is from 8:30 *till* 9:15 today.
	after that [ˌɑːftə 'ðæt]	danach	
	on Mondays [ɒn 'mʌndeɪz]	montags	! *on Mondays*, on Tuesdays ... = jeden Montag, jeden Dienstag ... (regelmäßig etwas tun!)
	netball ['netbɔːl]	Korbball	*Netball* is a popular girls' game at British schools.
	other ['ʌðə]	anders; andere/-r/-s; weitere	Is there only your family in your house, or are there *other* people too?

	right away [ˌraɪt‿əˈweɪ]	sofort; gleich	Can I watch TV now, Mum? – No, Dave. It's best to do your homework *right away*.
	often [ˈɒfn]	oft; häufig	At TTS there are *often* clubs after school.
	in the evenings [ɪn ði‿ˈiːvnɪŋz]	abends	We often watch TV *in the evenings*. You too?
	evening [ˈiːvnɪŋ]	Abend	*evening* ↔ morning
	sometimes [ˈsʌmtaɪmz]	manchmal	
	usually [ˈjuːʒli]	normalerweise; gewöhnlich; meistens	always – *usually* – often – sometimes – never
	long [lɒŋ]	lang	How *long* are lessons at TTS? *Fr.* long/longue; ***Lat.*** longus
	I'm dog-tired. [ˌaɪm ˌdɒgˈtaɪəd]	Ich bin hundemüde.	
	tired [taɪəd]	müde	I don't want to watch TV. I'm *tired*.
2	**What about …?** [ˈwɒt‿əbaʊt]	Wie wär's mit …?; Was ist mit …?	*What about* a new room in the loft? – For me? Wow! Great idea!
3	**afternoon** [ˌɑːftəˈnuːn]	Nachmittag	morning – *afternoon* – evening
6	to **look for** [ˈlʊk fɔː]	suchen nach	
7	to **snore** [snɔː]	schnarchen	
	roommate [ˈruːmmeɪt]	Zimmergenosse/Zimmergenossin	Jay can't sleep because his *roommate* snores.
	coach [kəʊtʃ]	Trainer/-in	A *coach* gives help in a sport.
	last [lɑːst]	letzte/-r/-s	*last* ↔ first
	tomorrow [təˈmɒrəʊ]	morgen	Today is Friday. *Tomorrow* is Saturday.

Prepositions

Prepositions of time

in	I get up early **in** the morning.	(Tageszeit)
at	I have breakfast **at** 8 o'clock.	(Uhrzeit)
on	I play football **on** Saturdays.	(Wochentag)

Prepositions of time and place

Zeitlich

vor	It's five **to** ten.	… fünf vor zehn.
	Please do your homework **before** lunch.	… vor dem Mittagessen.
nach	It's twenty **past** two.	… zwanzig nach zwei.
	Let's play football **after** breakfast.	… nach dem Frühstück.

Räumlich

Sherlock is **in front of** the TV.	… vor dem Fernseher.
Let's go **to** Greenwich.	… nach Greenwich.

Station 2: She gets on my nerves

	She gets on my nerves. [ʃi: ˌgets‿ɒn maɪ 'nɜ:vz]	Sie geht mir auf die Nerven.	
	granny ['græni]	Oma	! *Granny* wird nur als Name groß geschrieben: Hi, *Granny*! ABER: Where's Dave's *granny*?
	to **look after** [ˌlʊk‿'ɑ:ftə]	aufpassen auf; hüten; sich kümmern um	Luke is at school every day. So who *looks after* Sherlock?
	to **ask** [ɑ:sk]	fragen; bitten	Where's Sherlock? – Let's *ask* Luke.
	to **talk** [tɔ:k]	sprechen; reden	
	to **stop** [stɒp]	aufhören (mit); anhalten; stoppen	Skating is great, but I'm tired now. Let's *stop*!
	to **chat** [tʃæt]	plaudern; chatten *(sich online unterhalten)*	to speak – to talk – *to chat* *Fr.* chatter
	even ['i:vn]	sogar; selbst	Olivia is nice to her little sister. She *even* tidies Lucy's room.
	work [wɜ:k]	Arbeit	This is a very nice text, Olivia. Good *work*!
	vet [vet]	Tierarzt/Tierärztin	A *vet* knows lots about animals. *Fr.* vétérinaire *(m)*
	neighbour *(BE)* ['neɪbə]	Nachbar/-in	It's nice to have friendly *neighbours*.
	• to **take** [teɪk]	nehmen; mitnehmen; wegnehmen; bringen; mitbringen	Luke can't *take* Sherlock to school.
	• **pet** [pet]	Haustier	Sherlock is Luke's *pet*.
	surgery ['sɜ:dʒri]	Arztpraxis; Praxis; Praxisräume	The vet looks at people's pets in his/her *surgery*.
10	**why** [waɪ]	warum	*Why* is Aunt Frances here? – Because Granny hasn't got time.
12	**Be careful!** [ˌbi: 'keəfl]	Vorsicht!; Pass/Passt auf!	*Be careful*, Holly! Not so fast!
	mistake [mɪ'steɪk]	Fehler	That's wrong. It's a *mistake*.
14	**cooking** ['kʊkɪŋ]	Kochen	
18	**dialogue** ['daɪəlɒg]	Dialog; Gespräch	Let's act a *dialogue*!
	speaker ['spi:kə]	Redner/-in; Sprecher/-in	
	What is … about? [ˌwɒt‿ɪz‿ə'baʊt]	Worum geht es in/im …?	This is a great story! – *What's it about?* Tell me.
	to **be about** [bi‿ə'baʊt]	gehen um; handeln von	My new book *is about* dogs.
	to **find out** [ˌfaɪnd‿'aʊt]	herausfinden	Listen and *find out* what the text is about.
	situation [ˌsɪtju'eɪʃn]	Situation	What's the *situation*? It's Sunday. Olivia's in the kitchen with Lucy.

Skills: How to improve your speaking

	to **improve** [ɪm'pru:v]	sich verbessern; verbessern	I want to *improve* my English.
1	to **warm up** [ˌwɔ:m‿'ʌp]	aufwärmen; sich aufwärmen	First, let's *warm up*!
	mouth [maʊθ]	Mund	
	sound [saʊnd]	Ton; Geräusch; Klang	I like the *sound* of Jay's voice.

	to **get fit** [ˌget ˈfɪt]	in Form kommen; fit werden	You want to *get fit*? Do more sports!
2	**rhythm** [ˈrɪðm]	Rhythmus	*Fr.* rythme *(m)*
	to **stand up** [ˌstænd‿ˈʌp]	aufstehen *(von einer Sitzgelegenheit)*	! *to stand up* (from a chair) to get up (from bed)
	Clap your hands. [ˌklæp jɔː ˈhændz]	Klatsch/Klatscht in die Hände.	
	loud [laʊd]	laut	I like *loud* music.
	very much [ˌveri ˈmʌtʃ]	sehr	Thank you *very much*!
3	to **speak** [spiːk]	sprechen	Can you *speak* English? *to speak* → speaker
	clear [klɪə]	klar; deutlich	For presentations you need a *clear* voice.
	acting a scene [ˌæktɪŋ‿ə ˈsiːn]	eine Theaterszene spielen	
	too [tuː]	zu	Sorry, but I'm *too* tired to play with you. ! Achte auf die Satzstellung: *too* kann „auch" und „zu" heißen.

Unit task: Scenes from a typical day

	scene [siːn]	Szene	
	typical [ˈtɪpɪkl]	typisch	On a *typical* day, I go to school by bike. *Fr.* typique
	country [ˈkʌntri], **countries** *(pl)* [ˈkʌntriz]	Land	England and Germany are two different *countries*.
	interesting [ˈɪntrəstɪŋ]	interessant	My book about animals is very *interesting*. *Fr.* intéressant/-e
	to **describe** [dɪˈskraɪb]	beschreiben	
	to **look** [lʊk]	schauen; sehen; aussehen	Where's my ruler? – *Look* in your pencil-case. 
	in the mornings [ˌɪn ðə ˈmɔːnɪŋz]	morgens; vormittags	*In the mornings* I get up at seven. We have five different lessons *in the mornings*.
	to **act** [ækt]	spielen *(Theater)*	Take turns to *act* the scenes.
•	**help** [help]	Hilfe	*help* → to help
	to **be good at** [bi ˈgʊd‿ət]	gut sein in	*I'm good at* football.

Story: Luke is my pet

	to **wash** [wɒʃ]	waschen; sich waschen	Don't forget to *wash* your hands before lunch.
	face [feɪs]	Gesicht	This is a happy *face*: 
	to **make** [meɪk]	machen; tun; bilden	Olivia often *makes* models for her friends.
	early [ˈɜːli]	früh	*early* ↔ late
	goodbye [gʊdˈbaɪ]	auf Wiedersehen	*goodbye* ↔ hello
	to **bark** [bɑːk]	bellen	Dogs usually *bark* when they see a cat.

to **be scared (of)** [bi 'skeəd‿əv]	Angst haben (vor)	Cats *are* often *scared of* dogs.
to **run away** [ˌrʌn‿ə'weɪ]	wegrennen	Sid *runs away* when he sees Sherlock.
to **have fun** [ˌhæv 'fʌn]	Spaß haben; sich amüsieren	
to **listen for** ['lɪsn fə]	horchen auf	In the park, Sherlock *listens for* Luke's voice.
Sit! [sɪt]	Sitz! *(Befehl für Hunde)*	
around [ə'raʊnd]	um ... herum; umher	Sherlock often runs *around* in the park.
to **chase** [tʃeɪs]	jagen; nachjagen	Sherlock sometimes *chases* squirrels in the park. *Fr.* chasser
tail [teɪl]	Schwanz; Schweif	
a lot to learn [ə ˌlɒt tə 'lɜ:n]	viel zu lernen	Sherlock has got *a lot to learn*.
• to **put** [pʊt]	setzen; stellen; legen	Sherlock! *Put* the ball here!
drink [drɪŋk]	Getränk	Where are the *drinks*? – They're in the fridge.
to **fall over** [ˌfɔ:l‿'əʊvə]	hinfallen; umkippen	I sometimes laugh so much I *fall over*!
to **throw (at)** [θrəʊ]	werfen (nach)	In football, only one person can *throw* the ball!
• **shoe** [ʃu:]	Schuh	Luke! Please put your *shoes* away in the cupboard. – OK, Dad.
to **fall asleep** [ˌfɔ:l‿ə'sli:p]	einschlafen	When I'm in bed, I usually *fall asleep* right away.

Parts of the body

face	[feɪs]	Gesicht	head	[hed]	Kopf	foot, feet *(pl)*	[fʊt, fi:t]	Fuß
mouth	[maʊθ]	Mund	hair	[heə]	Haar(e)	leg	[leg]	Bein
eye	[aɪ]	Auge	**hand**	[hænd]	Hand	knee	[ni:]	Knie
ear	[ɪə]	Ohr	arm	[ɑ:m]	Arm	toe	[təʊ]	Zeh
nose	[nəʊz]	Nase	shoulder	['ʃəʊldə]	Schulter			

Across cultures 1 How to be polite in English

How to ... ['haʊ tə]	Wie man ...	You know *how to* say 'Hallo' in English.
to **visit** ['vɪzɪt]	besichtigen; besuchen	*to visit* → a visit *Fr.* visiter; ***Lat.*** visitare
important [ɪm'pɔ:tnt]	wichtig	This letter is *important*, Luke. Give it to your teacher. *Fr.* important/-e
page [peɪdʒ]	Seite	Open your books at *page* 11, please. *Fr.* page *(f)*; ***Lat.*** pagina *(f)*
what to ... ['wɒt tə]	was man ...	
English-speaking ['ɪŋglɪʃˌspi:kɪŋ]	englischsprachig	England is an *English-speaking* country.

2	**smile** [smaɪl]	Lächeln	With a *smile* on your face you look friendly. 
	Excuse me … [ɪk'skju:z mi]	Entschuldigung!; Entschuldigen Sie!	*Excuse me*. Where's the school, please? *Fr.* Excusez-moi …
	of course [əv 'kɔ:s]	natürlich; selbstverständlich	Can you play football? – *Of course* I can!
	to **have** *(a sweet)* [hæv]	*(ein Bonbon)* nehmen; *(ein Bonbon)* essen	Here, *have* a sweet. – Oh, thanks.
	You're welcome. [ˌjɔ: 'welkəm]	Bitte schön.; Nichts zu danken.; Gern geschehen.	Thank you. – *You're welcome.* ! *You're welcome* heißt nicht „Willkommen."
3	**way** [weɪ]	Weg; Art und Weise	This is a good *way* to do it.
	lemonade [ˌlemə'neɪd]	Limonade	Can I have a drink, please? – Yes, of course. Is *lemonade* OK?
	timetable ['taɪmˌteɪbl]	Stundenplan; Fahrplan	It shows you what lessons you have, and when.
	to **be in the way** [bi‿ɪn ðə 'weɪ]	im Weg sein/stehen	*Am I in the way?* – No, that's OK.
	bus station ['bʌs ˌsteɪʃn]	Busbahnhof	Let's meet at the *bus station*.
	person ['pɜ:sn], **people** *(pl)* ['pi:pl]	Person; Mensch	! one *person* – two people
	box [bɒks]	Box; Kasten; Schachtel; Kiste	My favourite games are in a *box* in my bedroom.
	to **open** ['əʊpn]	öffnen; aufmachen	Can you *open* the door for me, please?
	train [treɪn]	Zug	Let's take the next *train* to London.  *Fr.* train *(m)*
	window ['wɪndəʊ]	Fenster	Can we open the *window*? 

Prepositions of place

at	at home at school at the (bus/train) station	zu Hause in der Schule am (Bus-)Bahnhof	**on**	on the bus on the train ! in the car	im Bus im Zug im Auto
in	in Britain in Greenwich in the house in the park in the shop in the street	in Großbritannien in Greenwich im Haus im Park im Laden auf der Straße			

4	to **hold** [həʊld]	halten; festhalten	Tony always wants to *hold* Lou's hand.
	open ['əʊpn]	offen; geöffnet; aufgeschlagen	The shop is *open*. Let's go in.
	woman ['wʊmən], **women** *(pl)* ['wɪmɪn]	Frau	! Achtung Aussprache.
	man [mæn], **men** *(pl)* [men]	Mann	*man* ↔ woman

to **jump the queue** [ˌdʒʌmp ðə 'kjuː]	sich vordrängeln	Never *jump the queue*! Other people don't like it.
British ['brɪtɪʃ]	britisch; Brite/Britin	*British* people speak English.
escalator ['eskəleɪtə]	Rolltreppe	*Fr.* escalator *(m)*
to **stand** [stænd]	stehen	Please *stand* on the left.
to **walk** [wɔːk]	gehen; laufen	Let's *walk* to school today.

Focus 1 The United Kingdom

	castle ['kɑːsl]	Schloss; Burg	! Das „t" in *castle* wird nicht gesprochen.
	flag [flæg]	Flagge; Fahne	The colours of the British *flag* are red, white and blue.
	beach [biːtʃ]	Strand	
	sea [siː]	Meer	! the *sea* = **die** See, <u>nicht</u>: der See.
•	**cold** [kəʊld]	kalt	The sea around Britain is often *cold*.
	rock [rɒk]	Fels; Stein	
	special ['speʃl]	besonders; speziell	Let's do something *special*.
	shape [ʃeɪp]	Form	
	a lot of [ə 'lɒt‿əv]	viel/-e; eine Menge	I've got *a lot of* friends.
	high [haɪ]	hoch; groß	I live in that *high* building over there.
	mountain ['maʊntɪn]	Berg	
	forest ['fɒrɪst]	Wald	There are lots of trees in a *forest*. *Fr.* forêt *(f)*
	island ['aɪlənd]	Insel	Some *islands* are great for holidays.
1	**map** [mæp]	Stadtplan; Landkarte	Look at the *map* in your book.
	north [nɔːθ]	nördlich; im Norden	Let's go *north*. I think it's the right way.

Geography

north	[nɔːθ]	Norden, Nord-, nördlich	**rock**	[rɒk]	Fels, Stein	**lake**	[leɪk]	See
east	[iːst]	Osten, Ost-, östlich	**mountain**	['maʊntɪn]	Berg	**island**	['aɪlənd]	Insel
south	[saʊθ]	Süden, Süd-, südlich	**forest**	['fɒrɪst]	Wald	**sea**	[siː]	Meer
west	[west]	Westen, West-, westlich	**river**	['rɪvə]	Fluss	**map**	[mæp]	Landkarte, Stadtplan

Northern, eastern, southern und western können als Adjektive vor einem Nomen stehen: Northern Ireland is part of the UK.
Nur als Eigennamen werden Himmelsrichtungen großgeschrieben: Greenwich is in East London. England is south of Scotland. Wales is in the west of Britain.

	sheep, sheep *(pl)* [ʃi:p]	Schaf	
	separate ['seprət]	separat; getrennt; verschieden	Wales and England are *separate* countries. ***Lat.*** separatus/-a/-um

Activities

surfing	['sɜ:fɪŋ]	Surfen, Wellenreiten	**fishing**	['fɪʃɪŋ]	Angeln
hiking	['haɪkɪŋ]	Wandern	**pony trekking**	['pəʊni ˌtrekɪŋ]	Wanderreiten
mountain biking	['maʊntɪn ˌbaɪkɪŋ]	Mountainbikefahren	**shopping**	['ʃɒpɪŋ]	Einkaufen
skiing	['ski:ɪŋ]	Skifahren	**sightseeing**	['saɪtsi:ɪŋ]	Besichtigung von Sehenswürdigkeiten
canoeing	[kə'nu:ɪŋ]	Kanufahren			
camping	['kæmpɪŋ]	Camping, Zelten			

	museum [mju:'zi:əm]	Museum	Let's go to the clock *museum*. It's great! ***Fr.*** musée *(m)*
2	**capital** ['kæpɪtl]	Hauptstadt	London is the *capital* of England. ! Du kannst *capital* city sagen oder einfach *capital*. ***Lat.*** capitalis
	city ['sɪti]	Stadt; Großstadt	London is a *city*. A very big *city*!
	fact [fækt]	Fakt; Tatsache	I know a lot of *facts* about the UK. ***Lat.*** factum *(nt)*
3	**most famous** [ˌməʊst 'feɪməs]	berühmteste/-r/-s	One of London's *most famous* sights is Big Ben.
	famous ['feɪməs]	berühmt	I want to be *famous*. I want to be a star. ***Fr.*** fameux/fameuse; ***Lat.*** famosus
	sight [saɪt]	Sehenswürdigkeit; Anblick	A *sight* is an interesting thing to see in a city.
	queen [kwi:n]	Königin	The British king or *queen* lives in Buckingham Palace.
	river ['rɪvə]	Fluss	The Main and the Isar are *rivers*.
•	to **ride** [raɪd]	fahren; reiten	
4	**most interesting** [ˌməʊst‿'ɪntrəstɪŋ]	am interessantesten	I like a lot of books, but books about animals are *most interesting* to me. ***Fr.*** intéressant/-e
5	**town** [taʊn]	Stadt	If a *town* is very big, you can call it a city.
	near [nɪə]	nahe; in der Nähe von	Is your house *near* the school?
	village ['vɪlɪdʒ]	Dorf	*village* – town – city ***Fr.*** village *(m)*
	church [tʃɜ:tʃ]	Kirche	
	cinema ['sɪnəmə]	Kino	***Fr.*** cinéma *(m)*
	theatre ['θɪətə]	Theater	Is there a *theatre* in your town? ***Fr.*** théâtre *(m)*
	concert ['kɒnsət]	Konzert	

Unit 4 Let's do something fun

Check-in

	to **cost** [kɒst]	kosten	A day in London *costs* a lot!
	ship [ʃɪp]	Schiff	A *ship* is a big boat.
	over ['əʊvə]	hinüber; über	*over* ↔ under
	foot [fʊt], **feet** *(pl)* [fi:t]	Fuß	! one *foot* – two *feet* 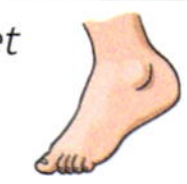
	pier [pɪə]	Pier; Hafendamm	You can watch the boats from the *pier*.
	to **start** [stɑ:t]	anfangen; beginnen; starten	School *starts* at 8 o'clock.
	across [ə'krɒs]	auf der anderen Seite von; über; hinüber; herüber; quer durch	The shop is *across* the street.
	free [fri:]	frei; kostenlos	1. There's no school on Saturday. It's my *free* day. 2. It's *free*! It costs no money.
	water slide ['wɔ:tə ˌslaɪd]	Wasserrutsche	
	leisure centre ['leʒə ˌsentə]	Freizeitzentrum	You can do a lot of fun things at a *leisure centre*.
3	**free time** [ˌfri: 'taɪm]	Freizeit	Olivia makes models in her *free time*.
4	**look** [lʊk]	Blick	*look* → to look

Station 1: Well, what's your idea?

	together [tə'geðə]	zusammen; miteinander; gemeinsam	
	at the weekend [ət ðə ˌwi:k'end]	am Wochenende	Saturday and Sunday = *the weekend*
	exciting [ɪk'saɪtɪŋ]	spannend; aufregend	I love *exciting* stories.
	What time? [ˌwɒt 'taɪm]	Um wie viel Uhr?	
•	**fine** [faɪn]	gut; in Ordnung; schön	Are you OK? – Yes, I'm *fine*.
	See you! ['si: jə]	Bis dann!; Bis ...	Bye. *See you* on Monday! 
4	to **close** [kləʊz]	schließen; zumachen	*to close* ↔ to open
	enough [ɪ'nʌf]	genug; genügend	Your skates aren't big *enough* for me!
5	**not ... either** [nɒt ... 'aɪðə; nɒt ... 'i:ðə]	auch nicht	He doesn't like her. She does*n't* like him *either*.
•	**Bye!** [baɪ]	Tschüss!	*bye* ↔ hello

Station 2: Does the farm look nice?

	to **spell** [spel]	buchstabieren	*Spell* 'Tony': T-O-N-Y
	at last [ət 'lɑ:st]	endlich; schließlich	*At last* I've got my own room in the loft!
	half-sister ['hɑ:fˌsɪstə]	Halbschwester	
	information *(no pl)* [ˌɪnfə'meɪʃn]	Information; *Informationen*	! *information* hat keine Mehrzahl (Pluralform): I've got a lot of *information* about Greenwich.
	all [ɔ:l]	alle/-s; ganz	1. *All* the children in my street are nice. 2. Don't play computer games *all* day!
	to **get there** ['get ðeə]	hinkommen	How can we *get there*? In the car?
	to **go by . . .** ['gəʊ baɪ]	fahren mit . . .	We can *go* there *by* bike or *by* bus.
	us [ʌs]	uns	Can you help *us*?
	to **answer** ['ɑ:nsə]	antworten; beantworten	! Achtung Aussprache: Bei *answer* ['ɑ:nsə] spricht man das „w" nicht. *to answer* ↔ to ask
	bad [bæd]	schlecht; böse; schlimm *(ugs.)*	*bad* ↔ good
	weather ['weðə]	Wetter	The *weather* is very nice today.
	to **keep your fingers crossed** [ˌki:p jɔ: ˌfɪŋgəz 'krɒst]	die Daumen drücken	I've got a test today, so *keep your fingers crossed* for me!
9	to **get to** ['get tə]	kommen zu; kommen nach; erreichen	How do we *get to* Cutty Sark?
	bus [bʌs]	Bus	! Vorsicht bei der Pluralform: *buses* [-sɪz]! *Fr.* bus *(m)*
10	to **talk to** ['tɔ:k tə]	reden mit	*Talk to* Pia about London.

Farm animals

pig	[pɪg]	Schwein	**lamb**	[læm]	Lamm	**goat**	[gəʊt]	Ziege
chicken	['tʃɪkɪn]	Huhn	**sheep, sheep** *(pl)*	[ʃi:p]	Schaf	**goose, geese** *(pl)*	[gu:s, gi:s]	Gans
horse	[hɔ:s]	Pferd	**cow**	[kaʊ]	Kuh	**duck**	[dʌk]	Ente

14	**tourist information centre** [ˌtʊərɪst ɪnfə'meɪʃn ˌsentə]	Touristeninformation	When I'm on holiday, I always go to the *tourist information centre*.
	to **need (to do)** [ni:d]	(tun) müssen	What do tourists *need to see* in Greenwich?
	I don't know! [ˌaɪ ˌdəʊnt 'nəʊ]	Ich weiß (es) nicht!	How old is Jake's brother? – *I don't know.*
15	**market** ['mɑ:kɪt]	Markt	You can go shopping in shops or at the *market*.
	to **get** [get]	bekommen; holen; bringen	Where can we *get* a brochure about our town?

Skills: How to talk to people in the street

3	**survey** ['sɜ:veɪ]	Umfrage; Studie	What do people think? – Find out with a *survey*.

Story: The captain and the cabin boy

captain ['kæptɪn]	Kapitän/-in; Mannschaftsführer/-in	Every ship needs a *captain*. ***Fr.*** capitaine *(m)*
cabin boy ['kæbɪn ˌbɔɪ]	Schiffsjunge	The *cabin boy* helps on a ship.
1 **aboard** [ə'bɔ:d]	an Bord	
sailor ['seɪlə]	Seemann; Matrose	*Sailors* work on ships.
visitor ['vɪzɪtə]	Besucher/-in	*visitor* → a visit → to visit ***Fr.*** visiteur *(m)*, visiteuse *(f)*
• **tea** [ti:]	Tee	***Fr.*** thé *(m)*
to **happen** ['hæpn]	geschehen; passieren	What *happens* in the story?
land [lænd]	Land	*land* ↔ sea
storm [stɔ:m]	Sturm	
wave [weɪv]	Welle	In a storm at sea there are big *waves*. 
wheel [wi:l]	Rad; Steuerrad; Steuer	A bike has got two *wheels*. 
to **reef the sails** [ˌri:f ðə 'seɪlz]	die Segel einholen	
to **shout** [ʃaʊt]	schreien; rufen	I can't hear you; can you *shout, please*?
to **climb** [klaɪm]	klettern; besteigen; steigen	
rigging ['rɪgɪŋ]	Takelage	Sailors sometimes climb the *rigging*.
dangerous ['deɪndʒrəs]	gefährlich	***Fr.*** dangereux/dangereuse
slow [sləʊ]	langsam	*slow* ↔ fast
brave [breɪv]	mutig; tapfer	***Fr.*** brave
to **come down** [ˌkʌm 'daʊn]	herunterkommen	
mate [meɪt]	Schiffsoffizier; Maat	! first *mate* = erster Offizier
• to **drink** [drɪŋk]	trinken	*to drink* → a drink
back [bæk]	zurück	After school you go *back* home.
to **hit** [hɪt]	schlagen; treffen	It can be very dangerous when a monster wave *hits* a ship.
to **fall** [fɔ:l]	fallen; hinfallen	Don't *fall* into the sea, Ben!
• to **swim** [swɪm]	schwimmen	You can *swim* in the sea. 
to **save** [seɪv]	retten; bergen	Help! *Save* me! ***Fr.*** sauver; ***Lat.*** salvare
lifebuoy ['laɪfbɔɪ]	Rettungsring	
lifeboat ['laɪfbəʊt]	Rettungsboot	A ship needs lifebuoys and *lifeboats*.
to **jump** [dʒʌmp]	springen	Let's *jump* into the water together!
to **stay** [steɪ]	bleiben	to come – *to stay* – to go
to **be wrong** [bi 'rɒŋ]	unrecht haben; sich irren	*to be wrong* ↔ to be right

to **be sorry** [bi 'sɒri]	leid tun	
to **make** [meɪk]	*hier:* ergeben	Brave people *make* good sailors.

Unit 5 Let's go shopping

Check-in

to **go shopping** [ˌgəʊ 'ʃɒpɪŋ]	einkaufen gehen	*to go shopping* → shop 
How much (is/are) ...? [ˌhaʊ 'mʌtʃ‿ɪz/ɑː]	Wie viel (kostet/kosten) ...?	I want to buy this T-shirt. *How much is it?*
It's .../They're ... [ɪts/ðeə]	Es kostet .../Sie kosten ...	*It's* 18 pounds.
pound (£) [paʊnd]	Pfund *(brit. Währungseinheit)*	! Das Zeichen „£" steht immer vor der Zahl, wird beim Sprechen aber nach der Zahl genannt.
expensive [ɪk'spensɪv]	teuer	If something is *expensive*, it costs a lot of money.
quality ['kwɒləti]	Qualität; Eigenschaft	Top-*quality* things are usually expensive. *Fr.* qualité *(f)*; ***Lat.*** qualitas *(f)*
cheap [tʃiːp]	billig; preiswert	*cheap* ↔ expensive
bottle ['bɒtl]	Flasche	! a *bottle* of water; a bag of sweets; ... *Fr.* bouteille *(m)*
Anything else? [ˌeniθɪŋ‿'els]	Sonst noch etwas?	*Anything else?* – No thanks. That's all.
can [kæn]	Dose; Büchse	You can get drinks in bottles or in *cans*.
coke [kəʊk]	Cola	
packet ['pækɪt]	Päckchen; Paket; Packung	Those biscuits are cheap. Let's get two *packets*. *Fr.* paquet *(m)*
That's ... [ðæts]	Das macht ...	How much is it? – *That's* £3 then.
I'm looking for ... [ˌaɪm 'lʊkɪŋ fə]	Ich suche nach ...	
present ['preznt]	Geschenk	You can buy a *present* or you can make one. 
bracelet ['breɪslət]	Armband	*Fr.* bracelet *(m)*
special offer [ˌspeʃl‿'ɒfə]	Sonderangebot	*Special offer* today: Jeans only £25.
1 **clothes** *(pl)* [kləʊðz]	Kleider; Kleidung	! Das englische Wort *clothes* steht immer im Plural: Olivia's *clothes* **are** nice.
snack bar ['snæk ˌbɑː]	Snackbar; Imbissstube	
jewellery ['dʒuːəlri]	Schmuck	Let's look at the bracelets in that *jewellery* shop.
penny, pence *(pl)* ['peni; pens]	Penny; Pence *(brit. Währungseinheit)*	! 1p is one *penny*. 5p is five *pence*. In Großbritannien spricht man *penny* oder *pence* immer als Kurzform ***p*** (wie den Buchstaben ***p*** [piː]): *one penny* = 1*p*, *five pence* = 5*p*.

	price [praɪs]	Preis	How much are these shoes? I can't find the *price*.
	euro ['jʊərəʊ]	Euro *(Währung)*	
	cent [sent]	Cent *(Währung)*	
2	**next** [nekst]	als Nächstes	What happens *next*? = What happens after that?
3	to **sell** [sel]	verkaufen	*to sell* ↔ to buy

British money

There are 100 pence (p) in a pound (£).

1p	one p (= penny)	**£1.50**	one (pound) fifty
25p	twenty-five p (= pence)	**£2**	two pounds
£1	one pound	**£3.70**	three (pounds) seventy

Station 1: Where can I get £90?

	glass [glɑ:s]	Glas	Can I have a *glass* of water, please?
	orange ['ɒrɪndʒ]	Orange	*Oranges* are usually orange. 
	juice [dʒu:s]	Saft	*Fr.* jus *(m)*
	at the moment [ət ðə 'məʊmənt]	im Moment; gerade	Is Luke at home? – No, he's in town *at the moment*.
•	**sad** [sæd]	traurig	*sad* ↔ happy
	to **earn** [ɜ:n]	verdienen	*to earn* – to buy – to pay – to sell
	flea market ['fli: ˌmɑ:kɪt]	Flohmarkt	You can sell things at the *flea market*.
	community centre [kə'mju:nəti ˌsentə]	Gemeindezentrum	Is there sometimes a flea market at your *community centre*?
	to **organise** ['ɔ:gənaɪz]	organisieren	Let's *organise* a flea market for our class!
	year [jɪə]	Jahr; Schuljahr	We go on holiday every *year*.
	charity ['tʃærɪti]	Wohltätigkeitsverein; wohltätige Zwecke; Wohlfahrt	A *charity* collects money to help people. *Lat.* caritas *(f)*
	toy [tɔɪ]	Spielzeug	Luke's brother Jamie has got a lot of *toys*.
	to **clear out** [ˌklɪər‿'aʊt]	ausräumen; entrümpeln	I want to *clear out* the fridge today.
	garage ['gærɑ:ʒ]	Garage	Luke's bike is in the *garage* next to the house.
	to **feel** [fi:l]	fühlen; sich fühlen	How do you *feel*? – I *feel* good/bad/sad …
	hopeful ['həʊpfl]	hoffnungsvoll	*hopeful* → hope
	to **ring** [rɪŋ]	klingeln; läuten	Listen, Olivia: Your phone *is ringing*.
1	to **make money** [ˌmeɪk 'mʌni]	Geld verdienen	*to make money* = to earn money
3	**full (of)** [fʊl‿əv]	voll (von)	Jamie's cupboard is *full of* cars.
	to **throw away** [ˌθrəʊ‿ə'weɪ]	wegwerfen	Don't *throw* those books *away*. They're for the flea market.

4	**e.g.** (= for example) [ˌiːˈdʒiː]	z. B. (= zum Beispiel)	I do lots of different sports, *e.g.* volleyball.
5	**coffee** [ˈkɒfi]	Kaffee	A lot of people drink tea or *coffee* in the morning.

Clothes

T-shirt	[ˈtiːʃɜːt]	T-Shirt
shoe	[ʃuː]	Schuh
jeans	[dʒiːnz]	Jeans
shirt	[ʃɜːt]	Hemd
pullover	[ˈpʊləʊvə]	Pullover

dress	[dres]	Kleid
shorts	[ʃɔːts]	Shorts, kurze Hose
skirt	[skɜːt]	Rock
jacket	[ˈdʒækɪt]	Jacke
coat	[kəʊt]	Mantel

7	**charity shop** [ˈtʃærɪti ˌʃɒp]	Second-Hand-Laden *(für wohltätige Zwecke)*	
	any [ˈeni]	irgendein/-e/-er; irgendwelche	Have you got *any* money?
8	**telephone** [ˈtelɪfəʊn]	Telefon	*Fr.* téléphone *(m)* 
	Too bad! [ˌtuː ˈbæd]	Zu dumm!; Schade!	I can't come, I'm busy today! – Oh, *too bad*!
	to **walk the dog** [ˌwɔːk ðə ˈdɒg]	den Hund ausführen; mit dem Hund spazieren gehen	My grandparents often *walk our dog*.

Shops

Where can you buy things?

- in a jewellery shop
- in a shoe shop
- in a clothes shop
- in a charity shop
- in a café / snack bar
- at the flea market
- at the supermarket
- at the market
- in a book shop
- in a sports shop

Station 2: That's what friends are for

That's what friends are for. [ˌðæts wɒt ˈfrendz‿ɑː ˌfɔː]	Dafür sind Freunde da.	
must [mʌst]	müssen	The phone is ringing. – That *must* be Granny.
to **be worth** [bi ˈwɜːθ]	wert sein	Jewellery can *be worth* a lot of money.
How many ...? [ˌhaʊ ˈmeni]	Wie viele ...?	
about [əˈbaʊt]	ungefähr; circa; etwa	I usually get up at *about* seven.
stuff [stʌf]	Zeug	We've got a lot of old *stuff* in the garage!
not ... any [nɒt‿eni]	kein/-e/-en	Jay has*n't* got *any* old toys for the flea market.

	a couple of [ə 'kʌpl‿əv]	ein paar	*a couple of* days = two or three days
	everything ['evriθɪŋ]	alles	*Everything* is OK.
	to **ask for** ['ɑ:sk fə]	fragen nach; bitten um	*Ask for* help if you need it.
	bargain ['bɑ:gɪn]	Schnäppchen	Only a pound for this pair of skates? That's a *bargain*!
	to **spend** [spend]	ausgeben *(Geld)*	I *spend* my money on computer games.
	a little [ə 'lɪtl]	ein wenig; etwas	I need *a little* help with my homework.
9	to **think of** ['θɪŋk‿əv]	halten von; denken über	What do you *think of* Greenwich, Pia? – It's great.
10	**anything** ['eniθɪŋ]	irgendetwas	
	nothing ['nʌθɪŋ]	nichts	*nothing* ↔ everything
	anybody ['eni,bɒdi]	jeder (beliebige); irgendjemand	
	somebody ['sʌmbədi]	jemand	*somebody* → some → something → sometimes
	nobody ['nəʊbədi]	niemand	
	someone ['sʌmwʌn]	jemand	*someone* = somebody
	anyone ['eniwʌn]	jeder (beliebige); irgendjemand	*anyone* = anybody
	no one ['nəʊ wʌn]	niemand	*no one* = nobody ! Achtung Rechtschreibung: Schreibe someone, anyone, nobody und nothing zusammen, aber *no one* getrennt.
11	**guitar** [gɪ'tɑ:]	Gitarre	

Skills: How to use the telephone

1	**answering machine** ['ɑ:nsrɪŋ mə,ʃi:n]	Anrufbeantworter	*answering machine* → to answer → answer
	message ['mesɪdʒ]	Botschaft; Nachricht	*Fr.* message *(m)*
	to **call** [kɔ:l]	anrufen; rufen	Luke isn't at home. Can you *call* again later?
	to leave a message [,li:v‿ə 'mesɪdʒ]	eine Nachricht hinterlassen	*Leave a message* for him. He can call you back.
	caller ['kɔ:lə]	Anrufer/-in	*caller* → to call
2	**phone call** ['fəʊn ,kɔ:l]	Anruf; Telefonanruf	*a phone call* → to call 
	to **answer the phone** [,ɑ:nsə ðə 'fəʊn]	einen Anruf entgegennehmen	Lots of people just say 'hello' when they *answer the phone*.
	to **put through** [,pʊt‿'θru:]	verbinden	Can you *put me through* to Mrs Elliot, please?
	left [left]	übrig	Can I have an orange? – Sorry, there aren't any oranges *left*.
3	**I'd like to ...** *(= I would like to)* [aɪd 'laɪk tə]	Ich möchte ...; Ich würde gern ...	! *I'd like to* ist höflicher als ***I want to***.
	to take a message [,teɪk‿ə 'mesɪdʒ]	eine Nachricht entgegennehmen; jmdm. etw. ausrichten	*to take a message* ↔ to leave a message
	I'll get her/him. [aɪl 'get hɜ:/hɪm]	Ich hole sie/ihn.	

Unit task: Our great flea market game

to **set up** [ˌset‿ˈʌp]	einrichten; aufbauen	First *set up* the tables, then put your things on them.
dictionary [ˈdɪkʃnri]	Wörterbuch	If you don't know a word in English, use a *dictionary*. *Fr.* dictionnaire *(m)*
buyer [ˈbaɪə]	Käufer/-in	*buyer* → to buy
seller [ˈselə]	Verkäufer/-in *(auf einem Flohmarkt)*	*seller* → to sell
half [hɑːf], **halves** *(pl)* **(of)** [hɑːvz]	die Hälfte	About *half* of the things for the flea market are old books.
goal [gəʊl]	Tor; Ziel	In this game, your *goal* is to sell lots of things. 

Story: Lucky Luke?

lucky ... [ˈlʌki]	... der/die Glückliche	! to be happy = glücklich sein to be *lucky* = Glück haben
wine [waɪn]	Wein	*Fr.* vin *(m)*; *Lat.* vinum *(nt)*
raffle [ˈræfl]	Tombola	Some people are always lucky at *raffles*.
prize [praɪz]	Preis; Gewinn	Are there any good *prizes* at the raffle? ! Nicht verwechseln: *prize* ≠ *price*
ticket [ˈtɪkɪt]	Los; Ticket; Eintrittskarte	You need a *ticket* for the cinema – or for a raffle.
each [iːtʃ]	pro Person; pro Stück	Tickets are a pound *each*.
to **hope** [həʊp]	hoffen	Luke *hopes* he can buy those expensive shoes.
to **think** [θɪŋk]	glauben	Luke doesn't *think* he can earn enough money.
still [stɪl]	noch; immer noch	It's 10 o'clock on Sunday morning and Dave is *still* in bed.
to **pull** [pʊl]	ziehen	If you want to open the door, just *pull*!
piece [piːs]	Stück	Oh no! The model is in *pieces*! *Fr.* pièce *(f)*
broken [ˈbrəʊkn]	gebrochen; kaputt	Don't sit on that chair – it's *broken*!
horrified [ˈhɒrɪfaɪd]	entsetzt	*Fr.* horrifié/-e
rubbish [ˈrʌbɪʃ]	Müll; Gerümpel	What can you do with *rubbish*? – Throw it away.
coin [kɔɪn]	Münze	
as ... as [əz ... əz]	so ... wie	Are rabbits *as* nice *as* guinea pigs?
not ... anything [ˌnɒt‿ˈeniθɪŋ]	nichts	I can buy something with a pound. I *can't* buy *anything* with that old coin.
more ... than [ˈmɔː ðən]	mehr ... als	Luke gets *more* pocket money *than* Jamie.
half [hɑːf]	halb	

	head [hed]	Kopf	A rabbit's *head*: 
	to **believe** [bɪ'li:v]	glauben	The first prize is for me? I can't *believe* it!
	to **hug** [hʌg]	umarmen	Luke *hugs* Sherlock because he's so happy.
	disappointed [ˌdɪsə'pɔɪntɪd]	enttäuscht	You can feel + happy, great, good, OK – awful, scared, tired, *disappointed*
2	**helpful** ['helpfl]	hilfsbereit; hilfreich	
	thankful ['θæŋkfl]	dankbar	*thankful* → to thank → thanks
	excited [ɪk'saɪtɪd]	aufgeregt; begeistert	*excited* → exciting
	helpless ['helpləs]	hilflos	*helpless* → helpful → to help

Check-out

1 •	**tomato** [tə'mɑ:təʊ], **tomatoes** *(pl)* [tə'mɑ:təʊz]	Tomate	For a pizza, you need *tomatoes* and cheese.  *Fr.* tomate *(f)*
	yoghurt ['jɒgət]	Joghurt	Many people like *yoghurt* for breakfast.

Across cultures 2 Food in the UK

	part [pɑ:t]	Teil; Stadtteil	England is a *part* of the UK. ***Fr.*** partie *(f)*; ***Lat.*** pars, partis *(f)*
	culture ['kʌltʃə]	Kultur	Different countries have different *cultures*. ***Fr.*** culture *(f)*; ***Lat.*** cultura *(f)*
1	**quick** [kwɪk]	schnell	Be *quick*! We're late.
	contest ['kɒntest]	Wettkampf; Wettbewerb	Let's have a song *contest*. Who wants to sing first?
2	**bacon** ['beɪkn]	Schinkenspeck; Speck	*Bacon* comes from pigs.
•	**bread** [bred]	Brot	Do you like brown *bread* or white *bread*? 
	cake [keɪk]	Kuchen; Torte	Lots of people like *cake* with tea in the afternoon.
•	**egg** [eg]	Ei	Let's have *eggs* and bacon for breakfast on Sunday!
•	**fish, fish** *(pl)* [fɪʃ]	Fisch	In Britain lots of people love *fish* and chips.
•	**fruit** [fru:t]	Frucht; Obst	! *fruit (sg)* = Obst *fruits (pl)* = Früchte
	pie [paɪ]	Kuchen; Pastete	There are fruit *pies*, fish *pies*, bacon-and-egg *pies* …
	strange [streɪndʒ]	fremd; seltsam; merkwürdig	Fish for breakfast? That's a *strange* idea.
3 •	**apple** ['æpl]	Apfel	Do you like *apple* pie? 
•	**butter** ['bʌtə]	Butter	

	cereal *(no pl)* ['sɪəriəl]	Frühstückszerealie; Getreideprodukt *(z. B. Cornflakes oder Müsli)*	
	• **chocolate** ['tʃɒklət]	Schokolade	Some dogs like *chocolate*, but it isn't good for them. *Fr.* chocolat *(m)*
	crisp *(BE)* [krɪsp]	Kartoffelchip	! *crisps* = German: Chips chips = German: Pommes frites
	• **ham** [hæm]	Schinken	I like *ham* and eggs for breakfast.
	nut [nʌt]	Nuss	Do you like chocolate with *nuts* in it?
	• **plum** [plʌm]	Pflaume	
	• **strawberry** ['strɔ:bri], **strawberries** *(pl)* ['strɔ:briz]	Erdbeere	
	sweet [swi:t]	süß	Chocolate and cakes are *sweet*.
	healthy ['helθi]	gesund	Burgers are OK, but it isn't *healthy* to eat too many of them.
	• **hot** [hɒt]	heiß	I like *hot* food for lunch.
4	**supermarket** ['su:pəˌmɑ:kɪt]	Supermarkt	*supermarket* → market → flea market *Fr.* supermarché *(m)*
	to **go together** [ˌgəʊ tə'geðə]	zueinander passen; zueinander gehören	Do cheese and chips *go together*?
	baked beans *(pl)* [ˌbeɪkt 'bi:nz]	weiße Bohnen in Tomatensoße	*Baked beans* on toast are popular in Britain.
	banana [bə'nɑ:nə]	Banane	Fruit: apples – oranges – mangoes – *bananas* *Fr.* banane *(f)*
	ready meal [ˌredi 'mi:l]	Fertiggericht	*Ready meals* aren't always healthy.
	• **salad** ['sæləd]	Salat	Fruit *salad* is great – and it's healthy too! *Fr.* salade *(f)*
	Indian ['ɪndiən]	Inder/-in; indisch	There's often curry in *Indian* food.
	chicken tikka masala [ˌtʃɪkɪn ˌtɪkə mə'sɑ:lə]	*indisches Hühnchengericht*	
	milk [mɪlk]	Milch	You make cheese and yoghurt from *milk*.
	young [jʌŋ]	jung	*young* ↔ old

Focus 2 English around the world

	world [wɜ:ld]	Erde; Welt	Football is popular around the *world*. 
	kind [kaɪnd]	Art; Sorte	What *kind* of music do you like?
2	**as** [æz]	wie	My favourite music is not the same *as* yours.
	to **make friends** [ˌmeɪk 'frendz]	Freundschaft schließen	It's easy for me to *make* new *friends*.

3 **independent** [ˌɪndɪ'pendənt]	unabhängig	*Fr.* indépendant/-e
American [ə'merɪkən]	Amerikanisch; amerikanisch; aus Amerika; Amerikaner/-in	*American* English isn't the same as British English.
government ['gʌvnmənt]	Regierung	
official language [əˌfɪʃl 'læŋgwɪdʒ]	Amtssprache	In India, English is an *official language*.
all around [ˌɔːl‿ə'raʊnd]	überall; rundherum; rings umher	
million ['mɪljən]	Million	1,000,000
first language [ˌfɜːst 'læŋgwɪdʒ]	Muttersprache	My *first language* is German.
technology [tek'nɒlədʒi]	Technologie	*technology*: computers, smartphones, machines etc.
to **communicate** [kə'mjuːnɪkeɪt]	kommunizieren; sich verständigen	*Lat.* communicare
although [ɔːl'ðəʊ]	obwohl	My father speaks good English *although* he's German.
not any more [ˌnɒt‿eni 'mɔː]	nicht mehr	Jay doesn't go to school in Enfield *any more*.
4 **the USA** *(United States of America)* [juːes'eɪ (juːˌnaɪtɪd ˌsteɪts‿əv‿ə'merɪkə)]	die USA *(die Vereinigten Staaten von Amerika)*	My uncle lives in the *USA*. ! Meistens sagt man „the US" statt „the *USA*". Achtung: the United States **is** … = die Vereinigten Staaten **sind** …
what else [ˌwɒt‿'els]	was sonst; was noch	I know she wants a new bag. *What else* does she want?

Unit 6 It's my party!

Check-in

costume ['kɒstjuːm]	Kostüm	People sometimes wear *costumes* at parties.
at the same time [ət ðə ˌseɪm 'taɪm]	zur selben Zeit; gleichzeitig	
bowling alley ['bəʊlɪŋ‿æli]	Bowlingbahn	Lots of people go to the *bowling alley* with friends.
to **give the bumps** [ˌgɪv ðə 'bʌmps]	hochleben lassen	On birthdays, people in England often *give* their friends *the bumps*.
to **celebrate** ['seləbreɪt]	feiern	How do you *celebrate* your birthday? – I usually have a party. *Fr.* célébrer; *Lat.* celebrare
• **birthday** ['bɜːθdeɪ]	Geburtstag	My *birthday* is on 3rd May. ! Geschrieben: **3rd May** oder **3 May** Gesprochen: **the third of May** oder **May the third**
ice rink ['aɪs ˌrɪŋk]	Eisbahn; Schlittschuhbahn	You can go skating at the *ice rink*.
to **blow out** [ˌbləʊ‿'aʊt]	ausblasen; auspusten	
candle ['kændl]	Kerze	Blow out the *candles* in the living room before you go to bed. 

	to **make a wish** [ˌmeɪk‿ə ˈwɪʃ]	sich etwas wünschen	When you blow out the candles on your birthday cake, you can *make a wish*.
	wish [wɪʃ]	Wunsch	
1	**Happy Birthday!** [ˌhæpi ˈbɜːθdeɪ]	Alles Gute zum Geburtstag!; Herzlichen Glückwunsch zum Geburtstag!	Let's sing: *Happy birthday* to you!
4	**date** [deɪt]	Datum	What's the *date* today? ***Fr.*** date *(f)*; ***Lat.*** datum *(nt)*

Ordinal numbers

1st **first** [ˈfɜːst]	11th **eleventh** [ɪˈlevnθ]	21st **twenty-first** [ˌtwentiˈfɜːst]
2nd **second** [ˈseknd]	12th **twelfth** [twelfθ]	22nd **twenty-second** [ˌtwentiˈseknd]
3rd **third** [ˈθɜːd]	13th **thirteenth** [θɜːˈtiːnθ]	23rd **twenty-third** [ˌtwentiˈθɜːd]
4th **fourth** [fɔːθ]	14th **fourteenth** [ˌfɔːˈtiːnθ]	24th **twenty-fourth** [ˌtwentiˈfɔːθ]
5th **fifth** [fɪfθ]	15th **fifteenth** [ˌfɪfˈtiːnθ]	…
6th **sixth** [sɪksθ]	16th **sixteenth** [ˌsɪkˈstiːnθ]	30th **thirtieth** [ˈθɜːtiəθ]
7th **seventh** [ˈsevnθ]	17th **seventeenth** [ˌsevnˈtiːnθ]	40th **fortieth** [ˈfɔːtiəθ]
8th **eighth** [eɪtθ]	18th **eighteenth** [ˌeɪˈtiːnθ]	50th **fiftieth** [ˈfɪftiəθ]
9th **ninth** [naɪnθ]	19th **nineteenth** [ˌnaɪnˈtiːnθ]	60th **sixtieth** [ˈsɪkstiɪθ]
10th **tenth** [tenθ]	20th **twentieth** [ˈtwentiɪθ]	100th **(one) hundredth** [ˈhʌndrədθ]

1st 2nd 3rd 4th

Months

January [ˈdʒænjuri]	Januar	**July** [dʒʊˈlaɪ]	Juli
February [ˈfebruri]	Februar	**August** [ˈɔːgəst]	August
March [mɑːtʃ]	März	**September** [sepˈtembə]	September
April [ˈeɪprɪl]	April	**October** [ɒkˈtəʊbə]	Oktober
May [meɪ]	Mai	**November** [nəʊˈvembə]	November
June [dʒuːn]	Juni	**December** [dɪˈsembə]	Dezember

5	**spring** [sprɪŋ]	Frühling	*Spring* comes after winter. It starts in March.
	summer [ˈsʌmə]	Sommer	The weather can be very hot in *summer*.
	autumn [ˈɔːtəm]	Herbst	*Autumn* is between summer and winter.
	winter [ˈwɪntə]	Winter	In *winter* I often go to the ice rink.

Station 1: I can't wait!

to **plan** [plæn]	planen	to make a plan
sleepover [ˈsliːpˌəʊvə]	Übernachtung	*sleepover* → to sleep
mustn't [ˈmʌsnt]	nicht dürfen	! You must. – Du musst. You *mustn't*. – Du darfst nicht.
like that [laɪk ˈðæt]	so	Please don't talk to me *like that*! I don't like it when you're rude.

	holidays *(pl)* ['hɒlədeɪz]	Ferien	*Holidays*! Great! No school.
	that [ðæt; ðət]	dass	! Anders als im Deutschen ist die Satzstellung in Haupt- und Nebensatz gleich: London is in England. I know *that* London is in England.
	theme [θi:m]	Thema; Motto	
	decorations *(pl)* [ˌdekə'reɪʃnz]	Dekoration; Schmuck	Let's buy the party *decorations*!  *Fr.* décoration *(f)*
	needn't ['ni:dnt]	nicht brauchen; nicht müssen	It's OK, you *needn't* go to the supermarket.
	to **invite** [ɪn'vaɪt]	einladen	I always *invite* all my friends to my birthday. ***Fr.*** inviter; ***Lat.*** invitare
	to **decorate** ['dekəreɪt]	dekorieren; verzieren; schmü-cken	*to decorate* → decorations ***Fr.*** décorer
	trifle ['traɪfl]	Trifle *(englischer Nachtisch)*	Let's make a *trifle* for the party!
	ice cream [ˌaɪs 'kri:m]	Eis; Eiscreme	
	all night [ˌɔ:l 'naɪt]	die ganze Nacht	
2	to **clean** [kli:n]	säubern; reinigen	It's OK, Holly. You needn't *clean* your windows.
3	to **get** [get]	besorgen; kaufen	You can *get* a new bike at the bike shop.
4	to **do our hair** [ˌdu:‿aʊə 'heə]	uns frisieren, unsere Haare machen	Come on, let's *do our hair* together for the party.
6	**invitation** [ˌɪnvɪ'teɪʃn]	Einladung	*invitation* → to invite ***Fr.*** invitation *(f)*; ***Lat.*** invitatio *(f)*
	size [saɪz]	Größe; Kleidergröße	These gloves are the wrong *size*. They're S, and I need M.
	locker ['lɒkə]	Schließfach; Spind	You can put your bag in your *locker*.
	without [wɪ'ðaʊt]	ohne	*without* ↔ with
	glove [glʌv]	Handschuh	You wear shoes on your feet and *gloves* on your hands.
10	to **move** [mu:v]	(sich) bewegen	Don't *move*. I'm taking a picture. *to move* → move
	at all [ət‿'ɔ:l]	überhaupt	Jay doesn't like homework *at all*.
	out [aʊt]	außerhalb; heraus; hinaus; draußen	You're *out*. = That's the end of the game for you. *out* → outside
	to **win** [wɪn]	gewinnen; siegen	My brother *wins* every game.
12	to **prepare** [prɪ'peə]	vorbereiten; zubereiten	Dad is *preparing* lunch. ***Fr.*** préparer; ***Lat.*** praeparare
	sponge [spʌndʒ]	Rühr-; Biskuit-	*sponge* fingers = Löffelbiskuits
	jelly ['dʒeli]	Tortenguss; Götterspeise; Wackelpudding; Gelee	
	custard ['kʌstəd]	Vanillesoße; Vanillepudding	All my family love jelly with *custard*!
	fresh [freʃ]	frisch	
	tinned [tɪnd]	Dosen-; aus der Dose	I don't like *tinned* fruit. I like it fresh.

cream [kri:m]	Creme; Sahne	I love cake with *cream*! *Fr.* crème *(f)*
to **break** [breɪk]	brechen; zerbrechen	*Break* the cake into pieces.
bowl [bəʊl]	Schale; Schälchen; Schüssel	You eat cereal from a *bowl*. 
to **slice** [slaɪs]	in Scheiben schneiden	Can you *slice* the apples for me, please?
on top [ɒn 'tɒp]	oben; obendrauf	Let's put cream *on top* of the cake.
to **leave it to cool** [ˌli:v‿ɪt tə 'ku:l]	kalt stellen	
to **pour** [pɔ:]	einschenken; eingießen; schütten	
to **whip** [wɪp]	(Sahne) schlagen	I can *whip* the cream for the cake, OK? 

Station 2: No problem!

*to **go wrong** [ˌgəʊ 'rɒŋ]	schiefgehen	*to go wrong* → wrong
in the end [ˌɪn ði‿'end]	schließlich; zum Schluss	First everything went wrong, but *in the end* I had a great party.
to **trip (over)** [ˌtrɪp‿'əʊvə]	stolpern (über)	Don't put your shoes there. I always *trip* over them.
*to **hurt** [hɜ:t]	verletzen; weh tun	I *hurt* my foot when I went skiing last winter.
yummy ['jʌmi]	lecker	This trifle is *yummy*!
bad luck [ˌbæd 'lʌk]	Pech; Unglück	to have *bad luck* ↔ to be lucky
15 **month** [mʌnθ]	Monat	day – week – *month* – year
yesterday ['jestədeɪ]	gestern	*Yesterday* I had some bad luck. *yesterday* – today – tomorrow

Station 3: An American party

postcard ['pəʊskɑ:d]	Postkarte	I love it when I get a *postcard* and not just an e-mail!
vacation *(AE)* [və'keɪʃn]	Ferien; Urlaub	*vacation (AE)* = holiday *(BE)*
barbecue ['bɑ:bɪkju:]	Grill; Grillparty	In summer we often have a *barbecue* in the garden.
fireworks *(pl)* ['faəwɜ:ks]	Feuerwerk	
awesome ['ɔ:səm]	super; spitze; beeindruckend	*awesome* = great
pancake ['pænkeɪk]	Pfannkuchen	In America people often have *pancakes* for breakfast.
normal ['nɔ:ml]	normal	These pancakes aren't *normal*. They're red, white and blue.
yard *(AE)* [jɑ:d]	Garten	*yard (AE)* = garden *(BE)*

	cookie *(AE)* ['kʊki]	Keks	*cookie (AE)* = biscuit *(BE)*
	fries *(pl) (AE)* [fraɪz]	Pommes frites	*fries (AE)* = chips *(BE)* 
	candy *(AE)* ['kændi]	Süßigkeiten	*candy (AE)* = sweets *(BE)*
	guy [gaɪ]	Typ; Kerl; *(Pl.)* Leute	Our new classmate is a really cool *guy*.
	to **want somebody to do something** [ˌwɒnt sʌmbədi tə 'du: sʌmθɪŋ]	wollen, dass jemand etwas tut	! Never use 'want' with 'that': Ich will, dass du bleibst. = I *want you to stay.*
20	**instead of** [ɪn'sted‿əv]	statt; anstatt; an Stelle von	Can I have toast *instead of* pancakes, please?
21	**Christmas** ['krɪsməs]	Weihnachten	We celebrate *Christmas* in our family every year.
	Easter ['i:stə]	Ostern	
	New Year's Eve [ˌnju: jɪəz‿'i:v]	Silvester	
	to **stay up** [ˌsteɪ‿'ʌp]	aufbleiben	On Christmas Eve I can *stay up* till late.
	midnight ['mɪdnaɪt]	Mitternacht	= twelve o'clock at night
22	**ago** [ə'gəʊ]	vor *(zeitlich)*	! *Ago* steht nach der Zeitdauer: I did my homework two days *ago*.

American English

In British and American English there are sometimes different words for the same things:

Sometimes the words are the same, but the spelling is different:

Dates are different in American English too. Americans write the month before the day:

German	British English	American English
Ferien	holidays	vacation
Garten	garden	yard
Keks	biscuit	cookie
Pommes frites	chips	fries
Süßigkeiten	sweets	candy
Fußball	football	soccer
Farbe	colour	color
Lieblings-	favourite	favorite
Zentrum	centre	center
Theater	theatre	theater
Mama	mum	mom
1. April	1st April	April 1st
4. Juli	4th July	July 4th

Skills: How to write and reply to party invitations

to **reply (to)** [rɪ'plaɪ]	antworten (auf); erwidern; entgegnen	Must I *reply* to Holly's invitation? *to reply* = to answer
1 • **Dear ...** [dɪə]	Lieber ...; Liebe ... *(Anrede in Briefen)*	! Persönliche Briefe beginnst du mit *Dear* und einem Namen. Danach schreibst du groß weiter.
*to **let** [let]	lassen	Can you come? Please *let* me know.
Love ... [lʌv]	Liebe Grüße *(am Briefende)*; Herzliche Grüße *(am Briefende)*	Some people write '*Love*' at the end of an e-mail, and some people just write 'See you' or 'CU'.
hat [hæt]	Hut	
greeting ['gri:tɪŋ]	Gruß	'Hello' is a *greeting*.
reply [rɪ'plaɪ]	Antwort; Erwiderung; Entgegnung	*reply* → to reply
*to **take place** [ˌteɪk 'pleɪs]	stattfinden	! *to take place* = stattfinden to sit down = Platz nehmen
would love [wʊd 'lʌv]	würde/-st/-n/-t sehr gern; hätte/-st-/-n/-t sehr gern	I *would love* to go to England on holiday.

Story: Don't they like me any more?

1 **suddenly** ['sʌdnli]	plötzlich; auf einmal	When Sherlock *suddenly* sees a cat, he starts to bark.
to **count (on)** ['kaʊnt‿ɒn]	zählen (auf)	My friends can *count on* me.
to **whisper** ['wɪspə]	flüstern	The girls *whisper*, so Jay can't hear them.
How are you? [ˌhaʊ‿'ɑ: jə]	Wie geht es dir?; Wie geht es euch?; Wie geht es Ihnen?	*How are you?* – OK, thanks. And you?
to **smile** [smaɪl]	lächeln	Don't look so angry. *Smile*!
to **hurry** ['hʌri]	eilen; sich beeilen	You needn't *hurry*! You've got lots of time. 
lonely ['ləʊnli]	einsam	I'm often alone, but I don't always feel *lonely*.
bored [bɔ:d]	gelangweilt	! to be boring = langweilig sein to be *bored* = gelangweilt sein
*to **be unlucky** [bi‿ʌn'lʌki]	Pech haben	*to be unlucky* ↔ to be lucky
*to **get into** [ˌget‿'ɪntə]	einsteigen; hineingelangen	We're late, Jay. *Get into* the car, please!
hungry ['hʌŋgri]	hungrig	When is lunch? I'm *hungry*.
better ['betə]	besser; lieber	! Ice cream is *better*. = Eis ist besser. I like ice cream *better*. = Eis mag ich lieber.
inside [ˌɪn'saɪd]	innen; im Innern; hinein; nach drinnen; in; drin	*inside* ↔ outside
after all [ˌɑ:ftər‿'ɔ:l]	doch; schließlich; immerhin	Great! Luke and the others are Jay's friends *after all*.

Check-out

2	**best** [best]	am besten; am liebsten	Which book is *best* for you?

Across cultures 3 Special days, special events

	event [ɪ'vent]	Ereignis; Veranstaltung	There are a lot of interesting *events* in our town every month.
	tradition [trə'dɪʃn]	Tradition	We always go swimming on 1st January. It's a *tradition*. ***Fr.*** tradition *(f)*; ***Lat.*** traditio *(f)*
1	**religious** [rɪ'lɪdʒəs]	religiös; gläubig	My grandpa is very *religious*. ***Fr.*** religieux/religieuse; ***Lat.*** religiosus
	national ['næʃnl]	national; landesweit	3rd October is a *national* holiday in Germany.
	wedding ['wedɪŋ]	Hochzeit	It's my sister's *wedding* next week. 
4	**historical** [hɪ'stɒrɪkl]	historisch; geschichtlich	***Fr.*** historique
	royal ['rɔɪəl]	königlich	The British *royal* family lives in London. 
	all over [ˌɔ:l‿'əʊvə]	überall (in)	*all over* the country = im ganzen Land
	bonfire ['bɒnfaə]	Lagerfeuer; Freudenfeuer	We always have a *bonfire* and fireworks on 5th November.
	background ['bækgraʊnd]	Hintergrund	I can't see you in the photo. – Look, that's me in the *background*.
	role [rəʊl]	Rolle	Which *role* do you want to play? ***Fr.*** rôle *(m)*
	another [ə'nʌðə]	ein/-e andere/-r/-s; noch ein/-e	*another* ↔ the same
	thousands of ['θaʊzndz‿əv]	Tausende (von)	*Thousands of* people live in Greenwich.
	Londoner ['lʌndənə]	Londoner/-in	a person from London
	whole [həʊl]	ganz	Do you want half of this pizza? Or can you eat the *whole* thing?
	international [ˌɪntə'næʃnl]	international	An Indian mother and an American father – that's very *international*.
	serious ['sɪəriəs]	ernsthaft; ernst	Don't laugh! This is *serious*. ***Fr.*** sérieux, sérieuse; ***Lat.*** serius
	colourful ['kʌləfl]	farbenfroh; bunt	People wear *colourful* costumes at Notting Hill Carnival.
5	**most important** [ˌməʊst‿ɪm'pɔ:tnt]	wichtigste/-r/-s	Look for the *most important* information in the text.
	Christian ['krɪstʃən]	christlich	Christmas is a *Christian* holiday.

Focus 3 A first look at the US

	stadium ['steɪdiəm]	Stadion	Let's watch football at the *stadium* on Saturday.
	down [daʊn]	entlang; herunter; hinunter	The ship is going *down* the river.
	mile [maɪl]	Meile *(brit. und amerikan. Längenmaß)*	1 *mile* = 1,609 metres
	up to ['ʌp tə]	bis zu	
	bottom ['bɒtəm]	Boden; unterer Teil; Grund	*bottom* ↔ top
	alligator ['ælɪgeɪtə]	Alligator	
	Native American [ˌneɪtɪv‿ə'merɪkən]	Ureinwohner/-in Amerikas; Indianer/-in; indianisch	*Native Americans* lived in North America long before British people went to live there.
	area ['eəriə]	Areal; Gebiet; Fläche	What sports events are there in your *area*?
	*to **mean** [mi:n]	bedeuten	What does it *mean*? = Was bedeutet es? ! to *mean* ≠ meinen
	*to **become** [bɪ'kʌm]	werden	Elizabeth *became* Queen in 1952 (nineteen fifty-two). ! to *become* ≠ bekommen
	state [steɪt]	Staat; Bundesstaat; Land	country or part of a country
	fair [feə]	Messe; Jahrmarkt	a special event, usually in a town, where there are often games for children, things to eat and all kinds of shows
	cow [kaʊ]	Kuh	
	also ['ɔ:lsəʊ]	auch	I like football and I *also* like basketball. = I like football and I like basketball too. ! *also* **(English)** ≠ *also* **(German)**
1	*to **be made up of** [bi ˌmeɪd‿'ʌp‿əv]	bestehen aus	The US *is made up of* 50 states.
2	**polar bear** ['pəʊlə ˌbeə]	Eisbär	
	*to **grow** [grəʊ]	anbauen; züchten	to *grow* corn = to produce corn
	to **produce** [prə'dju:s]	herstellen; produzieren	*to produce* = to make
	coast [kəʊst]	Küste	= where the land meets the sea

A US map

corn	[kɔ:n]	Korn, Mais, Getreide	cattle farm	['kætl ˌfɑ:m]	Viehzuchtbetrieb
wheat	[wi:t]	Weizen	cactus	['kæktəs]	Kaktus
cotton	['kɒtn]	Baumwolle	desert	['dezət]	Wüste
oil	[ɔɪl]	Öl	waterfall	['wɔ:təˌfɔ:l]	Wasserfall
wood	[wʊd]	Holz	factory	['fæktri]	Fabrik, Werk
peach	[pi:tʃ]	Pfirsich	airplane	['eəpleɪn]	Flugzeug
field	[fi:ld]	Feld, Wiese, Weide, Acker	rocket	['rɒkɪt]	Rakete

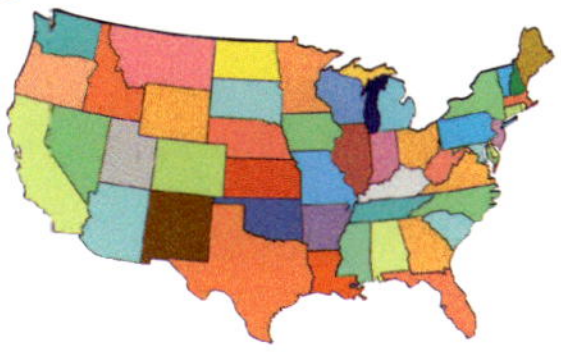

3	*to **be named after** [bi 'neɪmd‿ɑ:ftə]	benannt sein nach	Washington *is named after* the first president of the USA.
	president ['prezɪdnt]	Präsident/-in	! Watch the pronunciation!
	monument ['mɒnjəmənt]	Monument; Denkmal	In Washington you can visit lots of *monuments*. *Lat.* monumentum *(nt)*
	moon [mu:n]	Mond	
	space [speɪs]	Raum; Weltraum	1. Please leave some *space* for my picture on the wall. 2. The moon is in *space*.
	skyscraper ['skaɪskreɪpə]	Wolkenkratzer	A *skyscraper* is a very tall building.
	zoo [zu:]	Zoo; Tierpark	There are lots of animals in a *zoo*.
	the French *(pl)* [ðə 'frenʃ]	die Franzosen	
	freedom *(no pl)* ['fri:dəm]	Freiheit; Unabhängigkeit	*freedom* → free
4	to **enjoy** [ɪn'dʒɔɪ]	genießen; sich freuen an	The party was great. I really *enjoyed* it.
5	**dollar bill** ['dɒlə ˌbɪl]	Dollarnote; Dollarschein	

Dictionary

In dieser alphabetischen Wortliste findest du das gesamte Vokabular von *Green Line* 1. Namen stehen in einer extra Liste am Ende des ***Dictionary***. Einträge, die aus mehreren Wörtern bestehen, kannst du meist unter verschiedenen Stichwörtern nachschlagen. So ist z. B. *at home* unter *at* und unter *home* eingetragen. Die Fundstellen stehen immer hinter dem jeweiligen Wort und zeigen dir an, wo es zum ersten Mal vorkommt, z. B.:
always ['ɔ:lweɪz] immer; ständig **I U1**, 16 kommt zum ersten Mal vor in Band I, Unit 1, Seite 16
U = Unit, PU = Pick-up, AC = Across cultures, F = Focus
Die mit * gekennzeichneten Verben sind unregelmäßig.
Die mit ° gekennzeichneten Vokabeln sind rezeptiv.
Die Vokabeln mit **grünen** Fundstellen sind individueller Wortschatz.

English-German dictionary

A

a [ə] ein/-e **I PUA**, 8
  a couple of [ə 'kʌpl‿əv] ein paar **I U5**, 91
  a few [ə 'fju:] ein paar; wenige; einige **I U2**, 44
  a few minutes later [ə ˌfju: ˌmɪnɪts 'leɪtə] ein paar Minuten später **I U2**, 44
  a hundred [ə 'hʌndrəd; wʌn 'hʌndrəd] einhundert; hundert **I U1**, 20
  a little [ə 'lɪtl] ein wenig; etwas **I U5**, 91
  a lot [ə 'lɒt] viel **I U3**, 62
  a lot of [ə 'lɒt‿əv] viel/-e; eine Menge **I F1**, 68
  a lot to learn [ə ˌlɒt tə 'lɜ:n] viel zu lernen **I U3**, 62
a.m. [ˌeɪ'em] vormittags *(Uhrzeit)* **I U3**, 50
aboard [ə'bɔ:d] an Bord **I U4**, 80
about [ə'baʊt] ungefähr; circa; etwa **I U5**, 91
about [ə'baʊt] über; von **I U1**, 17
  What **about** …? ['wɒt‿əbaʊt] Was ist mit …?; Wie wär's mit …? **I U3**, 53
  What is … **about**? [ˌwɒt‿ɪz‿ə'baʊt] Worum geht es in/im …? **I U3**, 58
across [ə'krɒs] auf der anderen Seite von; über; hinüber; herüber; quer durch **I U4**, 71
  Across cultures [əˌkrɒs 'kʌltʃəz] Interkulturelles °**I U1**, 20
to act [ækt] spielen *(Theater)* **I U3**, 61
  Act … [ækt] Spiele/Spielt … °**I PUB**, 31
  to **act** out [ækt 'aʊt] nachspielen °**I F2**, 102
  acting a scene [ˌæktɪŋ‿ə 'si:n] eine Theaterszene spielen **I U3**, 59
action ['ækʃn] Handlung; Action; Aktion °**I U1**, 26
activity [æk'tɪvəti] Aktivität **I U4**, 71
to add [æd] hinzufügen; ergänzen **I U2**, 41
  Add … [æd] Füge/Fügt … hinzu. °**I U2**, 33
address [ə'dres] Adresse **I U1**, 21
after ['ɑ:ftə] nach *(zeitlich)* **I U1**, 24
  after all [ˌɑ:ftər‿'ɔ:l] doch; schließlich; immerhin **I U6**, 117
  after that [ˌɑ:ftə 'ðæt] danach **I U3**, 52
afternoon [ˌɑ:ftə'nu:n] Nachmittag **I U3**, 53
again [ə'gen] wieder; noch einmal; noch mal **I U1**, 19
ago [ə'gəʊ] vor *(zeitlich)* **I U6**, 114
ahoy [ə'hɔɪ] ahoi **I U4**, 80
airplane ['eəpleɪn] Flugzeug **I F3**, 122
alien ['eɪliən] Außerirdische/-r; außerirdisches Wesen **I U6**, 117
all [ɔ:l] alle/-s; ganz **I U4**, 74
  after **all** [ˌɑ:ftər‿'ɔ:l] doch; schließlich; immerhin **I U6**, 117
  all around [ˌɔ:l‿ə'raʊnd] überall; rundherum; rings umher **I F2**, 103
  all night [ˌɔ:l 'naɪt] die ganze Nacht **I U6**, 106
  all of them ['ɔ:l‿əv ˌðəm] alle °**I U2**, 37
  all over [ˌɔ:l‿'əʊvə] überall (in) **I AC3**, 121
  at **all** [ət‿'ɔ:l] überhaupt **I U6**, 109
bowling **alley** ['bəʊlɪŋ‿æli] Bowlingbahn **I U6**, 104
alligator ['ælɪgeɪtə] Alligator **I F3**, 122
alone [ə'ləʊn] allein; ohne fremde Hilfe **I U2**, 40
along [ə'lɒŋ] entlang °**I U6**, 105
alphabet ['ælfəbet] Alphabet **I PUA**, 13
already [ɔ:l'redi] schon; bereits **I U2**, 41
also ['ɔ:lsəʊ] auch **I F3**, 122
although [ɔ:l'ðəʊ] obwohl **I F2**, 103
always ['ɔ:lweɪz] immer; ständig **I U1**, 16
American [ə'merɪkən] amerikanisch; aus Amerika; Amerikaner/-in **I F2**, 103
  Native **American** [ˌneɪtɪv‿ə'merɪkən] Ureinwohner/-in Amerikas; Indianer/-in; indianisch **I F3**, 122
an [ən] ein/-e **I U1**, 16
and [ænd; ənd] und **I PUA**, 8
angry ['æŋgri] wütend; zornig; verärgert; böse **I U2**, 45
animal ['ænɪməl] Tier **I PUA**, 10
another [ə'nʌðə] ein/-e andere/-r/-s; noch ein/-e **I AC3**, 121
answer ['ɑ:nsə] Antwort **I U1**, 20
  short **answer** [ˌʃɔ:t‿'ɑ:nsə] Kurzantwort °**I U2**, 36
to answer ['ɑ:nsə] antworten; beantworten **I U4**, 74
  Answer … ['ɑ:nsə] Beantworte/Beantwortet … °**I U2**, 36
  to **answer** the phone [ˌɑ:nsə ðə 'fəʊn] einen Anruf entgegennehmen **I U5**, 93
  answering machine ['ɑ:nsrɪŋ məˌʃi:n] Anrufbeantworter **I U5**, 93
any ['eni] irgendein/-e/-er; irgendwelche **I U5**, 90
  not **any** more [ˌnɒt‿eni 'mɔ:] nicht mehr **I F2**, 103
  not … **any** [nɒt‿eni] kein/-e/-en **I U5**, 91
anybody ['eniˌbɒdi] jeder (beliebige); irgendjemand **I U5**, 92
anyone ['eniwʌn] jeder (beliebige); irgendjemand **I U5**, 92
anything ['eniθɪŋ] irgendetwas **I U5**, 92
  not … **anything** [ˌnɒt‿'eniθɪŋ] nichts **I U5**, 97
  Anything else? [ˌeniθɪŋ‿'els] Sonst noch etwas? **I U5**, 87
apple ['æpl] Apfel **I AC2**, 101
April ['eɪprl] April **I U6**, 105
Are you …? ['ɑ: ju] Sind Sie …?; Seid ihr … ?; Bist du … ? **I PUA**, 9
How **are** you? [ˌhaʊ‿'ɑ: jə] Wie geht es dir?; Wie geht es euch?; Wie geht es Ihnen? **I U6**, 116
area ['eəriə] Areal; Gebiet; Fläche **I F3**, 122
arm [ɑ:m] Arm **I U6**, 114
around [ə'raʊnd] um … herum; umher **I U3**, 62
  all **around** [ˌɔ:l‿ə'raʊnd] überall; rundherum; rings umher **I F2**, 103
Art [ɑ:t] Kunstunterricht **I U2**, 33
as [æz] wie **I F2**, 102
  as … **as** [əz … əz] so … wie **I U5**, 96
as [æz] während; indem **I AC3**, 120
to ask [ɑ:sk] fragen; bitten **I U3**, 55
  Ask … [ɑ:sk] Stelle/Stellt Fragen …; Frage/Fragt … °**I U1**, 15
  Ask about … ['ɑ:sk‿əˌbaʊt] Frage/Fragt nach … °**I U1**, 17
  to **ask** for ['ɑ:sk fə] fragen nach; bitten um **I U5**, 91
*to fall **asleep** [ˌfɔ:l‿ə'sli:p] einschlafen **I U3**, 63

at [æt; ət] in; auf; bei; an | **U1**, 14; um *(bei Uhrzeitangaben)* | **U3**, 51
at all [ət‿'ɔ:l] überhaupt | **U6**, 109
at home [ət 'həʊm] zu Hause | **U1**, 14
at last [ət 'lɑ:st] endlich; schließlich | **U4**, 74
at least [ət 'li:st] mindestens; wenigstens | **U6**, 112
at the back of [ət ðə 'bæk‿əv] hinten; am Ende; im hinteren Teil | **F1**, 69
at the moment [ət ðə 'məʊmənt] im Moment; gerade | **U5**, 88
at the same time [ət ðə ˌseɪm 'taɪm] zur selben Zeit; gleichzeitig | **U6**, 104
at the weekend [ət ðə ˌwi:k'end] am Wochenende | **U4**, 72
audio ['ɔ:diəʊ] Audio-; Hör- °| **U2**, 44
August ['ɔ:gəst] August | **U6**, 105
aunt [ɑ:nt] Tante | **U1**, 16
autumn ['ɔ:təm] Herbst | **U6**, 105
away [ə'weɪ] weg | **U3**, 62
right **away** [ˌraɪt‿ə'weɪ] sofort; gleich | **U3**, 52
*to run **away** [ˌrʌn‿ə'weɪ] wegrennen | **U3**, 62
*to throw **away** [ˌθrəʊ‿ə'weɪ] wegwerfen | **U5**, 89
awesome ['ɔ:səm] super; spitze; beeindruckend | **U6**, 112
awful ['ɔ:fl] schrecklich; furchtbar | **U1**, 24

B

baby ['beɪbi] Baby; Säugling | **U6**, 116
at the **back** of [ət ðə 'bæk‿əv] hinten; am Ende; im hinteren Teil | **F1**, 69
back to **back** [ˌbæk tə 'bæk] Rücken an Rücken °| **U5**, 90
back [bæk] zurück | **U4**, 80
background ['bækgraʊnd] Hintergrund | **AC3**, 121
bacon ['beɪkn] Schinkenspeck; Speck | **AC2**, 100
bad [bæd] schlecht; böse; schlimm *(ugs.)* | **U4**, 74
bad luck [ˌbæd 'lʌk] Pech; Unglück | **U6**, 110
Too **bad**! [ˌtu: 'bæd] Zu dumm!; Schade! | **U5**, 90
badminton ['bædmɪntən] Badminton | **PUA**, 11
bag [bæg] Tasche; Tüte | **U1**, 24
mixed **bag** [ˌmɪkst 'bæg] buntes Allerlei; bunte Mischung °| **U2**, 47
baked beans *(pl)* [ˌbeɪkt 'bi:nz] weiße Bohnen in Tomatensoße | **AC2**, 101
balcony ['bælkəni] Balkon | **U1**, 23
ball [bɔ:l] Ball | **PUA**, 8
banana [bə'nɑ:nə] Banane | **AC2**, 101
snack **bar** ['snæk ˌbɑ:] Café; Imbissstube | **U5**, 86
barbecue ['bɑ:bɪkju:] Grill; Grillparty | **U6**, 112
bargain ['bɑ:gɪn] Schnäppchen | **U5**, 91
to **bark** [bɑ:k] bellen | **U3**, 62
baseball ['beɪsbɔ:l] Baseball | **U6**, 112
basketball ['bɑ:skɪtbɔ:l] Basketball | **PUB**, 31
bath [bɑ:θ] Bad; Badewanne | **U1**, 15
bathroom ['bɑ:θrʊm] Bad; Badezimmer | **U1**, 14
*to **be** [bi:] sein | **U2**, 40
*to **be** about [bi‿ə'baʊt] gehen um; handeln von | **U3**, 58
*to **be** good at [bi 'gʊd‿ət] gut sein in | **U3**, 61
*to **be** in the way [bi‿ɪn ðə 'weɪ] im Weg sein/stehen | **AC1**, 67
*to **be** into [bi‿'ɪntə] mögen; stehen auf | **PUB**, 28
*to **be** jealous (of) [bi 'dʒeləs] eifersüchtig sein (auf); neidisch sein (auf) | **U2**, 44
*to **be** late [bi 'leɪt] zu spät dran sein; zu spät kommen | **U2**, 40
*to **be** lucky [bi 'lʌki] Glück haben | **U2**, 38
*to **be** made up of [bi ˌmeɪd‿'ʌp‿əv] bestehen aus | **F3**, 122
*to **be** named after [bi 'neɪmd‿ɑ:ftə] benannt sein nach | **F3**, 123
*to **be** right [bi 'raɪt] recht haben | **U2**, 45
*to **be** scared (of) [bi 'skeəd‿əv] Angst haben (vor) | **U3**, 62
*to **be** sorry [bi 'sɒri] leid tun | **U4**, 81
*to **be** unlucky [bi‿ʌn'lʌki] Pech haben | **U6**, 116
*to **be** worth [bi 'wɜ:θ] wert sein | **U5**, 91
*to **be** wrong [bi 'rɒŋ] unrecht haben; sich irren | **U4**, 81
Be careful! [ˌbi: 'keəfl] Vorsicht!; Pass/Passt auf! | **U3**, 56
Be polite. [ˌbi: pə'laɪt] Sei/Seid höflich. | **U2**, 36
Here you **are**. [ˌhɪə ju‿'ɑ:] Bitte schön. | **U2**, 36
How **are** you? [ˌhaʊ‿'ɑ: jə] Wie geht es dir?; Wie geht es euch?; Wie geht es Ihnen? | **U6**, 116
How much **is/are** ...? [ˌhaʊ 'mʌtʃ‿ɪz/ɑ:] Wie viel (kostet/kosten) ...? | **U5**, 86
I'**m** from ... [ˌaɪm frɒm] Ich bin aus ... | **PUA**, 8
beach [bi:tʃ] Strand | **F1**, 68
baked **beans** *(pl)* [ˌbeɪkt 'bi:nz] weiße Bohnen in Tomatensoße | **AC2**, 101
bear [beə] Bär | **PUA**, 10
polar **bear** ['pəʊlə ˌbeə] Eisbär | **F3**, 122
because [bɪ'kɒz] weil; da | **U2**, 47
*to **become** [bɪ'kʌm] werden | **F3**, 122
bed [bed] Bett | **U1**, 15
*to go to **bed** [ˌgəʊ tə 'bed] ins Bett gehen | **U3**, 51
bedroom ['bedrʊm] Schlafzimmer | **U1**, 14
before [bɪ'fɔ:] vor *(zeitlich)* °| **U2**, 32; bevor; vor *(zeitlich)* | **U2**, 44
behind [bɪ'haɪnd] hinter | **U1**, 19
to **believe** [bɪ'li:v] glauben | **U5**, 97
below [bɪ'ləʊ] unterhalb; unten | **U4**, 76
best [best] beste/-r/-s | **U1**, 24; am besten; am liebsten | **U6**, 119
better ['betə] besser; lieber | **U6**, 117
between [bɪ'twi:n] zwischen | **U6**, 113
big [bɪg] groß | **PUA**, 11
bike [baɪk] Fahrrad | **PUB**, 31
mountain **biking** ['maʊntɪn ˌbaɪkɪŋ] Mountainbikefahren | **F1**, 68
dollar **bill** ['dɒlə ˌbɪl] Dollarnote; Dollarschein | **F3**, 123
birthday ['bɜ:θdeɪ] Geburtstag | **U6**, 105
Happy **Birthday**! [ˌhæpi 'bɜ:θdeɪ] Alles Gute zum Geburtstag!; Herzlichen Glückwunsch zum Geburtstag! | **U6**, 104
biscuit ['bɪskɪt] Keks | **U1**, 14
black [blæk] schwarz | **PUA**, 12
*to **blow** out [ˌbləʊ‿'aʊt] ausblasen; auspusten | **U6**, 105
blue [blu:] blau | **PUA**, 12
board [bɔ:d] Tafel | **U2**, 35
boat [bəʊt] Boot | **PUA**, 13
boating lake ['bəʊtɪŋ ˌleɪk] See zum Rudern | **PUA**, 11
bonfire ['bɒnfaə] Lagerfeuer; Freudenfeuer | **AC3**, 121
book [bʊk] Buch | **PUB**, 31
exercise **book** ['eksəsaɪz ˌbʊk] Übungsheft | **U2**, 33
bored [bɔ:d] gelangweilt | **U6**, 116
boring ['bɔ:rɪŋ] langweilig | **PUB**, 28
bottle ['bɒtl] Flasche | **U5**, 87
bottom ['bɒtəm] Boden; unterer Teil; Grund | **F3**, 122
bowl [bəʊl] Schale; Schälchen; Schüssel | **U6**, 109
bowling alley ['bəʊlɪŋ‿æli] Bowlingbahn | **U6**, 104
box [bɒks] Box; Kasten; Schachtel; Kiste | **AC1**, 67
boy [bɔɪ] Junge | **PUA**, 8
cabin **boy** ['kæbɪn ˌbɔɪ] Schiffsjunge | **U4**, 80
bracelet ['breɪslət] Armband | **U5**, 87
brave [breɪv] mutig; tapfer | **U4**, 80
bread [bred] Brot | **AC2**, 100
break [breɪk] Pause | **U2**, 39
half-term **break** [ˌhɑ:ftɜ:m 'breɪk] Halbjahresferien °| **U3**, 54
lunch **break** ['lʌnʃbreɪk] Mittagspause | **U2**, 39
*to **break** [breɪk] brechen; zerbrechen | **U6**, 109
breakfast ['brekfəst] Frühstück | **U3**, 51
*to have **breakfast** [ˌhæv 'brekfəst] frühstücken | **U3**, 51
*to **bring** [brɪŋ] bringen; mitbringen | **U2**, 40
British ['brɪtɪʃ] britisch; Brite/Britin | **AC1**, 67
brochure ['brəʊʃə] Broschüre; Prospekt °| **U4**, 77
broken ['brəʊkn] gebrochen; kaputt | **U5**, 96
brother ['brʌðə] Bruder | **U1**, 16

brown [braʊn] braun **I PUA**, 12
budgie ['bʌdʒi] Wellensittich **I PUA**, 10
building ['bɪldɪŋ] Gebäude **I U2**, 38
*to give the **bumps** [ˌgɪv ðə 'bʌmps] hochleben lassen **I U6**, 105
burger ['bɜ:gə] Hamburger **I U5**, 88
bus [bʌs] Bus **I U4**, 75
bus station ['bʌs ˌsteɪʃn] Busbahnhof **I AC1**, 67
busy ['bɪzi] belebt; beschäftigt **I U1**, 24
but [bʌt] aber **I PUA**, 8
butter ['bʌtə] Butter **I AC2**, 101
*to **buy** [baɪ] kaufen **I U2**, 33
buyer ['baɪə] Käufer/-in **I U5**, 95
by *(bike)* [baɪ] mit *(dem Fahrrad)* **I U3**, 51
*to go **by** … ['gəʊ baɪ] fahren mit … **I U4**, 74
Bye! [baɪ] Tschüss! **I U4**, 73

C

cabin boy ['kæbɪn ˌbɔɪ] Schiffsjunge **I U4**, 80
cactus ['kæktəs] Kaktus **I F3**, 122
café ['kæfeɪ] Café **I F1**, 69
cafeteria [ˌkæfə'tɪəriə] Cafeteria **I U2**, 33
cake [keɪk] Kuchen; Torte **I AC2**, 100
phone **call** ['fəʊn ˌkɔ:l] Anruf; Telefonanruf **I U5**, 93
to **call** [kɔ:l] nennen **I U2**, 34; anrufen; rufen **I U5**, 93
caller ['kɔ:lə] Anrufer/-in **I U5**, 93
camping ['kæmpɪŋ] Camping; Zelten **I F1**, 68
can [kæn] Dose; Büchse **I U5**, 87
can [kæn; kən] können; dürfen **I PUA**, 13
can't [kɑ:nt] kann nicht; können nicht **I PUB**, 28
Can you name …? ['kæn jʊ ˌneɪm] Kannst du … nennen? **I PUA**, 13
I **can** see … [ˌaɪ ˌkən si:] Ich sehe …; Ich kann … sehen. **I PUA**, 13
candle ['kændl] Kerze **I U6**, 105
candy *(AE)* ['kændi] Süßigkeiten **I U6**, 112
canoeing [kə'nu:ɪŋ] Kanufahren **I F1**, 68
capital ['kæpɪtl] Hauptstadt **I F1**, 68
capital letter [ˌkæpɪtl 'letə] Großbuchstabe °**I U2**, 43
captain ['kæptɪn] Kapitän/-in; Mannschaftsführer/-in **I U4**, 80
car [kɑ:] Auto **I U1**, 19
card [kɑ:d] Karte; Spielkarte **I PUB**, 31
Be **careful!** [ˌbi: 'keəfl] Vorsicht!; Pass/Passt auf! **I U3**, 56
carrot ['kærət] Karotte; Möhre **I U2**, 36
castle ['kɑ:sl] Schloss; Burg **I F1**, 68
cat [kæt] Katze **I PUA**, 8
cattle farm ['kætl ˌfɑ:m] Viehzuchtbetrieb **I F3**, 122
to **celebrate** ['seləbreɪt] feiern **I U6**, 105
cellar ['selə] Keller **I U1**, 23
cent [sent] Cent *(Währung)* **I U5**, 86
centre ['sentə] Zentrum; Center **I U4**, 71
community **centre** [kə'mju:nəti ˌsentə] Gemeindezentrum **I U5**, 88
leisure **centre** ['leʒə ˌsentə] Freizeitzentrum **I U4**, 71
tourist information **centre** [ˌtʊərɪst‿ɪnfə'meɪʃn ˌsentə] Touristeninformation **I U4**, 78
cereal *(no pl)* ['sɪəriəl] Frühstückszerealie; Getreideprodukt *(z. B. Cornflakes oder Müsli)* **I AC2**, 101
chair [tʃeə] Stuhl; Sessel **I U1**, 15
character ['kærəktə] Charakter; Figur **I U2**, 8
charity ['tʃærɪti] Wohltätigkeitsverein; wohltätige Zwecke; Wohlfahrt **I U5**, 88
charity shop ['tʃærɪti ˌʃɒp] Second-Hand-Laden **I U5**, 90
lucky **charm** [ˌlʌki 'tʃɑ:m] Glücksbringer; Talisman **I PUB**, 29
to **chase** [tʃeɪs] jagen; nachjagen **I U3**, 62
video **chat** ['vɪdiəʊ ˌtʃæt] Videochat **I F2**, 102
to **chat** [tʃæt] plaudern; chatten *(sich online unterhalten)* **I U3**, 55
cheap [tʃi:p] billig; preiswert **I U5**, 86
to **check** [tʃek] überprüfen; prüfen; kontrollieren **I F1**, 69
Check … [tʃek] Überprüfe/Überprüft … °**I PUA**, 10
Check-in ['tʃekɪn] Einchecken °**I U1**, 14
Check-out ['tʃekaʊt] Auschecken °**I U1**, 27
cheese [tʃi:z] Käse **I U3**, 51
chicken ['tʃɪkɪn] Huhn; Hähnchen **I U4**, 77
chicken tikka masala [ˌtʃɪkɪn ˌtɪkə mə'sɑ:lə] *indisches Hühnchengericht* **I AC2**, 101
child [tʃaɪld], **children** *(pl)* ['tʃɪldrən] Kind **I U1**, 16
only **child** ['əʊnli ˌtʃaɪld] Einzelkind **I U1**, 16
chips *(pl) (BE)* [tʃɪps] Pommes frites **I U2**, 41
chocolate ['tʃɒklət] Schokolade **I AC2**, 101
Choose … [tʃu:z] Wähle/Wählt … aus. °**I PUA**, 10
Christian ['krɪstʃn] christlich **I AC3**, 121
church [tʃɜ:tʃ] Kirche **I F1**, 69
cinema ['sɪnəmə] Kino **I F1**, 69
circle ['sɜ:kl] Kreis; Ring °**I U4**, 73
city ['sɪti] Stadt; Großstadt **I F1**, 68
to **clap** [klæp] klatschen **I U3**, 59
Clap your hands. [ˌklæp jɔ: 'hændz] Klatsche/Klatscht in die Hände. **I U3**, 59
class [klɑ:s] Klasse; Schulklasse **I U2**, 44
class display ['klɑ:s dɪˌspleɪ] Ausstellung in der Klasse °**I U1**, 23
class poster ['klɑ:s ˌpəʊstə] Klassenposter °**I PUA**, 11
classmate ['klɑ:smeɪt] Klassenkamerad/-in; Mitschüler/-in **I U2**, 33
classroom ['klɑ:srʊm] Klassenzimmer **I U2**, 33
to **clean** [kli:n] säubern; reinigen **I U6**, 107
to **clear** out [ˌklɪər‿'aʊt] ausräumen; entrümpeln **I U5**, 88
clear [klɪə] klar; deutlich **I U3**, 59
clever ['klevə] schlau; klug; intelligent **I U1**, 17
to **climb** [klaɪm] klettern; besteigen; steigen **I U4**, 80
clock [klɒk] Uhr **I U1**, 15
o'**clock** [ə'klɒk] Uhr *(Zeitangabe bei vollen Stunden)* **I U3**, 50
to **close** [kləʊz] schließen; zumachen **I U4**, 73
Close … [kləʊz] Mach/t … zu. °**I PUA**, 8
close [kləʊs] eng; knapp **I PUA**, 10
That was **close**! [ˌðæt wɒz 'kləʊs] Das war knapp! **I PUA**, 10
clothes *(pl)* [kləʊðz] Kleider; Kleidung **I U5**, 86
club [klʌb] Klub; Verein; AG **I U3**, 51
Cooking **Club** ['kʊkɪŋ ˌklʌb] Koch-AG **I U3**, 51
coach [kəʊtʃ] Trainer/-in **I U3**, 54
coast [kəʊst] Küste **I F3**, 122
coat [kəʊt] Mantel **I U5**, 89
coffee ['kɒfi] Kaffee **I U5**, 89
coin [kɔɪn] Münze **I U5**, 96
coke [kəʊk] Cola **I U5**, 87
cold [kəʊld] kalt **I F1**, 68
to **collect** [kə'lekt] sammeln **I U1**, 15
colour ['kʌlə] Farbe **I PUA**, 12
What **colour** is …? [ˌwɒt 'kʌlər‿ɪz] Welche Farbe hat …? **I PUA**, 13
colourful ['kʌləfl] farbenfroh; bunt **I AC3**, 121
*to **come** [kʌm] kommen **I U3**, 51
*to **come** down [ˌkʌm 'daʊn] herunterkommen **I U4**, 80
Come on! [ˌkʌm‿'ɒn] Komm schon!; Komm jetzt! **I U2**, 44
to **communicate** [kə'mju:nɪkeɪt] kommunizieren; sich verständigen **I F2**, 103
community centre [kə'mju:nəti ˌsentə] Gemeindezentrum **I U5**, 88
to **compare** (with/to) [kəm'peə] vergleichen (mit) **I U4**, 71
Complete … [kəm'pli:t] Vervollständige/Vervollständigt … °**I U2**, 34
computer [ˌkəm'pju:tə] Computer **I PUB**, 28
concert ['kɒnsət] Konzert **I F1**, 69
contest ['kɒntest] Wettkampf; Wettbewerb **I AC2**, 100
cooker ['kʊkə] Herd **I U1**, 15
cookie *(AE)* ['kʊki] Keks **I U6**, 112
cooking ['kʊkɪŋ] Kochen **I U3**, 56
Cooking Club ['kʊkɪŋ ˌklʌb] Koch-AG **I U3**, 51
*to leave it to **cool** [ˌli:v‿ɪt tə 'ku:l] kalt stellen **I U6**, 109
cool [ku:l] cool; super **I U1**, 16
to **copy** ['kɒpi] abschreiben; kopieren **I U6**, 111
Copy … ['kɒpi] Schreibe/Schreibt … ab.; Kopiere/Kopiert … °**I U1**, 15
corn [kɔ:n] Korn; Mais; Getreide **I F3**, 122
Correct … [kə'rekt] Korrigiere/Korrigiert … **I U2**, 18

correct [kə'rekt] richtig; korrekt **I U2**, 41
*to **cost** [kɒst] kosten **I U4**, 70
costume ['kɒstju:m] Kostüm **I U6**, 104
cotton ['kɒtn] Baumwolle **I F3**, 122
to **count** (on) ['kaʊnt͜ ɒn] zählen (auf) **I U6**, 116
country, **countries** *(pl)* ['kʌntri] Land **I U3**, 60
a **couple** of [ə 'kʌpl͜ əv] ein paar **I U5**, 91
of **course** [əv 'kɔ:s] natürlich; selbstverständlich **I AC1**, 66
cousin ['kʌzn] Cousin/Cousine **I U1**, 16
cow [kaʊ] Kuh **I F3**, 122
crazy ['kreɪzi] verrückt **I PUA**, 9
cream [kri:m] Creme; Sahne **I U6**, 109
ice **cream** [ˌaɪs 'kri:m] Eis; Eiscreme **I U6**, 106
to **create** [kri'eɪt] schaffen; erschaffen; erfinden °**I U3**, 60
crisp *(BE)* [krɪsp] Kartoffelchip **I AC2**, 101
*to keep your fingers **crossed** [ˌki:p jɔ: ˌfɪŋgəz 'krɒst] die Daumen drücken **I U4**, 74
CU *(= See you)* ['si: ju] Bis dann!; Bis … **I PUB**, 28
cuddly toy ['kʌdli ˌtɔɪ] Stofftier **I U1**, 19
culture ['kʌltʃə] Kultur **I AC2**, 100
Across **cultures** [əˌkrɒs 'kʌltʃəz] Interkulturelles °**I U1**, 20
cupboard ['kʌbəd] Küchenschrank; Schrank **I U1**, 15
curry ['kʌri] Curry *(Gewürz oder Gericht)* **I U5**, 99
custard ['kʌstəd] Vanillesoße; Vanillepudding **I U6**, 109
cute [kju:t] niedlich; süß **I PUB**, 29
cycling ['saɪklɪŋ] Radfahren **I PUA**, 11

D

dad [dæd] Papa **I U1**, 16
to **dance** [dɑ:ns] tanzen **I U2**, 34
dangerous ['deɪndʒrəs] gefährlich **I U4**, 80
date [deɪt] Datum **I U6**, 105
day [deɪ] Tag **I PUB**, 28
Dear … [dɪə] Lieber …; Liebe … *(Anrede in Briefen)* **I U6**, 115
December [dɪ'sembə] Dezember **I U6**, 105
to **decide** [dɪ'saɪd] (sich) entscheiden **I U6**, 108
deck [dek] Deck **I U4**, 80
to **decorate** ['dekəreɪt] dekorieren; verzieren; schmücken **I U6**, 106
decorations *(pl)* [ˌdekə'reɪʃnz] Dekoration; Schmuck **I U6**, 106
to **describe** [dɪ'skraɪb] beschreiben **I U3**, 60
Describe … [dɪ'skraɪb] Beschreibe/Beschreibt … °**I U1**, 21
desert ['dezət] Wüste **I F3**, 122
diagram ['daɪəgræm] Diagramm °**I U6**, 116
dialogue ['daɪəlɒg] Dialog; Gespräch **I U3**, 58
Roll two **dice**. [ˌrəʊl ˌtu: 'daɪs] Würfle/Würfelt mit zwei Würfeln. °**I PUA**, 13

dictionary ['dɪkʃnri] Wörterbuch **I U5**, 94
difference ['dɪfrəns] Unterschied **I U5**, 89
different ['dɪfrnt] anders; unterschiedlich; verschieden **I PUA**, 9
ding-dong ['dɪŋdɒŋ] bim-bam °**I U1**, 24
dinner ['dɪnə] Abendessen **I U3**, 51
direction [dɪ'rekʃn] Richtung °**I U4**, 73
disappointed [ˌdɪsə'pɔɪntɪd] enttäuscht **I U5**, 97
to **discuss** [dɪ'skʌs] diskutieren °**I U6**, 108
class **display** ['klɑ:s dɪˌspleɪ] Ausstellung in der Klasse °**I U1**, 23
*to **do** [du:] machen; tun **I U2**, 40
*to **do** our hair [ˌdu:͜ aʊə 'heə] uns frisieren; unsere Haare machen **I U6**, 107
Don't translate … [ˌdəʊnt trænz'leɪt] Übersetze/Übersetzt nicht … °**I U2**, 38
Don't worry! [ˌdəʊnt 'wʌri] Keine Sorge! **I U1**, 24
dog [dɒg] Hund **I PUA**, 8
hot **dog** [ˌhɒt 'dɒg] Hot Dog *(Würstchen im Brötchen)* **I U6**, 112
to walk the **dog** [ˌwɔ:k ðə 'dɒg] den Hund ausführen; mit dem Hund spazieren gehen **I U5**, 90
I'm **dog-tired**. [ˌaɪm ˌdɒg'taɪəd] Ich bin hundemüde. **I U3**, 52
dollar bill ['dɒlə ˌbɪl] Dollarnote; Dollarschein **I F3**, 123
door [dɔ:] Tür **I U1**, 14
down [daʊn] entlang; herunter; hinunter **I F3**, 122
*to come **down** [ˌkʌm 'daʊn] herunterkommen **I U4**, 80
*to sit **down** [ˌsɪt 'daʊn] sich hinsetzen; sich setzen **I U3**, 51
*to write **down** [ˌraɪt 'daʊn] aufschreiben **I U2**, 43
*to **draw** [drɔ:] zeichnen **I U1**, 23
dress [dres] Kleid **I U5**, 89
drink [drɪŋk] Getränk **I U3**, 63
*to **drink** [drɪŋk] trinken **I U4**, 80
duck [dʌk] Ente **I U4**, 77
DVD [ˌdi:vi:'di:] DVD **I PUB**, 31

E

e. g. *(= for example)* [ˌi:'dʒi:] z. B. *(= zum Beispiel)* **I U5**, 89
each [i:tʃ] jede/-r/-s **I U5**, 94
each other [ˌi:tʃ͜ 'ʌðə] einander; sich; sich gegenseitig °**I U2**, 41
each [i:tʃ] pro Person; pro Stück **I U5**, 96
ear [ɪə] Ohr **I U3**, 63
early ['ɜ:li] früh **I U3**, 62
to **earn** [ɜ:n] verdienen **I U5**, 88
east [i:st] Osten; Ost- **I F1**, 68
easy ['i:zi] einfach; leicht **I U1**, 16
*to **eat** [i:t] essen; fressen **I PUA**, 10
egg [eg] Ei **I AC2**, 100
eight [eɪt] acht **I PUA**, 12
eighteen [ˌeɪ'ti:n] achtzehn **I U1**, 20

eighty ['eɪti] achtzig **I U1**, 20
not **either** [nɒt … 'aɪðə; nɒt … 'i:ðə] auch nicht **I U4**, 73
eleven [ɪ'levn] elf **I PUA**, 9
Anything **else**? [ˌeniθɪŋ͜ 'els] Sonst noch etwas? **I U5**, 87
what **else** [ˌwɒt͜ 'els] was sonst; was noch **I F2**, 103
e-mail ['i:meɪl] E-Mail **I U1**, 18
end [end] Ende; Schluss **I U2**, 42
in the **end** [ˌɪn ði͜ 'end] schließlich; zum Schluss **I U6**, 110
ending ['endɪŋ] Ende; Schluss *(einer Geschichte)* **I U1**, 25
English ['ɪŋglɪʃ] englisch; Englisch; aus England; Engländer/-in **I PUA**, 9
English-speaking ['ɪŋglɪʃˌspi:kɪŋ] englischsprachig **I AC1**, 66
I'm **English**. [aɪm͜ 'ɪŋglɪʃ] Ich bin Engländer/-in. **I PUA**, 9
to **enjoy** [ɪn'dʒɔɪ] genießen; sich freuen an **I F3**, 123
enough [ɪ'nʌf] genug; genügend **I U4**, 73
er [ɜ:] äh **I U2**, 34
escalator ['eskəleɪtə] Rolltreppe **I AC1**, 67
euro ['jʊərəʊ] Euro *(Währung)* **I U5**, 86
even ['i:vn] sogar; selbst **I U3**, 55
evening ['i:vnɪŋ] Abend **I U3**, 52
in the **evenings** [ɪn ði͜ 'i:vnɪŋz] abends **I U3**, 52
event [ɪ'vent] Ereignis; Veranstaltung **I AC3**, 120
every ['evri] jede/-r/-s **I U3**, 51
everyone ['evriwʌn] jeder; alle **I U2**, 34
everything ['evriθɪŋ] alles **I U5**, 91
everywhere ['evriweə] überall; überallhin **I U1**, 19
example [ɪg'zɑ:mpl] Beispiel **I PUA**, 13
excited [ɪk'saɪtɪd] aufgeregt; begeistert **I U5**, 97
exciting [ɪk'saɪtɪŋ] spannend; aufregend **I U4**, 72
Excuse me … [ɪk'skju:z mi] Entschuldigung!; Entschuldigen Sie! **I AC1**, 66
exercise ['eksəsaɪz] Übung; Aufgabe **I U2**, 43
exercise book ['eksəsaɪz ˌbʊk] Übungsheft **I U2**, 33
expensive [ɪk'spensɪv] teuer **I U5**, 86
to **explain** [ɪk'spleɪn] erklären **I AC1**, 67
Explain … [ɪk'spleɪn] Erkläre/Erklärt … °**I U1**, 20
to **explore** [ɪk'splɔ:] auf Entdeckungsreise gehen; sich umschauen; erkunden; erforschen **I U1**, 24
extra ['ekstrə] extra; zusätzlich **I U5**, 99
eye [aɪ] Auge **I U3**, 63

F

face [feɪs] Gesicht **I U3**, 62
Put … **face** down. [pʊt ˌfeɪs 'daʊn] Lege/Legt … umgedreht hin. °**I PUA**, 10

fact [fækt] Fakt; Tatsache I **F1**, 68
factory ['fæktri] Fabrik; Werk I **F3**, 122
fair [feə] Messe; Jahrmarkt I **F3**, 122
fair [feə] gerecht; fair I **U2**, 45
*to **fall** [fɔ:l] fallen; hinfallen I **U4**, 81
*to **fall** asleep [ˌfɔ:l‿ə'sli:p] einschlafen I **U3**, 63
*to **fall** over [ˌfɔ:l‿'əʊvə] hinfallen; umkippen I **U3**, 63
family ['fæmli] Familie I **U1**, 14
family tree ['fæmli ˌtri:] Stammbaum I **U1**, 16
famous ['feɪməs] berühmt I **F1**, 69
most **famous** [ˌməʊst 'feɪməs] berühmteste/-r/-s I **F1**, 69
fantasy ['fæntəsi] Fantasie; Traum- I **U1**, 23
farm [fɑ:m] Farm; Bauernhof I **U4**, 71
cattle **farm** ['kætl ˌfɑ:m] Viehzuchtbetrieb I **F3**, 122
fast [fɑ:st] schnell I **PUB**, 29
father ['fɑ:ðə] Vater I **U1**, 16
favourite ['feɪvrɪt] Lieblings- I **PUA**, 11
My **favourite** … [maɪ 'feɪvrɪt] Mein/-e Lieblings… I **PUA**, 11
What's your **favourite** …? ['wɒts jə ˌfeɪvrɪt] Was ist dein/-e Lieblings…? I **PUA**, 12
February ['februri] Februar I **U6**, 105
*to **feel** [fi:l] fühlen; sich fühlen I **U5**, 88
festival ['festɪvl] Festival; Fest I **F1**, 69
a **few** [ə 'fju:] ein paar; wenige; einige I **U2**, 44
field [fi:ld] Feld; Wiese; Weide; Acker I **F3**, 122
fifteen [ˌfɪf'ti:n] fünfzehn I **U1**, 17
fifty ['fɪfti] fünfzig I **U1**, 20
film [fɪlm] Film I **U2**, 32
*to **find** [faɪnd] finden; herausfinden I **U2**, 42
Find … [faɪnd] Finde/Findet … °I **PUA**, 10
*to **find** out [ˌfaɪnd‿'aʊt] herausfinden I **U3**, 58
fine [faɪn] gut; in Ordnung; schön I **U4**, 72
I'm **fine**. [ˌaɪm 'faɪn] Mir geht's gut. I **PUB**, 29
finger ['fɪŋgə] Finger I **U2**, 33
*to keep your **fingers** crossed [ˌki:p jɔ: ˌfɪŋgəz 'krɒst] die Daumen drücken I **U4**, 74
fireworks *(pl)* ['faəwɜ:ks] Feuerwerk I **U6**, 112
first [fɜ:st] zuerst; als Erstes I **U3**, 58; erste/-r/-s I **U2**, 43
first language [ˌfɜ:st 'læŋgwɪdʒ] Muttersprache I **F2**, 103
fish, fish *(pl)* [fɪʃ] Fisch I **AC2**, 100
fishing ['fɪʃɪŋ] Angeln; Fischen; Fischerei I **F1**, 69
*to **get fit** [ˌget 'fɪt] in Form kommen; fit werden I **U3**, 59
five [faɪv] fünf I **PUA**, 12
flag [flæg] Flagge; Fahne I **F1**, 68
flat [flæt] Wohnung I **U1**, 14
flea market ['fli: ˌmɑ:kɪt] Flohmarkt I **U5**, 88
floor [flɔ:] Fußboden I **U1**, 19
flyer ['flaɪə] Flyer I **U5**, 88
folder ['fəʊldə] Ordner; Mappe I **U1**, 23
food [fu:d] Essen; Lebensmittel I **U2**, 36
foot [fʊt], **feet** *(pl)* [fi:t] Fuß I **U4**, 71
football ['fʊtbɔ:l] Fußball I **PUA**, 11
for [fɔ:; fə] für I **PUA**, 11
forest ['fɒrɪst] Wald I **F1**, 68
*to **forget** [fə'get] vergessen I **U2**, 39
form [fɔ:m] Form I **U2**, 35
negative **form** ['negətɪv ˌfɔ:m] verneinte Form °I **U1**, 18
possessive **form** [pəˌzesɪv 'fɔ:m] Possessivform °I **U2**, 41
short **form** ['ʃɔ:t fɔ:m] Kurzform °I **U1**, 17
forty ['fɔ:ti] vierzig I **U1**, 20
four [fɔ:] vier I **PUA**, 12
Four and six is ten. [ˌfɔ:r‿ənd ˌsɪks‿ɪz 'ten] Vier plus sechs ist zehn. I **PUA**, 13
fourteen [ˌfɔ:'ti:n] vierzehn I **U1**, 20
free [fri:] frei; kostenlos I **U4**, 71
free time [ˌfri: 'taɪm] Freizeit I **U4**, 71
freedom *(no pl)* ['fri:dəm] Freiheit; Unabhängigkeit I **F3**, 123
French [frenʃ] Französisch I **U2**, 38
the **French** *(pl)* [ðə 'frenʃ] die Franzosen I **F3**, 123
fresh [freʃ] frisch I **U6**, 109
Friday ['fraɪdeɪ] Freitag I **U3**, 51
fridge [frɪdʒ] Kühlschrank I **U1**, 20
friend [frend] Freund/-in I **PUA**, 8
*to make **friends** [ˌmeɪk 'frendz] Freundschaft schließen I **F2**, 102
That's what **friends** are for. [ˌðæts wɒt 'frendz‿ɑ: ˌfɔ:] Dafür sind Freunde da. I **U5**, 91
friendly ['frendli] freundlich; nett I **U1**, 17
fries *(pl) (AE)* [fraɪz] Pommes frites I **U6**, 112
from [frɒm; frəm] aus; von I **PUA**, 9
from … to [frəm … tə] von … bis I **U1**, 20
Where … **from**? [ˌweə … 'frɒm] Woher …? I **PUA**, 9
in **front** of [ɪn 'frʌnt‿əv] vor I **U1**, 19
fruit [fru:t] Frucht; Obst I **AC2**, 100
full [fʊl] voll; ganz I **U5**, 89
full (of) [fʊl‿əv] voll (von) I **U5**, 89
fun [fʌn] Freude; Spaß I **PUA**, 11
*to have **fun** [ˌhæv 'fʌn] Spaß haben; sich amüsieren I **U3**, 62
It's **fun**. [ɪts 'fʌn] Es macht Spaß. I **PUA**, 11
fun [fʌn] lustig; witzig; fröhlich I **U2**, 40
funny ['fʌni] lustig; witzig I **U2**, 39

G

game [geɪm] Spiel I **PUB**, 28
gap [gæp] Lücke; Spalt; Abstand °I **U2**, 41
garage ['gærɑ:ʒ] Garage I **U5**, 88
garden ['gɑ:dn] Garten I **U1**, 19
Geography [dʒi'ɒgrəfi] Geografie; Erdkunde I **U2**, 38
German ['dʒɜ:mən] deutsch; Deutsch; aus Deutschland; Deutsche/-r I **PUA**, 8
*to **get** [get] bekommen; holen; bringen I **U4**, 78; besorgen; kaufen I **U6**, 107
*to **get** fit [ˌget 'fɪt] in Form kommen; fit werden I **U3**, 59
*to **get** into [ˌget‿'ɪntə] einsteigen; hineingelangen I **U6**, 117
*to **get** on people's nerves [ˌget‿ɒn pi:plz 'nɜ:vz] jemandem auf die Nerven gehen I **U3**, 55
*to **get** there ['get ðeə] hinkommen I **U4**, 74
*to **get** to ['get tə] kommen zu; kommen nach; erreichen I **U4**, 75
*to **get** up [ˌget‿'ʌp] aufstehen *(aus dem Bett)* I **U3**, 51
I'll **get** … [aɪl 'get] Ich hole … I **U5**, 93
Time to **get** up! [ˌtaɪm tə ˌget‿'ʌp] Es ist Zeit aufzustehen! I **U3**, 51
girl [gɜ:l] Mädchen I **PUA**, 11
a **girl** from Germany [ə ˌgɜ:l frəm 'dʒɜ:məni] ein Mädchen aus Deutschland I **PUA**, 11
*to **give** [gɪv] geben; schenken I **U2**, 45
*to **give** the bumps [ˌgɪv ðə 'bʌmps] hochleben lassen I **U6**, 105
glass [glɑ:s] Glas I **U5**, 88
glove [glʌv] Handschuh I **U6**, 108
*to **go** [gəʊ] gehen; fahren I **PUA**, 11
*to **go** by … ['gəʊ baɪ] fahren mit … I **U4**, 74
*to **go** on [ˌgəʊ‿'ɒn] weitergehen; weitermachen; weiterführen; fortfahren °I **U5**, 96
*to **go** shopping [ˌgəʊ 'ʃɒpɪŋ] einkaufen gehen I **U5**, 86
*to **go** swimming [ˌgəʊ 'swɪmɪŋ] schwimmen gehen I **PUB**, 31
*to **go** to bed [ˌgəʊ tə 'bed] ins Bett gehen I **U3**, 51
*to **go** together [ˌgəʊ tə'geðə] zueinander passen; zueinander gehören I **AC2**, 101
*to **go** with ['gəʊ wɪð] passen zu; gehören zu I **AC2**, 101
*to **go** wrong [ˌgəʊ 'rɒŋ] schiefgehen I **U6**, 110
goal [gəʊl] Tor; Ziel I **U5**, 95
goat [gəʊt] Ziege I **U4**, 77
good [gʊd] gut I **U1**, 14
*to be **good** at [bi 'gʊd‿ət] gut sein in I **U3**, 61
Good morning. [ˌgʊd 'mɔ:nɪŋ] Guten Morgen. I **U2**, 34
goodbye [gʊd'baɪ] auf Wiedersehen I **U3**, 62
goose Gans I **U4**, 77
government ['gʌvnmənt] Regierung I **F2**, 103
grammar ['græmə] Grammatik °I **U4**, 77
grandad ['grændæd] Opa I **U1**, 16
grandma ['grænmɑ:] Oma I **U1**, 16
grandparents *(pl)* ['grænˌpeərənts] Großeltern I **U2**, 36
granny ['græni] Oma I **U3**, 55
great [greɪt] großartig; toll; super I **PUA**, 11

It's **great** for … [ɪts ˈgreɪt fə] Es ist super zum/für … **I PUA**, 11
… is a **great** sport. [ɪz‿ə ˈgreɪt ˌspɔːt] … ist ein toller Sport. **I PUA**, 11
green [griːn] grün **I PUA**, 12
Greenwich Mean Time *(= GMT)* [ˌgrenɪdʒ ˈmiːn ˌtaɪm] westeuropäische Zeit **I U4**, 70
greeting [ˈgriːtɪŋ] Gruß **I U6**, 115
grey [greɪ] grau **I PUA**, 12
grid [grɪd] Gitter; Tabelle; Raster **I U2**, 42
group [gruːp] Gruppe; Klasse **I U2**, 36
a **group** of three [ə ˌgruːp‿əv ˈθriː] eine Dreiergruppe °**I U3**, 58
tutor **group** [ˈtjuːtə ˌgruːp] Klasse *(in einer englischen Schule)* **I U2**, 34
*to **grow** [grəʊ] anbauen; züchten **I F3**, 122
to **guess** [ges] raten; erraten; vermuten **I U2**, 37
Guess … [ges] Errate/Erratet … °**I PUA**, 8
guinea pig [ˈgɪniː ˌpɪg] Meerschweinchen **I U1**, 17
guitar [gɪˈtɑː] Gitarre **I U5**, 92
guy [gaɪ] Typ; Kerl; *(Pl.)* Leute **I U6**, 112

H

hair [heə] Haar; Haare **I U3**, 63
*to do our **hair** [ˌduː‿aʊə ˈheə] uns frisieren; unsere Haare machen **I U6**, 107
half [hɑːf], **halves** *(pl)* [hɑːvz] (of) die Hälfte **I U5**, 95
half [hɑːf] halb **I U5**, 97
half past [ˌhɑːf ˈpɑːst] halb *(bei Uhrzeitangaben)* **I U3**, 50
half-sister [ˈhɑːfˌsɪstə] Halbschwester **I U4**, 74
half-term break [ˌhɑːftɜːm ˈbreɪk] Halbjahresferien °**I U3**, 54
hall [hɔːl] Flur; Diele; Korridor **I U1**, 23
ham [hæm] Schinken **I AC2**, 101
hamster [ˈhæmstə] Hamster **I U5**, 92
hand [hænd] Hand **I U3**, 59
Clap your **hands**. [ˌklæp jɔː ˈhændz] Klatsche/Klatscht in die Hände. **I U3**, 59
handball [ˈhændbɔːl] Handball **I PUB**, 31
to **happen** [ˈhæpn] geschehen; passieren **I U4**, 80
happy [ˈhæpi] glücklich; froh; fröhlich **I PUB**, 28
Happy Birthday! [ˌhæpi ˈbɜːθdeɪ] Alles Gute zum Geburtstag!; Herzlichen Glückwunsch zum Geburtstag! **I U6**, 104
hat [hæt] Hut **I U6**, 115
*to **have** [hæv] haben **I U2**, 34
*to **have** breakfast [ˌhæv ˈbrekfəst] frühstücken **I U3**, 51
*to **have** fun [ˌhæv ˈfʌn] Spaß haben; sich amüsieren **I U3**, 62
*to **have** got [hæv ˈgɒt] besitzen; haben **I U2**, 34
*to **have** *(a sweet)* [hæv] *(ein Bonbon)* nehmen; *(ein Bonbon)* essen **I AC1**, 66

he [hiː] er **I U1**, 16
he's [hiːz] er ist **I U1**, 16
head [hed] Kopf **I U5**, 97
heading [ˈhedɪŋ] Überschrift; Titel **I U2**, 42
healthy [ˈhelθi] gesund **I AC2**, 101
*to **hear** [hɪə] hören **I U2**, 44
I **hear** … [aɪ ˈhɪə] Ich habe gehört, dass … **I U2**, 44
*to learn … by **heart** [ˌlɜːn baɪ ˈhɑːt] auswendig lernen **I U6**, 111
Hello. [helˈəʊ] Hallo. **I PUA**, 9
*to say **hello** (to) [ˌseɪ helˈəʊ tə] grüßen; Grüße ausrichten (an) **I U1**, 18
help [help] Hilfe **I U3**, 61
to **help** [help] helfen **I U1**, 15
helpful [ˈhelpfl] hilfsbereit; hilfreich **I U5**, 97
helpless [ˈhelpləs] hilflos **I U5**, 97
her [hɜː] ihr/-e; sie **I U1**, 14
here [hɪə] hier **I PUA**, 8
Here you are. [ˌhɪə ju‿ˈɑː] Bitte schön. **I U2**, 36
Here's … [hɪəz] Hier ist … **I PUA**, 8
Hey [heɪ] Hi.; He!; Hallo. **I PUB**, 29
Hi. [haɪ] Hi.; Hallo. **I PUA**, 9
high [haɪ] hoch; groß **I F1**, 68
hiking [ˈhaɪkɪŋ] Wandern **I F1**, 68
him [hɪm] ihn; ihm **I U2**, 34
his [hɪz] sein/-e **I U1**, 14
historical [hɪˈstɒrɪkl] historisch; geschichtlich **I AC3**, 121
History [ˈhɪstri] Geschichte **I U2**, 38
*to **hit** [hɪt] schlagen; treffen **I U4**, 80
hobby, hobbies *(pl)* [ˈhɒbi] Hobby **I PUB**, 28
*to **hold** [həʊld] halten; festhalten **I AC1**, 67
holiday [ˈhɒlədeɪ] Urlaub; Feiertag **I PUA**, 9
holidays *(pl)* [ˈhɒlədeɪz] Ferien **I U6**, 106
home [həʊm] Zuhause; Heim **I U1**, 14
at **home** [ət ˈhəʊm] zu Hause **I U1**, 14
home [həʊm] nach Hause **I U3**, 51
homework [ˈhəʊmwɜːk] Hausaufgabe(n) **I U2**, 40
to **hope** [həʊp] hoffen **I U5**, 96
hopeful [ˈhəʊpfl] hoffnungsvoll **I U5**, 88
horrified [ˈhɒrɪfaɪd] entsetzt **I U5**, 96
horse [hɔːs] Pferd **I U4**, 77
horse-riding [ˈhɔːsˌraɪdɪŋ] Reiten **I PUB**, 31
hot [hɒt] heiß **I AC2**, 101
hot dog [ˌhɒt ˈdɒg] Hot Dog *(Würstchen im Brötchen)* **I U6**, 112
hotel [həʊˈtel] Hotel **I F2**, 102
house [haʊs] Haus **I U1**, 14
how [haʊ] wie **I PUA**, 9
How are you? [ˌhaʊ‿ˈɑː jə] Wie geht es dir?; Wie geht es euch?; Wie geht es Ihnen? **I U6**, 116
How many …? [ˌhaʊ ˈmeni] Wie viele …? **I U5**, 91
How much (is/are) …? [ˌhaʊ ˈmʌtʃ‿ɪz/ɑː] Wie viel (kostet/kosten) …? **I U5**, 86
How old are you? [haʊ‿ˈəʊld‿ə juː] Wie alt bist du?; Wie alt sind Sie? **I PUA**, 9
How to … [ˈhaʊ tə] Wie man … **I AC1**, 66

this is **how** you do … [ˈðɪs‿ɪz haʊ jʊ ˌduː] so machst du … **I U3**, 51
to **hug** [hʌg] umarmen **I U5**, 97
hungry [ˈhʌŋgri] hungrig **I U6**, 117
to **hurry** [ˈhʌri] eilen; sich beeilen **I U6**, 116
*to **hurt** [hɜːt] verletzen; weh tun **I U6**, 110

I

I [aɪ] ich **I PUA**, 8
I can see … [ˌaɪ ˌkən siː] Ich sehe …; Ich kann … sehen. **I PUA**, 13
I don't know! [ˌaɪ ˌdəʊnt ˈnəʊ] Ich weiß (es) nicht! **I U4**, 78
I don't like … [aɪ ˈdəʊnt laɪk] Ich mag … nicht.; Ich mache … nicht gern. **I PUA**, 11
I hear … [aɪ ˈhɪə] Ich habe gehört, dass … **I U2**, 44
I like … [aɪ ˈlaɪk] Mir gefällt …; Ich mag … **I PUA**, 11
I like singing and dancing. [ˌaɪ laɪk ˌsɪŋɪŋ‿ənd ˈdɑːnsɪŋ] Ich singe und tanze gern. **I U2**, 34
I love … [aɪ ˈlʌv] Ich liebe …; Ich mag … total gern. **I PUA**, 10
I love you. [aɪ ˈlʌv ju] Ich liebe dich.; Ich mag dich. **I PUA**, 13
I'd like to … *(= I would like to)* [aɪd ˈlaɪk tə] Ich möchte …; Ich würde gern … **I U5**, 93
I'll get … [aɪl ˈget] Ich hole … **I U5**, 93
I'm … [aɪm] Ich bin … **I PUA**, 8
I'm (not) scared of … [ˌaɪm (nɒt) ˈskeəd‿əv] Ich habe (keine) Angst vor … **I PUA**, 10
I'm dog-tired. [aɪm ˌdɒgˈtaɪəd] Ich bin hundemüde. **I U3**, 52
I'm English. [aɪm‿ˈɪŋglɪʃ] Ich bin Engländer/-in. **I PUA**, 9
I'm fine. [ˌaɪm ˈfaɪn] Mir geht's gut. **I PUB**, 29
I'm from … [ˌaɪm frɒm] Ich bin aus … **I PUA**, 8
I'm sorry! [ˌaɪm ˈsɒri] Tut mir leid! **I PUB**, 29
ice [aɪs] Eis **I U6**, 105
ice cream [ˌaɪs ˈkriːm] Eis; Eiscreme **I U6**, 106
ice rink [ˈaɪs ˌrɪŋk] Eisbahn; Schlittschuhbahn **I U6**, 105
idea [aɪˈdɪə] Idee; Einfall **I U1**, 19
if [ɪf] wenn; falls; ob **I U3**, 52
to **imagine** [ɪˈmædʒɪn] sich (etwas) vorstellen **I U6**, 117
important [ɪmˈpɔːtnt] wichtig **I AC1**, 66
most **important** [ˌməʊst‿ɪmˈpɔːtnt] wichtigste/-r/-s **I AC3**, 121
to **improve** [ɪmˈpruːv] sich verbessern; verbessern **I U3**, 59
in [ɪn] in; im; rein; herein **I PUA**, 8
in front of [ɪn ˈfrʌnt‿əv] vor **I U1**, 19
in Greenwich Park [ˌɪn ˌgrenɪdʒ ˈpɑːk] im Greenwich-Park **I PUA**, 8

in the end [ˌɪn ðiˈend] schließlich; zum Schluss I U6, 110
in the evenings [ɪn ðiˈi:vnɪŋz] abends I U3, 52
in the middle (of) [ɪn ðə ˈmɪdl] in der Mitte (von); mitten in I U1, 19
in the mornings [ˌɪn ðə ˈmɔ:nɪŋz] morgens; vormittags I U3, 60
in the photo(s) [ˌɪn ðə ˈfəʊtəʊ(z)] auf dem Foto/den Fotos I U2, 37
in the street [ˌɪn ðə ˈstri:t] in der Straße; auf der Straße I U1, 14
independent [ˌɪndɪˈpendənt] unabhängig I F2, 103
Indian [ˈɪndiən] Inder/-in; indisch I AC2, 101
infinitive [ɪnˈfɪnətɪv] Infinitiv °I U6, 111
information *(no pl)* [ˌɪnfəˈmeɪʃn] Information; Informationen I U4, 74
inline skating [ˈɪnlaɪn ˌskeɪtɪŋ] Inlineskatefahren I PUA, 11
inside [ˌɪnˈsaɪd] innen; im Innern; hinein; nach drinnen; in; drin I U6, 117
instead of [ɪnˈsted‿əv] statt; anstatt; an Stelle von I U6, 113
instruction [ɪnˈstrʌkʃn] Instruktion; Anweisung I U6, 119
interesting [ˈɪntrəstɪŋ] interessant I U3, 60
most interesting [ˌməʊst‿ˈɪntrəstɪŋ] am interessantesten I F1, 69
international [ˌɪntəˈnæʃnl] international I AC3, 121
internet [ˈɪntənet] Internet I PUB, 31
interview [ˈɪntəvju:] Interview; Befragung I PUB, 30
into [ˈɪntə] in; in … hinein I U2, 40
*to be into [biˈɪntə] mögen; stehen auf I PUB, 28
You're into … [ˈjɔ:r‿ˌɪntə] Du magst …; Du stehst auf … I PUB, 28
Introduce … [ˌɪntrəˈdju:s] Stelle/Stellt … vor. °I PUA, 10
invitation [ˌɪnvɪˈteɪʃn] Einladung I U6, 108
to invite [ɪnˈvaɪt] einladen I U6, 106
irregular [ɪˈregjələ] unregelmäßig °I U6, 111
isn't (= is not) [ɪznt] ist nicht I U1, 16
island [ˈaɪlənd] Insel I F1, 68
it [ɪt] es I PUA, 11
It's …/They're … [ɪts/ðeə] Es kostet …/Sie kosten … I U5, 86
It's fun. [ɪts ˈfʌn] Es macht Spaß. I PUA, 11
It's great for … [ɪts ˈgreɪt fə] Es ist super zum/für … I PUA, 11
It's your turn. [ˌɪts ˈjɔ: tɜ:n] Du bist dran. I U2, 44
its [ɪts] sein/-e; ihr/-e I U1, 21

J

jacket [ˈdʒækɪt] Jacke I U5, 89
January [ˈdʒænjuri] Januar I U6, 105
*to be **jealous (of)** [bi ˈdʒeləs] eifersüchtig sein (auf); neidisch sein (auf) I U2, 44
jeans [dʒi:nz] Jeans I U5, 89
jelly [ˈdʒeli] Tortenguss; Götterspeise; Wackelpudding; Gelee I U6, 109
jewellery [ˈdʒu:əlri] Schmuck I U5, 86
job [dʒɒb] Arbeit; Aufgabe; Job I U2, 36
mouth jogging [ˈmaʊθ ˌdʒɒgɪŋ] Training für den Mund °I U3, 59
joke [dʒəʊk] Witz I U2, 44
juice [dʒu:s] Saft I U5, 88
July [dʒʊˈlaɪ] Juli I U6, 105
to jump [dʒʌmp] springen I U4, 81
to jump the queue [ˌdʒʌmp ðə ˈkju:] sich vordrängeln I AC1, 67
June [dʒu:n] Juni I U6, 105
just [dʒʌst] gerade; nur; einfach I U2, 44

K

*to **keep** [ki:p] behalten; aufbewahren; halten °I AC2, 100
*to keep your fingers crossed [ˌki:p jɔ: ˌfɪŋgəz ˈkrɒst] die Daumen drücken I U4, 74
key word [ˈki: ˌwɜ:d] Stichwort; Schlüsselbegriff I U6, 117
kind [kaɪnd] Art; Sorte I F2, 102
king [kɪŋ] König I U2, 44
kitchen [ˈkɪtʃɪn] Küche I U1, 14
knee [ni:] Knie I U3, 63
*to **know** [nəʊ] kennen; wissen I U2, 44
I don't know! [ˌaɪ ˌdəʊnt ˈnəʊ] Ich weiß (es) nicht! I U4, 78
You know how to … [ju: ˈnəʊ ˌhaʊ tə] Du weißt, wie man …; Ihr wisst, wie man … °I U1, 23

L

lake [leɪk] See I PUA, 11
boating lake [ˈbəʊtɪŋ ˌleɪk] See zum Rudern I PUA, 11
lamb [læm] Lamm; Lämmchen I U4, 77
lamp [læmp] Lampe; Leuchte I U1, 19
land [lænd] Land I U4, 80
language [ˈlæŋgwɪdʒ] Sprache I U1, 17
first language [ˌfɜ:st ˈlæŋgwɪdʒ] Muttersprache I F2, 103
official language [əˌfɪʃl ˈlæŋgwɪdʒ] Amtssprache I F2, 103
lassi [ˈlʌsi] Lassi I U6, 116
last [lɑ:st] letzte/-r/-s I U3, 54
at last [ət ˈlɑ:st] endlich; schließlich I U4, 74
late [leɪt] spät; zu spät I U2, 40
*to be late [bi ˈleɪt] zu spät dran sein; zu spät kommen I U2, 40
later [ˈleɪtə] später I U2, 44
Latin [ˈlætɪn] Latein I U2, 38
to laugh [lɑ:f] lachen I U2, 45
*to **learn** [lɜ:n] lernen I U2, 43
*to learn … by heart [ˌlɜ:n baɪ ˈhɑ:t] auswendig lernen I U6, 111
a lot to learn [ə ˌlɒt tə ˈlɜ:n] viel zu lernen I U3, 62
at least [ət ˈli:st] mindestens; wenigstens I U6, 112
*to **leave a message** [ˌli:v‿ə ˈmesɪdʒ] eine Nachricht hinterlassen I U5, 93
*to **leave it to cool** [ˌli:v‿ɪt tə ˈku:l] kalt stellen I U6, 109
on the left [ɒn ðə ˈleft] auf der linken Seite; links I U1, 19
left [left] übrig I U5, 93
leg [leg] Bein I U3, 63
leisure [ˈleʒə] Freizeit; Freizeit- I U4, 71
leisure centre [ˈleʒə ˌsentə] Freizeitzentrum I U4, 71
lemonade [ˌleməˈneɪd] Limonade I AC1, 67
lesson [ˈlesn] Unterrichtsstunde; Schulstunde; Unterricht I U2, 38
*to **let** [let] lassen I U6, 115
Let's … [lets] Lass/Lasst uns … I PUA, 11
letter [ˈletə] Buchstabe I U2, 42
capital letter [ˌkæpɪtl ˈletə] Großbuchstabe °I U2, 43
lifeboat [ˈlaɪfbəʊt] Rettungsboot I U4, 81
lifebuoy [ˈlaɪfbɔɪ] Rettungsring I U4, 81
to like [laɪk] mögen; gern haben I PUA, 11
would like [wʊd ˈlaɪk] würde/-st/-n/-t gern; hätte/-st/-n/-t gern I F3, 122
I don't like … [aɪ ˈdəʊnt laɪk] Ich mag … nicht.; Ich mache … nicht gern. I PUA, 11
I like … [aɪ ˈlaɪk] Mir gefällt …; Ich mag … I PUA, 11
I'd like to … *(= I would like to)* [aɪd ˈlaɪk tə] Ich möchte …; Ich würde gern … I U5, 93
like [laɪk] wie; als ob I PUA, 13
like that [laɪk ˈðæt] so I U6, 106
like this [laɪk ˈðɪs] so I U1, 19
line [laɪn] Linie; Zeile I U2, 34
time line [ˈtaɪm ˌlaɪn] Zeitstrahl °I AC3, 121
linking word [ˈlɪŋkɪŋ ˌwɜ:d] Verbindungswort °I U6, 117
list [lɪst] Liste I U2, 35
to listen (to) [ˈlɪsn] zuhören; anhören I U1, 19
Listen. [ˈlɪsn] Hör/Hört zu. °I PUA, 8
Listen again. [ˌlɪsn‿əˈgen] Hör/Hört noch einmal zu. °I U1, 17
to listen for [ˈlɪsn fə] horchen auf I U3, 62
listening [ˈlɪsnɪŋ] Hören °I PUA, 8
little [ˈlɪtl] klein I U1, 16
a little [ə ˈlɪtl] ein wenig; etwas I U5, 91
to live [lɪv] wohnen; leben I U1, 14
living room [ˈlɪvɪŋ rʊm] Wohnzimmer I U1, 14
locker [ˈlɒkə] Schließfach; Spind I U6, 108
loft [lɒft] Dachboden I U1, 19
Londoner [ˈlʌndənə] Londoner/-in I AC3, 121
lonely [ˈləʊnli] einsam I U6, 116
long [lɒŋ] lang I U3, 52
look [lʊk] Blick I U4, 71
to look [lʊk] schauen; sehen; aussehen I U3, 60

Look! [lʊk] Schau/Schaut mal! **I PUA**, 8
to **look** after [ˌlʊk‿'ɑ:ftə] aufpassen auf; hüten; sich kümmern um **I U3**, 55
to **look** at ['lʊk‿ət] anschauen; ansehen **I U2**, 41
Look at … ['lʊk‿ət] Schaut euch … an.; Schau dir … an. °**I PUA**, 9
to **look** for ['lʊk fɔ:] suchen nach **I U3**, 54
I'm **looking** for … [ˌaɪm 'lʊkɪŋ fə] Ich suche nach … **I U5**, 87
a **lot** [ə 'lɒt] viel **I U3**, 62
a **lot** of [ə 'lɒt‿əv] viel/-e; eine Menge **I F1**, 68
lots (of) ['lɒts‿əv] viel/-e; jede Menge **I U2**, 36
loud [laʊd] laut **I U3**, 59
Love … [lʌv] Liebe Grüße *(am Briefende)*; Herzliche Grüße *(am Briefende)* **I U6**, 115
to **love** [lʌv] lieben; gern mögen **I PUA**, 10
would **love** [wʊd 'lʌv] würde/-st/-n/-t sehr gern; hätte/-st-/-n/-t sehr gern **I U6**, 115
I **love** … [aɪ 'lʌv] Ich liebe …; Ich mag … total gern. **I PUA**, 10
I **love** you. [aɪ 'lʌv ju] Ich liebe dich.; Ich mag dich. **I PUA**, 13
Lower 48 [ˌləʊə fɔ:ti'eɪt] *Festlandstaaten der USA südlich von Kanada* **I F3**, 122
bad **luck** [ˌbæd 'lʌk] Pech; Unglück **I U6**, 110
lucky … ['lʌki] … der/die Glückliche **I U5**, 96
*to be **lucky** [bi 'lʌki] Glück haben **I U2**, 38
lucky charm [ˌlʌki 'tʃɑ:m] Glücksbringer; Talisman **I PUB**, 29
lunch [lʌnʃ] Mittagessen **I U2**, 33
lunch break ['lʌnʃbreɪk] Mittagspause **I U2**, 39

M

machine [mə'ʃi:n] Automat; Maschine; Apparat; Gerät **I U2**, 33
answering **machine** ['ɑ:nsrɪŋ məˌʃi:n] Anrufbeantworter **I U5**, 93
magazine [ˌmægə'zi:n] Zeitschrift **I PUB**, 31
main [meɪn] Haupt- °**I U3**, 60
*to **make** [meɪk] machen; tun; bilden **I U3**, 62; *hier:* ergeben **I U4**, 81
Make … [meɪk] Mache/Macht … °**I PUA**, 9
*to be **made** up of [bi ˌmeɪd‿'ʌp‿əv] bestehen aus **I F3**, 122
*to **make** a wish [ˌmeɪk‿ə 'wɪʃ] sich etwas wünschen **I U6**, 105
*to **make** friends [ˌmeɪk 'frendz] Freundschaft schließen **I F2**, 102
*to **make** money [ˌmeɪk 'mʌni] Geld verdienen **I U5**, 88
*to **make** notes [ˌmeɪk 'nəʊts] Notizen machen **I AC3**, 120
*to **make** trouble [ˌmeɪk 'trʌbl] Ärger machen; in Schwierigkeiten bringen **I U2**, 45
man [mæn], **men** *(pl)* [men] Mann **I AC1**, 67
mango ['mæŋgəʊ] Mango **I U5**, 99
many ['meni] viele **I U5**, 91
map [mæp] Stadtplan; Landkarte **I F1**, 68
mind **map** ['maɪnd mæp] Wörternetz *(eine Art Schaubild)* °**I U1**, 15
March [mɑ:tʃ] März **I U6**, 105
market ['mɑ:kɪt] Markt **I U4**, 78
flea **market** ['fli: ˌmɑ:kɪt] Flohmarkt **I U5**, 88
to **match** [mætʃ] zuordnen **I U1**, 25; passen zu; entsprechen **I U5**, 93
Match … [mætʃ] Ordne/Ordnet … einander zu. °**I U1**, 15
mate [meɪt] Schiffsoffizier; Maat **I U4**, 80
Maths *(infml)* [mæθs] Mathematik; Mathe **I U2**, 38
May [meɪ] Mai **I U6**, 105
maybe ['meɪbi] vielleicht **I U1**, 24
me [mi:] ich **I PUA**, 13; mich; mir **I U1**, 17
Me too. [ˌmi: 'tu:] Ich auch. **I PUB**, 31
ready **meal** [ˌredi 'mi:l] Fertiggericht **I AC2**, 101
*to **mean** [mi:n] bedeuten **I F3**, 122
mediation [ˌmi:di'eɪʃn] Sprachmittlung °**I U1**, 18
*to **meet** [mi:t] treffen; sich treffen **I PUB**, 28
message ['mesɪdʒ] Botschaft; Nachricht **I U5**, 93
*to leave a **message** [ˌli:v‿ə 'mesɪdʒ] eine Nachricht hinterlassen **I U5**, 93
*to take a **message** [ˌteɪk‿ə 'mesɪdʒ] eine Nachricht entgegennehmen; jmdm. etw. ausrichten **I U5**, 93
text (**message**) ['tekst ˌmesɪdʒ] SMS; Kurznachricht **I PUB**, 30
middle ['mɪdl] Mitte **I U1**, 19
in the **middle** (of) [ɪn ðə 'mɪdl] in der Mitte (von); mitten in **I U1**, 19
midnight ['mɪdnaɪt] Mitternacht **I U6**, 113
mile [maɪl] Meile *(brit. und amerikan. Längenmaß)* **I F3**, 122
milk [mɪlk] Milch **I AC2**, 101
million ['mɪljən] Million **I F2**, 103
mind map ['maɪnd mæp] Wörternetz *(eine Art Schaubild)* °**I U1**, 15
minute ['mɪnɪt] Minute **I U2**, 44
a few **minutes** later [ə ˌfju: ˌmɪnɪts 'leɪtə] ein paar Minuten später **I U2**, 44
mirror ['mɪrə] Spiegel **I U1**, 19
mistake [mɪ'steɪk] Fehler **I U3**, 56
mixed bag [ˌmɪkst 'bæg] buntes Allerlei; bunte Mischung °**I U2**, 47
model ['mɒdl] Modell; Tonmodell; Model **I U1**, 24
at the **moment** [ət ðə 'məʊmənt] im Moment; gerade **I U5**, 88
Monday ['mʌndeɪ] Montag **I U3**, 50
on **Mondays** [ɒn 'mʌndeɪz] montags **I U3**, 52
money ['mʌni] Geld **I U2**, 33
*to make **money** [ˌmeɪk 'mʌni] Geld verdienen **I U5**, 88
pocket **money** ['pɒkɪt ˌmʌni] Taschengeld **I U2**, 36
monster ['mɒnstə] Monster; Ungeheuer **I U4**, 80
month [mʌnθ] Monat **I U6**, 111
monument ['mɒnjəmənt] Monument; Denkmal **I F3**, 123
moon [mu:n] Mond **I F3**, 123
more [mɔ:] mehr; weitere **I U1**, 21
not any **more** [ˌnɒt‿eni 'mɔ:] nicht mehr **I F2**, 103
more … than ['mɔ: ðən] mehr … als **I U5**, 97
morning ['mɔ:nɪŋ] Morgen; Vormittag **I U3**, 52
in the **mornings** [ˌɪn ðə 'mɔ:nɪŋz] morgens; vormittags **I U3**, 60
Good **morning**. [ˌgʊd 'mɔ:nɪŋ] Guten Morgen. **I U2**, 34
(the) **most** [ðə 'məʊst] der/die/das meiste; die meisten **I F2**, 103
most famous [ˌməʊst 'feɪməs] berühmteste/-r/-s **I F1**, 69
most important [ˌməʊst‿ɪm'pɔ:tnt] wichtigste/-r/-s **I AC3**, 121
most interesting [ˌməʊst‿'ɪntrəstɪŋ] am interessantesten **I F1**, 69
mother ['mʌðə] Mutter **I U1**, 16
to **motivate** ['məʊtɪveɪt] motivieren °**I U4**, 81
mountain ['maʊntɪn] Berg **I F1**, 68
mountain biking ['maʊntɪn ˌbaɪkɪŋ] Mountainbikefahren **I F1**, 68
mouse [maʊs], **mice** *(pl)* [maɪs] Maus, Mäuse **I PUA**, 8
mouth [maʊθ] Mund **I U3**, 59
mouth jogging ['maʊθ ˌdʒɒgɪŋ] Training für den Mund °**I U3**, 59
to **move** [mu:v] (sich) bewegen **I U6**, 109
Mr ['mɪstə] Herr *(Anrede)* **I U1**, 19
Mrs ['mɪsɪz] Frau *(Anrede)* **I U1**, 19
much [mʌtʃ] viel **I U2**, 44
mum [mʌm] Mama **I U1**, 16
museum [mju:'zi:əm] Museum **I F1**, 68
music ['mju:zɪk] Musik **I PUB**, 30
must [mʌst] müssen **I U5**, 91
mustn't ['mʌsnt] nicht dürfen **I U6**, 106
my [maɪ] mein/-e **I PUA**, 8
My favourite … [maɪ 'feɪvrɪt] Mein/-e Lieblings… **I PUA**, 11
My name is … [maɪ 'neɪm‿ɪz] Ich heiße … **I PUA**, 9

N

name [neɪm] Name **I PUA**, 9
name day ['neɪm ˌdeɪ] Namenstag **I AC3**, 121
My **name** is … [maɪ 'neɪm‿ɪz] Ich heiße … **I PUA**, 9
What's your **name**? [ˌwɒts jə 'neɪm] Wie heißt du?; Wie heißen Sie? **I PUA**, 9
to **name** [neɪm] nennen; benennen **I U6**, 107

Name … [neɪm] Nenne/Nennt … °**I PUA**, 11
*to be **named** after [bi 'neɪmd‿ɑ:ftə] benannt sein nach **I F3**, 123
Can you **name** …? [ˌkæn jʊ 'neɪm] Kannst du … nennen? **I PUA**, 13
national ['næʃnl] national; landesweit **I AC3**, 120
national park [ˌnæʃnl 'pɑ:k] Nationalpark; Naturpark **I F3**, 122
Native American [ˌneɪtɪv‿ə'merɪkən] Ureinwohner/-in Amerikas; Indianer/-in; indianisch **I F3**, 122
near [nɪə] nahe; in der Nähe von **I F1**, 69
to **need** [ni:d] brauchen; benötigen **I U2**, 43
to **need** (to do) [ni:d] (tun) müssen **I U4**, 78
needn't ['ni:dnt] nicht brauchen; nicht müssen **I U6**, 106
negative ['negətɪv] negativ; verneint °**I U6**, 113
negative form ['negətɪv ˌfɔ:m] verneinte Form °**I U1**, 18
neighbour *(BE)* ['neɪbə] Nachbar/-in **I U3**, 55
*to get on people's **nerves** [ˌget‿ɒn pi:plz 'nɜ:vz] jemandem auf die Nerven gehen **I U3**, 55
netball ['netbɔ:l] Korbball **I U3**, 52
never ['nevə] nie; niemals **I U3**, 52
new [nju:] neu **I U1**, 15
next [nekst] nächste/-r/-s; der/die Nächste(n) **I U2**, 44
next [nekst] als Nächstes **I U5**, 87
next to ['nekst tə] neben **I U1**, 19
nice [naɪs] nett; schön; lieb **I PUA**, 9
night [naɪt] Nacht **I U6**, 106
all **night** [ˌɔ:l 'naɪt] die ganze Nacht **I U6**, 106
nine [naɪn] neun **I PUA**, 12
nineteen [ˌnaɪn'ti:n] neunzehn **I U1**, 20
ninety ['naɪnti] neunzig **I U1**, 20
no [nəʊ] kein/-e **I U2**, 34
no one ['nəʊ wʌn] niemand **I U5**, 92
no [nəʊ] nein **I PUA**, 9
nobody ['nəʊbədi] niemand **I U5**, 92
noisy ['nɔɪzi] laut **I U1**, 17
normal ['nɔ:ml] normal **I U6**, 112
north [nɔ:θ] Norden; Nord- **I F1**, 68
north [nɔ:θ] nördlich; im Norden **I F1**, 68
nose [nəʊz] Nase **I U3**, 63
not [nɒt] nicht **I PUA**, 8
not any more [ˌnɒt‿eni 'mɔ:] nicht mehr **I F2**, 103
not either [nɒt … 'aɪðə; nɒt … 'i:ðə] auch nicht **I U4**, 73
not … any [nɒt‿eni] kein/-e/-en **I U5**, 91
not … anything [ˌnɒt‿'eniθɪŋ] nichts **I U5**, 97
note [nəʊt] Notiz; Anmerkung **I F1**, 68
*to make **notes** [ˌmeɪk 'nəʊts] Notizen machen **I AC3**, 120
*to take **notes** [ˌteɪk 'nəʊts] sich Notizen machen **I U4**, 71
nothing ['nʌθɪŋ] nichts **I U5**, 92
November [nə'vembə] November **I U6**, 105
now [naʊ] jetzt; nun **I U1**, 19
number ['nʌmbə] Zahl; Nummer **I PUA**, 13
nut [nʌt] Nuss **I AC2**, 101

O

o'clock [ə'klɒk] Uhr *(Zeitangabe bei vollen Stunden)* **I U3**, 50
October [ɒk'təʊbə] Oktober **I U6**, 105
of [ɒv; əv] von **I U1**, 18
of course [əv 'kɔ:s] natürlich; selbstverständlich **I AC1**, 66
special **offer** [ˌspeʃl‿'ɒfə] Sonderangebot **I U5**, 87
office ['ɒfɪs] Büro **I U2**, 36
official language [əˌfɪʃl 'læŋgwɪdʒ] Amtssprache **I F2**, 103
often ['ɒfn] oft; häufig **I U3**, 52
oh [əʊ] null *(bei Telefonnummern und Uhrzeitangaben)* **I U3**, 50
Oh! [əʊ] O! **I PUA**, 8
oil [ɔɪl] Öl **I F3**, 122
OK [əʊ'keɪ] o.k.; in Ordnung **I PUA**, 10
old [əʊld] alt **I PUA**, 9
How **old** are you? [haʊ‿'əʊld‿ə ˌju:] Wie alt bist du?; Wie alt sind Sie? **I PUA**, 9
on [ɒn] auf; an; am; in; im **I PUA**, 9
on Mondays [ɒn 'mʌndeɪz] montags **I U3**, 52
on the left [ɒn ðə 'left] auf der linken Seite; links **I U1**, 19
on the right [ɒn ðə 'raɪt] auf der rechten Seite; rechts **I U1**, 19
on top [ɒn 'tɒp] oben; obendrauf **I U6**, 109
on your own [ˌɒn jər‿'əʊn] allein; für dich **I U6**, 108
Come **on**! [ˌkʌm‿'ɒn] Komm schon!; Komm jetzt! **I U2**, 44
once [wʌns] einmal; einst °**I AC1**, 67
one [wʌn] eins **I PUA**, 9
one hundred [ə 'hʌndrəd; wʌn 'hʌndrəd] einhundert; hundert **I U1**, 20
twenty-**one** [ˌtwenti'wʌn] einundzwanzig **I U1**, 20
only ['əʊnli] erst; bloß; nur **I U1**, 17
only child ['əʊnli ˌtʃaɪld] Einzelkind **I U1**, 16
Oops! [u:ps] Hoppla!; Huch! **I PUB**, 29
to **open** ['əʊpn] öffnen; aufmachen **I AC1**, 67
open ['əʊpn] offen; geöffnet; aufgeschlagen **I AC1**, 67
or [ɔ:] oder **I U1**, 21
orange ['ɒrɪndʒ] Orange **I U5**, 88
orange ['ɒrɪndʒ] orange **I PUA**, 12
order ['ɔ:də] Reihenfolge; Ordnung **I U1**, 25
word **order** ['wɜ:d‿ˌɔ:də] Wortstellung; Satzstellung °**I U3**, 53
to **organise** ['ɔ:gənaɪz] organisieren **I U5**, 88
other ['ʌðə] anders; andere/-r/-s; weitere **I U3**, 52
each **other** [ˌi:tʃ‿'ʌðə] einander; sich; sich gegenseitig °**I U2**, 41
the **others** [ði‿'ʌðəz] die anderen **I U3**, 60
our [aʊə; ɑ:] unser/-e **I U1**, 16
out [aʊt] außerhalb; heraus; hinaus; nach draußen **I U6**, 109
to clear **out** [ˌklɪər‿'aʊt] ausräumen; entrümpeln **I U5**, 88
outside [ˌaʊt'saɪd] nach draußen; draußen; außerhalb (von) **I U1**, 24
over ['əʊvə] hinüber; über **I U4**, 71
over there [ˌəʊvə 'ðeə] da drüben; dort drüben **I U2**, 42
own [əʊn] eigene/-r/-s **I U1**, 19
on your **own** [ˌɒn jər‿'əʊn] allein; für dich **I U6**, 108

P

p.m. [ˌpi:'em] nachmittags *(Uhrzeit)*; abends *(Uhrzeit)* **I U3**, 50
packet ['pækɪt] Päckchen; Paket; Packung **I U5**, 87
page [peɪdʒ] Seite **I AC1**, 66
to **paint** [peɪnt] anmalen; malen **I PUB**, 31
pair [peə] Paar **I U2**, 44
pancake ['pænkeɪk] Pfannkuchen **I U6**, 112
parents *(pl)* ['peərənts] Eltern **I PUA**, 9
park [pɑ:k] Park **I PUA**, 8
national **park** [ˌnæʃnl 'pɑ:k] Nationalpark; Naturpark **I F3**, 122
parrot ['pærət] Papagei **I PUA**, 10
part [pɑ:t] Teil; Stadtteil **I AC2**, 100
partner ['pɑ:tnə] Partner/-in **I PUA**, 8
party ['pɑ:ti] Party; Feier **I U6**, 104
past [pɑ:st] nach *(bei Uhrzeitangaben)* **I U3**, 50
half **past** [ˌhɑ:f 'pɑ:st] halb *(bei Uhrzeitangaben)* **I U3**, 50
quarter **past**/to ['kwɔ:tə pɑ:st/tə] Viertel nach/vor **I U3**, 50
pasta ['pæstə] Pasta; Nudeln **I AC2**, 101
*to **pay** (for) [peɪ] bezahlen **I U2**, 33
PE *(Physical Education)* [ˌpi:'i:] Sportunterricht **I U2**, 38
peach [pi:tʃ] Pfirsich **I F3**, 122
pen [pen] Füller **I U2**, 33
pencil ['pensl] Bleistift; Buntstift **I U2**, 33
pencil-case ['pensl ˌkeɪs] Federmäppchen; Mäppchen **I U2**, 33
penny ['peni], **pence** *(pl)* [pens] Penny *(brit. Währungseinheit)* **I U5**, 86
people *(pl)* ['pi:pl] Leute; Menschen **I PUA**, 12
person ['pɜ:sn], **people** *(pl)* ['pi:pl] Person; Mensch **I AC1**, 67
personal ['pɜ:snl] persönlich °**I AC2**, 101
pet [pet] Haustier **I U3**, 55
phone [fəʊn] Telefon; Handy **I PUA**, 13

to answer the **phone** [ˌɑːnsə ðə ˈfəʊn] einen Anruf entgegennehmen **I U5**, 93
phone call [ˈfəʊn ˌkɔːl] Anruf; Telefonanruf **I U5**, 93
photo [ˈfəʊtəʊ] Foto; Fotografie **I PUA**, 9
in the **photo**(s) [ˌɪn ðə ˈfəʊtəʊ(z)] auf dem Foto/den Fotos **I U2**, 37
photo story [ˈfəʊtəʊ ˌstɔːri] Fotostory; Bildgeschichte **I PUB**, 30
*to take **photos** [ˌteɪk ˈfəʊtəʊz] fotografieren; Fotos machen **I PUB**, 31
phrase [freɪz] Redewendung; Ausdruck; Satz **I PUB**, 30
Useful **phrases** [ˌjuːsfl ˈfreɪsɪz] nützliche Ausdrücke °**I U1**, 18
pick-up [ˈpɪkʌp] Pick-up; Wiederaufnehmen °**I U1**, 15
Pick-up [ˈpɪkʌp] *Einstiegslektion, die den Grundschulwortschatz aufgreift* °**I PUA**, 8
picnic [ˈpɪknɪk] Picknick **I U3**, 63
picture [ˈpɪktʃə] Bild; Foto **I PUA**, 12
pie [paɪ] Kuchen; Pastete **I AC2**, 100
piece [piːs] Stück **I U5**, 96
pier [pɪə] Pier; Hafendamm **I U4**, 71
pig [pɪg] Schwein **I U4**, 76
guinea **pig** [ˈgɪniː ˌpɪg] Meerschweinchen **I U1**, 17
pink [pɪŋk] pink; rosa **I PUA**, 12
pizza [ˈpiːtsə] Pizza **I U5**, 97
place [pleɪs] Ort; Stelle; Platz **I U2**, 43
*to take **place** [ˌteɪk ˈpleɪs] stattfinden **I U6**, 115
placemat [ˈpleɪsmæt] Placemat; Platzdeckchen °**I U6**, 108
plan [plæn] Plan; Entwurf °**I U1**, 23
to **plan** [plæn] planen **I U6**, 106
planner [ˈplænə] Handbuch; Kalender **I U2**, 32
role **play** [ˈrəʊl ˌpleɪ] Rollenspiel **I U3**, 54
to **play** [pleɪ] spielen **I PUB**, 28
to **play** a trick (on) [ˌpleɪ‿ə ˈtrɪk‿ɒn] einen Streich spielen **I U2**, 44
Please. [pliːz] Bitte. **I PUA**, 13
plum [plʌm] Pflaume **I AC2**, 101
plural [ˈplʊərl] Plural; Mehrzahl °**I U2**, 41
pocket money [ˈpɒkɪt ˌmʌni] Taschengeld **I U2**, 36
poem [ˈpəʊɪm] Gedicht **I U2**, 44
Point. [pɔɪnt] Zeige/Zeigt darauf. °**I PUA**, 12
Point to … [ˈpɔɪnt tə] Zeige/Zeigt auf … °**I U1**, 14
polar bear [ˈpəʊlə ˌbeə] Eisbär **I F3**, 122
polite [pəˈlaɪt] höflich **I U2**, 36
Be **polite**. [ˌbiː pəˈlaɪt] Sei/Seid höflich. **I U2**, 36
pony [ˈpəʊni] Pony **I U5**, 97
pony trekking [ˈpəʊni ˌtrekɪŋ] Wanderreiten; Ponyreiten im Gelände **I F1**, 69
popular [ˈpɒpjələ] beliebt; populär **I U2**, 44
possessive form [pəˌzesɪv ˈfɔːm] Possessivform °**I U2**, 41
possible [ˈpɒsəbl] möglich **I U5**, 97
post [pəʊst] Post *(Eintrag im Internet)* **I F3**, 122
postcard [ˈpəʊskɑːd] Postkarte **I U6**, 112
poster [ˈpəʊstə] Poster **I U5**, 91
class **poster** [ˈklɑːs ˌpəʊstə] Klassenposter °**I PUA**, 11
pound (£) [paʊnd] Pfund *(brit. Währungseinheit)* **I U5**, 86
to **pour** [pɔː] einschenken; eingießen; schütten **I U6**, 109
Word **power** [ˈwɜːd ˌpaʊə] die Kraft der Wörter *(Wortschatzübung)* °**I U1**, 16
to **practise** [ˈpræktɪs] üben; trainieren **I U2**, 43
practising [ˈpræktɪsɪŋ] Üben **I U3**, 59
to **prepare** [prɪˈpeə] vorbereiten; zubereiten **I U6**, 109
preposition [ˌprepəˈzɪʃn] Präposition °**I U3**, 53
pre-reading [ˌpriːˈriːdɪŋ] vor dem Lesen °**I U6**, 116
present [ˈpreznt] Geschenk **I U5**, 87
present progressive [ˌpreznt prəˈgresɪv] Verlaufsform des Präsens/der Gegenwart °**I U5**, 89
simple **present** [ˌsɪmpl ˈpreznt] Gegenwart; Präsens °**I U3**, 51
to **present** [prɪˈzent] präsentieren; vorstellen **I U3**, 60
Present … [prɪˈzent] Präsentiere/Präsentiert … °**I U1**, 23
presentation [ˌpreznˈteɪʃn] Präsentation; Vortrag **I U2**, 44
presenter [prɪˈzentə] Moderator/-in °**I U3**, 61
president [ˈprezɪdnt] Präsident/-in **I F3**, 123
price [praɪs] Preis **I U5**, 86
primary school [ˈpraɪmri ˌskuːl] Grundschule °**I U2**, 33
prize [praɪz] Preis; Gewinn **I U5**, 96
problem [ˈprɒbləm] Problem; Schwierigkeit **I U1**, 19
to **produce** [prəˈdjuːs] herstellen; produzieren **I F3**, 122
profile [ˈprəʊfaɪl] Profil; Porträt °**I PUA**, 9
present **progressive** [ˌpreznt prəˈgresɪv] Verlaufsform des Präsens/der Gegenwart °**I U5**, 89
project [ˈprɒdʒekt] Projekt **I U2**, 34
pronunciation [prəˌnʌnsiˈeɪʃn] Aussprache °**I U6**, 111
pudding [ˈpʊdɪŋ] Pudding; Nachtisch **I U2**, 36
to **pull** [pʊl] ziehen **I U5**, 96
pullover [ˈpʊləʊvə] Pullover **I U5**, 89
purple [ˈpɜːpl] violett; lila **I PUA**, 12
*to **put** [pʊt] setzen; stellen; legen **I U3**, 63
Put in … [pʊt‿ˈɪn] Setze/Setzt ein … °**I U1**, 18
Put it in … [ˌpʊt‿ɪt‿ˈɪn] Lege/Legt es in …; Stelle/Stellt es in … °**I PUB**, 31
*to **put** through [ˌpʊt‿ˈθruː] verbinden **I U5**, 93
Put … face down. [pʊt ˌfeɪs ˈdaʊn] Lege/Legt … umgedreht hin. °**I PUA**, 10
puzzle [ˈpʌzl] Rätsel **I PUA**, 10

Q

quality [ˈkwɒləti] Qualität **I U5**, 86
quarter past/to [ˈkwɔːtə pɑːst/tə] Viertel nach/vor **I U3**, 50
queen [kwiːn] Königin **I F1**, 69
question [ˈkwestʃən] Frage **I U2**, 34
queue [kjuː] Schlange; Warteschlange **I AC1**, 67
to jump the **queue** [ˌdʒʌmp ðə ˈkjuː] sich vordrängeln **I AC1**, 67
quick [kwɪk] schnell **I AC2**, 100
quiet [kwaɪət] still; ruhig; leise **I U1**, 17
quiz [kwɪz] Quiz; Rätsel **I U1**, 15

R

rabbit [ˈræbɪt] Kaninchen **I PUA**, 10
raffle [ˈræfl] Tombola **I U5**, 96
rafting [ˈrɑːftɪŋ] Schlauchbootfahren **I F3**, 122
rap [ræp] Rap **I PUA**, 13
to **rap** [ræp] rappen **I PUA**, 13
rat [ræt] Ratte **I PUA**, 10
RE *(Religious Education)* [ˌɑːr‿ˈiː] Religionsunterricht **I U2**, 38
*to **read** [riːd] lesen **I PUB**, 31
Read … [riːd] Lies/Lest … °**I PUA**, 13
reader [ˈriːdə] Leser/-in °**I U4**, 81
reading [ˈriːdɪŋ] Lesen **I PUB**, 30
ready meal [ˌredi ˈmiːl] Fertiggericht **I AC2**, 101
really [ˈrɪəli] wirklich **I U2**, 44
recording [rɪˈkɔːdɪŋ] Aufnahme; Aufzeichnung **I U2**, 44
recording studio [rɪˈkɔːdɪŋ ˌstjuːdiəʊ] Aufnahmestudio; Tonstudio **I U2**, 33
red [red] rot **I PUA**, 12
to **reef** the sails [ˌriːf ðə ˈseɪlz] die Segel einholen **I U4**, 80
regular [ˈregjələ] regelmäßig; gleichmäßig °**I U6**, 111
religious [rɪˈlɪdʒəs] religiös; gläubig **I AC3**, 120
to **remember** [rɪˈmembə] sich erinnern (an); sich merken; denken an **I U1**, 21
Repeat … [rɪˈpiːt] Wiederhole/Wiederholt … °**I PUA**, 9
reply [rɪˈplaɪ] Antwort; Erwiderung; Entgegnung **I U6**, 115
to **reply** (to) [rɪˈplaɪ] antworten (auf); erwidern; entgegnen **I U6**, 115
the **rest** [rest] der Rest °**I U4**, 74
restaurant [ˈrestrɒnt] Restaurant; Gaststätte **I U2**, 36
*to **retell** [ˌriːˈtel] nacherzählen; nochmals erzählen °**I U5**, 97
rhyme [raɪm] Reim °**I PUA**, 10

rhythm ['rɪðm] Rhythmus I **U3**, 59
*to **ride** [raɪd] fahren; reiten I **F1**, 69
rigging ['rɪgɪŋ] Takelage I **U4**, 80
right [raɪt] richtig; korrekt I **U1**, 25
*to be **right** [bi 'raɪt] recht haben I **U2**, 45
on the **right** [ɒn ðə 'raɪt] auf der rechten Seite; rechts I **U1**, 19
right away [ˌraɪt‿ə'weɪ] sofort; gleich I **U3**, 52
*to **ring** [rɪŋ] klingeln; läuten I **U5**, 88
ice **rink** ['aɪs ˌrɪŋk] Eisbahn; Schlittschuhbahn I **U6**, 105
river ['rɪvə] Fluss I **F1**, 69
rock [rɒk] Fels; Stein I **F1**, 68
rocket ['rɒkɪt] Rakete I **F3**, 122
rodeo [rə'deɪəʊ; 'rəʊdiəʊ] Rodeo I **F3**, 122
role [rəʊl] Rolle I **AC3**, 121
role play ['rəʊl ˌpleɪ] Rollenspiel I **U3**, 54
to swap **roles** [ˌswɒp 'rəʊlz] Rollen tauschen I **U5**, 95
Roll two dice. [ˌrəʊl ˌtu: 'daɪs] Würfle/Würfelt mit zwei Würfeln. °I **PUA**, 13
roof [ru:f] Dach I **U1**, 23
room [ru:m; rʊm] Zimmer; Raum I **U1**, 14
living **room** ['lɪvɪŋ rʊm] Wohnzimmer I **U1**, 14
roommate ['ru:mmeɪt] Zimmergenosse/Zimmergenossin I **U3**, 54
royal ['rɔɪəl] königlich I **AC3**, 121
rubber ['rʌbə] Radiergummi I **U2**, 33
rubbish ['rʌbɪʃ] Müll; Gerümpel I **U5**, 96
rude [ru:d] unhöflich; unverschämt I **U2**, 39
rug [rʌg] Vorleger; Teppich I **U1**, 19
rule [ru:l] Regel I **U2**, 32
What's the **rule** for ...? [ˌwɒts ðə 'ru:l fə] Was ist die Regel für ...? °I **U1**, 18
ruler ['ru:lə] Lineal I **U2**, 33
*to **run** [rʌn] rennen; laufen I **U2**, 40
*to **run** away [ˌrʌn‿ə'weɪ] wegrennen I **U3**, 62

S

sad [sæd] traurig I **U5**, 88
to reef the **sails** [ˌri:f ðə 'seɪlz] die Segel einholen I **U4**, 80
sailor ['seɪlə] Seemann; Matrose I **U4**, 80
salad ['sæləd] Salat I **AC2**, 101
the **same** [ðə 'seɪm] der-/die-/dasselbe; der/die/das gleiche I **PUA**, 11
sandwich ['sænwɪdʒ] Sandwich; belegtes Brot I **AC2**, 100
Saturday ['sætədeɪ] Samstag I **U3**, 51
to **save** [seɪv] retten; bergen I **U4**, 81
sax [sæks] Saxofon I **U3**, 52
saxophone ['sæksəfəʊn] Saxofon I **U3**, 52
*to **say** [seɪ] sagen; aufsagen; sprechen I **PUA**, 13
Say ... [seɪ] Sage/Sagt ... I **PUA**, 13
*to **say** hello (to) [ˌseɪ hel'əʊ tə] grüßen; Grüße ausrichten (an) I **U1**, 18
*to be **scared** (of) [bi 'skeəd‿əv] Angst haben (vor) I **U3**, 62
I'm (not) **scared** of ... [ˌaɪm (nɒt) 'skeəd‿əv] Ich habe (keine) Angst vor ... I **PUA**, 10
scene [si:n] Szene I **U3**, 60
acting a **scene** [ˌæktɪŋ‿ə 'si:n] eine Theaterszene spielen I **U3**, 59
school [sku:l] Schule I **PUA**, 11
primary **school** ['praɪmri ˌsku:l] Grundschule °I **U2**, 33
schoolbag ['sku:lbæg] Schultasche I **U2**, 34
Science [saɪəns] Naturwissenschaften I **U2**, 38
sea [si:] Meer I **F1**, 68
second ['seknd] zweite/-r/-s I **F2**, 103
*to **see** [si:] sehen I **PUA**, 13
See you! ['si: jə] Bis dann!; Bis ... I **U4**, 72
I can **see** ... [ˌaɪ ˌkən si:] Ich sehe ...; Ich kann ... sehen. I **PUA**, 13
Wait and **see**! [ˌweɪt‿ənd 'si:] Warte ab! I **U2**, 34
What can you **see** ...? [ˌwɒt kən ju 'si:] Was kannst du/könnt ihr ... sehen? °I **PUA**, 13
self-evaluation [ˌselfɪˌvælju'eɪʃn] Selbsteinschätzung °I **U1**, 27
*to **sell** [sel] verkaufen I **U5**, 87
seller ['selə] Verkäufer/-in *(auf einem Flohmarkt)* I **U5**, 95
*to **send** [send] schicken; senden I **U2**, 36
sentence ['sentəns] Satz I **U1**, 25
separate ['seprət] separat; getrennt; verschieden I **F1**, 68
September [sep'tembə] September I **U6**, 105
serious ['sɪəriəs] ernsthaft; ernst I **AC3**, 121
*to **set** up [ˌset‿'ʌp] einrichten; aufbauen I **U5**, 94
seven ['sevn] sieben I **PUA**, 12
seventeen [ˌsevn'ti:n] siebzehn I **U1**, 20
seventy ['sevnti] siebzig I **U1**, 20
shape [ʃeɪp] Form I **F1**, 68
she [ʃi:] sie I **U1**, 16
she's [ʃi:z] sie ist I **U1**, 16
shed [ʃed] Schuppen; Stall; Gartenhäuschen I **U1**, 23
sheep, **sheep** *(pl)* [ʃi:p] Schaf I **F1**, 68
shelf [ʃelf], **shelves** *(pl)* [ʃelvz] Regal; Regalbrett I **U1**, 19
ship [ʃɪp] Schiff I **U4**, 70
shirt [ʃɜ:t] Hemd; Shirt I **U5**, 89
shoe [ʃu:] Schuh I **U3**, 63
shop [ʃɒp] Geschäft; Laden I **U2**, 33
charity **shop** ['tʃærɪti ˌʃɒp] Second-Hand-Laden I **U5**, 90
shopping ['ʃɒpɪŋ] Einkaufen I **F1**, 69
*to go **shopping** [ˌgəʊ 'ʃɒpɪŋ] einkaufen gehen I **U5**, 86
short [ʃɔ:t] klein I **U1**, 17; kurz I **PUB**, 31
short answer [ˌʃɔ:t‿'ɑ:nsə] Kurzantwort °I **U2**, 36
short form ['ʃɔ:t fɔ:m] Kurzform °I **U1**, 17
shorts [ʃɔ:ts] Shorts; kurze Hose I **U5**, 89
shoulder ['ʃəʊldə] Schulter I **U3**, 63
to **shout** [ʃaʊt] schreien; rufen I **U4**, 80
talent **show** ['tælənt ˌʃəʊ] Talentwettbewerb I **U2**, 36
*to **show** [ʃəʊ] zeigen I **PUB**, 28
Show ... [ʃəʊ] Zeige/Zeigt ... °I **U1**, 23
shower ['ʃaʊə] Dusche I **U1**, 15
sight [saɪt] Sehenswürdigkeit; Anblick I **F1**, 69
sightseeing ['saɪtsi:ɪŋ] Besichtigung von Sehenswürdigkeiten I **F1**, 69
signal word ['sɪgnl ˌwɜ:d] Signalwort °I **U5**, 89
silly ['sɪli] dumm; doof; albern I **PUB**, 31
simple present [ˌsɪmpl 'preznt] Gegenwart; Präsens °I **U3**, 51
*to **sing** [sɪŋ] singen I **U2**, 34
sister ['sɪstə] Schwester I **U1**, 16
half-**sister** ['hɑ:fˌsɪstə] Halbschwester I **U4**, 74
*to **sit** [sɪt] sitzen I **U2**, 39
Sit! [sɪt] Sitz! *(Befehl für Hunde)* I **U3**, 62
*to **sit** down [ˌsɪt 'daʊn] sich hinsetzen; sich setzen I **U3**, 51
*to **sit** face to face [ˌsɪt feɪs tə 'feɪs] sich gegenüber sitzen °I **U4**, 73
situation [ˌsɪtju'eɪʃn] Situation I **U3**, 58
six [sɪks] sechs I **PUA**, 12
sixteen [ˌsɪk'sti:n] sechzehn I **U1**, 20
sixty ['sɪksti] sechzig I **U1**, 20
size [saɪz] Größe; Kleidergröße I **U6**, 108
to **skate** [skeɪt] Inlineskates fahren; Schlittschuh laufen I **PUB**, 29
skateboard ['skeɪtbɔ:d] Skateboard I **U1**, 19
skateboarding ['skeɪtbɔ:dɪŋ] Skateboardfahren I **PUA**, 11
skates *(pl)* [skeɪts] Inlineskates; Rollschuhe; Schlittschuhe I **PUB**, 28
(inline) **skating** ['ɪnlaɪn ˌskeɪtɪŋ] Inlineskatefahren I **PUA**, 11
skiing ['ski:ɪŋ] Skifahren I **F1**, 68
skill [skɪl] Fertigkeit; Geschick °I **U1**, 15
skirt [skɜ:t] Rock I **U5**, 89
skyscraper ['skaɪskreɪpə] Wolkenkratzer I **F3**, 123
*to **sleep** [sli:p] schlafen I **U3**, 51
sleepover ['sli:pˌəʊvə] Übernachtung I **U6**, 106
to **slice** [slaɪs] in Scheiben schneiden I **U6**, 109
slide [slaɪd] Rutschbahn I **U4**, 71
water **slide** ['wɔ:tə ˌslaɪd] Wasserrutsche I **U4**, 71
slow [sləʊ] langsam I **U4**, 80
small [smɔ:l] klein I **U1**, 15
smile [smaɪl] Lächeln I **AC1**, 66
to **smile** [smaɪl] lächeln I **U6**, 116
snack [snæk] Snack; Imbiss I **AC2**, 101
snack bar ['snæk ˌbɑ:] Café; Imbissstube I **U5**, 86
word **snake** ['wɜ:d ˌsneɪk] Wortschlange °I **U2**, 43

to **snore** [snɔ:] schnarchen **I U3**, 54
snowboarding ['snəʊbɔ:dɪŋ] Snowboarden **I PUB**, 31
so [səʊ] so; also **I PUB**, 29
soccer *(AE)* ['sɒkə] Fußball **I U6**, 114
sofa ['səʊfə] Sofa; Couch **I U1**, 15
solution [sə'lu:ʃn] Lösung **I U2**, 47
some [sʌm; səm] einige; ein paar; etwas **I U1**, 18
somebody ['sʌmbədi] jemand **I U5**, 92
someone ['sʌmwʌn] jemand **I U5**, 92
something ['sʌmθɪŋ] etwas **I U2**, 34
sometimes ['sʌmtaɪmz] manchmal **I U3**, 52
song [sɒŋ] Song; Lied **I U1**, 22
Sorry! ['sɒri] Entschuldigung!; Tut mir leid! **I PUA**, 9
*to be **sorry** [bi 'sɒri] leid tun **I U4**, 81
I'm **sorry**! [ˌaɪm 'sɒri] Tut mir leid! **I PUB**, 29
sound [saʊnd] Ton; Geräusch; Klang **I U3**, 59
to **sound** [saʊnd] klingen **I U6**, 112
south [saʊθ] Süden; Süd- **I F1**, 68
space [speɪs] Raum; Weltraum **I F3**, 123
*to **speak** [spi:k] sprechen **I U3**, 59
speaker ['spi:kə] Redner/-in; Sprecher/-in **I U3**, 58
speaking ['spi:kɪŋ] Sprechen °**I PUA**, 8
special ['speʃl] besonders; speziell **I F1**, 68
special offer [ˌspeʃl‿'ɒfə] Sonderangebot **I U5**, 87
speech bubble ['spi:tʃ ˌbʌbl] Sprechblase **I U3**, 51
*to **spell** [spel] buchstabieren **I U4**, 74
Spell … [spel] Buchstabiere/Buchstabiert … °**I PUA**, 13
spelling ['spelɪŋ] Rechtschreibung **I U2**, 43
*to **spend** [spend] ausgeben *(Geld)* **I U5**, 91
sponge [spʌndʒ] Rühr-; Biskuit- **I U6**, 109
sport [spɔ:t] Sport; Sportart **I PUA**, 11
… is a great **sport**. [ɪz‿ə 'greɪt ˌspɔ:t] … ist ein toller Sport. **I PUA**, 11
spring [sprɪŋ] Frühling **I U6**, 105
squirrel ['skwɪrəl] Eichhörnchen **I PUA**, 10
stadium ['steɪdiəm] Stadion **I F3**, 122
*to **stand** [stænd] stehen **I AC1**, 67
*to **stand** up [ˌstænd‿'ʌp] aufstehen *(von einer Sitzgelegenheit)* **I U3**, 59
star [stɑ:] Star; Stern **I PUA**, 13
to **stare** [steə] starren; anstarren **I U2**, 39
to **start** [stɑ:t] anfangen; beginnen; starten **I U4**, 71
Start. [stɑ:t] Fang/Fangt (so) an. °**I PUA**, 10
state [steɪt] Staat; Bundesstaat; Land **I F3**, 122
station ['steɪʃn] Haltestelle; Bahnhof; Station **I AC1**, 67
bus **station** ['bʌs ˌsteɪʃn] Busbahnhof **I AC1**, 67
to **stay** [steɪ] bleiben **I U4**, 81
to **stay** up [ˌsteɪ‿'ʌp] aufbleiben **I U6**, 113
steak [steɪk] Steak **I AC2**, 100
step [step] Stufe; Schritt **I U1**, 23
stepmum ['stepmʌm] Stiefmutter **I U3**, 52
still [stɪl] still **I U6**, 109
still [stɪl] noch; immer noch **I U5**, 96
to **stop** [stɒp] aufhören (mit); anhalten; stoppen **I U3**, 55
Stop and think [ˌstɒp‿ənd 'θɪŋk] Warte/Wartet und denk/denkt nach. °**I U1**, 24
Stop it! ['stɒp‿ɪt] Mach/Macht das aus!; Hör/Hört auf! **I U2**, 45
storm [stɔ:m] Sturm **I U4**, 80
story, stories *(pl)* ['stɔ:ri] Story; Geschichte; Erzählung **I U2**, 47
photo **story** ['fəʊtəʊ ˌstɔ:ri] Fotostory; Bildgeschichte **I PUB**, 30
strange [streɪndʒ] fremd; seltsam; merkwürdig **I AC2**, 100
strawberry, strawberries *(pl)* ['strɔ:bri] Erdbeere **I AC2**, 101
street [stri:t] Straße *(in der Stadt)* **I U1**, 14
in the **street** [ˌɪn ðə 'stri:t] in der Straße; auf der Straße **I U1**, 14
student ['stju:dnt] Schüler/-in; Student/-in **I U2**, 34
recording **studio** [rɪ'kɔ:dɪŋ ˌstju:diəʊ] Aufnahmestudio; Tonstudio **I U2**, 33
stuff [stʌf] Zeug **I U5**, 91
suddenly ['sʌdnli] plötzlich; auf einmal **I U6**, 116
summer ['sʌmə] Sommer **I U6**, 105
Sunday ['sʌndeɪ] Sonntag **I U3**, 51
supermarket ['su:pəˌmɑ:kɪt] Supermarkt **I AC2**, 101
sure [ʃʊə; ʃɔ:] sicher **I U2**, 44
surfing ['sɜ:fɪŋ] Surfen **I F1**, 68
surgery ['sɜ:dʒri] Arztpraxis; Praxis; Praxisräume **I U3**, 55
surprise [sə'praɪz] Überraschung **I U3**, 51
survey ['sɜ:veɪ] Umfrage; Studie **I U4**, 79
to **swap** roles [ˌswɒp 'rəʊlz] Rollen tauschen **I U5**, 95
sweet [swi:t] süß **I AC2**, 101
sweets *(pl)* [swi:ts] Süßigkeiten; Bonbons **I U2**, 33
*to **swim** [swɪm] schwimmen **I U4**, 81
swimming ['swɪmɪŋ] Schwimmen **I PUB**, 31
*to go **swimming** [ˌgəʊ 'swɪmɪŋ] schwimmen gehen **I PUB**, 31
symbol ['sɪmbl] Symbol **I F3**, 123

T

table ['teɪbl] Tisch **I U1**, 15
tail [teɪl] Schwanz; Schweif **I U3**, 62
*to **take** [teɪk] nehmen; mitnehmen; wegnehmen; bringen; mitbringen **I U3**, 55
*to **take** a message [ˌteɪk‿ə 'mesɪdʒ] eine Nachricht entgegennehmen; jmdm. etw. ausrichten **I U5**, 93
*to **take** notes [ˌteɪk 'nəʊts] sich Notizen machen **I U4**, 71
*to **take** out [ˌteɪk‿'aʊt] herausnehmen °**I U2**, 37
*to **take** photos [ˌteɪk 'fəʊtəʊz] fotografieren; Fotos machen **I PUB**, 31
*to **take** place [ˌteɪk 'pleɪs] stattfinden **I U6**, 115
Take turns. [ˌteɪk 'tɜ:nz] Wechselt euch ab. **I U1**, 17
talent ['tælənt] Talent **I U2**, 36
talent show ['tælənt ˌʃəʊ] Talentwettbewerb **I U2**, 36
to **talk** [tɔ:k] sprechen; reden **I U3**, 55
Talk. [tɔ:k] Sprich./Sprecht.; Rede/Redet. °**I PUA**, 10
to **talk** about ['tɔ:k‿əbaʊt] sprechen über; erzählen von **I U1**, 27
Talk about … ['tɔ:k‿əbaʊt] Sprich/Sprecht über …; Erzähle/Erzählt von … °**I PUA**, 8
to **talk** to ['tɔ:k tə] reden mit **I U4**, 75
Talk to … ['tɔ:k tə] Rede mit/Redet mit … °**I PUA**, 9
talking ['tɔ:kɪŋ] Sprechen °**I U2**, 36
tall [tɔ:l] groß; hoch **I U1**, 17
task [tɑ:sk] Aufgabe; Auftrag °**I U1**, 23
tea [ti:] Tee **I U4**, 80
teacher ['ti:tʃə] Lehrer/-in **I U2**, 35
team [ti:m] Team; Gruppe **I F3**, 122
technology [tek'nɒlədʒi] Technologie **I F2**, 103
teenager ['ti:nˌeɪdʒə] Teenager; Jugendliche/-r **I U6**, 104
telephone ['telɪfəʊn] Telefon **I U5**, 90
*to **tell** [tel] erzählen; sagen; mitteilen **I U1**, 17
Tell me about … ['tel mi‿əˌbaʊt] Erzähle mir von … **I U1**, 17
ten [ten] zehn **I PUA**, 9
tennis ['tenɪs] Tennis **I U3**, 53
terrace ['terɪs] Terrasse **I U1**, 23
test [test] Test; Klassenarbeit; Prüfung **I U2**, 34
text [tekst] Text **I U1**, 16
text (message) ['tekst ˌmesɪdʒ] SMS; Kurznachricht **I PUB**, 30
more … **than** ['mɔ: ðən] mehr … als **I U5**, 97
Thank you. ['θæŋk ju] Danke. **I PUA**, 10
thankful ['θæŋkfl] dankbar **I U5**, 97
Thanks. [θæŋks] Danke. **I U1**, 18
that [ðæt; ðət] dass **I U6**, 106
that [ðæt] das; jenes **I PUA**, 10
after **that** [ˌɑ:ftə 'ðæt] danach **I U3**, 52
like **that** [laɪk 'ðæt] so **I U6**, 106
That was close! [ˌðæt wəz 'kləʊs] Das war knapp! **I PUA**, 10
That's … [ðæts] Das macht … **I U5**, 87
That's what friends are for. [ˌðæts wɒt 'frendz‿ɑ: ˌfɔ:] Dafür sind Freunde da. **I U5**, 91
the [ðə; ði] der; die *(auch Pl.)*; das **I PUA**, 11
the others [ði‿'ʌðəz] die anderen **I U3**, 60
the rest [rest] der Rest °**I U4**, 74
the same [ðə 'seɪm] der-/die-/dasselbe; der/die/das gleiche **I PUA**, 11
theatre ['θɪətə] Theater **I F1**, 69

their [ðeə] ihr/-e *(Pl.)* **I U1**, 19
them [ðem] sie *(Pl.)*; ihnen **I U2**, 39
theme [θi:m] Thema; Motto **I U6**, 106
then [ðen] dann; danach **I U3**, 51
there [ðeə] da; dort; dahin; dorthin **I U1**, 19
over **there** [ˌəʊvə 'ðeə] da drüben; dort drüben **I U2**, 42
there is/are [ðər‿'ɪz/'ɑ:] da ist/sind; es gibt **I U1**, 19
these [ði:z] diese (hier) **I U2**, 42
they [ðeɪ] sie *(Pl.)* **I PUA**, 10
It's .../**They**'re ... [ɪts/ðeə] Es kostet .../ Sie kosten ... **I U5**, 86
They're ... [ðeə] Sie sind ... **I PUA**, 10
thing [θɪŋ] Ding; Sache **I PUA**, 13
*to **think** [θɪŋk] denken; nachdenken **I U2**, 45; glauben **I U5**, 96
Think! [θɪŋk] Denke/Denkt nach! °**I U2**, 40
Stop and **think** [ˌstɒp‿ənd 'θɪŋk] Warte/ Wartet und denk/denkt nach. °**I U1**, 24
*to **think** of ['θɪŋk‿əv] halten von; denken über **I U5**, 91
Think of ... ['θɪŋk‿əv] Denke/Denkt an ... °**I U1**, 23
third [θɜ:d] dritte/-r/-s **I U6**, 105
thirteen [ˌθɜ:'ti:n] dreizehn **I U1**, 16
thirty ['θɜ:ti] dreißig **I U1**, 20
this [ðɪs] dies; diese/-r/-s **I PUA**, 11
This is ... ['ðɪs‿ɪz] Das (hier) ist ... **I PUA**, 11
this is how you (do) ... ['ðɪs‿ɪz haʊ jʊ ˌdu:] so machst du ... **I U3**, 51
those [ðəʊz] diese dort; jene **I U2**, 42
thousands of ['θaʊzndz‿əv] Tausende (von) **I AC3**, 121
three [θri:] drei **I PUA**, 12
through [θru:] durch **I U6**, 104
*to **throw** (at) [θrəʊ] werfen (nach) **I U3**, 63
*to **throw** away [ˌθrəʊ‿ə'weɪ] wegwerfen **I U5**, 89
Thursday ['θɜ:zdeɪ] Donnerstag **I U3**, 50
ticket ['tɪkɪt] Los; Ticket; Eintrittskarte **I U5**, 96
to **tidy** *(a room)* ['taɪdi] aufräumen; in Ordnung bringen **I U3**, 50
till [tɪl] bis **I U3**, 52
time [taɪm] Zeit **I U2**, 44
at the same **time** [ət ðə ˌseɪm 'taɪm] zur selben Zeit; gleichzeitig **I U6**, 104
free **time** [ˌfri: 'taɪm] Freizeit **I U4**, 71
time line ['taɪm ˌlaɪn] Zeitstrahl °**I AC3**, 121
Time to get up! [ˌtaɪm tə ˌget‿'ʌp] Es ist Zeit aufzustehen! **I U3**, 51
What **time**? [ˌwɒt 'taɪm] Um wie viel Uhr? **I U4**, 72
What's the **time**? [ˌwɒts ðə 'taɪm] Wie spät ist es?; Wie viel Uhr ist es? **I U3**, 50
timetable ['taɪmˌteɪbl] Stundenplan; Fahrplan **I AC1**, 67
tinned [tɪnd] Dosen-; aus der Dose **I U6**, 109
tip [tɪp] Tipp; Ratschlag **I U2**, 43
tired [taɪəd] müde **I U3**, 52
to [tʊ; tə] zu; nach; auf; in **I U1**, 18; vor *(bei Uhrzeitangaben)* **I U3**, 50
from ... **to** [frəm ... tə] von ... bis **I U1**, 20
quarter past/**to** ['kwɔ:tə pɑ:st/tə] Viertel nach/vor **I U3**, 50
toast [təʊst] Toast **I AC2**, 101
today [tə'deɪ] heute **I U2**, 34
toe [təʊ] Zeh **I U3**, 63
together [tə'geðə] zusammen; miteinander; gemeinsam **I U4**, 72
toilet ['tɔɪlət] Toilette **I U1**, 15
tomato, tomatoes *(pl)* [tə'mɑ:təʊ] Tomate **I U5**, 99
tomorrow [tə'mɒrəʊ] morgen **I U3**, 54
2nite (= **tonight**) [tə'naɪt] heute Abend **I PUB**, 28
too [tu:] auch **I PUA**, 9; zu **I U3**, 59
Me **too**. [ˌmi: 'tu:] Ich auch. **I PUB**, 31
Too bad! [ˌtu: 'bæd] Zu dumm!; Schade! **I U5**, 90
You **too**? [ju: 'tu:] Du auch? **I PUA**, 9
top [tɒp] Spitze; oberer Teil; oberes Ende **I F1**, 69
on **top** [ɒn 'tɒp] oben; obendrauf **I U6**, 109
tourist ['tʊərɪst] Tourist/-in **I U4**, 78
tourist information centre [ˌtʊərɪst‿ ɪnfə'meɪʃn ˌsentə] Touristeninformation **I U4**, 78
town [taʊn] Stadt **I F1**, 69
toy [tɔɪ] Spielzeug **I U5**, 88
cuddly **toy** ['kʌdli ˌtɔɪ] Stofftier **I U1**, 19
tradition [trə'dɪʃn] Tradition **I AC3**, 120
train [treɪn] Zug **I AC1**, 67
to **translate** [trænz'leɪt] übersetzen **I U4**, 76
Don't **translate** ... [ˌdəʊnt trænz'leɪt] Übersetze/Übersetzt nicht ... °**I U2**, 38
translation [trænz'leɪʃn] Übersetzung **I U5**, 92
tree [tri:] Baum **I U1**, 16
family **tree** ['fæmli ˌtri:] Stammbaum **I U1**, 16
pony **trekking** ['pəʊni ˌtrekɪŋ] Wanderreiten; Ponyreiten im Gelände **I F1**, 69
trick [trɪk] Trick; Streich **I U2**, 44
to play a **trick** (on) [ˌpleɪ‿ə 'trɪk‿ɒn] einen Streich spielen **I U2**, 44
trifle ['traɪfl] Trifle *(englischer Nachtisch)* **I U6**, 106
trip [trɪp] Trip; Reise; Ausflug; Fahrt **I F3**, 123
to **trip** (over) [ˌtrɪp‿'əʊvə] stolpern (über) **I U6**, 110
*to make **trouble** [ˌmeɪk 'trʌbl] Ärger machen; in Schwierigkeiten bringen **I U2**, 45
to **try** [traɪ] versuchen; probieren **I PUB**, 28
Try ... [traɪ] Versuch es mal mit ...; Probier mal ... **I PUB**, 28
T-shirt ['ti:ʃɜ:t] T-Shirt **I U3**, 59
Tuesday ['tju:zdeɪ] Dienstag **I U3**, 50
tunnel ['tʌnl] Tunnel **I U4**, 71
It's your **turn**. [ˌɪts 'jɔ: tɜ:n] Du bist dran. **I U2**, 44
Take **turns**. [ˌteɪk 'tɜ:nz] Wechselt euch ab. **I U1**, 17
Your **turn**. ['jɔ: tɜ:n] Du bist dran. **I PUA**, 9
tutor ['tju:tə] Klassenlehrer/-in **I U2**, 32
tutor group ['tju:tə ˌgru:p] Klasse *(in einer englischen Schule)* **I U2**, 34
TV *(= television)* [ˌti:'vi: ('telɪvɪʒn)] Fernsehen; Fernseher **I U1**, 15
to watch **TV** [ˌwɒtʃ ti:'vi:] fernsehen **I PUB**, 31
twelve [twelv] zwölf **I PUA**, 12
twenty ['twenti] zwanzig **I U1**, 20
twenty-one [ˌtwenti'wʌn] einundzwanzig **I U1**, 20
two [tu:] zwei **I PUA**, 8
typical ['tɪpɪkl] typisch **I U3**, 60

U

u *(= you)* [ju:; jə] du; Sie; ihr **I PUB**, 28
uncle ['ʌŋkl] Onkel **I U1**, 16
under ['ʌndə] unter **I U1**, 14
*to **understand** [ˌʌndə'stænd] verstehen **I U5**, 93
uniform ['ju:nɪfɔ:m] Uniform **I U2**, 33
unit ['ju:nɪt] Lektion; Kapitel; Einheit °**I U1**, 14
*to be **unlucky** [bi‿ʌn'lʌki] Pech haben **I U6**, 116
*to get **up** [ˌget‿'ʌp] aufstehen *(aus dem Bett)* **I U3**, 51
up to ['ʌp tə] bis zu **I F3**, 122
us [ʌs] uns **I U4**, 74
to **use** [ju:z] benutzen; verwenden; gebrauchen **I U2**, 36
Use ... [ju:z] Benutze/Benutzt ...; Verwende/Verwendet ... °**I U1**, 18
useful ['ju:sfl] nützlich; hilfreich **I U4**, 81
Useful phrases [ˌju:sfl 'freɪsɪz] nützliche Ausdrücke °**I U1**, 18
usually ['ju:ʒli] normalerweise; gewöhnlich; meistens **I U3**, 52

V

vacation *(AE)* [və'keɪʃn] Ferien; Urlaub **I U6**, 112
verb [vɜ:b] Verb °**I PUB**, 31
very ['veri] sehr **I U1**, 18
very much [ˌveri 'mʌtʃ] sehr **I U3**, 59
vet [vet] Tierarzt/Tierärztin **I U3**, 55
video chat ['vɪdiəʊ ˌtʃæt] Videochat **I F2**, 102
viewing ['vju:ɪŋ] Hör-/Sehverstehen °**I U2**, 32
village ['vɪlɪdʒ] Dorf **I F1**, 69
visit ['vɪzɪt] Besuch **I U1**, 24
to **visit** ['vɪzɪt] besichtigen; besuchen **I AC1**, 66
visitor ['vɪzɪtə] Besucher/-in **I U4**, 80
vocabulary [və'kæbjələri] Vokabular; Wortschatz **I PUA**, 12
voice [vɔɪs] Stimme **I U2**, 44
volleyball ['vɒlibɔ:l] Volleyball **I PUA**, 11

W

to **wait** (for) [weɪt] warten (auf) **I U2**, 34
Wait and see! [ˌweɪt‿ənd ˈsiː] Warte ab! **I U2**, 34
to **walk** [wɔːk] gehen; laufen **I AC1**, 67
to **walk** the dog [ˌwɔːk ðə ˈdɒg] den Hund ausführen; mit dem Hund spazieren gehen **I U5**, 90
wall [wɔːl] Wand; Mauer **I U1**, 20
to **want** (to) [ˈwɒnt tə] wollen; mögen **I PUB**, 28
to **want** somebody to do something [ˌwɒnt sʌmbədi tə ˈduː sʌmθɪŋ] wollen, dass jemand etwas tut **I U6**, 112
wardrobe [ˈwɔːdrəʊb] Kleiderschrank **I U1**, 15
to **warm** up [ˌwɔːm‿ˈʌp] aufwärmen; sich aufwärmen **I U3**, 59
warm-up [ˈwɔːm‿ˌʌp] Aufwärmübung °**I AC1**, 66
to **wash** [wɒʃ] waschen; sich waschen **I U3**, 62
to **watch** [wɒtʃ] beobachten; (sich) ansehen; zuschauen **I PUB**, 31
to **watch** TV [ˌwɒtʃ tiːˈviː] fernsehen **I PUB**, 31
water [ˈwɔːtə] Wasser **I U4**, 71
water slide [ˈwɔːtə ˌslaɪd] Wasserrutsche **I U4**, 71
waterfall [ˈwɔːtəˌfɔːl] Wasserfall **I F3**, 122
wave [weɪv] Welle **I U4**, 80
way [weɪ] Weg; Art und Weise **I AC1**, 67
*to be in the **way** [biˌɪn ðə ˈweɪ] im Weg sein/stehen **I AC1**, 67
we [wiː; wi] wir **I PUA**, 9
We're from ... [ˈwɪə frəm] Wir sind aus ... **I PUA**, 9
*to **wear** [weə] anhaben; tragen *(Kleidung)* **I U2**, 40
weather [ˈweðə] Wetter **I U4**, 74
website [ˈwebsaɪt] Website; Internetauftritt **I U4**, 74
wedding [ˈwedɪŋ] Hochzeit **I AC3**, 120
Wednesday [ˈwenzdeɪ] Mittwoch **I U3**, 50
week [wiːk] Woche **I U2**, 44
weekend [ˌwiːkˈend] Wochenende **I U4**, 72
at the **weekend** [ət ðə ˌwiːkˈend] am Wochenende **I U4**, 72
Welcome! [ˈwelkəm] Willkommen! **I U4**, 76
You're **welcome**. [jɔː ˈwelkəm] Bitte schön.; Nichts zu danken.; Gern geschehen. **I AC1**, 66
well [wel] tja; nun **I U2**, 34
west [west] Westen; West- **I F1**, 68
what [wɒt] was **I PUA**, 9; welche/-r/-s; was für ein **I PUA**, 13
What about ... ? [ˈwɒt‿əbaʊt] Was ist mit ...?; Wie wär's mit ...? **I U3**, 53
What are ...? [ˈwɒt‿ɑː] Welche ... sind es? °**I PUA**, 12
What can you see ...? [ˌwɒt kən ju ˈsiː] Was kannst du/könnt ihr ... sehen? °**I PUA**, 13
What colour is ...? [ˌwɒt ˈkʌlər‿ɪz] Welche Farbe hat ...? **I PUA**, 13
what else [ˌwɒt‿ˈels] was sonst; was noch **I F2**, 103
What is ... about? [ˌwɒt‿ɪz‿əˈbaʊt] Worum geht es in/im ...? **I U3**, 58
What time? [ˌwɒt ˈtaɪm] Um wie viel Uhr? **I U4**, 72
what to ... [ˈwɒt tə] was man ... **I AC1**, 66
What's that? [wɒts ˈðæt] Was ist das? **I PUA**, 11
What's the rule for ...? [ˌwɒts ðə ˈruːl fə] Was ist die Regel für ...? °**I U1**, 18
What's your favourite ...? [ˈwɒts jə ˌfeɪvrɪt] Was ist dein/-e Lieblings...? **I PUA**, 12
What's your name? [ˌwɒts jə ˈneɪm] Wie heißt du?; Wie heißen Sie? **I PUA**, 9
What's the time? [ˌwɒts ðə ˈtaɪm] Wie spät ist es?; Wie viel Uhr ist es? **I U3**, 50
wheat [wiːt] Weizen **I F3**, 122
wheel [wiːl] Rad; Steuerrad; Steuer **I U4**, 80
when [wen] wenn; wann; als **I U2**, 41
where [weə] wo; wohin **I PUA**, 9
Where ... from? [ˌweə ... ˈfrɒm] Woher ...? **I PUA**, 9
which [wɪtʃ] welche/-r/-s **I U2**, 40
while [waɪl] während **I AC3**, 120
to **whip** [wɪp] *(Sahne)* schlagen **I U6**, 109
to **whisper** [ˈwɪspə] flüstern **I U6**, 116
white [waɪt] weiß **I PUA**, 12
who [huː] wer; wem; wen **I U1**, 24
Who ... for? [ˌhuː ˈfɔː] Für wen ...? **I U1**, 24
Who is it? [ˌhuː‿ˈɪz‿ɪt] Wer ist es? °**I PUA**, 8
whole [həʊl] ganz **I AC3**, 121
whoosh [wʊʃ] wusch **I U4**, 81
whose [huːz] wessen **I U2**, 37
why [waɪ] warum **I U3**, 55
*to **win** [wɪn] gewinnen; siegen **I U6**, 109
window [ˈwɪndəʊ] Fenster **I AC1**, 67
wine [waɪn] Wein **I U5**, 96
winter [ˈwɪntə] Winter **I U6**, 105
wish [wɪʃ] Wunsch **I U6**, 105
*to make a **wish** [ˌmeɪk‿ə ˈwɪʃ] sich etwas wünschen **I U6**, 105
with [wɪð] mit; bei **I PUA**, 9
without [wɪˈðaʊt] ohne **I U6**, 108
woman [ˈwʊmən], **women** *(pl)* [ˈwɪmɪn] Frau **I AC1**, 67
wood [wʊd] Holz **I F3**, 122
Woof! [wʊf] Wau! °**I PUA**, 8
word [wɜːd] Wort **I PUA**, 10
key **word** [ˈkiː ˌwɜːd] Stichwort; Schlüsselbegriff **I U6**, 117
linking **word** [ˈlɪŋkɪŋ ˌwɜːd] Verbindungswort °**I U6**, 117
signal **word** [ˈsɪgnl ˌwɜːd] Signalwort °**I U5**, 89
word order [ˈwɜːd‿ˌɔːdə] Wortstellung; Satzstellung °**I U3**, 53
Word power [ˈwɜːd ˌpaʊə] die Kraft der Wörter *(Wortschatzübung)* °**I U1**, 16
word snake [ˈwɜːd ˌsneɪk] Wortschlange °**I U2**, 43
work [wɜːk] Arbeit **I U3**, 55
to **work** [wɜːk] arbeiten **I U2**, 44
Work ... [wɜːk] Arbeite/Arbeitet ... °**I U2**, 34
workshop [ˈwɜːkʃɒp] Workshop **I U3**, 53
world [wɜːld] Erde; Welt **I F2**, 102
worm [wɜːm] Wurm **I PUA**, 10
Don't **worry!** [ˌdəʊnt ˈwʌri] Keine Sorge! **I U1**, 24
*to be **worth** [bi ˈwɜːθ] wert sein **I U5**, 91
would like [wʊd ˈlaɪk] würde/-st/-n/-t gern; hätte/-st/-n/-t gern **I F3**, 122
would love [wʊd ˈlʌv] würde/-st/-n/-t sehr gern; hätte/-st-/-n/-t sehr gern **I U6**, 115
Wow! [waʊ] Wow! **I U2**, 33
*to **write** [raɪt] schreiben **I U3**, 52
Write ... [raɪt] Schreibe/Schreibt ... °**I PUA**, 10
*to **write** down [ˌraɪt ˈdaʊn] aufschreiben **I U2**, 43
Write down ... [ˌraɪt ˈdaʊn] Schreibe/Schreibt ... auf. °**I U1**, 17
writing [ˈraɪtɪŋ] Schreiben °**I PUA**, 9
wrong [rɒŋ] falsch **I U1**, 18
*to be **wrong** [bi ˈrɒŋ] unrecht haben; sich irren **I U4**, 81
*to go **wrong** [ˌgəʊ ˈrɒŋ] schiefgehen **I U6**, 110

X

XOXO [ˌhʌgz‿ən ˈkɪsɪz] Umarmungen und Küsse *(am Ende von E-Mails und SMS)* **I U3**, 52

Y

yard *(AE)* [jɑːd] Garten **I U6**, 112
yeah *(infml)* [jeə] ja **I U2**, 45
year [jɪə] Jahr; Schuljahr **I U5**, 88
yellow [ˈjeləʊ] gelb **I PUA**, 12
yes [jes] ja **I PUA**, 9
yesterday [ˈjestədeɪ] gestern **I U6**, 111
yoghurt [ˈjɒgət] Joghurt **I U5**, 99
you [juː; jə] du; ihr; Sie **I PUA**, 9
Are **you** ...? [ˈɑː ju] Sind Sie ...?; Seid ihr ... ?; Bist du ... ? **I PUA**, 9
You know how to ... [juː ˈnəʊ ˌhaʊ tə] Du weißt, wie man ...; Ihr wisst, wie man ... °**I U1**, 23
You too? [juː ˈtuː] Du auch? **I PUA**, 9
You're ... [jɔːr] Sie sind ...; Du bist ... **I PUA**, 9
You're into ... [ˈjɔːr‿ˌɪntə] Du magst ...; Du stehst auf ... **I PUB**, 28
You're welcome. [ˌjɔː ˈwelkəm] Bitte schön.; Nichts zu danken.; Gern geschehen. **I AC1**, 66

young [jʌŋ] jung | **AC2**, 101
your [jɔ:; jə] dein/-e; euer/eure; Ihr/-e | **PUA**, 8
What's **your** name? [ˌwɒts jə 'neɪm] Wie heißt du?; Wie heißen Sie? | **PUA**, 9
Your turn. ['jɔ: tɜ:n] Du bist dran. | **PUA**, 9
yourself [jɔ:'self] dich (selbst) °| **PUA**, 8; du/dir/dich/Sie/sich (selbst); selber | **U3**, 57
yummy ['jʌmi] lecker | **U6**, 110

Z

zero ['zɪərəʊ] null | **PUA**, 12
zoo [zu:] Zoo; Tierpark | **F3**, 123

Boys' names

Ben [ben] | **U4**, 80
Bob [bɒb] | **U4**, 76
Damian ['deɪmiən] | **U1**, 16
Dave [deɪv] | **PUA**, 9
Desmond ['dezmənd] | **U4**, 74
Filip ['fɪlɪp] | **U1**, 16
Henry ['henri] | **U1**, 16
Jack [dʒæk] | **U1**, 16
Jahangir [dʒə'hʌŋgɪə] | **U2**, 34
Jamie ['dʒeɪmi] | **U1**, 16
Jay [dʒeɪ] | **U2**, 34
Luke [lu:k] | **PUA**, 9
Ryan [raɪən] | **U6**, 112
Shahid [ʃɑ:'hi:d] | **U2**, 36
Steve [sti:v] | **U1**, 17
Tony ['təʊni] | **PUA**, 8
Tyler ['taɪlə] | **U3**, 54

Girls' names

Alicia [ə'lɪsiə; ə'lɪʃə] | **U5**, 93
Amber ['æmbə] | **U1**, 17
Anna ['ænə] | **U1**, 16
Anne [æn] | **PUA**, 11
Beata [bi'ɑ:tə] | **U1**, 16
Carol ['kærəl] | **U1**, 16
Claire ['kleə] | **U3**, 52
Emily ['emɪli] | **U6**, 110
Frances ['frɑ:nsɪs] | **PUB**, 28
Holly ['hɒli] | **U1**, 14
Irina [ɪ'ri:nə] | **U1**, 16
Julie ['dʒu:li] | **U2**, 38
Laura ['lɔ:rə] | **AC1**, 67
Lily ['lɪli] | **U2**, 42
Lou [lu:] | **PUA**, 9
Lucy ['lu:si] | **U3**, 52
Mila ['mi:lə] | **U1**, 16
Olivia [ɒl'ɪviə] | **PUA**, 10
Pia ['pi:ə] | **PUA**, 9
Rose [rəʊz] | **U3**, 55
Sally ['sæli] | **U1**, 17
Seeta ['si:tə] | **U5**, 99

Surnames

Azad [ə'zɑ:d] | **U2**, 34
Briggs [brɪgz] | **U4**, 80
Elliot ['eliət] | **U1**, 16
Fraser ['freɪzə] | **U1**, 21
Green [gri:n] | **U4**, 76
Preston ['prestən] | **U3**, 55
Richardson ['rɪtʃədsn] | **U1**, 18
Swindon ['swɪndən] (leer) | **U2**, 32
Walker ['wɔ:kə] | **U5**, 93
Zajac ['zeɪdʒæk] | **U1**, 16

Place names

the **Bronx** [ðə 'brɒŋks] | **F3**, 123
Brook Lane [ˌbrʊk 'leɪn] | **U1**, 14
Brooklyn ['brʊklɪn] | **F3**, 123
Cologne [kə'ləʊn] Köln | **PUA**, 9
Cracow ['krækɒv; 'krɑ:kaʊ] Krakau | **U1**, 16
Enfield [en'fi:ld] | **U2**, 34
Everglades National Park [ˌevəgleɪdz ˌnæʃnl 'pɑ:k] | **F3**, 122
Greenwich Park [ˌgrenɪdʒ 'pɑ:k] | **PUA**, 8
Greenwich Pier [ˌgrenɪdʒ 'pɪə] | **U4**, 71
Hollywood ['hɒliwʊd] | **F2**, 103
Kidbrooke Gardens [ˌkɪdbrʊk 'gɑ:dnz] | **U3**, 56
London ['lʌndən] | **PUA**, 9
Manhattan [mæn'hætn] | **F3**, 123
Queens [kwi:nz] | **F3**, 123
South Street ['saʊθ ˌstri:t] | **U5**, 88
Staten Island [ˌstætn‿'aɪlənd] | **F3**, 123
Victoria Park [ˌvɪktɔ:riə 'pɑ:k] | **U4**, 73
Village Way ['vɪlɪdʒ ˌweɪ] | **U3**, 59
Washington ['wɒʃɪŋtən] | **U6**, 113
Wimbledon ['wɪmbldn] | **AC3**, 121

Geographical names

Alaska [ə'læskə] | **F3**, 122
America [ə'merɪkə] Amerika | **F2**, 103
Australia [ɒs'treɪliə] Australien | **F2**, 103
Bavaria [bə'veəriə] Bayern | **F1**, 69
Britain ['brɪtn] Großbritannien | **U2**, 38
Canada ['kænədə] Kanada | **F2**, 103
China ['tʃaɪnə] China | **U4**, 80
England ['ɪŋglənd] England | **U1**, 27
Florida ['flɒrɪdə] | **F3**, 122
Germany ['dʒɜ:məni] Deutschland | **PUA**, 9
Hawaii [hə'waɪi:] | **F3**, 122
India ['ɪndiə] Indien | **F2**, 102
Isle of Dogs [ˌaɪl‿əv 'dɒgz] | **U4**, 76
Northern Ireland [ˌnɔ:ðn‿'aələnd] Nordirland | **F1**, 68
Pakistan [ˌpɑ:kɪ'stɑ:n] | **U2**, 36
Poland ['pəʊlənd] Polen | **U1**, 16
Scotland ['skɒtlənd] Schottland | **F1**, 68
South Africa [ˌsaʊθ‿'æfrɪkə] Südafrika | **F2**, 103
Texas ['teksəs] | **F3**, 122
the **Thames** [ðə 'temz] die Themse | **F1**, 69
the **United Kingdom** (UK) [ði ju:ˌnaɪtɪd 'kɪŋdəm] das Vereinigte Königreich von Großbritannien und Nordirland | **F1**, 68
the **US** *(United States)* [ði ˌju:'es(ju:ˌnaɪtɪd 'steɪts)] die USA *(die Vereinigten Staaten)* | **F2**, 103
the **USA** *(United States of America)* [ði ˌju:es'eɪ (ju:ˌnaɪtɪd ˌsteɪts‿əv‿ə'merɪkə)] die USA *(die Vereinigten Staaten von Amerika)* | **F2**, 103
Wales [weɪlz] | **F1**, 68

Other names

Arches Leisure Centre [ˌɑ:tʃɪz 'leʒə ˌsentə] | **U4**, 71
Big Ben [ˌbɪg 'ben] | **F1**, 69
Buckingham Palace [ˌbʌkɪŋəm 'pælɪs] | **F1**, 69
the **Capitol** [ðə 'kæpɪtl] | **F3**, 123
Christmas ['krɪsməs] Weihnachten | **U6**, 113
2Cool Performing Academy [ˌtu:ku:l pəˌfɔ:mɪŋ ə'kædəmi] | **U3**, 54
Cutty Sark [ˌkʌti 'sɑ:k] | **U4**, 70
Diwali [dɪ'wɑ:li] *hinduistisches Lichterfest* | **AC3**, 121
Docklands Light Railway *(DLR)* [ˌdɒklændz ˌlaɪt 'reɪlweɪ] *Regionalbahn im Osten Londons* | **U4**, 74
Easter ['i:stə] Ostern | **U6**, 113
Eid [i:d] Opferfest *(islamisches Fest)* | **AC3**, 121; Fastenbrechen nach dem Fastenmonat Ramadan *(islamisches Fest)* | **AC3**, 121
For he's a jolly good fellow [fə ˌhi:z‿ə ˌdʒɒli gʊd 'feləʊ] *Volkslied* | **U6**, 117
Giant's Causeway [ˌdʒaɪənts 'kɔ:zweɪ] | **F1**, 68
Greenwich Foot Tunnel [ˌgrenɪdʒ 'fʊt ˌtʌnl] | **U4**, 71
Guy Fawkes Night ['gaɪ fɔ:ks ˌnaɪt] *Tag zum Gedenken an die Pulververschwörung gegen den englischen König und sein Parlament am 5.11.1605* | **AC3**, 121
Halloween [ˌhæləʊ'i:n] Halloween *Tag vor Allerheiligen* | **AC3**, 121
Hanukkah ['hʌnʊkə] Chanukka *(jüdisches Lichterfest)* | **AC3**, 121
Honey ['hʌni] | **U1**, 17
Independence Day [ˌɪndɪ'pendəns ˌdeɪ] Unabhängigkeitstag *(USA)* | **U6**, 112
London Eye [ˌlʌndən‿'aɪ] | **F1**, 69
Madame Tussauds [ˌmædəm tʊ'sɔ:dz] | **F1**, 69
Meridian Line [məˌrɪdiən 'laɪn] Nullmeridian | **U4**, 71
Mickey Mouse [ˌmɪki 'maʊs] | **PUA**, 13
Mother's Day ['mʌðəz ˌdeɪ] Muttertag | **AC3**, 121
Mr Fluff [ˌmɪstə 'flʌf] | **U1**, 17
Mudchute Farm [ˌmʌdʃu:t 'fɑ:m] | **U4**, 71
New Year's Eve [ˌnju: ˌjɪəz‿'ɪ:v] Silvester | **U6**, 113

Notting Hill Carnival [ˌnɒtɪŋ hɪl ˈkɑːnɪvl] *Karibischer Karneval in einem Stadtteil Londons* I **AC3**, 121
Pancake Day [ˈpænkeɪk ˌdeɪ] Faschingsdienstag I **AC3**, 121
Pentecost [ˈpentɪkɒst] Pfingsten I **AC3**, 121
Pets Corner [ˌpets ˈkɔːnə] I **U4**, 74
Royal Observatory [ˌrɔɪəl‿əbˈzɜːvətri] I **U4**, 71
Sherlock [ˈʃɜːlɒk] I **PUA**, 8
Shrove Tuesday [ˌʃrəʊv ˈtjuːzdeɪ] Faschingsdienstag I **AC3**, 121
Sid [sɪd] I **U3**, 55
star4ever [ˌstɑːfəˈrevə] I **U3**, 53
the Statue of Liberty [ˌstætʃuː‿əv ˈlɪbəti] die Freiheitsstatue I **U6**, 112
Sunny [ˈsʌni] I **U6**, 112
Tandoori [tænˈdʊəri] I **U2**, 36
Thomas Tallis School *(= TTS)* [ˌtɒməs ˈtælɪs ˌskuːl] I **U2**, 32
Valentine's Day [ˈvæləntaɪnz ˌdeɪ] Valentinstag I **AC3**, 121
Whitsun [ˈwɪtsn] Pfingsten I **AC3**, 121

Famous names

George Washington [ˌdʒɔːdʒ ˈwɒʃɪŋtən] I **F3**, 123;

German-English dictionary

A

Abend evening I **U3**, 52
heute **Abend** 2nite (= tonight) I **PUB**, 28
Abendessen dinner I **U3**, 51
abends in the evenings I **U3**, 52
abends *(Uhrzeit)* p.m. I **U3**, 50
aber but I **PUA**, 8
abschreiben to copy I **U6**, 111
acht eight I **PUA**, 12
achtzehn eighteen I **U1**, 20
achtzig eighty I **U1**, 20
Acker field I **F3**, 122
Adresse address I **U1**, 21
AG club I **U3**, 51
äh er I **U2**, 34
ahoi ahoy I **U4**, 80
Aktivität activity I **U4**, 71
albern silly I **PUB**, 31
alle everyone I **U2**, 34
alle/-s all I **U4**, 74
allein alone I **U2**, 40
allein on your own I **U6**, 108
alles everything I **U5**, 91
Alligator alligator I **F3**, 122
Alphabet alphabet I **PUA**, 13
als when I **U2**, 41
als ob like I **PUA**, 13
also so I **PUB**, 29
alt old I **PUA**, 9
Wie **alt** bist du? How old are you? I **PUA**, 9
Wie **alt** sind Sie? How old are you? I **PUA**, 9
am on I **PUA**, 9
am besten best I **U6**, 119
am liebsten best I **U6**, 119
am Wochenende at the weekend I **U4**, 72
aus Amerika American I **F2**, 103
Amerikaner/-in American I **F2**, 103
amerikanisch American I **F2**, 103
Amtssprache official language I **F2**, 103
sich amüsieren *to have fun I **U3**, 62
an on I **PUA**, 9; at I **U1**, 14
an Bord aboard I **U4**, 80
an Stelle von instead of I **U6**, 113
anbauen *to grow I **F3**, 122
Anblick sight I **F1**, 69
die anderen the others I **U3**, 60
andere/-r/-s other I **U3**, 52
ein/-e **andere**/-r/-s another I **AC3**, 121
anders different I **PUA**, 9; other I **U3**, 52
anfangen to start I **U4**, 71
Angeln fishing I **F1**, 69
Angst haben (vor) *to be scared (of) I **U3**, 62
Ich habe (keine) **Angst** vor … I'm (not) scared of … I **PUA**, 10
anhaben *to wear I **U2**, 40
anhalten to stop I **U3**, 55
anhören to listen (to) I **U1**, 19
anmalen to paint I **PUB**, 31
Anruf phone call I **U5**, 93
einen **Anruf** entgegennehmen to answer the phone I **U5**, 93
Anrufbeantworter answering machine I **U5**, 93
anrufen to call I **U5**, 93
Anrufer/-in caller I **U5**, 93
anschauen to look at I **U2**, 41
ansehen to look at I **U2**, 41
(sich) ansehen to watch I **PUB**, 31
anstarren to stare I **U2**, 39
anstatt instead of I **U6**, 113
Antwort answer I **U1**, 20; reply I **U6**, 115
antworten to answer I **U4**, 74
antworten (auf) to reply (to) I **U6**, 115
Apfel apple I **AC2**, 101
Apparat machine I **U2**, 33
April April I **U6**, 105
Arbeit job I **U2**, 36; work I **U3**, 55
arbeiten to work I **U2**, 44
Areal area I **F3**, 122
Ärger machen *to make trouble I **U2**, 45
Arm arm I **U6**, 114
Art kind I **F2**, 102
Art und Weise way I **AC1**, 67
Arztpraxis surgery I **U3**, 55
auch too I **PUA**, 9; also I **F3**, 122
auch nicht not either I **U4**, 73
Du **auch**? You too? I **PUA**, 9
Ich **auch**. Me too. I **PUB**, 31
auf on I **PUA**, 9; at I **U1**, 14; to I **U1**, 18
auf dem Foto/den Fotos in the photo(s) I **U2**, 37
auf der anderen Seite von across I **U4**, 71
auf der linken Seite on the left I **U1**, 19
auf der rechten Seite on the right I **U1**, 19
auf der Straße in the street I **U1**, 14
auf einmal suddenly I **U6**, 116
auf Wiedersehen goodbye I **U3**, 62
aufbauen *to set up I **U5**, 94
aufbleiben to stay up I **U6**, 113
Aufgabe job I **U2**, 36; exercise I **U2**, 43
aufgeregt excited I **U5**, 97
aufgeschlagen open I **AC1**, 67
aufhören (mit) to stop I **U3**, 55
aufmachen to open I **AC1**, 67
Aufnahme recording I **U2**, 44
Aufnahmestudio recording studio I **U2**, 33
aufpassen auf to look after I **U3**, 55
Pass/Passt **auf**! Be careful! I **U3**, 56
aufräumen to tidy *(a room)* I **U3**, 50
aufregend exciting I **U4**, 72
aufsagen *to say I **PUA**, 13
aufschreiben *to write down I **U2**, 43
aufstehen *(aus dem Bett)* *to get up I **U3**, 51
Es ist Zeit **aufzustehen**! Time to get up! I **U3**, 51
aufstehen *(von einer Sitzgelegenheit)* *to stand up I **U3**, 59

denken über *to think of I U5, 91
Denkmal monument I F3, 123
der the I PUA, 11
der-/die-/dasselbe the same I PUA, 11
deutlich clear I U3, 59
Deutsch German I PUA, 8
deutsch German I PUA, 8
Deutsche/-r German I PUA, 8
aus Deutschland German I PUA, 8
Dezember December I U6, 105
Dialog dialogue I U3, 58
die *(auch Pl.)* the I PUA, 11
die anderen the others I U3, 60
Diele hall I U1, 23
Dienstag Tuesday I U3, 50
dies this I PUA, 11
diese/-r/-s this I PUA, 11
diese (hier) these I U2, 42
diese dort those I U2, 42
Ding thing I PUA, 13
doch after all I U6, 117
Dollarnote dollar bill I F3, 123
Dollarschein dollar bill I F3, 123
Donnerstag Thursday I U3, 50
doof silly I PUB, 31
Dorf village I F1, 69
dort there I U1, 19
dort drüben over there I U2, 42
dorthin there I U1, 19
Dose can I U5, 87
aus der Dose tinned I U6, 109
Dosen- tinned I U6, 109
Du bist dran. It's your turn. I U2, 44
draußen outside I U1, 24
nach draußen outside I U1, 24; out I U6, 109
drei three I PUA, 12
dreißig thirty I U1, 20
dreizehn thirteen I U1, 16
drin inside I U6, 117
dritte/-r/-s third I U6, 105
da drüben over there I U2, 42
dort drüben over there I U2, 42
die Daumen drücken *to keep your fingers crossed I U4, 74
du you I PUA, 9
Bist du ... ? Are you ...? I PUA, 9
Du auch? You too? I PUA, 9
Du bist ... You're ... I PUA, 9
Du bist dran. It's your turn. I U2, 44
du/dir/dich/Sie/sich (selbst) yourself I U3, 57
dumm silly I PUB, 31
Zu dumm! Too bad! I U5, 90
durch through I U6, 104
dürfen can I PUA, 13
nicht dürfen mustn't I U6, 106
Dusche shower I U1, 15
DVD DVD I PUB, 31

E

Ei egg I AC2, 100
Eichhörnchen squirrel I PUA, 10
eifersüchtig sein (auf) *to be jealous (of) I U2, 44
eigene/-r/-s own I U1, 19
eilen to hurry I U6, 116
ein/-e a I PUA, 8; an I U1, 16
ein paar a few I U2, 44; a couple of I U5, 91
ein paar Minuten später a few minutes later I U2, 44
ein wenig a little I U5, 91
ein/-e andere/-r/-s another I AC3, 121
noch ein/-e another I AC3, 121
einfach easy I U1, 16
einfach just I U2, 44
Einfall idea I U1, 19
eingießen to pour I U6, 109
die Segel einholen to reef the sails I U4, 80
einhundert one hundred I U1, 20
einige some I U1, 18; a few I U2, 44
Einkaufen shopping I F1, 69
einkaufen gehen *to go shopping I U5, 86
einladen to invite I U6, 106
Einladung invitation I U6, 108
einrichten *to set up I U5, 94
eins one I PUA, 9
einsam lonely I U6, 116
einschenken to pour I U6, 109
einschlafen *to fall asleep I U3, 63
einsteigen *to get into I U6, 117
Eintrittskarte ticket I U5, 96
einundzwanzig twenty-one I U1, 20
Einzelkind only child I U1, 16
Eis ice I U6, 105; ice cream I U6, 106
Eisbahn ice rink I U6, 105
Eisbär polar bear I F3, 122
Eiscreme ice cream I U6, 106
elf eleven I PUA, 9
Eltern parents *(pl)* I PUA, 9
E-Mail e-mail I U1, 18
Ende ending I U1, 25; end I U2, 42
am Ende at the back of I F1, 69
endlich at last I U4, 74
eng close I PUA, 10
aus England English I PUA, 9
Engländer/-in English I PUA, 9
Englisch English I PUA, 9
englisch English I PUA, 9
englischsprachig English-speaking I AC1, 66
auf Entdeckungsreise gehen to explore I U1, 24
Ente duck I U4, 77
eine Nachricht entgegennehmen *to take a message I U5, 93
einen Anruf entgegennehmen to answer the phone I U5, 93
entgegnen to reply (to) I U6, 115
Entgegnung reply I U6, 115
entlang down I F3, 122
entrümpeln to clear out I U5, 88
(sich) entscheiden to decide I U6, 108
Entschuldigen Sie! Excuse me ... I AC1, 66
Entschuldigung! Sorry! I PUA, 9; Excuse me ... I AC1, 66
entsetzt horrified I U5, 96
entsprechen to match I U5, 93
enttäuscht disappointed I U5, 97
er he I U1, 16
Erdbeere strawberry, strawberries *(pl)* I AC2, 101
Erde world I F2, 102
Erdkunde Geography I U2, 38
Ereignis event I AC3, 120
erforschen to explore I U1, 24
ergänzen to add I U2, 41
sich erinnern (an) to remember I U1, 21
erklären to explain I AC1, 67
erkunden to explore I U1, 24
ernst serious I AC3, 121
ernsthaft serious I AC3, 121
erraten to guess I U2, 37
erreichen *to get to I U4, 75
erst only I U1, 17
erste/-r/-s first I U2, 43
als Erstes first I U3, 58
erwidern to reply (to) I U6, 115
Erwiderung reply I U6, 115
erzählen *to tell I U1, 17
erzählen von to talk about I U1, 27
Erzähle mir von ... Tell me about ... I U1, 17
Erzählung story, stories *(pl)* I U2, 47
es it I PUA, 11
Es ist super zum/für ... It's great for ... I PUA, 11
Essen food I U2, 36
essen *to eat I PUA, 10
(ein Bonbon) essen *to have *(a sweet)* I AC1, 66
etwa about I U5, 91
etwas some I U1, 18; something I U2, 34; a little I U5, 91
euer/eure your I PUA, 8
Euro *(Währung)* euro I U5, 86
extra extra I U5, 99

F

Fabrik factory I F3, 122
Fahne flag I F1, 68
fahren *to go I PUA, 11; *to ride I F1, 69
fahren mit ... *to go by ... I U4, 74
Fahrplan timetable I AC1, 67
Fahrrad bike I PUB, 31
Fahrt trip I F3, 123
fair fair I U2, 45
Fakt fact I F1, 68
fallen *to fall I U4, 81
falls if I U3, 52
falsch wrong I U1, 18
Familie family I U1, 14
Fantasie fantasy I U1, 23
Farbe colour I PUA, 12

Welche **Farbe** hat …? What colour is …? **| PUA**, 13
farbenfroh colourful **| AC3**, 121
Farm farm **| U4**, 71
Februar February **| U6**, 105
Federmäppchen pencil-case **| U2**, 33
Fehler mistake **| U3**, 56
Feier party **| U6**, 104
feiern to celebrate **| U6**, 105
Feiertag holiday **| PUA**, 9
Feld field **| F3**, 122
Fels rock **| F1**, 68
Fenster window **| AC1**, 67
Ferien holidays *(pl)* **| U6**, 106; vacation *(AE)* **| U6**, 112
Fernsehen TV *(= television)* **| U1**, 15
fernsehen to watch TV **| PUB**, 31
Fernseher TV *(= television)* **| U1**, 15
Fertiggericht ready meal **| AC2**, 101
Fest festival **| F1**, 69
festhalten *to hold **| AC1**, 67
Festival festival **| F1**, 69
Feuerwerk fireworks *(pl)* **| U6**, 112
Film film **| U2**, 32
finden *to find **| U2**, 42
Finger finger **| U2**, 33
Fisch fish, fish *(pl)* **| AC2**, 100
Fischen fishing **| F1**, 69
Fischerei fishing **| F1**, 69
fit werden *to get fit **| U3**, 59
Fläche area **| F3**, 122
Flagge flag **| F1**, 68
Flasche bottle **| U5**, 87
Flohmarkt flea market **| U5**, 88
Flugzeug airplane **| F3**, 122
Flur hall **| U1**, 23
Fluss river **| F1**, 69
flüstern to whisper **| U6**, 116
Flyer flyer **| U5**, 88
Form form **| U2**, 35; shape **| F1**, 68
in **Form** kommen *to get fit **| U3**, 59
Foto photo **| PUA**, 9; picture **| PUA**, 12
auf dem **Foto**/den **Fotos** in the photo(s) **| U2**, 37
Fotos machen *to take photos **| PUB**, 31
Fotografie photo **| PUA**, 9
fotografieren *to take photos **| PUB**, 31
Fotostory photo story **| PUB**, 30
Frage question **| U2**, 34
fragen to ask **| U3**, 55
fragen nach to ask for **| U5**, 91
die **Franzosen** the French *(pl)* **| F3**, 123
Französisch French **| U2**, 38
Frau woman, women *(pl)* **| AC1**, 67
Frau *(Anrede)* Mrs **| U1**, 19
frei free **| U4**, 71
Freiheit freedom *(no pl)* **| F3**, 123
Freitag Friday **| U3**, 51
Freizeit leisure; free time **| U4**, 71
Freizeitzentrum leisure centre **| U4**, 71
fremd strange **| AC2**, 100
fressen *to eat **| PUA**, 10
Freude fun **| PUA**, 11
Freudenfeuer bonfire **| AC3**, 121
sich **freuen** an to enjoy **| F3**, 123
Freund/-in friend **| PUA**, 8
freundlich friendly **| U1**, 17
Freundschaft schließen *to make friends **| F2**, 102
frisch fresh **| U6**, 109
uns **frisieren** *to do our hair **| U6**, 107
froh happy **| PUB**, 28
fröhlich happy **| PUB**, 28; fun **| U2**, 40
Frucht fruit **| AC2**, 100
früh early **| U3**, 62
Frühling spring **| U6**, 105
Frühstück breakfast **| U3**, 51
frühstücken *to have breakfast **| U3**, 51
Frühstückszerealie cereal *(no pl)* **| AC2**, 101
fühlen *to feel **| U5**, 88
sich **fühlen** *to feel **| U5**, 88
Füller pen **| U2**, 33
fünf five **| PUA**, 12
fünfzehn fifteen **| U1**, 17
fünfzig fifty **| U1**, 20
für for **| PUA**, 11
für dich on your own **| U6**, 108
Für wen …? Who … for? **| U1**, 24
furchtbar awful **| U1**, 24
Fuß foot, feet *(pl)* **| U4**, 71
Fußball football **| PUA**, 11; soccer *(AE)* **| U6**, 114
Fußboden floor **| U1**, 19

G

Gans goose **| U4**, 77
ganz all **| U4**, 74; full **| U5**, 89; whole **| AC3**, 121
die **ganze** Nacht all night **| U6**, 106
Garage garage **| U5**, 88
Garten garden **| U1**, 19; yard *(AE)* **| U6**, 112
Gartenhäuschen shed **| U1**, 23
Gaststätte restaurant **| U2**, 36
Gebäude building **| U2**, 38
geben *to give **| U2**, 45
es **gibt** there is/are **| U1**, 19
Gebiet area **| F3**, 122
gebrauchen to use **| U2**, 36
gebrochen broken **| U5**, 96
Geburtstag birthday **| U6**, 105
Alles Gute zum **Geburtstag**! Happy Birthday! **| U6**, 104
Herzlichen Glückwunsch zum **Geburtstag**! Happy Birthday! **| U6**, 104
Gedicht poem **| U2**, 44
gefährlich dangerous **| U4**, 80
Mir **gefällt** … I like … **| PUA**, 11
gehen *to go **| PUA**, 11; to walk **| AC1**, 67
gehen um *to be about **| U3**, 58
ins Bett **gehen** *to go to bed **| U3**, 51
Wie **geht** es dir/euch/Ihnen? How are you? **| U6**, 116
gehören zu *to go with **| AC2**, 101
zueinander **gehören** *to go together **| AC2**, 101
gelangweilt bored **| U6**, 116
gelb yellow **| PUA**, 12
Geld money **| U2**, 33
Geld verdienen *to make money **| U5**, 88
Gelee jelly **| U6**, 109
Gemeindezentrum community centre **| U5**, 88
gemeinsam together **| U4**, 72
genießen to enjoy **| F3**, 123
genug enough **| U4**, 73
genügend enough **| U4**, 73
geöffnet open **| AC1**, 67
Geografie Geography **| U2**, 38
gerade just **| U2**, 44; at the moment **| U5**, 88
Gerät machine **| U2**, 33
Geräusch sound **| U3**, 59
gerecht fair **| U2**, 45
Gern geschehen. You're welcome. **| AC1**, 66
gern haben to like **| PUA**, 11
gern mögen to love **| PUA**, 10
hätte/-st-/-n/-t sehr **gern** would love **| U6**, 115
Ich mache … nicht **gern**. I don't like … **| PUA**, 11
würde/-st/-n/-t sehr **gern** would love **| U6**, 115
Gerümpel rubbish **| U5**, 96
Geschäft shop **| U2**, 33
geschehen to happen **| U4**, 80
Geschenk present **| U5**, 87
Geschichte History **| U2**, 38; story, stories *(pl)* **| U2**, 47
geschichtlich historical **| AC3**, 121
Gesicht face **| U3**, 62
Gespräch dialogue **| U3**, 58
gestern yesterday **| U6**, 111
gesund healthy **| AC2**, 101
Getränk drink **| U3**, 63
Getreide corn **| F3**, 122
getrennt separate **| F1**, 68
Gewinn prize **| U5**, 96
gewinnen *to win **| U6**, 109
gewöhnlich usually **| U3**, 52
Gitarre guitar **| U5**, 92
Gitter grid **| U2**, 42
Glas glass **| U5**, 88
glauben *to think **| U5**, 96; to believe **| U5**, 97
gläubig religious **| AC3**, 120
der/die/das **gleiche** the same **| PUA**, 11
gleich right away **| U3**, 52
gleichzeitig at the same time **| U6**, 104
Glück haben *to be lucky **| U2**, 38
glücklich happy **| PUB**, 28
Glücksbringer lucky charm **| PUB**, 29
Götterspeise jelly **| U6**, 109
grau grey **| PUA**, 12
Grill barbecue **| U6**, 112
Grillparty barbecue **| U6**, 112
groß big **| PUA**, 11; tall **| U1**, 17; high **| F1**, 68
großartig great **| PUA**, 11

Größe size | **U6**, 108
Großeltern grandparents *(pl)* | **U2**, 36
Großstadt city | **F1**, 68
grün green | **PUA**, 12
Grund bottom | **F3**, 122
Gruppe group | **U2**, 36; team | **F3**, 122
Gruß greeting | **U6**, 115
Grüße ausrichten (an) *to say hello (to) | **U1**, 18
Herzliche **Grüße** *(am Briefende)* Love … | **U6**, 115
Liebe **Grüße** *(am Briefende)* Love … | **U6**, 115
grüßen *to say hello (to) | **U1**, 18
gut good | **U1**, 14; fine | **U4**, 72
am **besten** best | **U6**, 119
gut sein in *to be good at | **U3**, 61
Guten Morgen. Good morning. | **U2**, 34
Mir geht's **gut**. I'm fine. | **PUB**, 29

H

Haar hair | **U3**, 63
Haare hair | **U3**, 63
unsere **Haare** machen *to do our hair | **U6**, 107
haben *to have got; *to have | **U2**, 34
hätte/-st-/-n/-t sehr gern would love | **U6**, 115
Hafendamm pier | **U4**, 71
Hähnchen chicken | **U4**, 77
halb *(bei Uhrzeitangaben)* half past | **U3**, 50
halb half | **U5**, 97
Halbschwester half-sister | **U4**, 74
die **Hälfte** half, halves *(pl)* (of) | **U5**, 95
Hallo. Hello.; Hi. | **PUA**, 9; Hey! | **PUB**, 29
halten *to hold | **AC1**, 67
halten von *to think of | **U5**, 91
Haltestelle station | **AC1**, 67
Hamburger burger | **U5**, 88
Hamster hamster | **U5**, 92
Hand hand | **U3**, 59
Handball handball | **PUB**, 31
Handbuch planner | **U2**, 32
handeln von *to be about | **U3**, 58
Handschuh glove | **U6**, 108
Handy phone | **PUA**, 13
häufig often | **U3**, 52
Hauptstadt capital | **F1**, 68
Haus house | **U1**, 14
nach **Hause** home | **U3**, 51
zu **Hause** at home | **U1**, 14
Hausaufgabe(n) homework | **U2**, 40
Haustier pet | **U3**, 55
He! Hey! | **PUB**, 29
Heim home | **U1**, 14
heiß hot | **AC2**, 101
Ich **heiße** … My name is … | **PUA**, 9
Wie **heißen** Sie? What's your name? | **PUA**, 9
Wie **heißt** du? What's your name? | **PUA**, 9
helfen to help | **U1**, 15
Hemd shirt | **U5**, 89
heraus out | **U6**, 109
herausfinden *to find | **U2**, 42; *to find out | **U3**, 58
Herbst autumn | **U6**, 105
Herd cooker | **U1**, 15
herein in | **PUA**, 8
Herr *(Anrede)* Mr | **U1**, 19
herstellen to produce | **F3**, 122
um … **herum** around | **U3**, 62
herunter down | **F3**, 122
herunterkommen *to come down | **U4**, 80
Herzliche Grüße *(am Briefende)* Love … | **U6**, 115
heute today | **U2**, 34
heute Abend 2nite (= tonight) | **PUB**, 28
Hi. Hi. | **PUA**, 9; Hey! | **PUB**, 29
hier here | **PUA**, 8
Hilfe help | **U3**, 61
ohne fremde **Hilfe** alone | **U2**, 40
hilflos helpless | **U5**, 97
hilfreich useful | **U4**, 81; helpful | **U5**, 97
hilfsbereit helpful | **U5**, 97
hinaus out | **U6**, 109
hinein inside | **U6**, 117
hineingelangen *to get into | **U6**, 117
hinfallen *to fall over | **U3**, 63; *to fall | **U4**, 81
hinkommen *to get there | **U4**, 74
sich **hinsetzen** *to sit down | **U3**, 51
hinten at the back of | **F1**, 69
hinter behind | **U1**, 19
Hintergrund background | **AC3**, 121
hinüber over; across | **U4**, 71
hinunter down | **F3**, 122
hinzufügen to add | **U2**, 41
historisch historical | **AC3**, 121
Hobby hobby, hobbies *(pl)* | **PUB**, 28
hoch tall | **U1**, 17; high | **F1**, 68
hochleben lassen *to give the bumps | **U6**, 105
Hochzeit wedding | **AC3**, 120
hoffen to hope | **U5**, 96
hoffnungsvoll hopeful | **U5**, 88
höflich polite | **U2**, 36
Sei/Seid **höflich**. Be polite. | **U2**, 36
holen *to get | **U4**, 78
Holz wood | **F3**, 122
Hoppla! Oops! | **PUB**, 29
horchen auf to listen for | **U3**, 62
hören *to hear | **U2**, 44
kurze **Hose** shorts | **U5**, 89
Hot Dog *(Würstchen im Brötchen)* hot dog | **U6**, 112
Hotel hotel | **F2**, 102
Huch! Oops! | **PUB**, 29
Huhn chicken | **U4**, 77
Hund dog | **PUA**, 8
den **Hund** ausführen to walk the dog | **U5**, 90
mit dem **Hund** spazieren gehen to walk the dog | **U5**, 90
Ich bin **hundemüde**. I'm dog-tired. | **U3**, 52
hundert one hundred | **U1**, 20
hungrig hungry | **U6**, 117
Hut hat | **U6**, 115
hüten to look after | **U3**, 55

I

ich I | **PUA**, 8; me | **PUA**, 13
Ich auch. Me too. | **PUB**, 31
Ich bin aus … I'm from … | **PUA**, 8
Ich heiße … My name is … | **PUA**, 9
Ich mache … nicht gern. I don't like … | **PUA**, 11
Ich mag … nicht. I don't like … | **PUA**, 11
Ich möchte … I'd like to … *(= I would like to)* | **U5**, 93
Ich weiß (es) nicht! I don't know! | **U4**, 78
Ich würde gern … I'd like to … *(= I would like to)* | **U5**, 93
Idee idea | **U1**, 19
ihm him | **U2**, 34
ihn him | **U2**, 34
ihnen them | **U2**, 39
ihr you | **PUA**, 9
Seid **ihr** … ? Are you …? | **PUA**, 9
Ihr/-e your | **PUA**, 8
ihr/-e *(Pl.)* their | **U1**, 19
im in | **PUA**, 8; on | **PUA**, 9
im Greenwich-Park in Greenwich Park | **PUA**, 8
im Innern inside | **U6**, 117
im Moment at the moment | **U5**, 88
im Weg sein/stehen *to be in the way | **AC1**, 67
Imbiss snack | **AC2**, 101
Imbissstube snack bar | **U5**, 86
immer always | **U1**, 16
immer noch still | **U5**, 96
immerhin after all | **U6**, 117
in in | **PUA**, 8; on | **PUA**, 9; at | **U1**, 14; to | **U1**, 18; into | **U2**, 40; inside | **U6**, 117
in der Mitte (von) in the middle (of) | **U1**, 19
in der Nähe von near | **F1**, 69
in der Straße in the street | **U1**, 14
in … hinein into | **U2**, 40
in Ordnung OK | **PUA**, 10; fine | **U4**, 72
indem as | **AC3**, 120
Inder/-in Indian | **AC2**, 101
Indianer/-in Native American | **F3**, 122
indianisch Native American | **F3**, 122
indisch Indian | **AC2**, 101
Information information *(no pl)* | **U4**, 74
Informationen information *(no pl)* | **U4**, 74
Inlineskatefahren inline skating | **PUA**, 11
Inlineskates skates *(pl)* | **PUB**, 28
Inlineskates fahren to skate | **PUB**, 29
innen inside | **U6**, 117
Insel island | **F1**, 68
Instruktion instruction | **U6**, 119
intelligent clever | **U1**, 17
interessant interesting | **U3**, 60
international international | **AC3**, 121

Internet internet **I PUB**, 31
Internetauftritt website **I U4**, 74
Interview interview **I PUB**, 30
irgendein/-e/-er any **I U5**, 90
irgendetwas anything **I U5**, 92
irgendjemand anybody; anyone **I U5**, 92
irgendwelche any **I U5**, 90
sich **irren** *to be wrong **I U4**, 81

J

ja yes **I PUA**, 9; yeah *(infml)* **I U2**, 45
Jacke jacket **I U5**, 89
jagen to chase **I U3**, 62
Jahr year **I U5**, 88
Jahrmarkt fair **I F3**, 122
Januar January **I U6**, 105
Jeans jeans **I U5**, 89
jeder everyone **I U2**, 34
jeder (beliebige) anybody; anyone **I U5**, 92
jede/-r/-s each **I U5**, 94
jede/-r/-s every **I U3**, 51
jede Menge lots (of) **I U2**, 36
jemand somebody; someone **I U5**, 92
jene those **I U2**, 42
jenes that **I PUA**, 10
jetzt now **I U1**, 19
Job job **I U2**, 36
Joghurt yoghurt **I U5**, 99
Jugendliche/-r teenager **I U6**, 104
Juli July **I U6**, 105
jung young **I AC2**, 101
Junge boy **I PUA**, 8
Juni June **I U6**, 105

K

Kaffee coffee **I U5**, 89
Kaktus cactus **I F3**, 122
Kalender planner **I U2**, 32
kalt cold **I F1**, 68
kalt stellen *to leave it to cool **I U6**, 109
Kaninchen rabbit **I PUA**, 10
Kanufahren canoeing **I F1**, 68
Kapitän/-in captain **I U4**, 80
kaputt broken **I U5**, 96
Karotte carrot **I U2**, 36
Karte card **I PUB**, 31
Kartoffelchip crisp *(BE)* **I AC2**, 101
Käse cheese **I U3**, 51
Kasten box **I AC1**, 67
Katze cat **I PUA**, 8
kaufen *to buy **I U2**, 33; *to get **I U6**, 107
Käufer/-in buyer **I U5**, 95
Keine Sorge! Don't worry! **I U1**, 24
kein/-e no **I U2**, 34
kein/-e/-en not … any **I U5**, 91
Keks biscuit **I U1**, 14; cookie *(AE)* **I U6**, 112
Keller cellar **I U1**, 23
kennen *to know **I U2**, 44
Kerl guy **I U6**, 112
Kerze candle **I U6**, 105

Kind child, children *(pl)* **I U1**, 16
Kino cinema **I F1**, 69
Kirche church **I F1**, 69
Kiste box **I AC1**, 67
Klang sound **I U3**, 59
klar clear **I U3**, 59
Klasse group **I U2**, 36; class **I U2**, 44
Klasse *(in einer englischen Schule)* tutor group **I U2**, 34
Klassenarbeit test **I U2**, 34
Klassenkamerad/-in classmate **I U2**, 33
Klassenlehrer/-in tutor **I U2**, 32
Klassenzimmer classroom **I U2**, 33
klatschen to clap **I U3**, 59
Kleid dress **I U5**, 89
Kleider clothes *(pl)* **I U5**, 86
Kleidergröße size **I U6**, 108
Kleiderschrank wardrobe **I U1**, 15
Kleidung clothes *(pl)* **I U5**, 86
klein small **I U1**, 15; little **I U1**, 16; short **I U1**, 17
klettern to climb **I U4**, 80
klingeln *to ring **I U5**, 88
klingen to sound **I U6**, 112
Klub club **I U3**, 51
klug clever **I U1**, 17
knapp close **I PUA**, 10
Das war **knapp**! That was close! **I PUA**, 10
Knie knee **I U3**, 63
Koch-AG Cooking Club **I U3**, 51
Kochen cooking **I U3**, 56
kommen *to come **I U3**, 51
kommen nach *to get to **I U4**, 75
kommen zu *to get to **I U4**, 75
Komm jetzt! Come on! **I U2**, 44
Komm schon! Come on! **I U2**, 44
kommunizieren to communicate **I F2**, 103
König king **I U2**, 44
Königin queen **I F1**, 69
königlich royal **I AC3**, 121
können can **I PUA**, 13
kann nicht can't **I PUB**, 28
können nicht can't **I PUB**, 28
Ich **kann** … sehen. I can see … **I PUA**, 13
kontrollieren to check **I F1**, 69
Konzert concert **I F1**, 69
Kopf head **I U5**, 97
kopieren to copy **I U6**, 111
Korbball netball **I U3**, 52
Korn corn **I F3**, 122
korrekt right **I U1**, 25; correct **I U2**, 41
Korridor hall **I U1**, 23
kosten *to cost **I U4**, 70
Es **kostet** …/Sie **kosten** … It's …/ They're … **I U5**, 86
Wie viel **kostet**/**kosten** …? How much is/ are …? **I U5**, 86
kostenlos free **I U4**, 71
Kostüm costume **I U6**, 104
Küche kitchen **I U1**, 14
Kuchen cake; pie **I AC2**, 100
Küchenschrank cupboard **I U1**, 15

Kuh cow **I F3**, 122
Kühlschrank fridge **I U1**, 20
Kultur culture **I AC2**, 100
sich **kümmern** um to look after **I U3**, 55
Kunstunterricht Art **I U2**, 33
kurz short **I PUB**, 31
kurze Hose shorts **I U5**, 89
Kurznachricht text (message) **I PUB**, 30
Küste coast **I F3**, 122

L

Lächeln smile **I AC1**, 66
lächeln to smile **I U6**, 116
lachen to laugh **I U2**, 45
Laden shop **I U2**, 33
Lagerfeuer bonfire **I AC3**, 121
Lamm lamb **I U4**, 77
Lämmchen lamb **I U4**, 77
Lampe lamp **I U1**, 19
Land country, countries *(pl)* **I U3**, 60; land **I U4**, 80; state **I F3**, 122
landesweit national **I AC3**, 120
Landkarte map **I F1**, 68
lang long **I U3**, 52
langsam slow **I U4**, 80
langweilig boring **I PUB**, 28
lassen *to let **I U6**, 115
Lass/**Lasst** uns … Let's … **I PUA**, 11
Lassi lassi **I U6**, 116
Latein Latin **I U2**, 38
laufen *to run **I U2**, 40; to walk **I AC1**, 67
laut noisy **I U1**, 17; loud **I U3**, 59
läuten *to ring **I U5**, 88
leben to live **I U1**, 14
Lebensmittel food **I U2**, 36
lecker yummy **I U6**, 110
legen *to put **I U3**, 63
Lehrer/-in teacher **I U2**, 35
leicht easy **I U1**, 16
leid tun *to be sorry **I U4**, 81
Tut mir **leid**! Sorry! **I PUA**, 9; I'm sorry! **I PUB**, 29
leise quiet **I U1**, 17
lernen *to learn **I U2**, 43
auswendig **lernen** *to learn … by heart **I U6**, 111
viel zu **lernen** a lot to learn **I U3**, 62
Lesen reading **I PUB**, 30
lesen *to read **I PUB**, 31
letzte/-r/-s last **I U3**, 54
Leuchte lamp **I U1**, 19
Leute people *(pl)* **I PUA**, 12
lieb nice **I PUA**, 9
am **liebsten** best **I U6**, 119
Liebe/r … *(Anrede in Briefen)* Dear … **I U6**, 115
Liebe Grüße *(am Briefende)* Love … **I U6**, 115
lieben to love **I PUA**, 10
Ich **liebe** … I love … **I PUA**, 10
Ich **liebe** dich. I love you. **I PUA**, 13

lieber better I **U6**, 117
Lieblings- favourite I **PUA**, 11
Was ist dein/-e **Lieblings**…? What's your favourite …? I **PUA**, 12
Lied song I **U1**, 22
lila purple I **PUA**, 12
Limonade lemonade I **AC1**, 67
Lineal ruler I **U2**, 33
Linie line I **U2**, 34
links on the left I **U1**, 19
auf der **linken** Seite on the left I **U1**, 19
Liste list I **U2**, 35
Londoner/-in Londoner I **AC3**, 121
Los ticket I **U5**, 96
Lösung solution I **U2**, 47
lustig funny I **U2**, 39; fun I **U2**, 40

M

Maat mate I **U4**, 80
machen *to do I **U2**, 40; *to make I **U3**, 62
Fotos **machen** *to take photos I **PUB**, 31
sich Notizen **machen** *to take notes I **U4**, 71
so **machst** du … this is how you (do) … I **U3**, 51
Mädchen girl I **PUA**, 11
ein **Mädchen** aus Deutschland a girl from Germany I **PUA**, 11
Mai May I **U6**, 105
Mais corn I **F3**, 122
malen to paint I **PUB**, 31
Mama mum I **U1**, 16
manchmal sometimes I **U3**, 52
Mango mango I **U5**, 99
Mann man mæn, men *(pl)* men I **AC1**, 67
Mannschaftsführer/-in captain I **U4**, 80
Mantel coat I **U5**, 89
Mäppchen pencil-case I **U2**, 33
Mappe folder I **U1**, 23
Markt market I **U4**, 78
März March I **U6**, 105
Maschine machine I **U2**, 33
Mathe Maths *(infml)* I **U2**, 38
Mathematik Maths *(infml)* I **U2**, 38
Matrose sailor I **U4**, 80
Mauer wall I **U1**, 20
Maus, **Mäuse** mouse, mice *(pl)* I **PUA**, 8
Meer sea I **F1**, 68
Meerschweinchen guinea pig I **U1**, 17
mehr more I **U1**, 21
mehr … als more … than I **U5**, 97
Meile *(brit. und amerikan. Längenmaß)* mile I **F3**, 122
mein/-e my I **PUA**, 8
die **meisten** (the) most I **F2**, 103
der/die/das **meiste** (the) most I **F2**, 103
meistens usually I **U3**, 52
eine **Menge** a lot of I **F1**, 68
jede **Menge** lots (of) I **U2**, 36
Mensch person, people *(pl)* I **AC1**, 67
Menschen people *(pl)* I **PUA**, 12
sich **merken** to remember I **U1**, 21
merkwürdig strange I **AC2**, 100
Messe fair I **F3**, 122
mich me I **U1**, 17
Milch milk I **AC2**, 101
Million million I **F2**, 103
mindestens at least I **U6**, 112
Minute minute I **U2**, 44
ein paar **Minuten** später a few minutes later I **U2**, 44
mir me I **U1**, 17
Mir geht's gut. I'm fine. I **PUB**, 29
mit with I **PUA**, 9
mit *(dem Fahrrad)* by *(bike)* I **U3**, 51
mitbringen *to bring I **U2**, 40; *to take I **U3**, 55
miteinander together I **U4**, 72
mitnehmen *to take I **U3**, 55
Mitschüler/-in classmate I **U2**, 33
Mittagessen lunch I **U2**, 33
Mittagspause lunch break I **U2**, 39
in der **Mitte** in the middle (of) I **U1**, 19
mitteilen *to tell I **U1**, 17
mitten in in the middle (of) I **U1**, 19
Mitternacht midnight I **U6**, 113
Mittwoch Wednesday I **U3**, 50
Model model I **U1**, 24
Modell model I **U1**, 24
mögen to like I **PUA**, 11; to want (to); *to be into I **PUB**, 28
gern **mögen** to love I **PUA**, 10
Ich **mag** … I like … I **PUA**, 11
Ich **mag** dich. I love you. I **PUA**, 13
Ich **mag** … nicht. I don't like … I **PUA**, 11
Ich **mag** … total gern. I love … I **PUA**, 10
Ich **möchte** … I'd like to … *(= I would like to)* I **U5**, 93
möglich possible I **U5**, 97
Möhre carrot I **U2**, 36
im **Moment** at the moment I **U5**, 88
Monat month I **U6**, 111
Mond moon I **F3**, 123
Monster monster I **U4**, 80
Montag Monday I **U3**, 50
montags on Mondays I **U3**, 52
Monument monument I **F3**, 123
Morgen morning I **U3**, 52
Guten **Morgen**. Good morning. I **U2**, 34
morgen tomorrow I **U3**, 54
morgens in the mornings I **U3**, 60
Motto theme I **U6**, 106
Mountainbikefahren mountain biking I **F1**, 68
müde tired I **U3**, 52
Müll rubbish I **U5**, 96
Mund mouth I **U3**, 59
Münze coin I **U5**, 96
Museum museum I **F1**, 68
Musik music I **PUB**, 30
müssen must I **U5**, 91
nicht **müssen** needn't I **U6**, 106
(tun) **müssen** to need (to do) I **U4**, 78
mutig brave I **U4**, 80
Mutter mother I **U1**, 16
Muttersprache first language I **F2**, 103

N

nach to I **U1**, 18
nach *(bei Uhrzeitangaben)* past I **U3**, 50
nach *(zeitlich)* after I **U1**, 24
nach draußen outside I **U1**, 24; out I **U6**, 109
nach drinnen inside I **U6**, 117
nach Hause home I **U3**, 51
Nachbar/-in neighbour *(BE)* I **U3**, 55
nachdenken *to think I **U2**, 45
nachjagen to chase I **U3**, 62
Nachmittag afternoon I **U3**, 53
nachmittags *(Uhrzeit)* p.m. I **U3**, 50
Nachricht message I **U5**, 93
eine **Nachricht** entgegennehmen *to take a message I **U5**, 93
eine **Nachricht** hinterlassen *to leave a message I **U5**, 93
nächste/-r/-s next I **U2**, 44
der/die **Nächste(n)** next I **U2**, 44
als **Nächstes** next I **U5**, 87
Nacht night I **U6**, 106
die ganze **Nacht** all night I **U6**, 106
Nachtisch pudding I **U2**, 36
in der **Nähe** von near I **F1**, 69
nahe near I **F1**, 69
Name name I **PUA**, 9
Namenstag name day I **AC3**, 121
Nase nose I **U3**, 63
national national I **AC3**, 120
Nationalpark national park I **F3**, 122
natürlich of course I **AC1**, 66
Naturpark national park I **F3**, 122
Naturwissenschaften Science I **U2**, 38
neben next to I **U1**, 19
nehmen *to take I **U3**, 55
(ein Bonbon) **nehmen** *to have *(a sweet)* I **AC1**, 66
neidisch sein (auf) *to be jealous (of) I **U2**, 44
nein no I **PUA**, 9
nennen to call I **U2**, 34; to name I **U6**, 107
benannt sein nach *to be named after I **F3**, 123
jemandem auf die **Nerven** gehen *to get on people's nerves I **U3**, 55
nett nice I **PUA**, 9; friendly I **U1**, 17
neu new I **U1**, 15
neun nine I **PUA**, 12
neunzehn nineteen I **U1**, 20
neunzig ninety I **U1**, 20
nicht not I **PUA**, 8
auch **nicht** not either I **U4**, 73
nicht mehr not any more I **F2**, 103
nichts nothing I **U5**, 92; not … anything I **U5**, 97

Rolltreppe escalator | AC1, 67
rosa pink | PUA, 12
rot red | PUA, 12
rufen to shout | U4, 80; to call | U5, 93
ruhig quiet | U1, 17
Rühr- sponge | U6, 109
rundherum all around | F2, 103
Rutschbahn slide | U4, 71

S

Sache thing | PUA, 13
Saft juice | U5, 88
sagen *to say | PUA, 13; *to tell | U1, 17
Sahne cream | U6, 109
Salat salad | AC2, 101
sammeln to collect | U1, 15
Samstag Saturday | U3, 51
Sandwich sandwich | AC2, 100
Satz sentence | U1, 25; phrase | PUB, 30
säubern to clean | U6, 107
Säugling baby | U6, 116
Saxofon saxophone; sax | U3, 52
Schachtel box | AC1, 67
Schade! Too bad! | U5, 90
Schaf sheep, sheep *(pl)* | F1, 68
Schälchen bowl | U6, 109
Schale bowl | U6, 109
schauen to look | U3, 60
in Scheiben schneiden to slice | U6, 109
schenken *to give | U2, 45
schicken *to send | U2, 36
schiefgehen *to go wrong | U6, 110
Schiff ship | U4, 70
Schiffsjunge cabin boy | U4, 80
Schiffsoffizier mate | U4, 80
Schinken ham | AC2, 101
Schinkenspeck bacon | AC2, 100
schlafen *to sleep | U3, 51
Schlafzimmer bedroom | U1, 14
(Sahne) schlagen to whip | U6, 109
schlagen *to hit | U4, 80
Schlange queue | AC1, 67
schlau clever | U1, 17
Schlauchbootfahren rafting | F3, 122
schlecht bad | U4, 74
schließen to close | U4, 73
Schließfach locker | U6, 108
schließlich at last | U4, 74; in the end | U6, 110; after all | U6, 117
schlimm *(ugs.)* bad | U4, 74
Schlittschuh laufen to skate | PUB, 29
Schlittschuhbahn ice rink | U6, 105
Schlittschuhe skates *(pl)* | PUB, 28
Schloss castle | F1, 68
Schluss end | U2, 42
  zum **Schluss** in the end | U6, 110
Schluss *(einer Geschichte)* ending | U1, 25
Schlüsselbegriff key word | U6, 117
Schmuck jewellery | U5, 86; decorations *(pl)* | U6, 106
schmücken to decorate | U6, 106
Schnäppchen bargain | U5, 91
schnarchen to snore | U3, 54
in Scheiben schneiden to slice | U6, 109
schnell fast | PUB, 29; quick | AC2, 100
Schokolade chocolate | AC2, 101
schön nice | PUA, 9; fine | U4, 72
schon already | U2, 41
Schrank cupboard | U1, 15
schrecklich awful | U1, 24
schreiben *to write | U3, 52
schreien to shout | U4, 80
Schritt step | U1, 23
Schuh shoe | U3, 63
Schule school | PUA, 11
Schüler/-in student | U2, 34
Schuljahr year | U5, 88
Schulklasse class | U2, 44
Schulstunde lesson | U2, 38
Schultasche schoolbag | U2, 34
Schulter shoulder | U3, 63
Schuppen shed | U1, 23
Schüssel bowl | U6, 109
schütten to pour | U6, 109
Schwanz tail | U3, 62
schwarz black | PUA, 12
Schweif tail | U3, 62
Schwein pig | U4, 76
Schwester sister | U1, 16
Schwierigkeit problem | U1, 19
  in **Schwierigkeiten** bringen *to make trouble | U2, 45
Schwimmen swimming | PUB, 31
schwimmen *to swim | U4, 81
  schwimmen gehen *to go swimming | PUB, 31
sechs six | PUA, 12
sechzehn sixteen | U1, 20
sechzig sixty | U1, 20
Second-Hand-Laden charity shop | U5, 90
See lake | PUA, 11
  See zum Rudern boating lake | PUA, 11
Seemann sailor | U4, 80
die Segel einholen to reef the sails | U4, 80
sehen *to see | PUA, 13; to look | U3, 60
  Ich kann … **sehen.** I can see … | PUA, 13
  Ich **sehe** … I can see … | PUA, 13
Sehenswürdigkeit sight | F1, 69
  Besichtigung von **Sehenswürdigkeiten** sightseeing | F1, 69
sehr very | U1, 18; very much | U3, 59
sein *to be | U2, 40
  Sei/Seid höflich. Be polite. | U2, 36
Seite page | AC1, 66
  auf der anderen **Seite** von across | U4, 71
  auf der linken **Seite** on the left | U1, 19
  auf der rechten **Seite** on the right | U1, 19
selber yourself | U3, 57
selbst even | U3, 55
du/dir/dich/Sie/sich (selbst) yourself | U3, 57
selbstverständlich of course | AC1, 66
seltsam strange | AC2, 100
senden *to send | U2, 36
separat separate | F1, 68
September September | U6, 105
Sessel chair | U1, 15
setzen *to put | U3, 63
  sich **setzen** *to sit down | U3, 51
Shirt shirt | U5, 89
Shorts shorts | U5, 89
sicher sure | U2, 44
Sie you | PUA, 9
  Sie sind … You're … | PUA, 9
  Sind **Sie** …? Are you …? | PUA, 9
sie her | U1, 14; she | U1, 16
sie *(Pl.)* they | PUA, 10; them | U2, 39
sieben seven | PUA, 12
siebzehn seventeen | U1, 20
siebzig seventy | U1, 20
siegen *to win | U6, 109
singen *to sing | U2, 34
Situation situation | U3, 58
Sitz! *(Befehl für Hunde)* Sit! | U3, 62
sitzen *to sit | U2, 39
Skateboard skateboard | U1, 19
Skateboardfahren skateboarding | PUA, 11
Skifahren skiing | F1, 68
SMS text (message) | PUB, 30
Snack snack | AC2, 101
Snowboarden snowboarding | PUB, 31
so like this | U1, 19; so | PUB, 29; like that | U6, 106
  so … **wie** as … as | U5, 96
  so machst du … this is how you (do) … | U3, 51
Sofa sofa | U1, 15
sofort right away | U3, 52
sogar even | U3, 55
Sommer summer | U6, 105
Sonderangebot special offer | U5, 87
Song song | U1, 22
Sonntag Sunday | U3, 51
Sonst noch etwas? Anything else? | U5, 87
Keine Sorge! Don't worry! | U1, 24
Sorte kind | F2, 102
spannend exciting | U4, 72
Spaß fun | PUA, 11
  Spaß haben *to have fun | U3, 62
  Es macht **Spaß.** It's fun. | PUA, 11
spät late | U2, 40
  zu **spät** late | U2, 40
  zu **spät** dran sein *to be late | U2, 40
  zu **spät** kommen *to be late | U2, 40
  Wie **spät** ist es? What's the time? | U3, 50
später later | U2, 44
mit dem Hund spazieren gehen to walk the dog | U5, 90
Speck bacon | AC2, 100
speziell special | F1, 68
Spiegel mirror | U1, 19
Spiel game | PUB, 28
spielen to play | PUB, 28
  eine Theaterszene **spielen** acting a scene | U3, 59

einen Streich **spielen** to play a trick (on) **I U2**, 44
spielen *(Theater)* to act **I U3**, 61
Spielkarte card **I PUB**, 31
Spielzeug toy **I U5**, 88
Spind locker **I U6**, 108
Spitze top **I F1**, 69
spitze awesome **I U6**, 112
Sport sport **I PUA**, 11
Sportart sport **I PUA**, 11
Sportunterricht PE *(Physical Education)* **I U2**, 38
Sprache language **I U1**, 17
Sprechblase speech bubble **I U3**, 51
sprechen *to say **I PUA**, 13; to talk **I U3**, 55; *to speak **I U3**, 59
sprechen über to talk about **I U1**, 27
Sprecher/-in speaker **I U3**, 58
springen to jump **I U4**, 81
Staat state **I F3**, 122
Stadion stadium **I F3**, 122
Stadt city **I F1**, 68; town **I F1**, 69
Stadtplan map **I F1**, 68
Stadtteil part **I AC2**, 100
Stall shed **I U1**, 23
Stammbaum family tree **I U1**, 16
ständig always **I U1**, 16
Star star **I PUA**, 13
starren to stare **I U2**, 39
starten to start **I U4**, 71
Station station **I AC1**, 67
statt instead of **I U6**, 113
stattfinden *to take place **I U6**, 115
Steak steak **I AC2**, 100
stehen *to stand **I AC1**, 67
stehen auf *to be into **I PUB**, 28
Du **stehst** auf ... You're into ... **I PUB**, 28
steigen to climb **I U4**, 80
Stein rock **I F1**, 68
Stelle place **I U2**, 43
an **Stelle** von instead of **I U6**, 113
stellen *to put **I U3**, 63
Stern star **I PUA**, 13
Steuer wheel **I U4**, 80
Steuerrad wheel **I U4**, 80
Stichwort key word **I U6**, 117
Stiefmutter stepmum **I U3**, 52
still quiet **I U1**, 17; still **I U6**, 109
Stimme voice **I U2**, 44
Stofftier cuddly toy **I U1**, 19
stolpern (über) to trip (over) **I U6**, 110
stoppen to stop **I U3**, 55
Story story, stories *(pl)* **I U2**, 47
Strand beach **I F1**, 68
Straße *(in der Stadt)* street **I U1**, 14
auf der **Straße** in the street **I U1**, 14
in der **Straße** in the street **I U1**, 14
Streich trick **I U2**, 44
einen **Streich** spielen to play a trick (on) **I U2**, 44
Stück piece **I U5**, 96
pro **Stück** each **I U5**, 96
Student/-in student **I U2**, 34
Studie survey **I U4**, 79
Stufe step **I U1**, 23
Stuhl chair **I U1**, 15
Stundenplan timetable **I AC1**, 67
Sturm storm **I U4**, 80
suchen nach to look for **I U3**, 54
Süd- south **I F1**, 68
Süden south **I F1**, 68
super great **I PUA**, 11; cool **I U1**, 16; awesome **I U6**, 112
Es ist **super** zum/für ... It's great for ... **I PUA**, 11
Supermarkt supermarket **I AC2**, 101
Surfen surfing **I F1**, 68
süß cute **I PUB**, 29; sweet **I AC2**, 101
Süßigkeiten sweets *(pl)* **I U2**, 33; candy *(AE)* **I U6**, 112
Symbol symbol **I F3**, 123
Szene scene **I U3**, 60

T

Tabelle grid **I U2**, 42
Tafel board **I U2**, 35
Tag day **I PUB**, 28
Takelage rigging **I U4**, 80
Talent talent **I U2**, 36
Talentwettbewerb talent show **I U2**, 36
Talisman lucky charm **I PUB**, 29
Tante aunt **I U1**, 16
tanzen to dance **I U2**, 34
tapfer brave **I U4**, 80
Tasche bag **I U1**, 24
Taschengeld pocket money **I U2**, 36
Tatsache fact **I F1**, 68
Rollen tauschen to swap roles **I U5**, 95
Tausende (von) thousands of **I AC3**, 121
Team team **I F3**, 122
Technologie technology **I F2**, 103
Tee tea **I U4**, 80
Teenager teenager **I U6**, 104
Teil part **I AC2**, 100
im hinteren **Teil** at the back of **I F1**, 69
Telefon phone **I PUA**, 13; telephone **I U5**, 90
Telefonanruf phone call **I U5**, 93
Tennis tennis **I U3**, 53
Teppich rug **I U1**, 19
Terrasse terrace **I U1**, 23
Test test **I U2**, 34
teuer expensive **I U5**, 86
Text text **I U1**, 16
Theater theatre **I F1**, 69
eine Theaterszene spielen acting a scene **I U3**, 59
Thema theme **I U6**, 106
Ticket ticket **I U5**, 96
Tier animal **I PUA**, 10
Tierarzt/Tierärztin vet **I U3**, 55
Tierpark zoo **I F3**, 123
Tipp tip **I U2**, 43
Tisch table **I U1**, 15
Titel heading **I U2**, 42
tja well **I U2**, 34
Toast toast **I AC2**, 101
Toilette toilet **I U1**, 15
toll great **I PUA**, 11
Tomate tomato, tomatoes *(pl)* **I U5**, 99
Tombola raffle **I U5**, 96
Ton sound **I U3**, 59
Tonmodell model **I U1**, 24
Tonstudio recording studio **I U2**, 33
Tor goal **I U5**, 95
Torte cake **I AC2**, 100
Tortenguss jelly **I U6**, 109
Tourist/-in tourist **I U4**, 78
Touristeninformation tourist information centre **I U4**, 78
Tradition tradition **I AC3**, 120
tragen *(Kleidung)* *to wear **I U2**, 40
Trainer/-in coach **I U3**, 54
trainieren to practise **I U2**, 43
Traum- fantasy **I U1**, 23
traurig sad **I U5**, 88
treffen *to meet **I PUB**, 28; *to hit **I U4**, 80
sich **treffen** *to meet **I PUB**, 28
Trick trick **I U2**, 44
Trifle *(englischer Nachtisch)* trifle **I U6**, 106
trinken *to drink **I U4**, 80
Trip trip **I F3**, 123
Tschüss! Bye! **I U4**, 73
T-Shirt T-shirt **I U3**, 59
tun *to do **I U2**, 40; *to make **I U3**, 62
Tunnel tunnel **I U4**, 71
Tür door **I U1**, 14
Tüte bag **I U1**, 24
Typ guy **I U6**, 112
typisch typical **I U3**, 60

U

Üben practising **I U3**, 59
üben to practise **I U2**, 43
über about **I U1**, 17; over; across **I U4**, 71
überall everywhere **I U1**, 19; all around **I F2**, 103
überall (in) all over **I AC3**, 121
überallhin everywhere **I U1**, 19
überhaupt at all **I U6**, 109
Übernachtung sleepover **I U6**, 106
überprüfen to check **I F1**, 69
Überraschung surprise **I U3**, 51
Überschrift heading **I U2**, 42
übersetzen to translate **I U4**, 76
Übersetzung translation **I U5**, 92
übrig left **I U5**, 93
Übung exercise **I U2**, 43
Übungsheft exercise book **I U2**, 33
Uhr clock **I U1**, 15
Um wie viel **Uhr**? What time? **I U4**, 72
Wie viel **Uhr** ist es? What's the time? **I U3**, 50
Uhr *(Zeitangabe bei vollen Stunden)* o'clock **I U3**, 50

um *(bei Uhrzeitangaben)* at **I U3**, 51
um ... herum around **I U3**, 62
Um wie viel Uhr? What time? **I U4**, 72
umarmen to hug **I U5**, 97
Umarmungen und Küsse *(am Ende von E-Mails und SMS)* XOXO **I U3**, 52
Umfrage survey **I U4**, 79
umher around **I U3**, 62
umkippen *to fall over **I U3**, 63
sich umschauen to explore **I U1**, 24
unabhängig independent **I F2**, 103
Unabhängigkeit freedom *(no pl)* **I F3**, 123
und and **I PUA**, 8
ungefähr about **I U5**, 91
Ungeheuer monster **I U4**, 80
Unglück bad luck **I U6**, 110
unhöflich rude **I U2**, 39
Uniform uniform **I U2**, 33
unrecht haben *to be wrong **I U4**, 81
uns us **I U4**, 74
unser/-e our **I U1**, 16
unterer Teil bottom **I F3**, 122
unten below **I U4**, 76
unter under **I U1**, 14
unterhalb below **I U4**, 76
Unterricht lesson **I U2**, 38
Unterrichtsstunde lesson **I U2**, 38
Unterschied difference **I U5**, 89
unterschiedlich different **I PUA**, 9
unverschämt rude **I U2**, 39
Ureinwohner/-in Amerikas Native American **I F3**, 122
Urlaub holiday **I PUA**, 9; vacation *(AE)* **I U6**, 112
Seid ihr im **Urlaub**? Are you on holiday? **I PUA**, 9
Sind Sie im **Urlaub**? Are you on holiday? **I PUA**, 9

V

Vanillepudding custard **I U6**, 109
Vanillesoße custard **I U6**, 109
Vater father **I U1**, 16
Veranstaltung event **I AC3**, 120
verärgert angry **I U2**, 45
verbessern to improve **I U3**, 59
sich **verbessern** to improve **I U3**, 59
verbinden *to put through **I U5**, 93
verdienen to earn **I U5**, 88
Geld **verdienen** *to make money **I U5**, 88
Verein club **I U3**, 51
vergessen *to forget **I U2**, 39
vergleichen (mit) to compare (with/to) **I U4**, 71
verkaufen *to sell **I U5**, 87
Verkäufer/-in *(auf einem Flohmarkt)* seller **I U5**, 95
verletzen *to hurt **I U6**, 110
vermuten to guess **I U2**, 37
verrückt crazy **I PUA**, 9
verschieden different **I PUA**, 9; separate **I F1**, 68
sich verständigen to communicate **I F2**, 103
verstehen *to understand **I U5**, 93
versuchen to try **I PUB**, 28
verwenden to use **I U2**, 36
verzieren to decorate **I U6**, 106
Videochat video chat **I F2**, 102
Viehzuchtbetrieb cattle farm **I F3**, 122
viel much **I U2**, 44; a lot **I U3**, 62
viel zu lernen a lot to learn **I U3**, 62
viel/-e lots (of) **I U2**, 36; a lot of **I F1**, 68
viele many **I U5**, 91
vielleicht maybe **I U1**, 24
vier four **I PUA**, 12
Viertel nach/vor quarter past/to **I U3**, 50
vierzehn fourteen **I U1**, 20
vierzig forty **I U1**, 20
violett purple **I PUA**, 12
Vokabular vocabulary **I PUA**, 12
voll full **I U5**, 89
voll (von) full (of) **I U5**, 89
Volleyball volleyball **I PUA**, 11
von from **I PUA**, 9; about **I U1**, 17; of **I U1**, 18
von ... bis from ... to **I U1**, 20
vor in front of **I U1**, 19
vor *(bei Uhrzeitangaben)* to **I U3**, 50
vor *(zeitlich)* before **I U2**, 44; ago **I U6**, 114
vorbereiten to prepare **I U6**, 109
sich vordrängeln to jump the queue **I AC1**, 67
Vorleger rug **I U1**, 19
Vormittag morning **I U3**, 52
vormittags in the mornings **I U3**, 60
vormittags *(Uhrzeit)* a.m. **I U3**, 50
Vorsicht! Be careful! **I U3**, 56
vorstellen to present **I U3**, 60
sich (etwas) **vorstellen** to imagine **I U6**, 117
Vortrag presentation **I U2**, 44

W

Wackelpudding jelly **I U6**, 109
während while; as **I AC3**, 120
Wald forest **I F1**, 68
Wand wall **I U1**, 20
Wandern hiking **I F1**, 68
Wanderreiten pony trekking **I F1**, 69
wann when **I U2**, 41
warten (auf) to wait (for) **I U2**, 34
Warte ab! Wait and see! **I U2**, 34
Warteschlange queue **I AC1**, 67
warum why **I U3**, 55
was what **I PUA**, 9
was für ein what **I PUA**, 13
Was ist das? What's that? **I PUA**, 11
Was ist dein/-e Lieblings...? What's your favourite ...? **I PUA**, 12
Was ist mit ...? What about ...? **I U3**, 53
was man ... what to ... **I AC1**, 66
was noch what else **I F2**, 103
was sonst what else **I F2**, 103
waschen to wash **I U3**, 62
sich **waschen** to wash **I U3**, 62
Wasser water **I U4**, 71
Wasserfall waterfall **I F3**, 122
Wasserrutsche water slide **I U4**, 71
Website website **I U4**, 74
Weg way **I AC1**, 67
im **Weg** sein/stehen *to be in the way **I AC1**, 67
weg away **I U3**, 62
wegnehmen *to take **I U3**, 55
wegrennen *to run away **I U3**, 62
wegwerfen *to throw away **I U5**, 89
weh tun *to hurt **I U6**, 110
Weide field **I F3**, 122
weil because **I U2**, 47
Wein wine **I U5**, 96
weiß white **I PUA**, 12
weitere more **I U1**, 21; other **I U3**, 52
Weizen wheat **I F3**, 122
welche/-r/-s what **I PUA**, 13; which **I U2**, 40
Welche Farbe hat ...? What colour is ...? **I PUA**, 13
Welle wave **I U4**, 80
Wellensittich budgie **I PUA**, 10
Welt world **I F2**, 102
Weltraum space **I F3**, 123
wem who **I U1**, 24
wen who **I U1**, 24
Für **wen ...**? Who ... for? **I U1**, 24
ein wenig a little **I U5**, 91
wenige a few **I U2**, 44
wenigstens at least **I U6**, 112
wenn when **I U2**, 41; if **I U3**, 52
wer who **I U1**, 24
werden *to become **I F3**, 122
werfen (nach) *to throw (at) **I U3**, 63
Werk factory **I F3**, 122
wert sein *to be worth **I U5**, 91
wessen whose **I U2**, 37
West- west **I F1**, 68
Westen west **I F1**, 68
westeuropäische Zeit Greenwich Mean Time *(= GMT)* **I U4**, 70
Wettbewerb contest **I AC2**, 100
Wetter weather **I U4**, 74
Wettkampf contest **I AC2**, 100
wichtig important **I AC1**, 66
wichtigste/-r/-s most important **I AC3**, 121
wie like **I PUA**, 13; as **I F2**, 102
wie how **I PUA**, 9
Wie alt bist du? How old are you? **I PUA**, 9
Wie alt sind Sie? How old are you? **I PUA**, 9
Wie geht es dir? How are you? **I U6**, 116
Wie heißen Sie? What's your name? **I PUA**, 9
Wie heißt du? What's your name? **I PUA**, 9
Wie man ... How to ... **I AC1**, 66
Wie spät ist es? What's the time? **I U3**, 50

Wie viel (kostet/kosten) …? How much is/are …? **I U5**, 86
Wie viel Uhr ist es? What's the time? **I U3**, 50
Wie viele …? How many …? **I U5**, 91
Wie wär's mit …? What about …? **I U3**, 53
wieder again **I U1**, 19
auf **Wiedersehen** goodbye **I U3**, 62
Wiese field **I F3**, 122
Willkommen! Welcome! **I U4**, 76
Winter winter **I U6**, 105
wir we **I PUA**, 9
Wir sind aus … We're from … **I PUA**, 9
wirklich really **I U2**, 44
wissen *to know **I U2**, 44
Ich **weiß** (es) nicht! I don't know! **I U4**, 78
Witz joke **I U2**, 44
witzig funny **I U2**, 39; fun **I U2**, 40
wo where **I PUA**, 9
Woche week **I U2**, 44
Wochenende weekend **I U4**, 72
am **Wochenende** at the weekend **I U4**, 72
Woher …? Where … from? **I PUA**, 9
wohin where **I PUA**, 9
Wohlfahrt charity **I U5**, 88
wohltätige Zwecke charity **I U5**, 88
Wohltätigkeitsverein charity **I U5**, 88
wohnen to live **I U1**, 14
Wohnung flat **I U1**, 14
Wohnzimmer living room **I U1**, 14
Wolkenkratzer skyscraper **I F3**, 123
wollen to want (to) **I PUB**, 28
wollen, dass jemand etwas tut to want somebody to do something **I U6**, 112
Workshop workshop **I U3**, 53
Wort word **I PUA**, 10
Wörterbuch dictionary **I U5**, 94
Wortschatz vocabulary **I PUA**, 12
Worum geht es in/im …? What is … about? **I U3**, 58
Wow! Wow! **I U2**, 33
Wunsch wish **I U6**, 105
sich etwas **wünschen** *to make a wish **I U6**, 105
würde/-st/-n/-t sehr gern would love **I U6**, 115
Ich **würde** gern … I'd like to … *(= I would like to)* **I U5**, 93
Wurm worm **I PUA**, 10
Wüste desert **I F3**, 122
wütend angry **I U2**, 45

Z

z. B. *(= zum Beispiel)* e. g. *(= for example)* **I U5**, 89
Zahl number **I PUA**, 13
zählen (auf) to count (on) **I U6**, 116
Zeh toe **I U3**, 63
zehn ten **I PUA**, 9
zeichnen *to draw **I U1**, 23
zeigen *to show **I PUB**, 28
Zeile line **I U2**, 34
Zeit time **I U2**, 44
zur selben **Zeit** at the same time **I U6**, 104
Es ist **Zeit** aufzustehen! Time to get up! **I U3**, 51
Zeitschrift magazine **I PUB**, 31
Zelten camping **I F1**, 68
Zentrum centre **I U4**, 71
zerbrechen *to break **I U6**, 109
Zeug stuff **I U5**, 91
Ziege goat **I U4**, 77
ziehen to pull **I U5**, 96
Ziel goal **I U5**, 95
Zimmer room **I U1**, 14
Zimmergenosse/Zimmergenossin roommate **I U3**, 54
Zoo zoo **I F3**, 123
zornig angry **I U2**, 45
zu too **I U3**, 59
Zu dumm! Too bad! **I U5**, 90
zu to **I U1**, 18
zu Hause at home **I U1**, 14
zubereiten to prepare **I U6**, 109
züchten *to grow **I F3**, 122
zuerst first **I U3**, 58
Zug train **I AC1**, 67
Zuhause home **I U1**, 14
zuhören to listen (to) **I U1**, 19
zumachen to close **I U4**, 73
zuordnen to match **I U1**, 25
zurück back **I U4**, 80
zusammen together **I U4**, 72
zusätzlich extra **I U5**, 99
zuschauen to watch **I PUB**, 31
zwanzig twenty **I U1**, 20
zwei two **I PUA**, 8
zweite/-r/-s second **I F2**, 103
zwischen between **I U6**, 113
zwölf twelve **I PUA**, 12;

In the classroom

You can say

Before / after the lesson

Good morning Mr / Mrs …	Guten Morgen, Herr / Frau …
Hello Mr / Mrs …	Hallo, Herr / Frau …
Goodbye.	Auf Wiedersehen.
See you tomorrow / next week.	Bis morgen / nächste Woche.

Asking for help

Can you help me, please?	Kannst du / Können Sie mir bitte helfen?
How do you do this exercise?	Wie macht man diese Übung?
Is this right? I'm not sure.	Ist das richtig? Ich bin mir nicht sicher.
Sorry, I don't know. Ask …	Tut mir leid, das weiß ich nicht. Frage …
Sorry. Can you say that again, please?	Wie bitte? Kannst du / Können Sie das bitte wiederholen?
What's for homework?	Was haben wir als Hausaufgabe auf?

Asking for information

What's that in English / German?	Was heißt das auf Englisch / Deutsch?
What does that mean?	Was bedeutet das?
How do you spell … , please?	Wie schreibt man … , bitte?
Is it OK to …?	Ist es in Ordnung, wenn ich / wir …?

Working in class with each other

Thank you. / Thanks.	Danke.
You're welcome.	Bitte. / Bitte schön!
Now it's your turn.	Jetzt bist du an der Reihe.
Let's make / draw a …	Lasst uns ein / eine / einen … machen / zeichnen.

Your teacher can say

Open your books at page …	Öffnet eure Bücher auf Seite …
Do exercise … on page … for homework.	Macht Übung … auf Seite … als Hausaufgabe.
Sit down, please.	Setz dich / Setzt euch bitte.
Say that again, please.	Wiederhole / Wiederholt es bitte.
That's very good!	Das ist sehr gut!
Stop it!	Lass(t) das! / Hör(t) auf!

Vocabulary for instructions and activities

Act (out) one of the scenes. / Act (out) the dialogues.	Spielt eine der Szenen. / Spielt die Dialoge.
Add more words / ideas.	Füge weitere Wörter / Ideen hinzu.
Ask your partner questions.	Stelle deinem Partner / deiner Partnerin Fragen.
Answer the questions.	Beantworte die Fragen.
Check your partner's text.	Überprüfe den Text deines Partners / deiner Partnerin.
Choose one part of the story.	Wähle einen Teil der Geschichte aus.
Collect ideas.	Sammle Ideen.
Compare English and German.	Vergleiche das Englische und das Deutsche.
Complete the answers.	Vervollständige die Antworten.
Copy the grid / the mind map.	Schreibe die Tabelle / das Wörternetz ab.
Correct the wrong sentences.	Korrigiere die falschen Sätze.
Describe your room.	Beschreibe dein Zimmer.
Draw a picture.	Zeichne ein Bild.
Explain your answer.	Erkläre deine Antwort.
Find the rule / the right order.	Finde die Regel / die richtige Reihenfolge.
Guess the new words.	Errate die neuen Wörter.
Learn your text by heart.	Lerne deinen Text auswendig.
Listen and repeat.	Höre zu und sprich nach.
Listen to the dialogue.	Höre dir den Dialog an.
Look at the picture / the examples / the map.	Schau dir das Bild / die Beispiele / die Landkarte an.
Make a poster / a grid / a mind map.	Fertige ein Poster / eine Tabelle / ein Wörternetz an.
Make sentences.	Bilde Sätze.
Match the sentence parts.	Ordne die Satzteile einander zu.
Name more sports.	Nenne mehr Sportarten.
Plan the scenes.	Plane die Szenen.
Play a game.	Spielt ein Spiel.
Point to the things in the classroom.	Zeige auf die Dinge im Klassenzimmer.
Practise your scenes / the dialogues.	Übe deine Szenen / die Dialoge.

Present your ideas / scenes.	Präsentiere deine Ideen / Szenen.
Put in the correct forms.	Setze die richtigen Formen ein.
Read (out) the text (to the class).	Lies den Text (der Klasse laut vor).
Repeat the words.	Wiederhole die Wörter.
Say the words / the sounds.	Sage die Wörter / Sprich die Laute.
Show your pictures.	Zeige deine Bilder.
Start. / Start like this.	Fange an. / Fange so an.
Swap roles.	Tauscht die Rollen.
Take a card.	Nimm eine Karte.
Take notes.	Mache dir Notizen.
Take turns.	Wechselt euch ab.
Talk about yourself.	Sprich über dich selbst.
Talk with your partner.	Sprich mit deinem Partner / deiner Partnerin.
Tell your partner about your hobby.	Erzähle deinem Partner / deiner Partnerin von deinem Hobby.
Think about the story.	Denke über die Geschichte nach.
Think of a new sentence.	Überlege dir einen weiteren Satz.
Use the vocabulary. / Use the information from the text.	Verwende die Vokabeln. / Verwende die Informationen aus dem Text.
Watch the film.	Schau dir den Film an.
Work with a partner or in a group.	Arbeite mit einem Partner / einer Partnerin oder in einer Gruppe.
Write dialogues / a short text.	Schreibe Dialoge / einen kurzen Text.
Write about your friends.	Schreibe über deine Freunde.
Write down school words.	Schreibe Wörter zum Thema „Schule" auf.

Useful words

activity	Aktivität
answer	Antwort
class display	Ausstellung in der Klasse
dialogue	Dialog
dice	Würfel
dictionary	Wörterbuch
example	Beispiel
folder	Ordner; Mappe
game	Spiel
grid	Gitter; Tabelle; Raster
heading	Überschrift
information	Information(en)
list	Liste
mind map	Wörternetz
order	Reihenfolge
phrase	Redewendung; Ausdruck
puzzle	Rätsel; Puzzle
question	Frage
quiz	Quiz; Rätsel
rhyme	Reim
role play	Rollenspiel
rule	Regel
scene	Szene
sound and spelling	Aussprache und Rechtschreibung
story	Geschichte; Erzählung
task	Aufgabe
tip	Tipp
unit	Lektion; Kapitel
useful phrases	nützliche Ausdrücke
vocabulary	Vokabular; Wortschatz
word order	Wortstellung; Satzstellung
word snake	Wortschlange

Check-out solutions

Unit 1 Page 27

Exercise 1
- In A there is a cat on the bed. In B there isn't a cat on the bed.
- In A there is a blue clock on the table. In B there is a red clock on the table.
- In A there are three big cars on the cupboard. In B there are four small cars on the cupboard.
- In A there is a chair behind the table. In B there is a chair in front of the table.

Exercise 2
Lösungsvorschlag: I'm Luke Elliot and I'm eleven. My friends are Dave, Holly and Olivia. I live with my parents, my sister and my little brother. My father is English and my mother is from Poland. My sister is thirteen. Her name is Irina. My brother Jamie is eight. Sherlock is our dog. He's my friend. Our house is in Brook Lane in Greenwich. My new room is in the loft. It's my own room.

Exercise 3
a) 1. Is Holly's father in London too?; 2. Are Luke and Jamie brothers?; 3. Is Anna Elliot from England?; 4. Are Irina and Amber sisters?; 5. Are the Richardsons English?; 6. Is Sherlock Olivia's dog?; 7. Is a bedroom in the loft Tony's idea?

b) 1. Yes, he is. 2. Yes, they are. 3. No, she isn't. She's from Poland. 4. No, they aren't. Irina is Luke's sister and Amber is Holly's sister. 5. Yes, they are. 6. No, he isn't. He's Luke's dog. 7. No, it isn't. It's Mrs Elliot's idea.

Unit 2 Page 47

Exercise 1
1. Holly's pen is pink. 2. The Richardsons' flat isn't big. 3. Jay's school uniform is nice. 4. Holly's favourite colour is pink. 5. Jay's three hobbies are singing, dancing and talent shows. 6. Tony's house is in TTS. 7. The Elliots' friends are very nice. 8. Jamie's cars are everywhere.

Exercise 2
1 What; 2 've; 3 brother; 4 are; 5 There; 6 Have; 7 have; 8 Has; 9 has; 10 he's; 11 own; 12 got; 13 haven't; 14 has; 15 two; 16 What; 17 this; 18 that; 19 're

Exercise 3
Lösungsvorschlag: 1. We can draw nice pictures in the Art room. 2. Don't play football in the classroom! 3. Don't use your phone at school! 4. We can sing in the recording studio.

Exercise 4
Lösungsvorschlag: My school is a big 'Gymnasium' in Frankfurt. My tutor's name is Mrs Schneider. She is my German teacher too. We've got a cafeteria at our school. We have lunch there.

Unit 3 Page 65

Exercise 1
Lösungsvorschlag:
1. I get up at (a) quarter past seven. 2. Then I have my breakfast. 3. After that I go to school. 4. I usually come home at 4 o'clock. 5. First I play a computer game. 6. Then I do my homework.

Exercise 2
Lösungsvorschlag: She goes swimming. She plays the saxophone. She listens to music. She draws pictures. She makes models.

Exercise 3
1. Sherlock sometimes chases squirrels. 2. Dave and Jay often play computer games. 3. Holly is usually at home in the evenings. 4. Luke never goes to Art Club. 5. Dave's parents are often busy. 6. The guinea pigs usually get up late.

Unit 4 Page 83

Exercise 1
1 Do; 2 don't; 3 Does; 4 does; 5 don't; 6 do; 7 Does; 8 doesn't; 9 doesn't

Exercise 2
1. When does the farm close? 2. How do I get to Pets Corner? 3. Where do the pigs live? 4. What does the big rabbit eat?

Exercise 3
1 Do; 2 is; 3 ship; 4 an; 5 open; 6 a.m.; 7 of; 8 stories; 9 about; 10 boy; 11 doesn't; 12 thinks; 13 too; 14 finds; 15 wrong; 16 storm; 17 hit; 18 falls; 19 because; 20 swim; 21 isn't; 22 doesn't; 23 lifeboat; 24 jumps; 25 saves; 26 takes; 27 they; 28 says; 29 last/the end; 30 brave.

Unit 5 Page 99

Exercise 1
a) 1 is chatting; 2 goes; 3 buys; 4 stops; 5 talks; 6 are working; 7 help; 8 get; 9 have; 10 is standing; 11 are making

b) 1 any; 2 any; 3 any; 4 some; 5 any; 6 some; 7 some

Exercise 2
1 something; 2 everything; 3 anything; 4 anything; 5 something; 6 something; 7 nothing; 8 something; 9 Nothing

Unit 6 Page 119

Exercise 1
1 can; 2 can't / mustn't; 3 can't / mustn't; 4 must; 5 must; 6 needn't; 7 mustn't; 8 needn't

Exercise 2

1 was; 2 got; 3 bumps; 4 gave; 5 blew; 6 cake; 7 made; 8 opened; 9 was; 10 with; 11 game; 12 had; 13 went; 14 looked; 15 watched; 16 loved; 17 were; 18 liked; 19 dinner

Exercise 3

1. What did you do last Saturday? – We went to the cinema. 2. Where did you go on holiday last summer? – Last summer we went to Scotland. 3. When did Emily and Ryan watch fireworks? – They watched the fireworks on 4th July. 4. What did Emily and Ryan eat on 4th July? – They ate red, white and blue things. 5. Did Sunny see the fireworks too? – No, she didn't. She was at home. 6. Did she sleep? – Yes, she did.

Grammar solutions

Unit 1

G1 Nomen im Singular und Plural

1.	homes	[z]	5.	clocks	[s]
2.	squirrels	[z]	6.	schools	[z]
3.	houses	[ɪz]	7.	wardrobes	[z]
4.	streets	[s]	8.	flats	[s]

G2 Die Personalpronomen und die Formen von *be*

1. I'm [your name]. / My name is [your name]. I'm ten / eleven. 2. I'm from [name of your town]. 3. You're nice. / You're a nice person. 4. He's / She's nice.

G3 Die Verneinung von *be*

1. I'm not eight. 2. We aren't from London. 3. It isn't big. 4. They aren't crazy.

G4 Entscheidungsfragen und Kurzantworten mit be

1. Are you from [name of your town]? – Yes, I am. / No, I'm not. 2. Are you from [name of your town]? – Yes, we are. / No, we aren't. 3. Are your friends nice? – Yes, they are. / No, they aren't. 4. Is Tony a guinea pig? – No, he isn't. 5. Are we at home? – Yes, we are. / No, we aren't

G5 Fragen mit Fragewörtern

1. Who are you? – I'm [your name]. / I'm a student. 2. What's your favourite colour? – My favourite colour is [name of the colour]. 3. Where are you from? – I'm from [name of your town]. 4. How old are you? – I'm ten / eleven. 5. What's in your (bed)room? – There's a bed, a chair, a table, …

G6 Die Possessivbegleiter

1. My (bed)room is small. 2. Our living room is big. Its walls are white. 3. My big sister is nice. 4. Lou and her family live in Greenwich. Their flat is good / great for mice. 5. His flat is in the loft. His flat is in Brook Lane. / It's in Brook Lane.

G7 Aussagesätze, Fragen und Kurzantworten mit *there is / there are*

1. There are three cars on the table. 2. Is there a football under the chair? – Yes, there is. 3. Are there two biscuits under the bed? – No, there aren't. 4. Is there a biscuit on the chair? – Yes, there is. 5. There's a clock on the table.

Unit 2

G8 Der unbestimmte Artikel

a cousin, an aunt, a fridge, an idea, an answer, a loft, an address

G9 Der bestimmte Artikel

[ðə]: dog, house, shop; [ði]: Art room, exercise book, ending

G10 Besitz und Zugehörigkeit mit *have got* ausdrücken

1. I've got a question. 2. My teacher has got a big bag. 3. We've got a computer room. 4. The computer room has got ten computers.

G11 Die Verneinung von *have got*

Lösungsvorschlag: I've got a pencil-case and three books in my bag. I haven't got a mouse in my bag.

G12 Entscheidungsfragen und Kurzantworten mit *have got*

1. Have you got a pet? – Yes, I have. / No, I haven't. Have you got a sister or a brother? – Yes, I have. / No, I haven't. / I've got a sister, but I haven't got a brother. / I've got two brothers, but I haven't got a sister. Have you got a big (bed)room? – Yes, I have. / No, I haven't. Have you got a pencil? – Yes, I have. / No, I haven't.

2. **Lösungsvorschlag:** Where is he / she from? How old is he / she? Is he / she in our class? Has he / she got a brother or a sister? Has he / she got a blue / red / green T-shirt? Has he / she got a dog / cat / rabbit?

G13 Die Fragewörter *who, what* und *whose*

1. What's in your room? 2. Who can you see in the house? 3. What has Luke got in his room? 4. Whose school uniform is blue? 5. Who has got a guinea pig? 6. Whose dog is this?

G14 Die Modalverben *can* und *can't*

a) 1. We can buy sweets in the cafeteria. 2. We can't eat in the classroom(s). 3. We can't bring pets to school. 4. I can play badminton.

b) 1. Can you show me the cafeteria? – Yes, I can. / No, I can't. 2. Can I use your ruler? – Yes, you can. / No, you can't. 3. Can my friend use your phone? – Yes, he / she can. / No, he / she can't. 4. Can you skate? – Yes, I can. / No, I can't.

G15 Der Imperativ

1. Write (down) your name. 2. Don't forget your homework. 3. Don't be rude. / Be nice. / Be polite.

G16 Die Besitzform bei Nomen und Namen (Der s-Genitiv)
1. Elliots'; 2. Luke's; 3. Holly's; 4. girls'; 5. Holly and Olivia's

G17 Die Besitzform mit *of*
1. This is the end of the lesson. 2. Z is the last letter of the alphabet. 3. Luke's dog is black and white. 4. The Elliots' house is small. 5. The colour of the door is green. 6. The name of the street is Brook Lane.

G18 Die Demonstrativpronomen *this / that* und *these / those*
1. 1 This; 2 That; 2. 3 This; 4 that 3. 5 These; 6 that; 4. 7 that; 5. 8 this; 9 Those; 6. 10 that

Unit 3

G19 Die einfache Form der Gegenwart
1. I meet my friends every day. 2. I go to Football Club on Tuesdays. 3. My friend / He / She plays the sax. 4. My friend / He / She watches TV in the evenings. 5. My sister and I / We tidy our (bed)room on Fridays.

G20 Die Satzstellung in Aussagesätzen
1. I get up at 7 o'clock every morning. / Every morning I get up at 7 o'clock. 2. I have / eat breakfast in the kitchen. 3. I take the bus at quarter to eight (7:45 a.m.). / At quarter to eight (7:45 a.m.) I take the bus. 4. I go to Football Club after school. / After school I go to Football Club. 5. I'm dog-tired in the evenings. / In the evenings I'm dog-tired.

G21 Häufigkeitsadverbien
1. Sid always likes his breakfast. 2. He's usually in the house. 3. He sometimes plays outside. 4. He often goes outside in the evenings.

Unit 4

G22 Entscheidungsfragen und Kurzantworten mit *do / does*
1. Do you know Greenwich Park? – Yes, I do. / No, I don't.
2. Do you like inline skates? – Yes, I do. / No, I don't.
3. Does your dad / father / brother like museums? – Yes, he does. / No, he doesn't. 4. Do your friends play football? – Yes, they do. / No, they don't. 5. Does you mother/mum come from England? – Yes, she does. / No, she doesn't. Is your mother / mum from England? – Yes, she is. / No, she isn't. Is your mother / mum English? – Yes, she is. / No, she isn't. 6. Can you play badminton? – Yes, I can. / No, I can't.

G23 Verneinte Aussagesätze in der einfachen Gegenwart
1. I don't go to school by bike. 2. My brother can't help me with my homework. 3. I don't do sport(s) every day. 4. I haven't got a pet. 5. My friend / He / She doesn't like cats. 6. Mudchute Farm isn't in Greenwich.

G24 Objektformen der Personalpronomen
1. them, me; 2. it; 3. it, them; 4. him, you; 5. them, her; 6. us, me

G25 Fragen mit Fragewörtern und *do / does*
1. Where's the boating lake? – It's in Greenwich Park. 2. How do I get to Greenwich Park? – You can walk there. It's over there. 3. What can I / you do in Greenwich Park? – You can go to the boating lake, play football or visit the Royal Observatory. 4. When does the Royal Observatory open on Saturdays? – It opens at 10 o'clock. 5. Who is this? / Who's this? – Oh, that's my dog. Her name is Molly. 6. Why do you live in Greenwich? – Because it's a nice part of London. I work here.

Unit 5

G26 Mengenangaben mit *of*
Lösungsvorschlag: She's got a chicken, a box of eggs, a packet of cheese, two cans of baked beans, two bags of crisps, three bottles of milk and a bag of sugar.

G27 Die Verlaufsform der Gegenwart
a) 1. Olivia is playing the sax. 2. Jay is singing and dancing. 3. Holly and Amber are doing their homework. 4. Luke and Jamie aren't playing football in the garden. 5. Dave isn't playing a computer game at the moment.

b) **Lösungsvorschlag:** What are they selling? – They're selling toys, clothes and books.
Are they selling football shoes? – No, they aren't.
Is Luke buying new football shoes? – No, he isn't. He's buying old / second-hand football shoes.
What is the boy holding in his hands?– He's holding a car in his hands.

G28 Die Mengenwörter *some, any* und *no*
1 any; 2 some; 3 some; 4 some; 5 any; 6 some

G29 Zusammensetzungen mit *some, any, every* und *no*
1. Everything is OK. 2. Nothing is happening. 3. Does anyone / anybody want to sell a game? 4. Do you know anyone / anybody here? 5. Maybe I can find something at the flea market.

G30 Die Mengenwörter *much, many* und *a lot of*
1. How much pocket money do you get? – A lot. / Not much.
2. How much homework do you get? – A lot. / Not much.
3. How much free time have you got? – A lot. / Not much.
4. How many books have you got? – A lot. / Not many.
5. How many friends have you got? – A lot. / Not many.

G31 Die Mengenwörter *a few, a little* und *a couple of*
1. a few / a couple of; 2. a little; 3. a few / a couple of; 4. a few / a couple of; 5. a little; 6. a few / a couple of

Unit 6

G32 Die Modalverben *can, can't* und *mustn't*
1. can; 2. can; 3. can; 4. can't; 5. mustn't; 6. can't; 7. mustn't / can't; 8. can

G33 Die Modalverben *must* und *needn't*

You **mustn't** invite too many friends. Tell your friends they **needn't** be scared of our dog. You **needn't** spend your own money on decorations. We can give you some money for balloons and things. You **mustn't** play the music too loud. Your friends **must** go home before nine o'clock. You **must** prepare some games, and prizes for the winners. We **needn't** prepare all the food. You can ask your friends to bring a cake or a salad.

G34 Die einfache Form der Vergangenheit

liked, wanted, invited, gave, played, did, made, went, were, was

G35 Fragen in der einfachen Vergangenheit

1. Were you at home on Sunday? – Yes, I was. / No, I wasn't.
   Did you stay at home on Sunday? – Yes, I did. / No, I didn't.
2. Did you watch TV? – Yes, I did. / No, I didn't.
3. What did you do yesterday? – I went to the park / cinema …
4. Did you like it? – Yes, I did. / No, I didn't.
5. When did you go to bed? – I went to bed at 9 p.m.

G36 Die Verneinung in der einfachen Vergangenheit

1. I didn't go to the skater park on Monday. I went there on Tuesday. 2. My teacher didn't give us a lot of homework last Thursday. He / She gave us a lot of homework on Wednesday. 3. I didn't like the football game yesterday. I liked the football game last week. 4. We weren't at home on Saturday evening. We were at the bowling alley. 5. The girls didn't have a sleepover last week. They had a skater party. 6. Dave wasn't in New York three weeks ago. He was in London.

G37 Haupt- und Nebensätze

1. He had lots of fun **because/when** he was at his friend's sleepover. 2. He knows **that** I'm his friend. 3. He tripped over Jamie's car, **but** he didn't hurt his foot.

Bildquellennachweis

Cover.1 February Films (Andrew Kemp), London; **Cover.2** shutterstock.com (Jose AS Reyes), New York, NY; **2.1** shutterstock.com (suicidecrew), New York, NY; **2.1–3** February Films (Andrew Kemp), London; **3.1; 3.3** February Films (Andrew Kemp), London; **3.2** February Films (Elke Bock), London; **4.1; 4.2** February Films (Elke Bock), London; **5.1; 5.2** February Films (Andrew Kemp), London; **6.1–6.3** February Films (Andrew Kemp), London; **7.1–7.3** February Films (Andrew Kemp), London; **8.1; 8.2** February Films (Andrew Kemp), London; **9.–3** February Films (Andrew Kemp), London; **9.4** Getty Images (Photolibrary), München; **10.1–4** February Films (Andrew Kemp), London; **11.1–3** February Films (Andrew Kemp), London; **11.4** Thinkstock (iStockphoto), München; **11.5** Klett-Archiv (Cornelia Donth-Schäffer), Stuttgart; **14.1** February Films (Andrew Kemp), London; **15.1–15.4** February Films (Andrew Kemp), London; **16.1** February Films (Andrew Kemp), London; **16.2** Klett-Archiv (Weccard), Stuttgart; **16.3** Avenue Images GmbH (Photo Alto), Hamburg; **16.4** Klett-Archiv (Viktor Justratow), Stuttgart; **16.5** Thinkstock (Jupiterimages), München; **16.6** February Films (Elke Bock), London; **16.7** Thinkstock (Comstock), München; **16.8; 16.10** Avenue Images GmbH (Banana Stock), Hamburg; **16.9** iStockphoto (RF/Steve Luker), Calgary, Alberta; **17.1** shutterstock.com (Erika Cross), New York, NY; **17.2** iStockphoto (Kemter), Calgary, Alberta; **17.3** February Films (Andrew Kemp), London; **17.4** iStockphoto (Bobbie Osborne), Calgary, Alberta; **18.1** February Films (Andrew Kemp), London; **22.1; 22.2** February Films (Andrew Kemp), London; **23.1; 23.2** Hath, Jessica Alice, Freiburg; **25.1** February Films (Andrew Kemp), London; **26.1–7** February Films, London; **27.1** February Films (Andrew Kemp), London; **28.1–4** February Films (Andrew Kemp), London; **29.1; 29.3–5; 29.6** February Films (Andrew Kemp), London; **29.2** February Films (Elke Bock), London; **30.1; 30.2** February Films (Andrew Kemp), London; **31.1** shutterstock.com (Monkey Business Images), New York, NY; **31.2** Fotolia.com (Phattman), New York; **31.3** Fotolia.com (teressa), New York; **31.4** shutterstock.com (GWImages), New York, NY; **31.5** Thinkstock (BananaStock), München; **31.6** Thinkstock (Brand X Pictures), München; **32.1; 32.2** February Films (Elke Bock), London; **32.3; 32.4** Klett-Archiv, Stuttgart; **33.1–4** February Films (Andrew Kemp), London; **35.1** February Films (Andrew Kemp), London; **36.1** Hath, Jessica Alice, Freiburg; **36.2** February Films (Elke Bock), London; **36.3** iStockphoto (travellinglight), Calgary, Alberta; **37.1** February Films (Elke Bock), London; **37.2** February Films (Andrew Kemp), London; **39.1–39.5** February Films (Andrew Kemp), London; **40.1** February Films (Elke Bock), London; **46.1–5** February Films, London; **48.1** Avenue Images GmbH (Photo Alto), Hamburg; **50.1–4** February Films (Elke Bock), London; **51.1–3** February Films (Elke Bock), London; **52.1** February Films (Elke Bock), London; **52.2** shutterstock.com (beboy), New York, NY; **53.1** February Films (Andrew Kemp), London; **54.1** February Films (Elke Bock), London; **54.2** shutterstock.com (lemony), New York, NY; **56.1** February Films (Andrew Kemp), London; **57.1** panthermedia.net (Elmar Tomasi), München; **58.1** February Films (Elke Bock), London; **59.1–3** Hath, Jessica Alice, Freiburg; **60.1; 60.2** Hath, Jessica Alice, Freiburg; **61.1; 61.2** Hath, Jessica Alice, Freiburg; **64.1–6** February Films, London; **67.1** February Films, London; **68.1** Getty Images (Photolibrary/roy james Shakespeare), München; **68.2** Alamy Images (Photoshot License Ltd), Abingdon, Oxon; **68.3** Getty Images (National Geographic), München; **68.4** Thinkstock (Stephen Meese), München; **68.5** Dream Maker Software (RF), Colorado; **68.6–8** Fotolia.com (Claudio Divizia), New York; **69.1** shutterstock.com (StockStudio), New York, NY; **69.2** Getty Images, München; **69.3** laif (Polaris Images), Köln; **70.1** February Films (Andrew Kemp), London; **70.2** shutterstock.com (QQ7), New York, NY; **71.1** Getty Images (AFP), München; **71.2** shutterstock.com (r.nagy), New York, NY; **71.3** Picture-Alliance (Natalie Teppe), Frankfurt; **71.4** Thinkstock (istcok/ Gennadiy Poznyakov), München; **72.1** February Films (Andrew Kemp), London; **75.1** Hath, Jessica Alice, Freiburg; **76.1** shutterstock.com (gorillaimages), New York, NY; **77.1** Alamy Images (Patrick Ward), Abingdon, Oxon; **77.2–6** February Films (Andrew Kemp), London; **78.1** Hath, Jessica Alice, Freiburg; **79.1** February Films (Andrew Kemp), London; **82.1–6** February Films, London; **83.1** February Films (Andrew

Kemp), London; **84.1** Bananastock, Watlington/Oxon; **86.1; 86.2** February Films (Andrew Kemp), London; **87.1; 87.2** February Films (Andrew Kemp), London; **87.3** Getty Images RF (PhotoDisc), München; **87.4** shutterstock.com (Nikolay Postnikov), New York, NY; **87.5** Fotolia.com (Ilona Baha), New York; **87.6** Avenue Images GmbH (Ingram Publishing), Hamburg; **90.1** Avenue Images GmbH (Comstock), Hamburg; **90.2** shutterstock.com (karelnoppe), New York, NY; **90.3** shutterstock.com (ResolutionDigital), New York, NY; **90.4** iStockphoto (Beyond Foto), Calgary, Alberta; **90.5** Getty Images (Blend Images), München; **90.6** February Films (Andrew Kemp), London; **90.7** iStockphoto (Linda Steward), Calgary, Alberta; **94.1** Hath, Jessica Alice, Freiburg; **95.-3** Hath, Jessica Alice, Freiburg; **98.1-6** February Films, London; **100.1** Fotolia.com (A.L), New York; **100.2** shutterstock.com (msheldrake), New York, NY; **100.3** Thinkstock (Monkey Business), München; **100.4** shutterstock.com (Joe Gough), New York, NY; **100.5** Fotolia.com (Joe Gough), New York; **100.6** Thinkstock (iStockphoto), München; **101.1-4** February Films, London; **102.1; 102.2** February Films, London; **103.1** Thinkstock (Ramon Purcell), München; **103.2** Interfoto (NG Collection), München; **104.1** February Films (Andrew Kemp), London; **104.2** Avenue Images GmbH (Digital Vision, RF), Hamburg; **105.1** Getty Images (Stone/Lars Borges), München; **105.2** iStockphoto (Liz Leyden), Calgary, Alberta; **105.3** Getty Images (Flickr Open), München; **107.1; 107.2** February Films (Andrew Kemp), London; **108.1** Picture-Alliance (Zentralbild/Marco Kohlmeyer), Frankfurt; **109.1** Thinkstock (iStock/Tasia12), München; **109.2** shutterstock.com (Hristo Svinarov), New York, NY; **109.3** iStockphoto (filo), Calgary, Alberta; **110** shutterstock.com (pdesign), New York, NY; **112.1** shutterstock.com (Steve Cukrov), New York, NY; **114.1** Corbis (Stewart), Berlin; **114.2** iStockphoto (RF/Cathleen Clapper), Calgary, Alberta; **114.3** Fotolia.com (Lane Erickson), New York; **114.4** shutterstock.com (Vertes Edmond Mihai), New York, NY; **116.1; 116.2** February Films (Andrew Kemp), London; **118.1-6** February Films, London; **119.2** shutterstock.com (Syda Productions), New York, NY; **120.1-3** February Films, London; **120.4** dreamstime.com (trentham), Brentwood, TN; **120.5** Corbis (Stephane Cardinale/People Avenue), Berlin; **120.6** Fotolia.com (goodluz), New York; **121.1** iStockphoto (Jean-Francois Guignard), Calgary, Alberta; **121.2** iStockphoto (Daniel Troutman Photography), Calgary, Alberta; **121.3** shutterstock.com (Lisa F. Young), New York, NY; **121.4** shutterstock.com (Ievgenii Meyer), New York, NY; **122.1** Corbis (Mark Goldman/Icon SMI), Berlin; **122.2** Corbis (John and Lisa Merrill), Berlin; **122.3** shutterstock.com (Brberrys), New York, NY; **122.4** Alamy Images (RGB Ventures/SuperStock), Abingdon, Oxon; **122.5** iStockphoto (nazlisart), Calgary, Alberta; **123.1** Thinkstock (Cazi), München; **123.2** Getty Images (Photographer's Choice/Patti McConville), München; **123.3** iStockphoto (RF/Timothy Babasade), Calgary, Alberta; **123.4** Picture-Alliance (AP Photo/Gene J.Puskar), Frankfurt; **123.5** Thinkstock (paulprescott72), München; **125.1** shutterstock.com (Patricia Marks), New York, NY; **125.2** shutterstock.com (MaszaS), New York, NY; **126.1** Alamy Images (Graham Franks), Abingdon, Oxon; **126.2** Getty Images (Britain On View/martin leigh), München; **126.3** Alamy Images (Sylvie JARROSSAY), Abingdon, Oxon; **127.1** Marika Hildebrandt, Berchtesgaden; **127.2** Ullstein Bild GmbH (Prisma/Fürmann Hans), Berlin; **128.1** Hath, Jessica Alice, Freiburg; **128.2** February Films (Andrew Kemp), London; **133.1** February Films (Andrew Kemp), London; **134.1** February Films (Elke Bock), London; **135.1** iStockphoto (miralex), Calgary, Alberta; **135.2** Thinkstock (Hemera), München; **135.3** Thinkstock (iStockphoto), München; **135.4** shutterstock.com (BESTWEB), New York, NY; **136.1** Hath, Jessica Alice, Freiburg; **137.1** February Films (Elke Bock), London; **138.1; 138.2** February Films (Andrew Kemp), London; **139.1** February Films (Andrew Kemp), London; **140.1** dreamstime.com (Noamfein), Brentwood, TN; **140.2** shutterstock.com (pio3), New York, NY; **140.3** Imago, Berlin; **140.4** February Films (Andrew Kemp), London; **145.1** shutterstock.com (travellight), New York, NY; **148.1** shutterstock.com (g-stockstudio), New York, NY; **148.2** shutterstock.com (stock-227852623.jpg), New York, NY; **148.3** Fotolia.com (WavebreakmediaMicro), New York; **148.4** shutterstock.com (Africa Studio), New York, NY; **148.5** Fotolia LLC (corbis_micro), New York; **153.1** Picture-Alliance (EPA/PHIL NIJHUIS/POOL), Frankfurt; **154.1** Alex's Lemonade Stand Foundation, Wynnewood,; **156.1** Getty Images (George Pimentel/WireImage), München; **160.1** February Films (Andrew Kemp), London; **161.1** February Films (Andrew Kemp), London; **162.1** February Films (Andrew Kemp), London; **163.1; 163.2** February Films (Andrew Kemp), London; **164.1; 164.2** February Films (Andrew Kemp), London; **165.1** February Films (Elke Bock), London; **166.1** February Films (Andrew Kemp), London; **167.1** February Films (Elke Bock), London; **167.2; 167.3** February Films (Andrew Kemp), London; **169.1** February Films (Elke Bock), London; **170.1** February Films (Elke Bock), London; **171.1** February Films (Elke Bock), London; **171.2** February Films (Andrew Kemp), London; **172.1-3** February Films (Andrew Kemp), London; **174.1** February Films (Elke Bock), London; **176.1** February Films (Elke Bock), London; **177.1** February Films (Andrew Kemp), London; **182.1** February Films (Andrew Kemp), London; **183.1** February Films (Elke Bock), London; **183.2** February Films (Andrew Kemp), London; **190.1** shutterstock.com (irur), New York, NY; **193.1** Thinkstock (iStock/Redcup2), München; **194.1** February Films (Andrew Kemp), London; **205.1-7** February Films (Andrew Kemp), London; **227.1** Klett-Archiv, Stuttgart; **228.1** Fotolia.com (erwinova), New York; **269.1** February Films (Elke Bock), London; **282.1-3** February Films (Andrew Kemp), London; **283.1; 283.2** February Films (Andrew Kemp), London

Textquelle:

93 Song „Ring Ring Ring: Ha ha hey" Text: Brookhouse, Julian Godfrey/Drummond, Michael John/Huston, Paul E./Jolicoeur, David J./Mason, Vincent Lamont/Mercer, Kelvin/Skinner, Glenn Francis/Thorp, Nicholas Bernard/Volpeliere-Pierrot, Ben © Chelsea-Music Publishing Co Ltd/Curio Sounds Ltd/Caisy Age Music/Prinse Pawl Music, Rolf Budde Musikverlag GmbH, Berlin/Universal Music Publishing GmbH, Berlin/Neue Welt Musikverlag GmbH, Hamburg; **109** Webseite: Staatliche Schlösser und Gärten Baden-Württemberg; **126** Victor Djumpah, London; **127** Webseite: Berchtesgadener Land Tourismus GmbH; **145** Webseite: Durham University, UK

Sollte es in einem Einzelfall nicht gelungen sein, den korrekten Rechteinhaber ausfindig zu machen, so werden berechtigte Ansprüche selbstverständlich im Rahmen der üblichen Regelungen abgegolten.

Irregular verbs

Infinitiv	simple past	Deutsch
be [bi:]	was / were [wɒz / wɜ:]	sein
become [bɪ'kʌm]	became [bɪ'keɪm]	werden
blow (out) [bləʊ]	blew [blu:]	(aus)blasen, (aus)pusten
break [breɪk]	broke [brəʊk]	(zer)brechen, kaputt machen
bring [brɪŋ]	brought [brɔ:t]	(mit)bringen
buy [baɪ]	bought [bɔ:t]	kaufen
choose [tʃu:z]	chose [tʃəʊz]	(aus)wählen
come [kʌm]	came [keɪm]	kommen
cost [kɒst]	cost [kɒst]	kosten
do [du:]	did [dɪd]	machen, tun
draw [drɔ:]	drew [dru:]	zeichnen
drink [drɪŋk]	drank [dræŋk]	trinken
eat [i:t]	ate [et]	essen
fall [fɔ:l]	fell [fel]	fallen
feel [fi:l]	felt [felt]	fühlen
find [faɪnd]	found [faʊnd]	finden
forget [fə'get]	forgot [fə'gɒt]	vergessen
get [get]	got [gɒt]	bekommen, hinkommen, werden
give [gɪv]	gave [geɪv]	geben
go [gəʊ]	went [went]	gehen, fahren
grow [grəʊ]	grew [gru:]	wachsen, anbauen
have [hæv]	had [hæd]	haben
hear [hɪə]	heard [hɜ:d]	hören
hit [hɪt]	hit [hɪt]	schlagen, treffen
hold [həʊld]	held [held]	halten
hurt [hɜ:t]	hurt [hɜ:t]	verletzen, weh tun
keep [ki:p]	kept [kept]	(auf)bewahren, behalten
know [nəʊ]	knew [nju:]	kennen, wissen
learn [lɜ:n]	learned [lɜ:nd] / learnt [lɜ:nt]	lernen
leave [li:v]	left [left]	(ver)lassen
let [let]	let [let]	lassen
make [meɪk]	made [meɪd]	machen, tun
mean [mi:n]	meant [ment]	bedeuten, meinen
meet [mi:t]	met [met]	treffen
pay [peɪ]	paid [peɪd]	(be)zahlen
put [pʊt]	put [pʊt]	legen, setzen, stellen

Infinitiv	simple past	Deutsch
read [ri:d]	read [red]	lesen
retell [ˌri:ˈtel]	retold [ˌri:ˈtəʊld]	nacherzählen
ride [raɪd]	rode [rəʊd]	reiten, fahren
ring [rɪŋ]	rang [ræŋ]	klingeln, läuten
run [rʌn]	ran [ræn]	laufen, rennen
say [seɪ]	said [sed]	sagen
see [si:]	saw [sɔ:]	sehen
sell [sel]	sold [səʊld]	verkaufen
send [send]	sent [sent]	senden, verschicken
set up [ˌset‿ˈʌp]	set up [ˌset‿ˈʌp]	erbauen, errichten
show [ʃəʊ]	showed [ʃəʊd]	zeigen
sing [sɪŋ]	sang [sæŋ]	singen
sit [sɪt]	sat [sæt]	sitzen
sleep [sli:p]	slept [slept]	schlafen
speak [spi:k]	spoke [spəʊk]	sprechen
spell [spel]	spelt [spelt]	buchstabieren
spend [spend]	spent [spent]	ausgeben, verbringen
stand (up) [stænd]	stood (up) [stʊd]	(auf)stehen
swim [swɪm]	swam [swæm]	schwimmen
take [teɪk]	took [tʊk]	nehmen
tell [tel]	told [təʊld]	erzählen
think [θɪŋk]	thought [θɔ:t]	(nach)denken, glauben
throw [θrəʊ]	threw [θru:]	werfen
understand [ˌʌndəˈstænd]	understood [ˌʌndəˈstʊd]	verstehen
wear [weə]	wore [wɔ:]	anhaben, tragen
win [wɪn]	won [wʌn]	gewinnen, siegen
write [raɪt]	wrote [rəʊt]	schreiben

THE BRITISH ISLES

ENGLISH AROUND THE WORLD

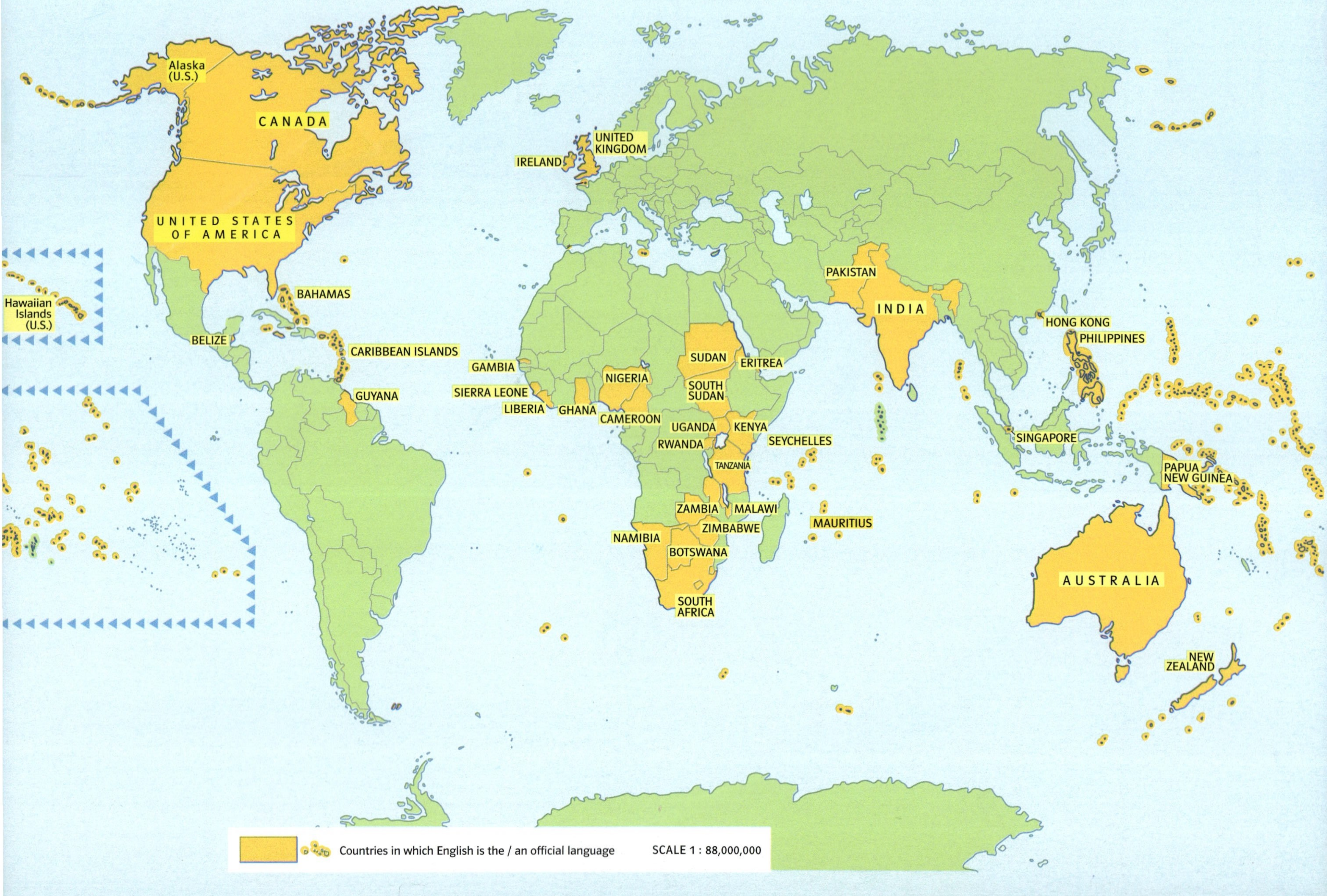

THE UNITED STATES OF AMERICA

Olivia Fraser
- 11 years old
- lives with her dad, her stepmum and her half-sister Lucy (5)
- likes netball, cycling and creative activities

Luke Elliot
- 11 years old
- has a sister, Irina (13), and a brother, Jamie (8)
- has a dog, Sherlock
- likes football and jokes

Jahangir ("Jay") Azad
- 11 years old
- has one brother, Shahid (17)
- his uncle and aunt have a restaurant
- likes singing and dancing